D1474193

ABOUT BREAKFAST IN NUDIE SUITS

'It ended too soon for me, I wanted more.'

'..Straight from the heart.'
Billy Ray Herrin, 'Hickory Wind Music'

'Ian Dunlop is a masterful storyteller, who bore witness to and
participated in the birth of country rock.'
Holly George-Warren, author, music journalist and co-editor
The Rolling Stone Encyclopedia of Rock & Roll

'This isn't a book. It's a journey, the trip through the '60s we all
either dreamed about, lied about or actually took. Coolest road
read since Kerouac left the Flamingo Bar.'
Pete Gallagher, WMNF Radio

'Part Kerouac, part Tom Robbins, it's a transcendental
road trip down a lost highway that leads to the roots of the
Americana music movement.'
Jim White, musician, writer. Presenter of the BBC film
'Searching for the Wrong-eyed Jesus'

'I know what you're thinking: just what the world needs, another
memoir by another musician. Well, the world needs this one.
Forget the cliche that if you can remember the '60s, you weren't
there. Fortunately, Ian remembers, and his accounts of his
adventures are frequently inspiring and often hilarious.
He makes me wish I'd been there too.'
Scott Schinder, writer, Time Out, New York.

CLARKSDALE

Published by Clarksdale an imprint of Ovolo Books Ltd
Text © Ian Dunlop 2011
This edition © Ovolo Books Ltd 2011

Publisher: Mark Neeter
Cover illustration: Ian Dunlop
Cover design: Poppublishing

ISBN: 978 1 9059594 0 2
Printed in the UK

www.clarksdalebooks.co.uk

Visit these sites for music, film, art and information.
Music downloads of Ian Dunlop recordings including free download to readers:
http://iand.bandcamp.com/
Performances, gigs, music: http://www.myspace.com/iandunlop
Art, music-related artwork, exhibitions, art for sale:
http://www.iandunlopart.com
The 'Church of Elvis' exhibition by ian D.:
http://www.churchofelvis.com

Films by ian D.
http://www.youtube.com/idastudio

BREAKFAST IN NUDIE SUITS

IAN DUNLOP

CLARKSDALE

Foreword

Jam at Brandon DeWilde's house in Topanga Canyon, LA, 1968. Left to right: Mickey Gauvin, Barry Tashian and Gram Parsons. Ink sketch by Ian Dunlop

WHEN THE AUDIENCE runs for the exit as if you're singing a tear gas song and the record companies reply with the cold shoulder, it might be a sign that you are doing something right but at the wrong time. After your knuckles are too bruised to keep knocking on the wrong doors the best pain relief is to grab the steering wheel and hit the road. Hollywood shrinks to the size of a monopoly board compared to the knock-out majesty of the Joshua Tree desert and hooting owls in Utah make more sense than A & R men in New York.

This book is a collage of events and adventures that took place between September 1965 and June 1968. It was a period of intense experiences, excitement and musical alchemy that was heightened by choosing an alternative path with a few other people who were not afraid to go against contemporary trends. Gram Parsons and the International Submarine Band began an exploration of an American music style that had been relegated to the hinterland with very little exposure in the urbane media. At the time, Country Music was hugely unfashionable, unpalatable and dismissed by the slaves to fashion. The floundering ISB was the prequel to country-rock, alternative country and contemporary Americana music. The band embarked upon an exasperating upstream journey, swimming against a tide of opposition, rejection and astonishment from the establishment but their music reverberates into the twenty-first century. It was a wonderful, enriching experience but also a rough road, that is the way nonconformity works.

The ISB and Parsons recordings from the period sunk without a trace but have subsequently been discovered and released decades later. Parson's recordings sell in increasingly greater numbers as he has become recognized as a major influence on country and rock music. His flamboyant life style has grown to mythological proportions in rock chic. This book contains a glimpse into the Parsons legend that has never been offered before; a look at the life-line on his palm, an ear to his spontaneous banter and a candid portrait sketched during a formative, creatively productive and happy era of his life. The ISB was the crash-test dummy that helped to design the Parsons legacy.

Much of the details, imagery and information included have been derived from sketchbooks and journals that I kept during these years. I have chosen to narrate this journey with the voice and the vision I possessed at the time and have rigorously avoided including any element of hindsight or knowledge of events that transpired after June 1968. This book is a trip through then.

> 'And this was really the way my whole road experience began, and the things that were to come are too fantastic not to tell. Somewhere along the line I knew there would be girls, visions, everything; somewhere along the line the pearl would be handed to me.' *Jack Kerouac*

> 'Memory takes a lot of poetic licence it omits details; others are exaggerated according to the emotional value of the articles it touches for memory is seated predominantly in the heart.' *Tennessee Williams*

This story has been in my heart for a bit too long.

Ian Dunlop, Cornwall, March 2011

I extend thanks to those who have helped me to complete this writing. Thanks to; Karen Townshend for encouraging me to begin this book and Holly George-Warren for reminding me to continue with the book. Also, the poet Katherine Solomon, the screenwriter Chris Tuff for acting as sounding posts, David Roberts for double checking and my friend and former band-mate, Barry Tashian for lending me his sketchbook from the 1967-1968 period. And a dubious thanks to all the managers and record companies who because of their rejection and indifference made the journey so much more rewarding. ID

CAST OF CHARACTERTS

In alphabetical order,

Mike Bloomfield – musician, bandleader

The Blues Magoos – band; psychedelic–pop

William Briggs – musician, piano, hot rodder

The Byrds – band; folk-rock

Freddie Cannon – teen-pop star

Jon Corneal – musician, drummer

David Crosby – musician, Byrd

'Indian Ed' Davis – musician, guitar

Brandon DeWilde – actor, Broadway, Hollywood, closet musician

Ian Dunlop – artist, musician, narrator

Peter Fonda – actor; Hollywood

Chester Fox – manager, promoter

The Flying Burrito Brothers – roots band, hard working – short-lived

Mickey Gauvin – musician, drummer

Dennis Hopper – actor; Hollywood

The International Submarine Band – band, pre-country-rock

Bobby Keys – musician, loud sax

Buzzy Linhart – musician, eccentric

Arthur Lee – musician, Love

Junior Markham – musician, dust-bowl blues

Hugh Masekela – musician, producer

Mimi – groupie

John Nuese – musician, upside-down guitar

Gram Parsons – musician, songwriter

The Remains – America's lost band

Leon Russell – musician, producer

Lawrence Spector – manager

Barry Tashian – musician, songwriter, campfire cook

The Turtles – band, chart toppers

John Zacherley – TV Vampire

Plus many others who show up along the way

Chapter 1
HOLLYWOOD EXIT
May 10th 1968

RT. 66

AMBOY

PALMDALE

RT. 138

LUCERNE

RT. 18

CAJON

JOSHUA TREE

TOPANGA

SMOG

L.A.

JOSHUA TREE NAT'NL MON.

SAN BERNADINO

Pacific Ocean

ANEHEIM

R.P.A.

N
W E
S

0 10 20 30 40 50

Spider

Santa Catalina

Good 'bye, so long.

Heading east, anywhere
The keys to the highway: Roadmap,
sleeping-bag, a tank of gas,
10 lbs of pinto beans, 8 onions
and $200.

The sleepy engine wakes and coughs into a willing Bum-bum-bum-bum-bum-bum-bum. I'm ready to go. After handshakes, hugs and good-byes, I climb into the microbus and open the sliding window.

"See ya, somewhere in the land of a million items."

"Good luck, I hope you find it," Brandon laughs.

"Thanks, I'll send a postcard from the desert."

"'Bye."

I coast down Waveview Drive, turn up onto Topanga Canyon road and start heading east, away from the Pacific Ocean, California dreamin' and my Hollywood hangover. Winding up through Topanga Canyon, I pass a dumpy looking roadhouse-bar, the Topanga Corral, a place I had played a dozen times or more during the last year. It's a great morning for leaving California. Spring is the season to turn over new ground, plant seeds, watch 'em grow and mature, bear fruit.. or, is it vegetables? Either one would be fine.

The old VW bus is rattling along, it's slow but it seems to be going okay. It went fine a few weeks ago, when I drove one hundred and fifty miles up to Lake Isabella, in the Sierra Nevada foothills, to go camping with Gram Parsons for a couple of days. He had just come back from a short tour with the Byrds and we had always wanted to see Bakersfield, even from a distance. It was really just a dusty, big farm-town but, in the past, we had held it in over-glorified esteem because of the mid-60s country music that came out of there. The Bakersfield Sound had inspired us when we were in the International Submarine Band and had begun a bizarre adventure into country music. The run up to Lake Isabella was fun, Gram and I had enjoyed seeing each other again, talking, catching-up and it was the trial run for the rebuilt VW engine.

Near the ridge, just ahead, is Mulholland Drive, the twisty hill top road I used to drive, late at night, after a gig on my way home to Laurel Canyon. I'm not taking it today. I'm not going back to Laurel Canyon. I'm going to skirt round the Valley, head up to Palmdale then over to Cajon and we'll probably get to Joshua Tree by mid-afternoon. I'll be glad to get out there, after that, who knows what route we'll take. It could be anywhere, as long as it's east of LA.

My buddies, Barry and Briggs, are on the road up ahead of me driving their ancient Chevy panel van. We're going to try and stay together or, at least, hope to catch sight of each other, over the one hundred-and-seventy-five miles on the road today. Both of the funky vans are at least twenty-five years old and cost about two-hundred-dollars each. We fixed them up, got enough work done to make them legal and hope that they splutter their way across the U.S.A. We're not rushing. We've planned to stay in the slow-lane for awhile, the three of us have had enough of Hollywood. It's time for recess. The Flying Burrito Brothers are on-tour, well, more of a pilgrimage really.

I got the itch to get on the road and get out of Hollywood a couple of months ago. One day I had gone over to visit Gram and while talking with my buddy over a couple of beers I began thinking about getting out of town. It's funny how you can see what you're really feeling after that second beer.

Afternoon Los Angeles sun dazzles me driving down from Laurel Canyon. I fish around in the glove compartment trying to hook some shades, cross over Sunset on to Sweetzer and park a few blocks down. Up the steps to the second floor apartment, I knock.

"Hey. Come-on in."

"Hey man. Good to see ya."

"Yeah, yeah. How 'bout a beer?" Gram offers, opening the fridge. "Let's see. M-m, yeah, here a' those li'l culprits, hidin' behind the orange juice. Mexican, ya want a Mexican?"

"Sure man, sure."

"So, what's happenin', how ya doin'?" He asks as he pops off the bottle tops.

"Ah, okay. Okay, ya know." I took a swig of the Dos Equis.

"A-a-ah, yeah." We pull out a couple of chairs and sit down at the table. "We had a weird time, last night. Weirdness, man!"

"Hey that's what we're here for, weird times. Were you guys doin' a gig?"

"Yeah, out at that place in south LA, Peacock Alley. Y' know the place, didn't you come out once, when we were there awhile ago?"

"Um, which one was it, that place down by Watts? With the Burrito Brothers?"

"Yeah, that's it. We just finished another week there, shit. So, last night we were driving back, about two-thirty, an' just down the block there was a guy, lyin' right in the middle of the road. Drunk, shot, O-D'ed, dead? I don't know. We didn't stop, there was a bunch of guys over on the sidewalk, just didn't look too cool. Down the street a bit more, there were two cops hasslin' a couple of black guys, you know, pushin' them up against the wall. What a place! A bit later, we're at a stoplight, an' get this, two guys come up to the van and started yellin'. They looked crazy. Wild hair, wearin' army jackets, one of them had a gash on his face. I mean the whole side of his face looked smashed-up. They were grabbin' at the door handle and one started reachin' 'round behind him like he might have had a gun or something, we just floored-it and went right through the red light. Jesus! It's like a battlefield at night, sometimes."

"Hey, that's what happens when you go out of Beverly Hills. There's just too much heat under the soup and it's always boilin' over. Makes you want to stay home, jump in bed an' pull the covers over ya head, huh."

"Yeah. Man, LA is a fuckin' crazy place."

"And getting' crazier everyday," Gram agreed. "You know that place, The Prelude, out in the Valley, where you guys play sometimes. Well the guy downstairs was out there the other night, he went and saw a, sort of, psychedelic blues band playin'. An' after the gig, he's out in the parking lot, he hears an engine start-up and this chocolate-colored Cadillac comes roarin' across the parking lot. No lights, he has to jump outta the way and it doesn't stop, it just crashes into the back wall. The front end goes right into it, like it's cardboard, and like, breaks through, sticking right out onto the stage! He said he couldn't believe it. The car door opens and this tall, oriental-lookin' babe gets out and she's not hurt or anything. She just looks around, like turns around a couple of times and wobbles on her stilettos. She pulls out a cigarette and says, 'You got a light?' He's just standin' there with his mouth open, like still shakin'. She's got a long silver lamé scarf, an' she wraps it round her neck a couple times, gets back in the car, pushes in the lighter, slams it in reverse, burns rubber, screeching, backing the Caddy outta the wall! She stops, lights-up her cigarette, then peels outta there with the bumper draggin' an' sparks flying everywhere. The only thing she cared about was lightin' her cigarette!"

"She musta been loaded, or full a coke."

"Hey, she's just tryin' to have a night on the town in LA."

"I'll drink to that."

"So what's up with you, did you finish-off the recording?"

"Um, well, hm, the recording. I'm really finished with the recording, in more ways than one," Gram replied, rather mysteriously. "Somethin' else has happened. It looks like I'm gonna be doing something with the Byrds."

"No shit! Really? Since when?"

"Well, I've met with them a few times, played some things, you know. Yeah, I'm tryin' to get them into country music, we'll see. They've got another album to do and they need somebody since Crosby left. I told them that I'd want to do some of my songs though. We're talkin' about it."

"Hey that's great! Yeah, great. Wow! What about the Submarine Band album, what's gonna happen to that?"

"Well. Corneal and the other guys are still hangin' in there. There might be some tracks to finish up. It's, sort of, up to them, if they wanna pick-up the ball and run with it. I gotta go see Larry to find out about some legal stuff."

"Ha, I've got an appointment with Larry too. Next week. It might be about some acting work or something. I did some last week, as an extra."

"Acting. Hey! Its Hollywood." Gram used one of our favourite catch phrases, applicable to almost anything.

"Yeah, yeah. The work was really stupid. With Tim Conway, ya know from that TV show, ah, whatever it was called, um, Gilligan's Island, no another one, a-ah.. whatever. I sat around for hours, waiting for the scene, bummin" cigarettes from a make-up man, who maybe thought I was comin'-on to him. They got to the scene I'm supposed be in and the guest star, Nancy Wilson, gets to her spot and the director doesn't like the color of her dress! So they stop everything and we have to wait around for another hour while someone goes out to find her a new outfit. When they were ready to roll again, it really didn't look any fuckin' different. You know, like so what! The show was completely dull, the comedy routines and the script were so bad that they'll probably have to use canned laughter."

"Har-har-har-har."

"Yeah. So, I don't know, that's show biz."

"An' long may it reign."

"All hail, Holy Hollywood."

"A toast to the entertainment industry!" We clinked our beer bottles together in salute.

"I went out to the desert about a week ago. Just drove out there and stayed for the afternoon, out by Joshua Tree. Ya know it's so big and, well, calm. I just didn't want to come back. I've been thinking about getting' a camper or a van and a tent, just to go out somewhere like that and stay for a bit."

"Ian, you're always pissed-off with LA," Gram laughed.

"Yeah, I ought to take a break. It's getting crazier every day." "Well, all I can recommend is to have another beer and we can cry about it."

I like distance driving, I always have. I drove out to LA in early '67 when we moved out to Hollywood. We were in a rush then, there were already potential gigs in the pipeline and interest in The International Submarine Band from the music people, managers and record companies. We had stopped at Nashville on the way to California, just to get a little taste of the country music capital but that was the only deviation from the beeline to LA. Driving across America is always such a wild trip, an experience full of weird, wonderful sights and places, a draining but elevating journey on that long road. I had done the drive across a couple of times before. I was seventeen the first time and that trip was like a ritualistic passage from Boy to, not quite, Man. A ceremony, appropriate in the early '60s for space age American kids and reverential to the country where the car is king, or, at least if not a reigning monarch, a cherished member of your immediate family.

The Submarine Band had been in New York for over a year. We had done a lot of gigs, a few big concerts and had released a couple of singles. We were ambitious, things never moved quickly enough for us, particularly for Gram and so, we went to California. Everybody needs to go to a California, it's not so much a place, it's a concept. We all want that California dream, just gotta have it. The desire has been sold to us and, before you know it, you're chanting 'we're on our way to Cal-a-for-ni-ay', just like they all have been doing for decades. It's been happening for over a century, the 1848 gold rush never really ended. People keep pouring into that juicy well of promises, LA, the Venus flytrap, to slurp it up. Yum, yum, yum, real sweet, oh yes, oh yes. Since I've been in LA, I have hardly met anyone who is not from out of town, or somewhere else, they just keep coming, full of dreams. We were dreamers. There should be a border post where you have to stop, roll down the window and they say, 'Let's see your dreams.' Dreams are the valid entry visa for California.

California sunshine was seductive and the novelty of warm nights reinforced our choice of relocating and leaving the freezing New York winter three thousand miles behind. We had leased an unusual house in Laurel Canyon, high up in the hills. It sprawled on different levels, nestling into the folds of the land. The driveway led through a mysterious grove of tall eucalyptus trees and the landscaped hillside areas around the house were covered with semitropical plants, creating an exotic retreat. Meandering stone paths and steps connected the multileveled patios, garden and roof terrace. Under an arbor, covered by a shady kumquat tree, large stone seats were built into a retaining wall that spewed and drooled vines and ferns. It was a property with character and privacy. Low-end luxury, with a hint of jungle, but what else would you expect.

Hey, it's Hollywood.

Willow Glen Road was a typical Hollywood neighborhood and most all of the residents had some claim to celebrity. Everybody had done something in the movies or TV and, in true show-biz form, they would tell you about it. The old lady living down opposite our driveway was the 'ornithologist' in Hitchcock's movie The Birds, the old guy across the road from her had written songs for the mid-'30s Gold Diggers movies with Dick Powell and Joan Blondel. Down at the Laurel Canyon Country Store I'd see Cass Elliot or Jim Morrison buying oranges or Twinkies. Another neighbor, a petite dark woman, often curiously overdressed for the LA climate, wrote a lot of novelty songs about hot rods and cars. Songs like 'Go Little Cobra' and 'Go Little Honda', I remembered them, they had been hits when I was in High school.

Our landlord, Pat White, an elderly English gent and probably out of work, told me that he was the guy in some buccaneer movie, that I'd never heard of, who came on deck just as the cut-throat pirates were swarming aboard and shouted, 'It's all hands for themselves now Captain!' He assumed that I would remember that crucial scene and, for his sake, I appeared suitably impressed. The guy who did some yard work and property maintenance had just done a couple of days shooting on Hell's Angels Meet the Apaches. He had dressed up in buckskins, moccasins, a black wig and war paint and yelled 'Woo-woo-woo', I guess this was considered a speaking role.

Jim was 'the Marlboro Man', once. He straddled his palomino, wore a big white Stetson and dragged on a filter cigarette. Andy was a stunt driver who swerved, skidded or crashed cars, sometimes jumping out of the flaming wrecks, in costume, doubling for the star. At the supermarket I overheard 'Bones', Star Trek's easy-going medic, complaining, 'Oh, we've already had chicken this week', as his wife picked up a packet of drumsticks. There were balding childstars, ex-Mouse-ka-teers, cameramen, writers, occasional vampires, professional hippies. The whole neighborhood had once been famous and were waiting for their agent to phone, sometime soon.

The Hollywood crowd made New Yorkers look so anemic, ill, and riddled with anxiety. No pale, bad skin here, everyone was bronzed and wore gold chains to complement the tans. The California sun enabled people to be seen almost year-round, sitting at sidewalk cafes, riding in cars with the tops down and lazing at the beaches. New Yorkers, wrapped in ankle-length coats, scarves and fur hats, were hunched-over against the snow flurries and biting winds as they sloshed through the dirty snow in their lined boots. LA footwear was sparkling, gold, skimpy sandals, loafers or tennis shoes. People wore as few clothes as possible, mostly for decoration rather than protection. Just about everybody looked good, or they were working on it, it was a culture of beautiful bodies.

It was good to be in LA, with my buddies again. Brandon DeWilde had left New York several months ago, thinking that a move to California would help to invigorate his acting career, since most of the work he was offered was coming from LA. He had been dormant for too long, New York wasn't buzzing and it was difficult for him, having been such a renowned Broadway childstar. A tough act to follow.

Gram had gone out to LA to visit Brandon for a couple of weeks towards the end of '66 and dove into the new scene headfirst, before flying back to do some gigs we had booked in New York and Boston. When Gram returned to New York he had already decided that LA was where it's at and had convinced me and the other guys in the band to move out there with him. We did the east coast gigs and Gram flew back to LA by the end of the year. I hadn't seen him for a month or more.

Gram had leased an economy car, a yellow Toyota, that didn't fit-in very well, driving around on Santa Monica or Sunset Boulevard, with all the flashy cars. Nobody walked, except when strolling around while shopping. Shoes weren't as important as cars, convertibles, Corvettes, Porsches, those Mercedes with gull-wing doors and the limos. The traffic glided slowly along Sunset at a promenade pace. The convertible was the perfect exhibition space for people to show-off as the car crawled ahead, slowly, so they didn't have to worry about their hair styling getting mussed.

The Toyota car radio was tuned to an LA radio station K-RLA that played non-stop West Coast music; Buffalo Springfield, Jefferson Airplane, Byrds, Grateful Dead and the Doors. Jim Morrison crooned 'Crystal Ship'. Gram and I had seen the Doors a few months ago at Ondine, an east-side, New York club where we had also played. The Doors weren't that well known in New York when we saw them, we had been told that they were big on the west coast. I was surprised that a lot of the LA and 'Frisco bands hadn't had much air play back East. It made California seem like a different country, the state that wrote its own rules, did its own thing and had its own music. They had their own way of speaking. There was a southern Californian accent, that I had begun to perceive, delivered in a droopy-lidded, half awake and sun-baked lilt.

Gram had made some new friends and connections in his short time in LA. There were several meetings lined up so, as soon as we were settled-in, we started rehearsing at the house in Laurel Canyon. The house became the band's center with enough space to rehearse and accommodation for three of us. Gram had rented an apartment on Sweetzer Avenue about ten minutes away. He had decided that he wanted to live with his new girl friend Nancy Ross. Women never seemed to fit the package in homes dominated by a band.

A stream of people came to the house to hear the band, offer services and talk music biz. A booking agent, Ronnie Herrin, a perky, go-getter, young woman came to check us out. She heard us play and soon got back to us on the phone about gigs she had lined up at some of the LA showcase venues. She booked the Submarine Band into the Hollywood Palladium, the Hullabaloo, the Valley Music Center and other clubs in the greater Los Angeles area.

The first gig was at the Seal Beach Auditorium on the sea front down by Long Beach.

We drove down to the gig in a new, green, V-8 van that we had leased from Hollywood Dodge, all very simple and quick, right off the shelf. Somehow we had acquired a guy who acted as driver and roadie and wheeled us on our way. The Freeway system revealed how massive LA was with miles and miles of development that stretched off beyond the horizon. As we drove further south the darkening landscape became an industrial zone of construction sites, freight yards and factories, bathed in orange lighting. We passed junkyards, scrap heaps and oil fields with hundreds of pumping rigs and flaring vents, adjacent to stockyards full of cattle. A city-sized industrial complex near Downey was where the rockets and capsules for the space launches were built. We drove at least thirty miles and we were still within greater Los Angeles.

After a sound check, we went to a back-stage dressing room.

"What are we going to play? We need a set list, let's put something together," John Nuese the guitar player suggested.

"Well now, what should we play for the fine young folks in Seal Beach?" Gram mused.

We had plenty of material, it was a matter of which way we tailored it and how much of the country style music we could throw in.

"Yeah okay, let's start with 'One Day Week' or 'I Don't Care.'"

"They probably want surf music."

"Yeah, it still could be big down here at Seal Beach."

'I'm gonna take you surfin' tonight, Oo-w wee oo-w woo,' Gram and I sang.

"Gee, we don't do that one kids."

"'Truck Drivin' Man', 'Buckaroo', uh, 'Lazy Day.'"

"Hold on, I'm writing this down."

Suddenly there was a burst of muffled, echoing music as the opening band, Dave and The Disciples began their set. It sounded like they could have been playing 'Route 66'. Their next number was 'Surfin' U.S.A.'

"Oh shit! They DO like surf music."

"Hey we're right on the beach, there's probably a bunch of them out in the parkin' lot right now, waxin'-down their boards and hangin' ten."

"I'll bet we're going to have to play 'Wipe-Out' if we want to get out of here and get paid." Everybody's gone surfin', surfin' you- ess- ay.

On stage, our first couple of numbers went okay. It was a big space, I couldn't hear much of our vocals and had to keep turning-up the bass amp. Gram announced the next one;

"Okay, thank you. Now we're gonna do a little number about drivin' trucks..."

One guy in a group of blonde teenaged surfers cupped his hand to his mouth and yelled, 'Get outta here with your trucks!'

"…And this one's 'specially for one of our fans down here in front. Okay, one two, one two three four."

We altered the set, scrubbed 'That's All It Took' and 'Blue Eyes', a couple of country songs and replaced them with 'Good Golly Miss Molly' and 'In the Midnight Hour' to give the crowd a bit more of the energetic, rocky stuff. It looked like they weren't into the country music in LA, either.

Peter Fonda had been over to hear us rehearse at Laurel Canyon. He was going to do some sessions for Hugh Masekela's label, Chisa Records and was considering cutting one of Gram's songs. There was also talk that the Submarine Band might do some sound track music for his new movie that would be shot next month. One afternoon a few days later, Brandon and I drove over to Coldwater Canyon to visit Peter. Brandon and Peter were friendly and shared the same personal management. At Peter's house we sat on a long, low, couch passing a joint back and forth. It tasted sharp, acrid and potent. Peter called the stuff Ice Bag. The dealer had packaged the pot in white bags, like those used in ice machines. The bag had images of cubes and said ICE. The coffee table was lo-o-n-n-n-ng and lo-o-w-w-w and so was the room and the whole house, the swimming pool, the lawn and the cars parked on the long driveway. This lanky, stretchy style must have been the design-look that defined success in LA. In New York height was more important, not width. Skyscrapers and apartment buildings, the higher the floor the better, the penthouse apartment was supreme. Just another fundamental difference between the two cities: New York was vertical, sprawling reigned in LA.

We smoked more Ice Bag, settled deeper into the couch as the room silently expanded and the carpet grew into a meadow.

"Man, that stuff is, ah, strong."

"Oh-h, yeah-h-h."

"It's knocking me right out man, shit."

We put our feet up on the coffee table, slumped back into an

LA sprawl and watched the spinning colors of a beach ball, blown slowly across the pool.

On the road, near Lucerne Valley, at a crossroads with nothing much more than a few houses and a gas station, I can see the blinker on the white van and I pull over as well.

"How's it goin', is everything alright?"

"We just want to have a better look at the map. There's
a junction, up here. See it? I think we just, sort of, go straight,
on to this other road," Briggs said with his finger on the map.

"Yeah. Man, it looks like there's nothing else along this way." The map showed a lot
of empty space and a couple of small roads.

"An-nd then it leads, just about, right into Joshua Tree."

"How far do you think it is, about an hour?" Asked Barry.

"Yeah, maybe fifty miles, about."

"God, I can't believe that we got outta there! We're on the road now." I was happy.

"Yeah, finally."

"Goodbye Hollywood."

Barry and Briggs had come out to the West Coast during the summer of '67 after the
Submarine Band had been settled in LA for about six months. We had originally known
each other from Boston then later we had all moved to New York. Their band, The
Remains, were big back east. They had done a lot of college and university gigs, had a
couple of singles that charted and were on the cusp of becoming the next big thing.
That's what the word had been. In the summer of '66 they had toured with The Beatles
and played the biggest venues and arenas in the U.S. But by the time I had left New York
the band had broken up, in spite of all their major achievements and the notches-on-
their-gun. Six months later they came out for a visit, had a taste of the West Coast and
decided to stay. Laurel Canyon seemed a better place to hang out than back east. When
you're waiting for that phone to ring, you might as well do it in the sun and, at least the
weather is much, much, better for barbecues.

I look around at the lopsided buildings, the flat dry range dotted with a few scruffy
bushes and the distant mountains, glazed orange by the afternoon sun. A puff of wind
stirs-up dust, I close my eyes and get a feel of the space and silence.

"I'm glad we're out of there. The last week, staying at Topanga was a bit weird."

"What do ya mean, did something happen?" I wondered.

"No nothing like that, it was just that the guys where we were staying were
rehearsing, working on some of the things they were writing. They were all full of how
good they were sounding, and what the manager was telling 'em. You know, the usual
bull. And, it was hard to keep my mouth shut and not come-out with something like,
hey we've been there and heard all the same crap, watch out, don't get too excited yet,
they're mostly all liars."

"I guess everybody has just gotta have at least one big swig from that bottle. You
know how much people want it," I said. "They can drink-up all they want, I'm moving

over and let them stand at the bar."

"Don't speak too soon, maybe we'll be turning-back in a week from now. Maybe less."

"No man, not that soon! Hey, I'm gaspin' for some of that mountain air, I just need to see if there's still someplace left that's safe to breathe."

Barry looked around. "Looks like it's getting better already."

"So-o-o, shall we get rollin'?"

"Lets go, I'll see you in Joshua Tree."

A few miles further down this minor road I see a sign, a piece of plywood with drunken lettering, 'U F O'. I peer down along the track but can't see any flying saucers that have landed and parked for the afternoon. I won't be able to see them anyway, I haven't resided in California long enough for my vision to be attenuated. Plenty of other people claim to see them all the time, it's just a common, everyday or everynight occurrence in California.

One evening, a few weeks after I had settled into the Laurel Canyon house, Gram had invited me to a small party that he and his girlfriend, Nancy were having for a few friends. There were drinks, something to smoke, snacks, candles and new faces. I nibbled and talked to some of them. Several of the guests were new acquaintances Gram had made at a spiritual and meditation group he had recently frequented. Wednesday night drifting.

I spoke with Susan, very soft, sweet and sincere. She asked, so I gave her a bit of a run-down on what had brought me here. After reflecting and twinkling, she responded with her interpretation.

"Wow, you're a really beautiful person Ian, that's why you have been guided to LA." She expostulated on her theory that LA was a new spiritual center on our planet and people were gathering here for the next renaissance, the new era. They were coming from all over the world, being led, whether they realized it or not, by a force that was beyond their power to resist. Part of the reason that people were arriving was due to their respective past lives and reincarnations. It seemed the man she studied with had been a keeper of the royal birds at a temple in ancient Atlantis. He tended the splendid aviary wearing radiant robes that came with the job. A woman Susan knew had been Joan of Arc in a former life and had been bequeathed an unusual birthmark in the shape of a flame.

"What about you? Tell me where have you been during the ages?" I couldn't remember an emperor's crown, the Pharaoh's court, the skyline of Babylon or the thin air of the Inca kingdom. Nothing so glamorous or romantic as her friends. Maybe I had been Howdy Doody's aunt, a black-and-white barn cat or, at most, a tail fin on Jonah's whale. I had never had a glimpse into any interesting, exotic past lives. "Well, let me look at your hand, come on, let's see. You can tell an awful lot by the palm." She studied my up-turned hand for a minute. "Oh wow! You're so new, so pure, that's so, so beautiful. You're beautiful." She had appraised me and approved, like examining a piece of fruit, evidently I was unbruised but not quite ripe yet.

"Are you going to the love-in on Sunday? It's at Griffith Park." Tall, blonde Natalie wore a burgundy velvet caftan trimmed with gold thread that patterned the hem and loose sleeves, her skullcap was of the same material. "Someone said The Doors might be there. Something very magical will happen, I know it. When you get hundreds and hundreds of beautiful people all together their spiritual energies can combine and if that happens... it can create an aural tunnel that opens-up into the astral level of being."

"Oh Yeah? Wow" I couldn't take what she was talking about seriously but she looked great, shit.

"Yeah really, it can pull you right out of your body. It's so beautiful to float in absolute purity, it's like being up in silvery clouds then you just fly-y-y. Wouldn't you like to do that?"

Fuck, she was making me dizzy, looking into her enchanting, jade eyes while trying to dredge-up an encouraging response from my slightly cynical stance. "Why don't you come with us? It'll be so beautiful." She fiddled with a silver filigree butterfly on the thin chain round her neck.

"Um-m, maybe, yeah maybe." I didn't want to bring her down or frighten her away by revealing what an earth-bound sort of guy I was. I liked motorcycles, the blast of wind in my face, leaning into corners, feeling the surge when you twist the grip but I didn't know about this disembodied flight, sounds a bit soft, too Dairy Queen. I was entranced by her lips and the movement of her moist tongue. I lost the thread of her delivery about the ethereal, Tinkerbell stuff. "Yeah, okay. Thanks. Maybe I'll see you there."

I drifted over to the other side of the room, beginning to feel stoned. I had taken several drags on the different joints that had been passed to me during a circuit of the room. The chatter began to take a rubber ball rhythm. Gram was sitting at a table with two others, staring into a crystal ball. They had turned off the lights in that end of the room and candle light licked, warm, soft, occasionally stuttering or darting when the flames were disturbed by passing strangers.

"You have to be ready to search through a lot of the stuff in your life." A slender girl with long dark hair and prominent teeth cooed to Gram. Her lids low, over unfocused eyes. "Just wait, it takes time...Sometimes something happens, almost right away......."

Other times, too many shrouds. Relax.... Go to the center, into the center...... Look into the ball.....Just look, try not to think.....That's right, look into the ball.....I can see-e-e, movement......Something....Waves...It's water. The ocean?...No, a lake.....It's not water.... Something else...A drink, someone's drinking...Thirsty...... Thirsting.......Is it you?...You want something. ....You need it....There's a hand, it's reaching across....It's covering the liquid, it's taking something,..... away.....Oh! It's gone now. Wow. Oh, wait a sec. I have to recover." She slumps back in the chair and shakes her head, slowly. "Ah-h-h. Sometimes it's so-o draining that I can't do anything for hours. I have had to call up my friend Julie to come over, because I was too exhausted to feed Karma, my cat. He's a very holy, Hindu cat. Ah-h-h. Now I feel better. Uh-h. Did that mean anything for you?"

Gram smiled and nodded but didn't act like any of that was crucial information. A woman, slightly older than the rest of the guests, with a round face, fleshy body and dark, styled-and-sprayed hair, caught my eye. She had been watching the crystal ball session.

"I didn't see anything but the tablecloth," she whispered.

"No, me neither. I guess you have to be a believer to see the show."

Outside in a courtyard, shared by the apartments that had been built in a Ye Olde English-movie-set style, I looked up and could see a few stars and the flashing of air traffic.

"The sky is so, so beautiful at night." It was soft-Sue from the party, standing in a darkened part of the garden.

"Yeah, nice." I gazed up again and saw a meteorite. "Wow! Look at that, must be a shooting star."

"Or a space-ship," she suggested. "We see them all the time. They are really interested in us. Sometimes I've seen three or four at one time."

"Oh yeah?" There were all sorts of things flying around overhead. LA International Airport was only a few miles away and there were jets, private planes, small air-strips all over the place and police helicopters, news teams and traffic reports. Funny, how lots of UFO sightings were often out west.

"Once, when the Byrds were playing at the Hollywood Bowl, the sky was full of them. They were sending messages that night. They must have known that there were thousands of groovy people all together in one place."

"What! Were they using groove sonar that night?"

"You can laugh but that is one of the reasons why they won't come down, they know that we have to be ready to accept them. We're just not there yet, a lot of people have to evolve and get much higher before the aliens are going to have anything to do with us.

They're just keeping track of things. You can feel it." She looked back up at the night sky and sighed. "It won't be long before we enter the new era."

I was saying goodbye, it was late but I didn't have far to drive, just Sweetzer to Laurel Canyon.

"You met some people, did you have a good time Ian?" Gram asked.

"Yeah, it was good. Thanks. What happened with the crystal ball, see your future?"

"Hey, a lot of stuff comes out of the mist, we don't know how much is out there. I like to keep lookin'. I met some of these people at this sort of class, like a meditation group. It's with a great man, Jacques. He's a visionary. He can see all sorts of things, yeah. I've learned a lot goin' there. I thought that you might like to come along sometime, maybe have an aura reading. Hey, I'll treat ya, a present. Come on man, it won't hurt, you might dig it."

"Yeah, okay man, thanks."

Hey, it's Hollywood.

The deal for the Submarine Band to appear in Peter Fonda's movie, The Trip, worked out. It sounded like it would be fun. Peter was playing the part of a guy going on an acid trip, the script was written by Jack Nicholson and Susan Strasberg and Dennis Hopper were in it as well. The Submarine Band would be doing a couple of scenes.

"Yeah, okay, you go on through, it's set number six." We were on the list and drove the van through the gates to the studio. The road went past rows of buildings the size of hangers, the third on the right was number six, like the guard told us. Inside, people were milling around and clanking tools that created an assembly plant, industrial feel. Technicians and lighting men on stepladders connected power cables to huge floodlights, others erected gantries or pushed sound booms and baffles into place. Small groups of people were talking, drinking coffee and looking through folders. Off to one side was a bar and two big movie cameras, I realized that it was a set and not catering, all the bottles were probably filled with colored water or 7-Up, with a little golden dye, to resemble beer.

"You guys are the band? Right, I'll get you in position, just follow me, this way, down here. Yeah, up on the stage there, try and get the equipment right in the back. Okay?"

As we set-up, more people, extras, arrived filling the floor area, it was a club scene. Some electricians were arranging colored lights and strobes for a light show. A speaker or megaphone crackled.

'Attention. Quiet on the set! Scene sixteen.' A crowd knotted around the bar area.

'Quiet on the set!' The lighting around the bar went on like an explosion, so intense and bright that I could just about count the hairs on people's eyelashes from across the room. Peter Fonda walked into the bar room, past a couple of tables, up to the bar, paused, slowly turned and scanned the room, then held that pose. The lights went out, the people and the bar decayed to gray.

Two naked women appeared and climbed up onto the stage, one stood next to me.

"Ah, hel-l-l-o-o." I greeted. Her body was painted with orange and green stripes and swirls, one eddying pattern radiated from her left nipple.

"What are you doing, who are you 'sposed to be?"

"I'm a dancer." She actually meant, 'I'm a dancer, stupid.'

"Well I hope the paint's enough to keep ya warm." I got a bit of a smile out of her then.

"It won't take long, it's just this scene," she replied.

"Do you do this a lot?"

"No, not with the paint."

She raised a hand, casually inspecting the purple polish on her long nails and settled into a relaxed, on-standby stance. She was used to hanging around. She was probably a topless dancer, working six nights a week at bars and clubs. Some of the Valley bars featured topless lunch-hour shows. She had big tits and looked a bit too old to still have dreams of becoming a starlet or hope that, today, she would catch an assistant director's eye and he'd offer her a role that might include clothing. There were dozens of fresh, young chicks on the set, a few of them were adorable.

'Quiet!' The lights blazed again and Peter repeated the scene walking to the bar.

Gram offered me a Winston, we lit them.

"He-y-y, how ya doin'?" He smiled at the painted dancer. She barely acknowledged him, just raised her eyebrows.

"Takes them an hour just to shoot a minute, huh"

"Maybe we'll be next, who knows."

"They can switch everybody off-and-on. Off...on...off...on...now you're he-e-r-re...no-o-w-w you'r-r-e...not! That's it...go to sleep," Gram drawled.

"Yeah when the lights go on the puppets start movin'," I agreed.

"Filming a set-up and trying to make us believe it. That's why TV is so stupid."

"Yeah, if you take out the canned laughter it really is dumb. Like on Ozzie and Harriet when the porky guy, Wally, Ricky's buddy, walked into the dining room and there would always be a big applause, as if there were a couple a hundred people sittin' around the house, in the kitchen or on the stairs. 'Hey Mrs Nelson, leave some a that cake for me.' Ha-ha-ha-ha-ha."

"Yeah. If Ozzie had to take a pee, he'd have to walk round saying, 'scuse me, oops, pardon me, lemme get past ya there,' just to get to the can. Hey well, it's all keepin' Mr and Mrs America happy."

"Keep watchin' folks."

"And buy your TV Dinners," Gram resolved.

'Quiet!' the megaphone demanded. Lights again, but we couldn't see what they were filming this time.

The cameras, lights and crowd moved closer to the stage end of the set.

'Okay! All you people dancing, get closer to the stage. Groupies, get right up front, lean on the stage.' I picked up my bass guitar, ready to act.

'Sound track! We're ready for the soundtrack, lets run it.' A tape began.

'Yeah, louder! More of the track!' The crowd danced, the colored light-rig flashed, the topless gal jiggled a bit, wisely holding back until the real take.

'Okay, hold it, hold it! You people dancing, we want more action than that, don't ya like to dance?'

A guy assumed the role of spokesman for a group in the dancing crowd. He was a bit too old for the part, I thought, really grizzly, skinny with a potbelly and was wearing striped tights, beads and fur, like Sonny and Cher.

'We don't know this song, man,' he explained.

We had recorded the song for the movie soundtrack a couple of weeks ago at Sunset Sound studio. The spot for the Submarine Band in The Trip was put together by Lawrence Spector Associates, some of the people involved, including Peter Fonda were under Larry Spector's management. He liked to work it that way, keeping it all in the family, spreading the bounty around for his clients, if and when that gilded ship came cruisin' in.

The session hadn't gone well, we had some problems recording 'Lazy Day'. The band had not settled into a groove that suited the sleepy, good-ol'-boy lyrics that Gram had written, back in New York. Hugh Masekela, the producer and another of Larry's clients, had suggested a harder, rock feel. We put down a wobbling rhythm track that was at odds with the lyrics that evoked a scene of sittin' on the front porch, swattin' them pesky m'skeeters, yawnin' and watchin' the day roll by. Maybe we picked the wrong song but there wasn't really much of a chance for success. Trying to come up with a psychedelic sound track using a South African jazz musician to produce a band that normally played country rock wasn't the right formula. It just wouldn't all fit in the same box. Like hitching a camel to a Pontiac and expecting a watermelon to take the wheel, it doesn't work. Since the beginning, the Submarine Band had been plagued by recording sessions that did not gel and producers that had no empathy or understanding of what we were trying to do. We had hoped that we would meet the right person, one day, some time, some place and it would all make sense.

On the set, the hippie dancers suggested that they do their own backing and, miraculously, out from under the furs and beads, a couple of bongos materialized and sparked off a minute of tribal dancing action. The cameras and lights rolled closer to the stage ready to shoot the band scene.

'Okay everybody. Quiet! Lights. Roll the track. Action!'

The colored spots winked and the strobes flashed. Through the dancing bodies a camera advanced slowly toward the stage flanked by a guy furiously puffing on two cigarettes and blowing smoke in front of the lens. I plonked on my mute bass and moved around simulating someone in a rock group. The painted dancer pumped her ass, pistoned her arms up and down and waggled her tits. She blossomed with a toothy smile and shut her eyes, conjuring the perfect expression of ecstatic abandon as she strobed in and out of existence. Mesmerized by the blipping painted dancer, I forgot that we were supposed to be lip-syncing and jumped over to the mic in time for the chorus. Arms waved in the strobe lights and someone grabbed at my leg. At my feet, on the stage edge, was a beautiful, petite girl, a little Audrey Hepburn, beaming up at me with adoration, desire and mouthing perfect kisses.

'A-a-nd CUT!'

Hey, it's Hollywood.

A couple of wigs from Capitol Records came out to the house at Willow Glen a few days later to hear us play. They were about forty, very self-assured and clean cut. Clark had wavy brown hair and wore a pale yellow knitted short sleeved shirt like a golfer and was an A & R man. Stephen was a vice president of something. They were both tanned, like they had spent the weekend cruising to Santa Catalina on their yachts. Clark was an outgoing guy, he shook hands and asked about the movie shoot. Stephen said hello then began looking around at the house, out of the windows, seeing what the surroundings were like, as if he were a real estate agent sizing up the place to put a value on it.

"What were you doing in New York?" Clark asked. "It's probably changed a lot since I left, that's the City for you. I used to be there, in publicity. It would take one Hell of an offer to get me back there now."

"It was good, yeah, we did a lot of things but we sort of reached that place where we just kept going round in the same circle, played the same clubs, got to feeling that there had to be something else. The world seemed to be getting a bit flat, you know. It pancaked-out, with maybe too much molasses," Gram answered.

We played a few songs for them, kept it short. Clark seemed entertained, nodding his head and tapping his Weejuns, Stephen remained straight-faced and occasionally gazed out the windows. It was a bit frigid playing for two guys, or really one-and-a-half, in the living room at four in the afternoon, with the sun blazing down outside.

"Yeah, yeah thanks. That was good. Those were your songs?" We should have had some drinks ready so we could sit around and talk, it would have broken the ice if we had offered them a beer or something. Maybe we could have rolled a joint and had a smoke but it wasn't like they were friends or anything. They weren't wearing them, but they were the guys in suits, from that fraternity of management and business.

"I like it, you sound good," Clark judged and weighed it up. "I'll tell you what though, I can picture a guy who's buying albums and he's got on a T-shirt, wearing his worry beads... he shakes his head and says, 'Man, I just don't dig that country an' western music, it's not what's happenin'.' That's how he'll see it. But there's something about what you guys are doing here that I like," Clark continued. "I'll tell you what, I think you can develop some of these, uh, ideas and maybe it'll be closer to some thing we might be looking for. Stay in touch, give me a call if you work-up some new material, I'd be interested, okay. Phone me in about a month or so."

We had a pretty good hold on Clark's take about country music already. It wasn't the latest breaking news or anything. Little hints and reminders about how far we were going in the wrong direction weren't that hard to pick up on. Pretty easy really, all we needed was to go out and play to get a good taste of the lions and Christians thing. We had another couple of meetings with other record company people that, pretty much, followed the same script. There must have been a record executives' training manual that they all had to study before being promoted to any position of responsibility. It contained a chapter including; 'Awkward decisions: Ten water-tight excuses'.

The Submarine Band's focus began to waver by the summer of '67. The rehearsal schedule slackened and we began to amuse ourselves individually. Mickey, the drummer, began screwing around with a Theremin sound oscillator, filling the house with eerie electronic sounds, ascending er-rr-rr-rr-rr-rr-rrs, wobbly woo-oow-wee-ooos and gargantuan, prolonged belches and burps. I began working on a sculptural construction, something that could go on stage, an addition to some of our music. It was a bit like an altar to some wino God of nightlife and advertising that incorporated flashing lights, mirrors, aluminum foil and dangling dolls. John took his guitar apart again. Gram kept trying to write songs and went to his meditation group.

Some nights the tape recorder rolled when Brandon, Mickey and I got together to swap lines, make up songs and stir-up a concoction of off-the-top-of-our-heads mish mash as we continued with the random home recording sessions that we had begun in New York over a year ago. In front of the mic, the three of us became a multitude of guests at a never-ending talk show. We adopted and developed fantasy roles for a wide spectrum of characters, animals, machines and attitudes. We would set up the microphones, get a balance, start the tape and just leap, never knowing where the action would take us or how the story lines would develop.

One night Mickey had moved the dialogue around to suggest several soldiers dug-in, ducking an artillery barrage in a fox hole.

"Phew. I don't know when this is going to end, Sarge. How long are we gonna be out here?"

"I just can't tell, Private Malooney. There's no way a-knowin'. We're just doin' our job an' bein' good soldiers. Just keep your powder dry and your hair curlers on," Sgt. DeWilde answered.

"But Sarge, I think we're the only ones left from our company."

"Come on soldier, no time for talk like that. We've got a war to win."

"Sure Sarge, but how long has it been goin' on? I can't remember. I was seventeen when it started, now I'm fifty-two. I could understand Viet Nam, Cambodia and then China but now…England!? Man, what the Hell is Lyndon Johnson gonna do next?"

Sometimes Gram would join us in one of the late night sessions as we explored our theater of the unknown. We would run the tapes back at another session and it was usually a surprise where the skits and dialogues went. Brandon thought they had potential if we edited the tapes and picked out the sections that worked and he wanted to make a demo to see if he could get any show biz interest in our alternative comedy.

The next Submarine Band gig was with Love and Iron Butterfly at The Valley Music Center in Encino. The concert hall featured a round, rotating stage where a band could set-up while another performed. Non-stop assembly-line shows, really smooth. Iron Butterfly opened up the show. They were very psychedelic and played long songs with marathon guitar solos building up to doubled-up, frantic rhythms. From my view back stage I could see the lighting man getting into it. He tried to follow them, clicking switches, blinking the stage lights off and on, dit-dit-dit-dit-dit. It wasn't really syncopated but it added to the trippy mood. The guitar player hunched down and his hair draped over the neck getting knotted in his fingers until he straightened up, arched his back and shook his head. The Butterfly finished with a climax of drums and guitar licks but the lighting guy missed it and kept flashing the lights up and down after they had stopped but no one really noticed it, they had done a good show.

The Submarine Band opened up with a couple of up-tempo country rock songs and got a good reception. They liked the look of us, different from the tie-dye shirts and beads. It might have been the first time Gram wore his new Nudie suit, a loud stage outfit styled on the glittering costumes that the country & western stars usually wear. Gram had found out that Nudie Cohn's Rodeo Tailors, the main man of flashy country wardrobes, was based in Hollywood. Wearing fancy, loud outfits was a very mainstream country music thing. Some of the c 'n' w stage outfits they wore were killers, often with wild designs that usually sprung from the musicians' whims. The stage suits were usually personalized; Porter Wagoner had one with wagon wheels and cactus, Hank Williams had worn a white suit covered with staves and notes. Others featured stars, flowers, sunsets or an image from one of their big songs. Gram had gone for the submarine theme. The suit was pink with turquoise, rhinestoned submarines and torpedoes. I wore a 1950s cowboy shirt embroidered with red roses and pistols that I had recently found at a swap meet. It was another way of showing that we were deep into country music, having fun with it and really dug the Webb Pierce sense of fashion.

We played a couple of our favorite old rock 'n' roll numbers, Gram switched back and forth between rhythm guitar and keyboard depending on the song. We had agreed that we would finish the set with an unrehearsed, free-form thing. The scene changed completely. The lighting man dipped the lights, candles were lit on stage, inducing a different mood. Gram began playing around on a Hohner clavinet, Mick started-up the whooping Theremin generating electro-ripples and I plugged-in my flashing altar-piece sculpture. Gram and I added random, arbitrary vocals. John, the guitar player, stepped back; it wasn't his sort of thing. The audience was mystified. We hadn't really thought where this was going, it wasn't rehearsed, there was no real progression, no definite beginning or end; that wasn't the idea. The performance didn't go on too long and ended in a roar of cacophony. The audience was perplexed at hearing rock 'n' roll, country and avant-garde all in one set and maybe slightly relieved to be let off so easy. It could have been worse.

There was some sparse applause in response to the 'thank you, good night, thank you'. The kids certainly weren't standing on their seats and screaming for more. We really hadn't thought about how a mainstream audience would react to such an awkward mix of music. It might have worked somewhere else but not tonight, in this place, with a teenaged crowd. I was reminded of the last gigs we did in Boston, where we did just about whatever we felt like on stage. The band was challenging people and, at the same time, taking the risk of alienating them. We seemed to have a tendency to keep doing that. Love, the main act, played some of their hit songs as we took down our gear, I recognized 'My Little Red Book'. They were a popular band, that's who most of the crowd came to see and the kids must have been relieved at getting rid of those guys wearing cowboy suits, playing country music followed by a mish-mash of noise.

At the back stage loading bay there were dozens of fans and groupies. A stunning, platinum-blonde chick wearing shorts and a top that must have been vacuum fitted, pointed at Arthur Lee and mouthed to her friend, 'I'm going home with him.' A guy from the Butterfly was holding a guitar case as his other hand cradled the butt of a girl with long, absolutely straight dark hair. Gram was talking to a couple of chicks and holding Nancy's hand.

"Hey Ian. You want to go to a party?" Gram asked, as a way of introducing me to the girls.

"Hi-i-i Ian," said white lipstick and big eyes. "We liked your show, cowboy"

"Why don't you come with us," suggested her friend.

"Well, after we load-up, I was going to drive the van back," I demurred.

"Oh come on, don't be shy!"

"Yeah, come on, let's have some fun. Get some one else to drive your van," said big eyes.

"Okay, sure. Yee-haw! Let's go. What's your name?"

Hey, it's Hollywood.

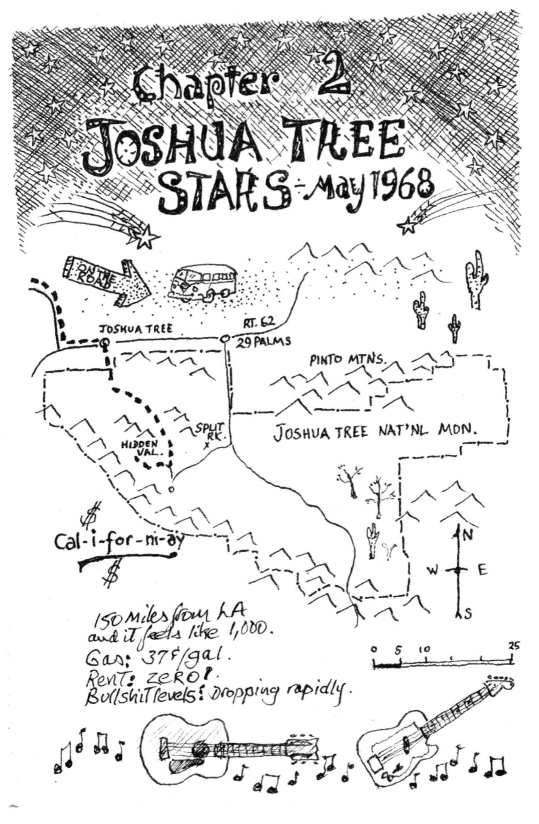

On the road, we roll off Highway 62 just after passing the straggle of buildings pretending to be a town. Joshua Tree, the beginning of the high desert, the edge of wilderness. A gravel road leads into the national park, further along, a sign points to Hidden Valley. That has a good sound to it, a promising place to camp, maybe. I could definitely use some hiding out for a few days, or more. We have taken a meandering route to get here and that reinforces the feeling of being distanced from Los Angeles, turning this morning's exit into a bigger event. Even though we are only about a hundred miles away from the city, it's a different world, an entrance to another era. We're bumping along in the Old West that lies hidden, between the hills, passing through cactus and big mounds of smooth boulders.

We are finally on the road and even better, we're heading off into the interior. From the city to the wilderness in one afternoon: easier than you imagine when you decide to do it. Passing a sign for Lost Horse Valley, we take another road at a wedding-aisle pace towards Split Rock. A mile further on, I spot a seldom used track trailing off behind a hill of large boulders, golden glowing, warm in the western sun. They have been waiting for me, I've been prophesying them. We meet at last. Behind this beckoning hill we'll be off the road, and out of sight.

"This looks mighty fine, I could stay here for a bit." Barry T approves.

"Yeah man, it's great! Here it is, we've arrived!" I enthuse.

"Yeah, it's beautiful! Wow, everything is so massive and ancient!"

"God! look at the size of these boulders, stacked-up there. Almost like they were huge constructions once, like temples or pyramids that have been slowly falling apart for a million years."

"So, how did the van go?' I ask Briggs.

"Yeah okay, we're not goin' to be breaking any records, won't have to worry about getting pulled-over for speeding. Hey, we got this far."

I yank open the rear door of my van, excited about pitching camp and trying out the gear we have collected in anticipation of a setting like this. A couple of weeks ago when we were working on the vans, the idea of being in a place like Joshua Tree seemed remote, a fantasy.

I look at the hills and the sky and remember the last couple of times I was here.

Once, in the fall, last year, I was driving around with Brandon and Mickey in a camper we borrowed from Larry Hagman. We had spent the afternoon out in the hills by Yucca Valley. The silence had seemed almost physical, like sense deprivation. There was no noise, nothing, as if any lurking sound had been eaten alive. We yelled to penetrate its permanence and were surprised by the vivid echoes, encouraging us to shout out words that we didn't often use. They bounced back, echoing, sounding ridiculous and a bit embarrassing.

'HE-E-L-L-LP…HE-E-L-L-LP'

'TA-AKE A-ACID…TA-AKE A-CID'

A few months before that shouting trip, in the summer of '67, a bunch of us had gone out to Joshua Tree at night. I had seen, on the news, that an unusual meteor shower had been predicted for southern California. Because of this special occasion I had spontaneously organised a shooting-star tour. I phoned Gram to let him know what might be up and the romantic prospect of a night sky, raining stars, appealed to him. Later that afternoon, we packed-up some blankets, sleeping bags and snacks and drove out here hoping for a spectacular show. All aboard, all aboard for the night star show! It was the first time Gram had been to Joshua Tree.

Gram and I had been friends and had worked together for almost two years by then. We had done a lot together since we first met in Cambridge, Massachusetts in September of '65. There had been loads of gigs and recordings, it had been a crazy trip, a lot of fun.

In '65 there was a small music scene happening in Cambridge. There weren't a whole lot of us and it hadn't taken long to figure out what was going on, what venues there were and who was doing anything. Gram had walked into a shop, where a friend of mine was working, looking for a birthday present for his sister. While browsing he had mentioned that he was a musician and was trying to make some connections. My friend had suggested that he come over to meet some of the musicians she knew. He did. At the time we didn't have any idea that we would eventually work together.

After first meeting him, I used to hang out with Gram in his students room at Harvard. We would often listen to music, have a couple of drinks or smoke a joint that led to talking and laughter. Gram was underage in Massachusetts, you had to be twenty-one to buy booze, but he had figured out a method to get around that little obstacle. He would 'phone in an order to a package store that provided a delivery service, pay by credit card and they never would bother to ask for an ID. Bingo! The booze was delivered by a friendly young student, working a part-time job and not concerned about law enforcement. We'd sip a bit of whiskey and listen to records, they could be by Ray Charles, Bill Evans, The Beatles or others. Sometimes, on one of those autumn nights, Gram would show me a song he was working on, pick up his acoustic guitar and sing. His songs were lyrical, poetic, sometimes mournful and occasionally they seemed a bit too long. He sang and played in a folk style. He had been influenced by spending time in New York that summer and being around the Greenwich Village folk scene. He talked about wanting to arrange some of the songs for a band, going electric rather than solo acoustic, like most of the folk singers and songwriters were doing.

Gram had been rehearsing with a group of guys from the Berkley School of Jazz, in Boston who had answered an ad that he had tacked-up on a couple of student bulletin boards. He had invited me over to one of their next sessions at the Harvard Student Union and I sat back listening as four guys, on guitar, drums, bass and electric piano, played through some of Gram's songs. It sounded proficient, maybe over-complicated or a bit stiff, the solos and instrumental bits were jazzy and congested. Folk rock without the rock.

After the rehearsal Gram, Tom Snow, the piano player, and I went back to Gram's dorm to have a smoke and hang-out for a bit.

"Hey, wait 'til you try this stuff."

"Wha' cha got there?"

"It's a last little piece of hash from New York."

"Okay, let's try it on for size."

"Here's a light."

Gram put a Beatles LP on the turntable. They sang about hiding love away.

"What did you think the rehearsal sounded like tonight?" Gram wondered.

"Um-m, I don't know. I think the rhythms might have been a bit, uh-h, bouncy, Maybe."

"Um-m-m."

"It, sort of, sounded a bit jazzy to me. Maybe that's what you want? All those guys could play well."

"You know what I like about this track? There isn't much on it.

It starts off without, hardly, any backing...you know…. just a tambourine and acoustic guitar." Gram said, listening.

"Yeah that's kinda cool isn't it."

"They do some great recording things. I like how you can hear the different instruments." Tom said.

"Yeah man, the way they recorded that stereo sounds really great."

"Yeah."

"M-m-m."

"Hey, it always sounds good…. when you're stoned…. like this."

"Yeah, cool."

Later, Tom Snow decided he had to split and walk down to Harvard square to catch the M.T.A. back over the river to Boston.

"Tom's a good player, man."

"Yeah, I like his feel.... an' the chords he uses. I don't know about a couple of the other guys though. What do you think?" He asked me.

"I thought they were.. well, too busy, or played too fast or something."

"Yeah. Um-m-m. Maybe we could try something, with you and a couple of those guys you know?" Gram suggested.

"Okay man, sure. You could come over to my place and we could jam.. I've got a bass over there. I'm not a busy bass player, that's for shit-sure."

"Yeah? Maybe that's good. Why's that?"

"Well, I've been a sax player and singer all the time. I only just got a bass awhile ago."

Shortly after that rehearsal at Harvard, Gram had come over with his guitar to visit me where I was living on Kinnard Street, a low-rent neighborhood in Cambridge, one of the areas where bohemians, musicians and black people lived. Several musicians were staying in the same house; John Nuese, Michael Cain, 'Bananas' and others. The residents and their instruments changed, floating in and out depending on circumstances. We were all involved in some way or other with music, either in bands or trying to get something together.

I was still doing a few gigs with my outfit, The Refugees, the band I had been fronting since I was fifteen. We had started by playing at very local small-town gigs, birthdays, beach parties, store openings and high school dances, but over the last few years had moved-on to do gigs at the numerous colleges, universities and fraternity house parties around the Boston and New England area. It was good work, playing rock 'n' roll and r 'n' b standards for a bunch of students who wanted to go nuts on the weekends, drink beer and yell the A-a-ays and O-o-ohs to 'Wha'd I Say'. But, like Gram, I was looking for something different, whatever that might be.

The expectations of most musicians were changing as more and more records were released by the companies and new labels. The era of American Bandstand-type music was at an end and the accent was on groups. Boston was beginning to feel like a scene, there were a lot of bands coming together, a few of them were talking about deals with labels and more of the coffee houses and folk clubs were becoming rock music venues. The Lost and Barry & the Remains were both signing record deals.

We jammed at Kinnard Street with a couple of guitars and a bass, strumming along with a few of Gram's tunes. It was cool, playing with songs that were originals and weren't completely formed or finished. One of Gram's songs, 'November Night', had a tempo change that made it different and it had a bit of a Beatles feel to it. It was a change from playing all the old r 'n' b covers; Chuck Berry, Jimmy Reed or Solomon Burke. The song wasn't a blues twelve-bar, the lyrics were romantic, full of impressionist imagery and I had to find a bass part that fit. Some aspects of his songs seemed a bit too gentle or soft but there was also a feel of something a bit different. We all enjoyed messing around with them and Gram liked some of the moods that we managed to conjure up.

Someone suggested a smoke of some new pot they had just picked up. All of us were in favor of that. We passed a pipe around, whooshing and coughing. Gram talked about his plan to rehearse several of his songs, getting some arrangements worked out and going into a recording studio to get them down on tape. Gram had recorded one or two of the songs a couple of months ago but he had done them acoustic solo and he wanted to get more of an electric sound in them, some push and shove.

I was excited by the prospects of going into a recording studio one day. The only recording I had done was on a primitive domestic tape recorder that had a small white plastic mic on a short lead and flashing green neon fish-eye, volume-level gauge. The recordings we tried always resulted in a distorted, rhythmic fuzz when played back on the recorder's built-in two-inch speaker. My only experience in a studio had been recording an instrumental rock 'n' roll song of mine at the W-ARA radio studio in '62 when the Refugees had won a talent contest in Massachusetts.

Gram, feeling more positive about the songs and the sound, went on with a bit more detail and mentioned a New York manager who might be able to put a deal together for him with RCA. It sounded like the real thing, a major league deal. It was just a matter of getting some of his songs worked out and recorded so the demos could be presented to the record company and he could move on to an exciting future.

"Wow man, that's great!" I congratulated.

"You feel like gettin' together again sometime, what do you think? Maybe something might just happen."

"Shit yeah! Sure."

The guitar player that day was John Nuese. I had met him in Providence when I was at RISD in '64. Providence was one of the smaller jewels in the alternative culture's crown in the early '60s. Greenwich Village, Woodstock, Cambridge, San Francisco, Taos, some place in Colorado, maybe Boulder, Provincetown and a few other places were hideouts for the hip culture. When I first met John he had just returned from London and was all fired up about bands, groups and rock music. He had pretty much traded his acoustic Martin for a Telecaster. John had wanted to try and put a band together and over the next few months we stayed in touch, but apart from talking over possibilities, and listening to our favorite records, nothing really had come together. At the end of the summer of '65 we were both living in Cambridge. John was doing some gigs with a Cambridge band, The Trolls that had just reformed after a split with their singer.

During that same time period I had gone with friends over to South Washington Street in Boston, a night club district where there were a lot of bars and clubs. The bands that played over there were good and we could see some hot stuff. Most of the bands worked on a club circuit, travelling and playing a week here, a week there, in the sleazier parts of the cities. Washington Street could be a rough part of town and they called it the War-Zone. There were usually lots of sailors, drunks, fights and cops on the street. It was a completely different thing than Harvard Square in Cambridge, with its huge student population, bookshops, coffee houses and folk clubs. Cambridge had the Club 47 with Dick and Mimi Fariña, singing peace songs or bluegrass by Keith & Rooney. Washington Street had Louie's Lounge with the Ferraris, pumping out rock 'n' roll, and go-go girls wearing sparkling, fringed bikinis. We had heard about a band playing over there, at the Intermission Lounge, called Roger Pace & the Pacemakers, they were supposed to be unbelievable.

A few of us decided to go over and check them out and it was something else. Washington Street was busy, the gaggles of people roaming up and down the sidewalks glowed under the neon lights of bars and clubs. I stopped in front of a store that had a window full of garish clothes; lavender-and-black, frilly-front shirts, iridescent peacock-blue jackets with black satin lapels and Valentine-red satin, lacy underwear sets. It looked like a shop where a small-time magician would get his stage outfits. I wondered who would want to wear a bow tie the size of a vampire bat. We came to a club that had big plate glass windows on one side of the door, you could see who was on stage and hear them. A small speaker was mounted above the entrance blaring the sound of the band onto the street. It was distorted and when the singer grabbed the mic the speaker spouted a honking drone. One couple danced up near to the band. The woman was wearing a black shiny mini skirt that flashed as she shook. She raised her arms slowly like a weight lifter and swished her hair side to side.

Roger Pace was charged with high-tension energy. He danced, sang, screamed and sweated underneath a teased-up pile of reddish hair; practically a bouffant. During a song he would spin around, pluck up an alto sax and blow an intro or solo, dance with the spinning mic-stand, or juggle the microphone. The Pacemakers were playing soul music. They did stuff by Joe Tex, Wilson Pickett and long medleys of James Brown songs. Their sets were energetic, and frantic. There was never any discussion as to what they were going to play next. They never stopped and ran one song into the next, linking them up with a few hyped-up bars of 'Hold It', the old Bill Doggett instrumental.

It was only a quartet but they sounded like so much more. They were very tight and the drummer was amazing, he played very differently from anything I had heard before, it was weird. He seemed to accent the oddest places of the beat, turning it inside-out but always coming out on top. The bass player was hot, playing all over the neck of his Fender jazz bass. He was tall, with dark hair and very white skin, like he never saw the sun, but he couldn't stop smiling. He looked like a very happy, well-adjusted vampire. They ended their set, all of them trotting in place, to a blistering version of 'Hold It', while Roger glided across the stage on one foot, while screaming, 'We gotta run, we gotta run'. Wow! What a show!

During their break we went over and congratulated Roger and the band on such a whacked-out show, had a drink with them and gabbed. They seemed Southern to me but were from Baltimore and had been gigging in Virginia the week before they came up to Boston. The Intermission had booked them again. They were crowd pleasers. The place wasn't too busy at the moment, it was still early and they probably went on 'til two. Roger and the Pacemakers were going to be in Boston for another week and had a matinee spot on Sunday at a club south of Boston and invited us to come down there and sit-in.

Gram and I drove down to the Pacemaker's Sunday gig in his Austin Healy. It was a warm day and we had the roof down, our hair whipped around on the Southeast Expressway out of Boston. I got up on stage with the Pacemakers, sang 'Johnny B. Goode' and Nuese played guitar. Roger and the band might have thought we were sort of corny, playing such a worn-out song but we all got a kick out of it. Gram got talking to Mickey Guavin their drummer and a few days later he came over to Cambridge to check out Kinnard Street. He met some of the crowd that came by, smoked the pot that was going around and decided that he would finish-up the week at the Intermission Lounge, quit the Pacemakers and get into this crazy Cambridge scene. There was room for him somewhere, people were always coming and going.

A week or so later, Gram let the guys from the Berkley jazz band go, except for Tom Snow, the pianist, and we began rehearsing. Gram started writing some more material and revamped other things into a form that might be more suitable for a band. He put off going to classes or missed lectures and would show up at our next session and sing a new tune that he'd just finished. A few of them showed promise and worked out, others did not, songwriting is like that.

The news from New York was that Gam's manager expected to book a date for recording, probably soon. Gram was very happy about the way things were falling together and his optimism was contagious. At the end of October we rented a station wagon, loaded the gear and headed out of Boston. I was driving the tail-heavy wagon down Storrow Drive and getting use to the mushy ride. John, in the back seat, was criticising my overtaking, when Gram lit a joint and passed it over.

"Hey this'll help make the trip a bit more interesting."

Yeah, okay, why not. We got on Route 24 and awhile later 95 on our way to New York and cruised down there in a cloud.

We were booked into a studio in midtown Manhattan to record a few demos for RCA and got there okay, in time for our afternoon slot.

We wheeled our gear into the studio and quickly set up, got in tune and tried to hype ourselves up. I had not been in a studio as sophisticated as this before and I wasn't the only one. The New Yorkers probably didn't mean it but the studio people seemed abrupt and impersonal. Somehow the clock or the pulse started racing. Everything happened too quickly and seemed to be out of control. When the red recording-in-progress light went on it radiated like a warning, rather than an invitation to do something good. We had a bit of trouble laying down the backing tracks and reacted by playing very cautiously. I could only hear a bit of what we were doing. My earphones had the fidelity of an elevator sound system producing a thin, watery version of what we were playing and they kept slipping off.

"Okay guys. We're going to call that one a run through," said the engineer through the headset. "I'm going to run the tape back and we'll roll it again. Okay? What do you call this one?"

"'November Night', officer." Replied Gram.

We cut a couple of things that afternoon, 'I Just Can't Take It Anymore' and 'November Night'. It took us about a half-hour to set up and maybe two hours, or less, to record. It was over before we knew it.

"Okay boys, thank you."

Maybe we were only booked in for a couple of hours, it was a demo session. We listened to the songs being played back as we packed up. I guess the songs sounded better than when we first started rehearsing them a few weeks ago. We just left the songs there at the studio, abandoned them believing that the engineers would work some technical magic and the tracks would be the first of many for RCA. Really, it was more like the tracks were about to be kidnapped or exiled to Siberia. We never heard that stuff again.

Gram had delivered on his end of the deal and we were proud to get that done. There was a 'Hey, wow, we've recorded in New York!' feeling of achievement, it was a good buzz. Later that night we celebrated at Brandon's fifteenth-floor apartment on the upper West Side. We had an order of Chinese food delivered and followed the fried rice and Moo Go Gai Pang with Lebanese Red and smoked ourselves silly.

As the night went on we picked up some instruments and started fooling around. Brandon had a decent quality Tandberg tape recorder set up in his living room and had been using it as a home studio, recording songs he had been writing. We plugged in a couple of microphones and started the tape rolling. Brandon had figured out how to get a wonderful echo effect, a bit like the old Sun Records sound, by using open mics with a bit of fold-back into the room.

'Hey!'...hey....hey......hey, how's that?...that...that...that

'Yeah, great...great.....great......great.'

The living room had suddenly been transformed into a completely different place, a new space, an echo chamber. The four walls seemed to have melted. Every sound, voices, snapping fingers, clapping, scratching or whistles, became embellished and animated with a theatrical, reverberating richness.

'Wow, wonderful....full....full......full'

We played off-the-cuff, goofy music, jamming, following ideas and themes that surfaced, just going with whatever happened. Gram picked up a Fender Mustang and we played a mangled conglomeration of surf-music. He grinned sheepishly, pulled faces and bit his tongue as he staggered through lead-guitar clichés. We sang; 'We're hangin' nine on our woodies, catchin' the pipeline, Woo-Ooo.' Mick put together an instant percussion kit, trying out different sounds made by playing items picked up around the house; a cereal box, shoes, wooden spoons or a hairbrush, what ever worked. We joked between the music and soon characters, alter egos, began to develop. Brandon and Gram became, Pelbert J. Long and Lulu Round. Dickens' Tiny Tim appeared, with his strident, squeaky voice. An interviewer questioned Ogg the caveman who responded in a guttural language and grunts until he was chased-off by Wild Bill Hickok's TV sidekick, Jingle Jones, shooting a bazooka. Mrs Santa Claus, relaxing in her bubbling bath, revealed her prize-winning walrus pizza recipe and the old Senator, Everet

Dirkson, croaked-out political jargon, accompanied by a cloud of humming angels. We went on, until the tape ran out.

"Okay, sounds good, let's over-dub it," said Brandon as he rewound the tape. He enjoyed doing this, he was an actor. It was fun, recording in such a loose uninhibited way. I reflected on the Submarine Band's midtown session, earlier this afternoon. The mood and the atmosphere at the studio had been completely contrary to having fun. It had been so technical and restrained. We had been like greenhorns, intimidated by technicians, nothing like what had just happened here. Creating scenarios and music out of thin air wouldn't have happened back there in that studio. Maybe the session would have been more successful if they had left the tape recorder running and then took-off for a long lunch break.

"Man! Why couldn't the recording studio have been a bit more like this?" I suggested to Gram.

"Well, they were just busy, tryin' to be New Yorkers, lookin' at their watches every six minutes-and-forty-two seconds, makin' sure they still existed. Once you stop doin' that, Aunt Jemima might quit makin' pancakes and you have to line up for bagels again. Yeah...that musta been why."

At two in the morning, Gram and I stepped out of the elevator and walked outside onto 92nd Street, into the chilly New York night. We headed towards 10th Avenue, tired and zonked-out-stoned. We were approached by a Hispanic prostitute.

"Can I do anytheeng for you boys?" She smiled.

"No, nadda. We're fucked-up enough already."

A Checker cab took us flying down 10th Avenue, through an Edward Hopper nightscape, past flashing stoplights and steaming manholes. We both gripped the seat like it was a roller coaster, wide-eyed and silent until we reached 4th Street where we wobbled out of the cab. Walking towards the street corner, I heard roaring voices and a crash, like a garbage can being knocked over in a street brawl. We slowed and stalled as a monstrous silhouette loomed around the corner. An enormous lion, walking upright, approached, making us freeze. We were spooked. In that instant, another monster or robot followed the lion, banging and clanking as he lurched towards us. The Tin Man and the Cowardly Lion bellowed with laughter at the two petrified wimps glued to the sidewalk.

"Happy Halloween boys!" they cheered.

"Hm-m, I guess we're not in Kansas anymore, Ian." Gram slurred.

At our campsite in Hidden Valley the tents are set up. A plank bench serves as a kitchen counter. We have gathered fuel, gleaned around Joshua Tree. Scrubby branches, dried out cactus and dead leaves from the stubby desert palms, are piled up where we will have our campfire. Barry T and I sail a Frisbee back and forth. F-f-f-f-fw-w-w-wup, he scales one over, I catch it, spin it backhand, in his direction. F-f-f-f-f-fw-w-w-up. I tell him about my last trip to Joshua Tree, trying to remember it.

"We might have been around here somewhere, maybe. Don't know where though, it was dark. We drove off the road a bit and stopped, we came out here to see the shooting stars. There were a bunch of us, Gram, Nancy, a couple of others maybe." F-f-f-f-fw-w-w-wup. I have to run for that one. "The shooting stars thing must have been just before you and Briggs came out to LA, yeah. I guess we probably didn't get this far into the park on that night." F-f-f-fw-w-w-wup. "I can't remember if Brandon came to see the stars? Hum-m, maybe not, he might have been away." F-f-f-f-w-w-w-wup. "I remember that Gram and I were talking about how we couldn't recollect seeing any stars when we were living in New York."

"Well, you're too busy watchin' out for traffic in the City, you can't spend much time looking up. There's too much happening at street level in New York. You're either going to get crushed by a crowd in a stampede to cross the street or hit by a taxi as soon as the light has changed or have your wallet stolen by a pickpocket. Doesn't leave a lot of time for looking at stars." Barry T figured.

The Submarine band moved to New York early in '66, said 'bye to Cambridge, Kinnard Street and Harvard and cut-out for the brighter lights of the city. Our new base was up in the Bronx, in a big house with plenty of space to live and rehearse. We put together a band room, under the roof on the third floor, thumbtacked as many egg crates as we could get to the walls and started playing. We only practiced live with amps and drums during the day, never at night. We didn't need to get any visits from the cops or neighbors complaining about noise.

During the few months of rehearsals, recording sessions and hanging out together, our energy had changed. We had come together as a few guys backing up a singer in a few months but had evolved into a band. Tom Snow did not want to make the move to New York and Marty Erlichman's fabled RCA deal seemed to have gone cold, leaving the four of us to decide where to go next. We shuffled the deck and made suggestions for new material to play, rather than restricting ourselves to Gram's folk-rock songs.

What we came up with was a change, a different direction and we needed a name, an identity for the band. Back in Cambridge, Gram had tossed around the idea of using 'Gram Parsons & the Like'. The name didn't grab me that much, a bit flat, but it summed-up the project at the time. It can be difficult if you think too much about titles and names, nothing is perfect. One day Mick and I had been watching an old black-and-white Buck Rogers outer-space thing on TV and we began talking about the TV shows we had seen when we were kids. I remembered one of the Little Rascals films I saw on TV in the '50s and the cumbersome name they had used for their comedy orchestra. It was sort of cool. I shortened it to The International Submarine Band. The title was clumsy but catchy, it contained humor, a hint of mystery and was slightly underground and alternative, it could work. None of the other guys in the band said no.

It didn't take long to put a couple of sets together using a few originals, some covers and old rockers. We wanted to get out there and start gigging. Gram knew some club managers from the time he had spent in the Village playing on the folk scene and most of them were looking for bands now. It was good timing for us. We auditioned and pulled a week-long gig at The Night Owl in the Village. That was our New York debut.

The Night Owl had become a happening club and was right in the centre of the Greenwich Village club scene on Bleecker Street, a great place to start. There was always a buzz. The streets were busy with people looking around to see what was going on or what might be trendy in New York. 'What's happening', that's what they wanted to know. At the club we were greeted by Jack the freaky doorman, a Village fixture, wearing his button, pin and badge-encrusted straw hat and vest. He had strange eyes, definitely weird looking. Jack was a walking advertisement, proclaiming the alternative tone of the club, sending a message that something different might be going on inside. The Night Owl was a small place with a stage down the far end and a dressing room the size of a phone box but it had a history and a reputation as a showcase venue. A lot of musicians had started there, including The Lovin' Spoonful.

We usually did two or three sets at The Night Owl, sometimes alternating with another act. Gram and I would swap singing the lead vocals and backing each other. We played a bit of rock 'n' roll; 'Rip it Up', 'Sweet Little Sixteen', some r 'n' b and soul, 'the Midnight Hour', 'I Can Tell' and a few crossover country songs, 'As Long As I Live' and 'Just As Long As You Love Me'. We went down well. It was mostly up-tempo stuff, a lot of covers and maybe a couple of Gram's folk-rock songs. We sounded like a rock band. The front of the club had windows onto the street, people could see the band and hear the sound pouring out of the open door, they could check-out what was on sale and we managed to pull 'em in. At the end of our first week the club wanted us to come back the week after. Okay! That would give us some time to make a few calls, hustle some music biz people and get in more rehearsals. New York was looking good, we had found our foothold at The Night Owl.

Our next week at The Night Owl was playing back-to-back with The Strangers, a New York based outfit. We would only catch a bit of the other band's set as usually we would go for a drink somewhere else to see what was happening at other clubs or meet people. One night The Strangers were finishing their set and they did some Motown covers. The singer-guitarist was a dark-haired, burley guy and looked like a wrestler. I knew Jay, the drummer, from Cambridge. Tonight he was playing like he was bored and wanted this last set finished. It was a quiet mid-week night. The Strangers left the stage and almost immediately a bunch of guys, looking like a gang from West Side Story, climbed up. They wore uniform, lavender, frilly-front shirts, black slacks with satin ribbon down the outside leg and dark, slicked-back hair. It was the '50s again! Where did they come from? They moved the mic stands around but didn't seem to have any instruments with them. It was an audition. The club owner must have suggested that they come over and he'd see what they sounded like. They were probably Italian kids from Jersey or Queens and were right in there with that late '50s, white, doo-wop look; like Dion and The Belmonts, Danny and The Juniors or the Elegants. This was a blast from the past, no one played that sort of old stuff any more! Sure enough, they started singing;

'Ba-wah-da-da-da-da, ba-wah-da-da;

Oh my baby, my sweet, sweet darling,

you'll never know, oh no no no,

how much I love you so, Ba-wah-da-da'.

Gram and I could not help smiling and enjoying their enthusiasm. They must have been in a coma for the last few years or buried so deep in lasagne in Newark or Long Island that they were unaware that the era of Brylcreem and doo-wop was long gone, like, in the grave. Their shiny black shoes kept in-step with a dance routine and, snapping their fingers, a row of four guys sang back-up harmonies.

"Man, this has gotta be some sort of time warp." I guessed.

"Yeah. Look out New York, here we come!" Gram laughed.

"They do look like they're dressed up to go to a '50s costume party."

We clapped and cheered when they finished.

"Yeah! More! More!"

"And now Sal's gonna do one for all you love birds here tonight," they announced and started into a slow ballad.

"Hey, at least they're not goin' to go through a lot of anxiety about getting a record deal." Gram whispered. I guess they didn't get the gig. We never saw them again.

After finishing our last set Gram and I were going out to score some hash. That afternoon Serge, a jazz drummer and dealer, had 'phoned putting the word around that he had just got hold of some Lebanese and it was powerful stuff. There was always Mexican grass available here and there but we preferred hash. It didn't stink-up the place so much, it wasn't so common or recognizable and we could smoke it mixed with tobacco poked back into a regular filter cigarette. A couple of drags and the hash would be gone. We called them tippers, very convenient when running around town.

Going out to score could be pretty creepy, so occasionally we dealt with a guy who did a home delivery service. The trouble with him was he'd bring his guitar and, after sampling the goods, we'd feel obliged to sit through one of his guitar-raga performances that normally went on for about ten minutes too long. Tonight was going to be one of those eerie, Film Noir trips, down towards Canal Street.

We took the subway from Washington Square. It was still early enough for the subway not to look like a train full of lost souls riding to Hell. Those special trains would begin arriving at the station in about an hour from now. As we rocked on the subway seats our late night visages were reflected in the tunnel-blacked window opposite and our ghosts would disappear when the train threw up blue electric flashes and sparks.

We emerged from the underworld onto Spring Street, walked down 6th Avenue, locked-up and dim, and onto Grand Street, a desolate warehouse district. Silent, empty brick buildings loomed up on both sides of the deserted street. Our footsteps rang out, echoing as we picked up the pace and crossed over toward a dark alley. Gram flicked a lighter revealing the rust-and-green metal door, I grabbed the handle and it creaked open. The metal gate of the freight elevator slammed. Gram reached out to the controls, turned to me and said,

"What floor do you require, sir?" The elevator lurched and began a groaning ascent. In the metal cage, the orange light illuminated the passing bricks and cement. It was like travelling up a giant chimney.

"Second floor. Ladies department; underwear, negligees."

"Third floor. Sporting goods; baseball bats, guns and knives."

"Fourth floor. Drugs department; pills, marijuana, hashish. Everybody out, please."

"Hey." Serge welcomed, from the lighted end of the huge loft. We made our way through boxes, crates and mysterious forms. A large gas heater, whooshing blue flames, hung on chains from the ceiling, suspended sheets created room divisions. A drum kit and guitars stood in a corner. An industrial sink, a fridge and a table, covered with pots and pans, boxes of cereal, packets and jars were beyond the sitting area. Serge sat in a big dusty ripped easy chair, Gram and I sat down on a couch with wildly mismatched cushions. Through the fabric drapes I could make out a figure in a brass double bed, a shape under layers of covers.

"We were rehearsing earlier, Buzzy's got a couple of new songs, we're starting to get 'em together. Yeah, you gotta come down and hear us some time," Serge suggested.

Buzzy Linhart had been on the club scene in the Village, Gram knew him and had said that he was good and had a soulful voice. He wrote wacky songs and was getting a band together. I think he was having trouble though, he was a bit nuts, a character. Maybe he'd been to Vietnam or had taken just a bit too much acid, something like that.

Serge was wearing a long-john top, jeans and sandals. The straw hat, short beard and sunken cheeks made him look like a Vincent Van Gogh self-portrait.

"Okay. You want to try some of this stuff, yeah?" He unwrapped a cloth revealing a round, hamburger-sized lump of brick-colored hash.

"Wow! Look at the size of that thing."

"Hey now, don't be greedy boys," Serge smiled as he prised off a little chunk, lit a match and crumbled the hash into the skull shaped bowl of a small pipe. He struck another match and proffered the pipe across the coffee table.

"Okay, now who's gonna be first?"

That Lebanese had whacked us! Was it powerful shit or what! Man, were we zonked-out. The freight elevator seemed to grate and stutter as we descended like miners, down, down the long shaft, past miles of brick wall, for two hundred floors, to the knee-bending clunk of the ground. The steel door, now six inches thick, seemed welded shut and reluctantly gave way with a metallic roar. The two a.m. street was breathless and empty: silent and black. We were blind. I could hear the faint rustle of our clothing and the beating of my heart as we cautiously shuffled along the uneven sidewalk on our concrete legs, struggling to lift leaden shoes. We crept along making very little headway as shapes of the surrounding city jungle began to materialize, rear up, forming an endless tunnel of sky-high brick punctuated by gaping caves and mouths. My foot nudged something. An open manhole, a bear trap? It clanged on the sidewalk. A tin can. It sounded more like a large, metal trash can. Man! Why did we get so wasted! This was no-mans land, limbo. We were hardly moving. Gravitational force was growing stronger every second. We might grind to a halt and solidify, becoming statues, overwhelmed by the concrete, until we fused with the bricks.

I had a revelation. We actually had a choice, if we could break the spell.

"Hey, uhm-m, ah, we gotta get movin', man. Just get movin'. I don't want to get stuck here in Vampire City all night." I whispered.

"Yeah, ah, we sorta got a little glued here", Gram agreed, "seems like the old sidewalk just won't let me go."

"Yeah it has me too. Let's see if we can walk a bit better." I took a bigger step. "Yeah….. See, that's better.……Yeah. Now we're moving, aren't we."

"Hey, yeah, it's not so hard if you get into it."

"No, we're doin' okay, we're doin' okay…..Yeah, that's better."

"Now we're flying along, hey."

"Yeah! I can see street lights way up there, we're gonna make it."

"Walk towards the light, walk towards the light."

Lower Broadway beckoned. If we kept going we could get the subway. Of course, by now, it definitely would be the time for the Lost Souls Express. Maybe we could get a taxi? As we got closer to Broadway the light filtered onto the dark street and I could make out a group of people on the sidewalk. Oh shit! Now what? Muggers, zombies, cannibals? Walk faster, just keep going. Two or three of them were huddled in a doorway off the main avenue, wrapped up, like they could have been bodies, just dumped out of a hit man's Caddy. One of them muttered as we went by. They were alive, or close to it anyway, probably winos.

Broadway was quiet, only a bit of traffic as we turned on to the avenue and into the shower of streetlights.

"Well, this is a bit better."

"Yeah, we're doin' Okay."

A police cruiser passed us at a night prowling pace. One of the cops looked us over, causing a subconscious, animal reaction of fear and adrenaline to well up from my chest, skitter up my neck to dance on my scalp.

"Hell-ll-ll-o officer." Gram said under his breath. The cruiser continued on its way. "Yeah, those boys got more important things to worry about than us, with our li'l chunk of hash. But, let's find a taxi."

"Okay. Swing low sweet chariot, an' let this boy ride."

We're sitting in a pool of campfire glow, the rocks and scrubby plants occasionally catch the warm flickers and define the edge of our gypsy settlement.

"Seems just about the right time for a cowboy song," Barry T drawls.

'Oh give me a home where the buffalo roam,

where the deer and the antelope play,

where seldom is heard a discouraging word,

and the skies are not cloudy all day.'

I walk a few paces off into the dark and look back at Barry and Briggs sitting by the fire. Yeah, this is like a cow punchers' trail camp but with old vans rather than a chuck wagon and, if they were both wearing cowboy hats, it would look pretty convincing. The desert sky over Joshua Tree is burning with bright cold stars. As my eyes adjust, I begin to see faint shapes of boulders and the Joshua trees.

The night of the shooting star trip, about a year ago, had been dark like this, no moon. We had huddled in blankets waiting for the meteorites. No cowboy songs. We talked as we lay stretched-out looking up at the sky trying to name the familiar constellations and whimsically renaming others.

"See that one over there?" Gram pointed at the sky.

"What d' you mean, the one on the other side of the Big Dipper?"

"No, more to the right. It's got, uh, three bright ones in a row an' next to it is a bunch of 'em, yeah? It's a guy catching a fish, The Fisherman."

"Oh yeah, it is." I agreed. "This one over here looks like a big W, and below that is an F."

"W, F. Woof, woof."

"Where's the dog?"

"Where's the bone?"

"Hey there's a banjo. That row, an' a bunch at the bottom, well, sort of a square banjo."

"Bluegrass, The Hillbilly, yeah."

"Look at that bright one. Way over there, all by its self."

"Yeah. Mr. Lonely."

'Ow-wnly the lonely.

'Dum-dum-dee-dooby-do-wah,' I joined Gram singing the old Roy Orbison song.

'Know the way I feel tonight,

'Oh yea-yea-yea-yeah,

'Only the lonely

'know the fee-eelin' just ain't right.'

Gram and I had been singing together for almost two years, harmonising, a, sort of, partnership. We had begun after we first met and we sang together when we had moved to New York, getting songs together for gigs but it developed much more as we began playing country music. The vocal harmonies were an important part of that tradition and style. On most nights, if we were not out gigging, we'd sing and play acoustically, to keep the noise down at night. We'd toss around a few oldies from the '50s, do some of the Everlys' and other old stuff. We tried to remember other country songs we might have heard when we were younger and were only half listening.

Anyone who grew up the '50s had been exposed to music that had a country influence. Elvis had been pretty much country back then. There were plenty of others, besides the early Rockabillys, that crossed-over into the pop charts; Conway Twitty, Brenda Lee, Don Gibson, Cowboy Copas, Floyd Cramer, dozens of them. I used to listen to W-WVA from Wheeling, West Virginia, a show called The Jamboree with all the country and bluegrass acts playing live. It only came through at night when the ionosphere effect enabled AM radios to pick up distant stations. All of us who liked music listened, late at night, to the far away broadcasts. The radios would be turned down real low or hidden under the pillow, we'd pretend to be asleep but we'd be filling our heads with late-night music.

Ray Charles had released a new LP. We were big fans of 'the Genius' and listened to this new record, Modern Sounds in Country Music vol. 1, Country and Western meets Rhythm 'n' Blues. Ray had covered some country stuff in the past, like Hank Snow's 'I'm Movin' On', but this was a whole album of country material, including some Buck Owens numbers. Buck's records soon went on our turntable, it was good stuff, very electric and lean, like that funkier honky tonk style of the '50s, a style that Nashville had disowned in favour of Jim Reeves and the easy listening sound. We started hunting down country records, they were not easy to find in New York.

We learned more country songs, practised them with the band but also did a lot of acoustic playing. Gram and I sang, exploring, searching for the right phrasing and harmonies while John played guitar fills and solos. John had a feel for country, he had played a lot of acoustic mountain music in the past and liked the way the contemporary country guitarists were playing those Telecasters, with plenty of bite. The nights we spent learning all this new country material were magic. In one of the bedrooms of the house, the subtly of the acoustic guitars, the vocal harmonies and the excitement of discovering something new, filled the small space. It was good.

"Hey, let me play you this one." Gram strummed his Martin. "Okay, I haven't got all of the words yet. You're gonna love it."

"What is it?" I asked.

"Man, it's great. One of those songs by ol' mister-r Webb Pierce. It's on the album I found in that big record store on Twenty-first street."

"Yeah?"

"Yeah, it's called 'Back Street Affair', about this couple, runnin' around behind other peoples' backs. A cheatin' song. The lyrics are great. Here, let's see." He strummed, looking for the key.

"You didn't know I wasn't free,
when you fell in love with me
and with all your young heart
you learned to care."
"Cool."
"Yeah, like, really a tragedy. Ill-fated love, meeting in strange places, where no one recognizes you. Hiding, hangin' up the phone, if the wrong person answers. Here, try singing this line with me."
"Yes, they call our love
a back-street affair."
"That's cool man. Let's try and work that one out."
"There's another one of his, 'In the Jailhouse Now'." Gram sang a bit of it.
"'Well I told him once or twice,
about playin' cards and shootin' dice.
He's in the jailhouse now.
"Ha. That's a great line isn't it?"
"Yeah. Sleazy, huh."
"That's what he's into, I think. Like, low-life. There's another one of Webb's, 'I Don't Care'. It goes something like, "I don't care, if I'm not the first love, you've had". Like who's a virgin any more?"
"Yeah. You know, it's not low-life, it's just, like, reality."
"That's what's cool about country, it's real. Real American life."
Those were great nights, back in New York when we were learning to find our way around country music. Too bad we never recorded any of those explorations, we should have. They are all lost in the ether now. Some of it was good, a great feel, soulful and done pretty much the way you'd think country was played, by a few people sitting around on the front porch or inside, near a wood-stove, whiling away a lonely night.

We'd run through dozens of them, anything. Hank Williams, Everlys, Webb Pierce, George Jones, Merle Haggard, Buck Owens, it was exciting finding this wealth of stuff. We also did some of the gospel things. Country music was loaded with that gospel tradition and sentiment. There were lots of lyrics like; 'Oh Lord forgive me, I know momma will be waitin' up in heaven, after I go to the electric chair for them bad things the devil done made me do'. Or, 'give me the power to believe that some day, high on a hilltop together we'll pray'.
Gram and I had both been exposed to fundamentalist, baptisin', Bible-totin', scripture

quotin' church experiences as kids. Those messages had implanted the same fear of God in us as in all of those country guys, who sang about their evil ways and thoughts. That tricky ol' Satan, always enticing us away from the righteous path of the Lord and throwing everything our way to tempt us; wine, whiskey, loose women, money and gamblin'. You couldn't let go of Jesus' word or take your eyes off of his Holy face for a minute. If you did, you'd begin a long slide, down, down, away from your family, friends and neighbors. Away from the loved ones, who were earnestly praying that you'd repent your wicked ways and were pleading in Jesus' name that the lost lamb would return to the fold and renounce the devil.

Eight or ten years ago, as boys, Gram and I had been in different congregations, absorbing. Wearing our best suits, hair combed-back and parted, holding that black Bible with our names embossed on the cover in little gold letters, we had sung,

'I've got a home in glory land

that out-shines the sun.

Do Lord, oh do Lord,

do remember me,

Way beyond the stars.'

We knew a lot of these country sentiments by heart. We both had heard the preaching for years and there was an inherent familiarity about it. Maybe, for us, playing this music was an exorcism, it certainly was therapeutic.

Mainstream, solid country music was just about unheard of and, so far, uncharted in the contemporary music scene. Loads of bands were borrowing from cultures alien to themselves. Yankees, white boys, English, Europeans and maybe even Japanese were playing blues even though it was from a world away in Chicago or the Delta. We'd begun to hear sitars and other influences from the East and India.

There had been some bluegrass, mountain, and old-timey music in the folk scene in the early '60s but, so far, no urban rock band had gone into the one-hundred-percent country and western style, with all the truck drivin' and I'm a sinner stuff, thrown in for flavor. It was a no-man's land, unexplored by hippies and longhairs. This uniqueness was very compelling, we gave in to it and started going down that crazy, bizarre, rocky road. At least, we would be doing something different.

"Whoa! There's one!" I pointed as a meteorite zipped across the sky and fizzled toward the horizon.

"Hey, finally saw one." At least the shooting star tour wouldn't be a total wash-out.

"Yeah, I thought that there would be more of 'em than this."

It hadn't been much of a spectacle so far and a couple of our gang had pulled their sleeping bags over their heads, given up and gone to sleep.

Gram and I chattered back and forth, gazed up at the stars and pondered the vastness of the universe. How significant were we in this infinity? Were the stars just God exhaling? Did the scale of the stars extend down through us to where there might be proportionately minuscule beings in our cells who were looking up, tonight, at their own stellar infinity show? Worlds within worlds, within worlds.

"Well, I don't know Doc, maybe."

"Maybe, when you get a headache, it's some comet travelling across your brain... their sky."

"Yeah, think of all that smog they get when we have a cigarette."

"Yeah, poor li'l folks down there, we should treat 'em better."

"It's awful being a God, all this creatin' an' destroyin'."

"Yeah, sure is a job."

Gram and I had recently parted from the Submarine Band, he was going ahead with an album deal that Lee Hazlewood had offered. I had hoped that the talks I had been having with Mothers Records might have developed. They were a new outfit, part of Jay Ward's animation company. Jay Ward must have made a load of money with Rocky and Bullwinkle and was branching out into music, there could have been a deal for the ISB. There had been no animosity when we split, just a difference of opinion. We still remained close friends and hung-out even though we were working with different bands now.

While looking at the stars, Gram had told me that he would be going to Florida soon. Occasionally he'd have to go down there and sign some papers, something to do with his family's estate. He didn't look forward to it but he'd be able to see his younger sister. I had been down there with him once before, in March of '66, when we had done a short tour.

After a couple of week-long stints at The Night Owl, we were told about a promoter/ manager who was putting together a package to tour Florida during the Easter Spring Break, when loads of college students went south. Buzzy and Serge were going to do it and there would also be a couple of Florida bands. The tour headliner would be Freddy Cannon, a bit of a has-been from the early '60s. Sort of a Frankie Avalon look-a-like, Freddy had enjoyed success with a bunch of top twenty records; 'Transistor Sister', 'Way Down Yonder' and 'Palisades Park' but that was back when I was in high school. The idea of touring with Freddy 'Boom-Boom' Cannon made us chuckle but the promoter had a few dates set up. It could be fun and with Serge being on the scene there would be plenty to smoke. Gram figured that he might know some club owners, back in his old neighborhood, who might give us a few more dates. Hey why not?

We travelled down South in two groups. John and Mickey went on the train with the equipment, Gram and I drove down in his Austin Healey sports car. We drove straight through, taking turns at the wheel, sleeping if we could, stopping along the route to drink gallons of coffee, listening to the radio and talking until we arrived in central Florida, completely shot, about fifteen-hundred miles later.

After making it down South and re-grouping we drove over from Winter Haven in central Florida to Daytona Beach on the Atlantic coast. We had a Chevy station wagon, loaded-down with all the gear and we got there allowing enough time for meetings and rehearsal. They had suggested that we arrive a couple of days before the first night to do some promotion and publicity. We were booked into one of the beach hotels and all met-up at a cocktail party in a hotel lounge.

The tour manager, Chester Fox, was a short, red-headed guy, all smiles and bursting with enthusiasm.

"Lemme tell ya, it's great to meet you boys, I've heard so much about ya, this is gonna be a great show and Freddy's really lookin' forward to workin' with ya, yeah it's gonna be great. Here, I wancha to meet the rest of the folks."

He introduced us to a thin, balding, anaemic looking guy in a suit, the accountant, and a couple of sun tanned, paunchy 'investors', Gary and Rex. They were accompanied by their wives, both in cocktail dresses and supporting enormous beehives that must have exhausted several cans of hair spray earlier in the afternoon.

"John, Mickey, Ian and Gram, great names, I really like 'em, yeah, this gonna be great, great, I love it already. Let's have a drink, come on, let your hair down, get ta know each other. Lemme just call Buzzy's room, I want to get them down here, I told 'em six-thirty, we got a lot to do. Be right back." Chester had the road manager hustle going.

"So, you boys are doing well in New York?" asked one of the guys. He was wearing a sky-blue blazer, yellow slacks and white loafers with gold effect buckles, a golfer, I guessed.

"Yeah, playing the clubs in Greenwich Village, strumming the guitars up in old New York." Gram chuckled back.

"And, we've been recording." I added, figuring they would want to hear some big-city credentials, even though I couldn't quite figure out what role these people were really playing.

"Oh, we just can't wait to hear you, we're really looking forward to it," giggled one of the hair-do wives. She was tanned, a pearl necklace glowed against her bronzed, freckled chest. Her coral-tone lipstick left behind a faint crescent on the rim of her martini glass. Blinking mechanically, black lashes on blue ovals of eye shadow, she raised her eyebrows and asked me:

"What sort of music do you play? is it like The Beatles? I like them better than The Rolling Stones."

"Well no, not exactly. It's rock music, some of our own songs and other things we like doing, it's okay, 'long as I can wear my silver shoes and yell." She blinked again and smiled.

Chester Fox scurried back over to our group clutching the briefcase he hadn't put down since we arrived.

"Great you're all getting to know each other, good, good. Freddy's gonna be arriving soon, we'll see him later. Now let me tell ya what's happening, okay? I've got interviews set with both of the Daytona stations, Mitch the Man on W-DAY and the other one, what's it, ah, I'll find it later, both of 'em tonight so a couple a you can go to one an' the other guys to the other, okay?" He rattled it off. "Now tomorrow we're gonna do a parade, right down along the beach, everybody will see ya, Rex and Garry fixed that up for us. Then we'll rehearse with Freddy so you....Hey! Here's Buzzy and the guys. Hey! Come on over."

Buzzy, Serge and their bass player, Steve, looked like they had been dragged out of bed or had just got off a long flight. They reluctantly shuffled over and greeted us, Buzzy hugging Gram and repeating, 'Hey man, hey man.' He had long curly hair, thinning so it formed three bunches, one on the top, one on each side and a wide, smiling mouth a bit like The Joker on Batman. He was wearing those old-fashioned black sneakers, P.F. Flyers or Keds, they were scuffed and torn. Serge smiled or grimaced through clenched teeth and somehow managed to talk without moving his jaws, like a ventriloquist. Their bass player, by contrast, appeared quite clean-cut and subdued. The golfer's beehive babe was checking out Serge, she gave him a bit more room and then increased that to a wide berth, her smile moved down a couple of notches. Rex suggested that we all have another drink.

Later Chester gathered the guys from the bands around a long table.

"Okay, let's work-out a couple a things here," Chester said, beaming round at everyone. "Freddy's gonna want to rehearse tomorrow afternoon at the hall, so we'll get set for two. Okay?"

"Is his band here yet?" Gram wondered. Chester looked blank, like he didn't understand.

"No, he's not bringin' a band. No, one of you is gonna back him, didn't ya know that?"

"No, we didn't know that, no one said anything about it."

Chester looked questioningly at Serge, who answered with an indeterminate, lock-jawed grunt. Gram and I looked at each other open-mouthed. John shook his head. Buzzy wore the same enthusiastic smile.

"What about the local band, can't they do it?"

Chester glanced very quickly, left, right and lowered his voice like he wanted to keep this misunderstanding confidential.

"No. Look, none of 'em are stayin' with us on the tour, it'll be a different bunch every night. We gotta have this thing runnin' smooth, one of you has gotta do it. No other way."

"We're only a trio, with no lead guitar, he's gonna want lead guitar." Serge was getting them off the hook.

"Yeah, I think he's right. Freddy's gonna want to have the best, or the biggest, I mean." Chester affirmed.

"Oh, no."

"Well, I guess we're Freddy's boys." Gram shrugged his shoulders with a why worry, why fight it, no-sweat gesture.

After discussing the radio spots and seeing each of the other guys, for one reason or another, decline because of shyness or clenched teeth, it fell to Gram and I to be the promo-team. We went in different directions, one of us to each of the two competing stations. Gram was going to regale Mitch the Man and I'd do 'Wild Bill's Beach Party' on, 'All Hits Eight-Fifty, The Sound of the Florida Coast.'

"Hey and after this I've got a SPECIAL guest down from NEW YORK, Ian Dunlop. He's gonna be telling you about the International Submarine Band, hey, I LIKE the name, and the BIG concert at the Daytona Beach Auditorium TOMORROW night, right after Tommy James and The Shondells do THIS!" Wild Bill pulled down the fader, removed his earphones, puffed out his cheeks and blew as he swivelled his chair toward me.

"Hey, how ya doin'? Why don't ya pull your seat up a bit closer. Yeah, up to the mic, an' try on them earphones, I'll just get a level. Are you pushing a single?"

"No, not yet. We've done some sessions but nothing's out yet."

"Okay, well I found a Freddy Cannon thing we'll play. I had to search around in the store room to find it."

"Yeah, I guess Freddy's a bit dusty by now."

"My Baby Does the Hanky Panky!" Wild Bill was back on the mic. His eyelids dropped.

"So, my GUEST tonight is Ian Dunlop, in town with the International Submarine Band, and we're gonna talk about that date they're doing at the Daytona Beach Auditorium. Welcome Ian and I'm sure everybody wants to know what's the LATEST up in the Big Apple?" Wild Bill turns to me and his eyes pop open expectantly, the size of baseballs, Boi-oi-oi-oi-oing.

"Yeah, okay Bill, great to be here, I like it, yeah. New York, well…" I start wondering; (what is going on in New York? We smoke a lot of dope? Take LSD. Make crazy, rambling tape recordings? Go shopping down at the Jewish bakery on the Fordham Road. Take LSD, listen to whacky, old fashioned country music, paint the walls of my bedroom in dazzling stripes, go out collecting junk on the streets to make sculptures in the living room, play all week at The Night Owl? Yeah, The Night Owl, that's a bit more like it.) "There's a great club scene, 'specially down in the Village.."

"That's GREENWICH Village, that WAY-OUT, CRAZY part of the City, right Ian?"

"Yeah, that's it Bill, we play down there a lot, you know, lots of clubs, lots of bands. Yeah, great scene." (I guess that sounded like I'm on the right track.)

"And you guys are going to be bringing that GREENWICH- VILLAGE- SOUND to the Daytona Beach Auditorium TOMORROW night at 9 p.m., right?"

"Yeah Bill, that's right. We gonna be… (What? We haven't even met Freddy Cannon yet, or rehearsed his stupid, out of date, golden oldie stuff. I don't even know what the Hell Buzzy and Serge do or what they sound like. FUCK, who knows? Man, what have we got ourselves into here? And the local band? I'm not even sure who they are.)… doing the music that we've been playing, at The Night Owl. There's another band from the New York scene…(what are they called? I don't even know…) uh, The Buzzy Linhart Band… and Freddy Cannon's gonna be doing his big hits."

"We're going to play one of them right now and let EVERYBODY know what to expect, here's FREDDY CANNON. 'Let Me Take You Where the ACTION IS!" Bill puts on the 45 and I get a chance to hear what I'm supposed to be playing by this time tomorrow night. Freddy sings in his nasal tone, 'It's so nice to take your baby where the action is.' Wild Bill takes off his 'phones and repeats the puffing, chair swivelling and leans back.

"Great. Thanks for comin' by." That must be it. I get up and shake Wild Bill's hand.

"Okay, thanks a lot Bill."

I see Chester Fox's face pressed up against the glass of the studio door, he's grinning and nodding, mouthing 'Great, great.' As I push through he's still saying, "Great, that was great."

I wonder how Gram did on his radio slot, over on the other side of town, with Mitch the Man?

Wham, wham, wham. Morning thumping on the hotel room door. Wham, wham. "Hey, come on! Aren't you guys up? Hey in there?'" Wham, wham. "Hey, in there! It's a great day out here, you gotta see the beach, God!"

"Hey Chester! Take it easy, okay?"

"Come on out! Meet me down the hotel café. You can get some coffee, breakfast, I'll see you down there. Yeah, it's a great day!"

"U-u-gh." The sun was blasting on the orange and white scallop shell curtains. We got into a bit of a smoke-athon last night on Serge's Pakistani Black. It made you cough and it certainly induced sleep. We were all quite high on just being here, in such a different place and embarking on a nutty and, so far, comic adventure, like a corny TV situation-comedy, cast with loony caricatures. I pulled the curtains open. Wow, bright! The platinum beach was vast, at least a quarter-mile wide down to the sea and it stretches away in each direction as far as I can see. There were people out walking or lying on colourful beach towels and big groups hanging around the seawalls and benches. A few guys were throwing a football back and forth, another bunch sailed Frisbees across the sand. God! There were loads of chicks.

"Here you are at last! Here sit down, ya want coffees, yeah? What about a Danish or something? I just had one, they're great, come on sit down, we got plenty to talk about. I'm gonna tell you the news, okay?"

"Sock it to us Chester."

"Donald, the accountant, has been on the 'phone with the ticket office and they been sellin' seats for both nights. That's great boys, great. Coulda been that radio you did last night, ya never can tell. I'm gonna 'phone the station in Cocoa Beach, see if we can do an interview down there before Tuesday, okay? Ah, here's the coffees! Yeah, thanks. Okay, so we're gonna do the parade a bit earlier, 'bout an hour maybe. See, there are loads a kids around now an' probably more soon, we want to get 'em before they all go swimming or something." So, the cars are gonna pick you up out front at twelve okay?

"Okay. Twelve o'clock, parade!" we started humming and blowing the tune, 'Seventy-Six Trombones' and tapping-out rhythm on the table with spoons.

"Great, great, you boys kill me!"

About noon we gathered around the hotel entrance. Chester emerged from the doors with Freddy Cannon. Chester was porky, his shirt buttons straining, one had come undone. The white shirt and dark suit was not the right outfit for a rock 'n' roll promoter. Chester looked like an undertaker and Freddy Cannon's purple shirt and black pants reminded me of a plush coffin lining.

"Hey guys! Come an' meet Freddy."

"How aw ya, good ta meecha." Freddy smiled and shook hands. I recognised his flat, Bawhstin (Boston) accent. He was from around there somewhere. I could remember him doing local gigs around Massachusetts in the early '60s. He had been reinvigorated, a year or so ago, by having a hit with the theme song of pop-music TV show. 'Oh baby come on, Lemme take ya where the action is, Oh baby come on.'

Several convertibles were pulled up to the door.

"Okay everybody, let's go. Freddy you get in this one with me. Boys, you get in this other one here, okay. Buzzy, you guys go in that one over there, okay everybody, let's GO!"

Chester's motorcade proceeded down the main drag of Daytona to a Winn Dixie supermarket parking lot where we met up with a town motor cycle cop and one of the investors. Another guy began taping signs to the car doors; 'TONIGHT, Freddy Cannon, Daytona Hall, 9 p.m.'

"That looks great! Okay everybody, look like you're enjoyin' it, wave, smile, right!" Chester got back into the lead car then raised his hand and waved us forward, like a D-Day General, in a jeep.

The cop started his Harley, switched on the flashing lights and we headed back up the main street at about five miles per hour, sitting up on the backs of the convertibles' rear seats. To help attract attention, Chester had suggested that all the car radios should be turned up loud. The beachfront street was a long strand of stores selling pizza, ice cream and seashells. We waved to the curious kids on the sidewalks and yelled out greetings. The car radio was blaring, distorted, we had to shout above it.

"Hey! how are you. How ya doin'! Hey, honey you're lookin' GOOD! Hey, come to the gig tonight! Please! Do you have a friend?"

We cruised on past bars, bikinis and burger joints, acting like astronauts or politicians, with big jack o' lantern grins, waving and campaigning.

"Vote for me! 'Don't forget to vote next week! A vote for me is a vote wasted! Waste your vote! Vote wasted! Vote for the Wasted Party! Vote! Vote! Vote! Vote for the Wasted Party! Vote! Vote! Vote!"

The Beach Auditorium was the biggest venue we had played so far; a thousand seats fanned-out and upward. Each empty, red theatre seat, rows and rows of them, compounded silence and emptiness.

Ba-Boom! Mick kicked the bass drum, hit the snare, did some rolls and cymbal crashes. Dr-r-r-r-r Ka-sh-sh-sh-sh-sh! Ba-boom! Ba-boom! He whacked them, challenging the room, showing who was in charge even if it was a big space. He could do it. He was a powerful, aggressive drummer, a small guy who perched so high on the drum-stool that his heels didn't touch the ground, enabling him to deliver all the power in his legs to the balls of his feet when he tromped down on the foot pedals. Mick was critical of drummers who sat down low, their knees up in the air, heels on the ground tapping with their toes. He thought that they were lazy. He really should have been playing with a big jazz band. He was never, never tentative, indecisive or ambivalent and played with an authority that sometimes carried very obvious messages, codes, and responses to the immediate situation.

"Sounds good man."

"Let's do something." Mick wanted some action.

"Okay, uhm, how about 'Buckaroo'?"

"Let's go." Tick. Tick. Tick, tick, tick, tick.

We went into a country- rock instrumental.

"TURN IT UP!" Mickey yelled, "LOUDER!"

The music brought people into the wings and some onto the stage, Chester, Freddy, some of the entourage and a soundman who began setting-up mic-stands and plugging in cables.

"Great, boys! I love it! You're gonna sound good tonight. How 'bout you run through some stuff with Freddy. I told the other bands to hold on for awhile, they can set up when you guys are through. It's all happenin'! Great, great, this is gonna be good."

'Thum, thum. Testing, Testing, one, two, three.'

Freddy came over with some papers, song lists, that we looked over.

"We can knock this off pretty quick. You'll know the songs. Be easy, no sweat, okay. Lemme see, okay, ya know this? 'Land of a Thousand Dances', ya know, Na, na-na-na-na, na-na-na-na," he sang, "right?" It was the Cannibal and the Headhunters' song.

"Are you two guys the singers? Ya just do the na-na stuff with me, okay? What about the other guys? They sing?" John shook his head. "No, okay. Hey we'll be fine. You okay drummer? Watch me." Freddy slapped out the count on his thigh and we tried it.

"Okay, okay, hold it. Hold it! See, when we come to chorus, everybody lay out, okay? Just the drums, okay drummer. Try it."

'Na, na-na-na-na,'

"Whoa, whoa, whoa! Drummer, I just want a simple back-beat. Okay, just keep a back-beat, no fancy stuff, okay? Try it again, same place, okay." Mick returned an expressionless face and knocked out an exaggeratedly flat, mechanical rhythm. "Yeah! That's it perfect! Okay, okay, we got that knocked. Now I wanna run through 'Palisades Park', you gotta know that one don'cha?" 'Palisades Park' was a bit more complex, with a couple of chords we had to work out. It was a hit song for Freddy a few years ago, about a guy meeting a girl at an amusement park, going on the roller-coaster, the loop-d-loop and the tunnel of love. I had heard it but never took much notice. The intro was odd, a sort of fair-ground circus sound and originally had been done with an organ. The long, descending melody line threw John completely.

"Ah, what was that again?" he asked.

Freddy sang the line "Da, da-da, du, da-da-da, da-da."

The guitar played a bit.

"No! Like this, Da, da-da, DUH, DA, DA, DA, DA!"

"Wait, let's see if I got that bit." He played a few notes.

"NO!! Duh, da, da, DA !!"

"I'm going to have to sit down and work this out." That was John's best offer. Freddy was beginning to get pissed-off at the delay and affronted that someone didn't know one of his biggest hits.

"Hey Freddy, It'll be alright, he'll get it. We'll work on it. Okay?" Gram reassured, to cool things down.

"Yeah man, we'll be okay. The other stuff sounds good." I added. Freddy flicked his wrist and checked his watch. Maybe he only had allowed an hour, maximum, for running through songs with the back-up-bands, or Chester and the investors had arranged for him to judge a bikini contest down on the beach.

"Yeah, well. I'll see ya guys tonight then, take it easy."

"'Bye Freddy."

The Night Crawlers from Orlando opened up the show. They were young, lively and played a set covering a few Rolling Stones' songs and a couple songs of their own. The hall was busy, at least half-full, and people were still arriving. One of The Night Crawlers' guitar players stood, legs apart, slightly on his toes, with both feet swivelling like crushing-out a cigarette butt. He kept it up, the same movement for their entire set, either nervous or really enjoying himself.

Buzzy's group went on wearing the same clothes they had arrived in, the funky old sneakers and T- shirt, Serge's battered straw hat and one of those Mexican thick-weave waistcoats. They were quiet compared to the Crawlers and I was amazed to see Serge using brushes and just pattering around on the top of the drum kit. Buzzy had an expressive, very emotional vocal style and would stretch some of the lyrics, shaping them into unusual, even grotesque sounds. Gorilla blues. Maybe he didn't have time, or forgot to adjust the mic-stand, it was very low and he crouched as he sang 'Yellow Cab'.

The audience was wondering if this was the latest thing from New York, unsure if they wanted it.

I went back into the dressing room backstage to see how the other guys were doing and have a tune up. There were a few people in there, Gram was talking to a guy and his girlfriend and laughing, he was feeling good about it. John was in the corner playing something on his Telecaster, as I get closer I could hear him trying to work out that Palisades intro.

"How's it goin'?"

"Do you think we could convince him NOT to play that song."

"Hey man, he's gonna do it. It's one of his things. It'll be okay. Just don't let it fuck you up. Just play what ever you got figured out, don't worry about it." John could get nervous. I left him to it and checked out the bass guitar.

"I'm going out to see what Buzzy's doin'," Gram said, "You never know what he might get up to. Once, at the Café Wah? he got up to do two numbers, that's what they told him, 'Two numbers Buzzy, that's it.' An' he went on and on. Shit, the second one musta been about a half-hour long, hah, that's Buzzy. He just doesn't think that way. Yeah."

It seemed like only a couple of minutes later when Gram popped back into the dressing room and grabbed his guitar.

"They must have changed their set or something, they're already doin' their last number. I guess we're gonna have to get our little party clothes on."

We walked on stage to; 'And, now, from New York, The International Submarine Band!!' We waved and smiled, the audience responded, with applause, whistles, probably for our clothing. John was wearing an English Norfolk belted jacket, Mick had on a bright scarlet velvet jacket. I had a cobalt blue cape-top with rows of brass buttons, a fur collar, knee-high black suede boots and grey striped jeans. Gram was wearing a very sharp, double-breasted, fawn-and-charcoal striped suit and finely-shaped brown boots, a real French, high-fashion outfit from Le Dernier Cri, a boutique in New York. We definitely looked like we were from out of town.

We played an up-tempo set that included some of the country crossover numbers that we had begun to call country rock. When Gram and I sang together on the first chorus the audience cheered, making us feel more relaxed, accepted and able to project more personality into the room. We both stepped right into that role and played to the young crowd that had filled the hall. We finished with an old rock 'n' roll song, 'Rip it Up'. Freddy was waiting it the wings, probably glad that we had warmed-up the crowd but they wouldn't let us go and we went back on and did another. When Freddy trotted on to the stage the announcer's intro was 'Now, Freddy Cannon AND The International Submarine Band!'. A crowd up in front cheered, Gram and I smiled at them and simultaneously shrugged our shoulders. They were glad to see us playing again. Maybe the clothes had something to do with it.

We got through Freddy's set, since we were now at ease with the audience. Gram and I fooled around, playing with the role of back-up singers and threw-in some extra oo-oos, ah-ahs and ya-da-ya-das, laughing at it. Mick pulled one on Freddy, getting back at him for the rehearsal earlier, and played a real show-off bit of drumming when he was meant to stick to the simple back-beat. Just a couple of bars, enough to say, 'Yeah, fuck you.' When it came to the awkward 'Palisades Park' intro, we covered the uncertainty by singing Da, da-da, du, da-da-da. We got a quick, surprised glance from Freddy but he didn't have anything to gripe about. He'd had a good show even though he was beginning to look a bit like Dean Martin and was wearing a corny Las Vegas outfit that been given my 'DELUXE' award, earlier.

At the after-show party in the hotel lounge, the atmosphere was up. Everyone was charged-up by the show's success.

"Lemme tell ya. You boys were a big hit! Great, really great, what a first night! This is gonna be great! You're gonna be big! Soon as we get back to New York we gotta get together, we gotta get together, I got some great ideas, you're gonna love 'em! It could be great!"

"Yeah, Chester, sure, we'll do that, we wanna keep the sun shinin'." A couple of guys from the Night Crawlers desperately had to know where they could buy clothes like ours, what shop they were in, where did the boots come from?

"Hey, it's not that simple, a lot of our stuff was 'specially made," we explained. Yeah, it was. In a place, way outside of Florida, where we came from.

In the morning I wander away from our camp at Joshua tree and pick up what looks like a trail through the flat valley. Even though this is called a desert, I'm walking through a stubby sort of woods and can't see beyond the grove of cactus and Joshua trees that surround me. A couple of small birds flap away, startled. The plants look tough and dangerous, armed with spikes, prickles and spines like a street gang. A few small plants on the ground are sprouting shoots with peach colored blossom. My footsteps crunch on the gravel as I walk slightly uphill to a small rise. I can see the valley ahead and the hills surrounding it. Looking back, I see the faded red roof of my van, about a half-mile away. On a rise in the distance, against the warm glow of boulders, there is a dark shape of timber cabin. The trail leads in that direction, off the rise.

The tilting cabin is the only structure within sight. There are no roads, no trucks, no blondes wearing sunglasses and driving Pontiac convertibles, no stereos, no Lonely Hearts Club Band. I stop on the trail and listen. Nothing, but a slight whisper of a breeze. Just on the edge of the trail is a brassy-backed beetle that climbs over a small stone that is in his way.

"Hey, how's it going, bug?" He keeps forging ahead. It has been a long time since I have been out of range, out of sight, out of communication and without the constant background roar of people and machines. I take several deep breaths, relieved by my release from LA. I have managed to swim to the placid edge of the whirlpool, escaping the swirling brew of clichés, empty bottles, special offers and the raucous laughter of all the satisfied customers floating in the Babylon Stew.

'The recipe for Babylon Stew: Take a few million people, tenderize them with non-stop TV ads and censorship. After not stirring, empty the contents into a hot concrete bowl and cover with a thick layer of smog. Put them in a low oven to fester. Now, you can get to work on the sugar coating for the war dessert. Remember to add an extra portion of flag-waving to prevent the war from turning sour. Now, check the oven. The stew should be bland. If not, add more TV game shows and sports. Check the stew occasionally for any signs of bubbling or rising. If so, throw in more consumer goods, golf courses and a measure of Desire and, for even better results, a good portion of Greed. Stand back, and you will have a perfect Babylon Stew'. I breathe another sigh of relief and walk along the dusty path that weaves through the desert plants.

The old abandoned cabin is leaning but still standing. The plank siding is warped and gray, like driftwood. Maybe it was a ranch bunkhouse or, more likely, a prospector's place. There could be an old gold mine, or zinc? Silver? What ever it was they were digging for, they gave up or burned out. About fifty feet away from the place is their dump, probably just about the distance a bottle could be thrown. A one-house collection, or exhibition, of trash. Glass jars, broken bottles, metal and a few tortured, leather boots make a small heap. The sole and the uppers on a large work boot have parted and it seems to be smiling and has a face like Goofy. There are a lot of tin cans, all of them opened by those old-fashioned stab-and-lift can openers that leave saw-toothed flares around the lid, like an elementary school kid's cut-out of the sun. I pick up one of the cans, the lid, with it's zig-zags, is still attached. I have a feeling the can is ancient. All the old glass bottles are unrecognizable, none have the familiar shape of a Heinz ketchup or Coke bottle. The boots look like they could be from the 1800s, with big nails in the soles. In most places, all of the cans and leather would have crumbled to dust by now. Maybe it hardly ever rains here. I turn the can around in my hand, some parts of it still have a dull tin sheen. The can wasn't supposed to be this permanent, it only contained pork 'n' beans or Melba peaches for a few months. It's still hanging around, empty, with nothing to do but sit in the desert. Maybe I ought to take it with me in the van and throw it out somewhere else where it can rust in peace.

The fifth night on the Florida tour was down by Melbourne, about thirty miles south of Cocoa Beach where we had played the night before. The Crawlers had done the show again and I had hung-out with some of the guys 'til late. Serge had got a couple of the Florida boys very stoned and they were funny, good-natured guys who reminded Gram of some people he used to know when he was younger and lived in Florida. We slept late and walked on the golden beach for breakfast.

In the late afternoon, after packing up the gear, we were searching for the Holiday Inn, tonight's venue. We must have driven past it and when we turned around, retracing our route. I saw the Holiday Inn sign and underneath it:

TONIGHT

Freddy CAN &

NEW YOrK

SUBMaRINES

Well, close enough. This must be the place. We went to reception and found our rooms. Chester found us.

"Here you are, great, I was beginning to worry about you. You boys okay? Great. Lemme tell ya 'bout tonight. It's a dinner show, early start, seven-thirty, couple hours, but you need to get the amps in there before people arrive, okay? Great. It's gonna be fine, fine. Get the stuff in there soon. We're down in the other wing, number twelve, room twelve, okay. Great, see you later."

Around seven-thirty Gram, Mick and I went down to the dining room and leaned-back against the bar, sitting on stools and sippin' our drinks. The room was almost empty except for a few tables up by the small stage and several older couples, scattered around the room, having supper. Donald, the dorky-looking accountant walked on stage and went up to the mic.

"Good evening, ladies and gentlemen. Ah, welcome to the Holiday Inn. Tonight's show will, ah, start now with, ah, someone you'll enjoy, ah, please welcome Miss Patricia MacSalvey." There was a sparse applause.

"Jesus, who is this?"

"Hey what's going on?"

"Ya think we're in the right place?"

"I didn't see any other room, did you?" I asked Gram.

"No, I didn't either. I think this is it guys. Hum, lookin' like we're gonna be playin' to ghosts. Maybe Sinatra's doing a show somewhere else in town tonight, hah."

"Yeah, right. It's almost empty here."

"I hope Granny, over there, turns her hearin'-aid up."

"Hum, I'm not sure, we don't need those senior citizens gettin' too worked-up or there could be trouble at the Holiday Inn." A woman came on-stage, banged her acoustic guitar against the mic-stand, making a loud CLUNK! and started singing.

'Five hundred miles, five hundred miles, five hundred mi-yi-yi-yi-iles,

I can hear the whistle blow, five hundred miles.'

"Holy shit?"

"Maybe she's the accountants wife, or somethin'?"

"Man, I miss The Night Crawlers."

Buzzy and Serge started their set.

'Oh ba-ya-ya-bee plee-ee-z-z-z doan go-o-o, yeah, yeah, yeah.'

We applauded and whistled to encourage them but they seemed fine, okay, not worried at all. Buzzy just did what he did in that world of his. He wagged his head, shook his hair, closed his eyes and worried-out his songs. Chester was wandering through the dining room, looking back at the stage and around the room, he spotted us and bustled over to the bar.

"There ya are boys! I been lookin' for ya everywhere. Look! Change of plans. This isn't goin' too well. Ya gotta get up there and save the show! Maybe if you guys go on, you can bring 'em in. Ya gotta SAVE THE SHOW! I'll let Buzzy do another one. You boys get ready to come right on, okay!' It seemed like a pointless change of plan, there wasn't a traffic jam of cars flooding into the parking lot full of people who would suddenly come bursting through the doors. It was more like desperation, like wearing a bottle-cap on your head in a cloudburst.

"Sure, Chester we'll come right on. Okay."

"What the Hell. We're already here."

"I got a feelin' this isn't going last too long," Mickey whispered.

We got up and played, a few more people wandered in and sat down, they had probably been allowed in for free or maybe had to pay on the way out. I saw Freddy stick his head round the door and have a look, clocking the room. He shook his head. Chester gestured toward the stage, ran his hand over his scalp, rubbing his head, said something more to Freddy, looked back over his shoulder, pointed to us then held his hands out, pleading. Freddy looked up in the air and shrugged his shoulders. They reached some sort of a deal. We stayed on stage, Chester pointed at Freddy and gave us the okay sign. Freddy came up on stage but we only did two songs with him before he walked off.

'Oh baby come on, let me take you where the action is!'

Back in our room there were clouds of smoke and a bit of coughing. We were laughing about the evening, imitating the folk singer and the awkward accountant doing his M C debut.

"Yeah, Melbourne sure is a wild place."

"Gonna have to get it in the diary for next year."

"Maybe I'll go down an' check it out with the manager, see if we can get an advance."

"While you're at it, get 'em to send up some food."

"Yeah! I'm hungry."

"Room service!"

Gram and I decided to see if we could get a sandwich or something and check-out what was going on with Chester. We found room twelve, there were several people in there and they were arguing. Chester spotted us and came over looking worried.

"Come on boys, step outside, come 'ere with me. Now look, this has been a big mess-up. What a night! We tried to tag this date on the end, things were goin' so great, you know, so we thought, why not? Only got it organized yesterday, shit! They didn't do any publicity, what a mess, what a mess. Now they're saying they want to charge us for the hall! No way I'm telling' 'em, no way. They didn't do any radio plugs, nothing! I'm sorry 'bout this boys, really sorry. Shit!'

"Hey Chester, cool-out, it's okay."

"Yeah man, don't worry, so what? We're all okay," we soothed.

"You boys are great! You did a wonderful job, lemme tell you, you're a bunch of great guys. But it gets worse! Yeah. Now they are saying they want to charge us for the rooms as well! That wasn't the deal, we were havin' the rooms and we were splitting the money on the door! Now, on top of everythin', they wanna charge for the rooms. Forget about it! We're not makin' anything! I tell ya what. You boys go back into that hall and get your stuff out. Now! We don't want 'em grabbing your gear or something crazy. No! Load it up and get outta here! Okay?"

"Gee, I guess you're right. Hum, this is getting' pretty crazy."

"Yeah, okay, we'll split."

"Go on boys, get your stuff and get outta here, quick! I'll be in touch to sort everythin' out, okay! Just get goin'! I'll call ya! Great."

"Okay, 'bye Chester, see ya when the shootin' stops."

We did a bunk, had everything in the wagon in less than fifteen minutes and were soon lazily heading north east on a small road in the warm Southern night. Spanish moss, misty-green in the headlights, draped the roadside. We passed a few small houses set back from the road, dull light issuing from open doorways, silhouette figures settled on the front steps. Rolling through a village, a floodlight playing on a big chicken-shaped sign reminded us that we were hungry and enticed us off the dark road. We pulled into the fried chicken joint where dizzy moths swarmed around the light over a serving counter and a couple of people sat at a plank table, swatting insects. We ordered a big cardboard bucket of breasts, drumsticks and some coffees from the big laughing black woman. We drove away munching. Yeah, Southern fried.

"God, I still can't believe that! Ha. What a night."

"I know crazy or what, huh?"

"It was like a Marx Brothers' movie, with the bumbling characters, Freddy feeling so insulted, the stammering accountant guy. Man! Some night."

"Yeah. In some ways it was great. Funny, or what? Jesus!"

"Poor ol' Chester. Man, I hope he gets outta there soon."

"Yeah. I don't know, he probably is gettin' in to scrapes like that all the time."

"What about Buzzy and them?"

"Man, I don't know, they'll probably want to get back to New York, where everything isn't so loopy."

"Yeah, maybe."

"You know what? Did we get paid for the night before?"

"Nope. Chester said he'd figure it out tomorrow. Well, today. That was before the shit hit the fan."

"I guess we kiss that good bye."

"You know what, I don't think so. I think He likes us, I bet we'll be hearing from him when the dust settles down a bit."

"Anybody want another piece of chicken, it's a big bucket."

"Yeah, man."

"Huh, huh… what a great night."

"Yeah, classic."

We twiddled the radio and, magically, found W-LAC. John R purred in his mesmerising, warm, easygoing way. He played the best music I'd ever heard on a single radio show. One after another. Beautiful stuff, by artists that we'd never heard up north and lots of music from Memphis. Most of the show was sponsored by mail order record companies offering bargain packages on the records John R was airing. After playing a few he'd say;

'Now that's the 'Weekend Blu-ues Special', You kin have all-a dem, those fahv great recurds, that ah jest played for y-all, Randy's gonna let ya have all of 'em, what ya jes' heard, fo' the prahce o' three. Five records for the price a three! Only two dollahs an' forty nahn cents. The weekend Blu-ues special from Randy's records, Gallatin, Tennessee. This is John R, way down South in Dixie. Wha' we gonna play for ya now? Mercy.'

One of his other sponsors was a mail order chicken outfit, who dispatched baby chicks all over the place by delivery; 'The Red Top Chick' company.

'Nah y-all jest wraht to them 'nclosin' ya money ordah, an' jest a few days laytah, you gonna have dem chicks. Red Top Chicks are guaran-nteed to grow-up to be dee-licious, m-m-um! I can jest taste them golden drumsticks now, man it's makin' me hungry talkin' 'bout 'em. Now, looka here, Mistah Sam 'n' Dave.'

John R played more fantastic, incredible music. Easy, relaxed, laid back, wow! The essence of the South. Exciting, yet so easy-going, just no rush to get anywhere, simple rhythms and horn sections, an Otis Redding song, endless, great grooves.

The next show on W-LAC played country music. The same sort of format as John R. Mail order record companies and the Red Top Chicks peeped up again. This guy sounded almost the same as John R, except he referred to the listeners as 'Naybuhs' all the time. He played great soulful country music. We couldn't believe how good this was. The soul music and the country sat just-right together and expressed common themes about longing, heartbreak, distrust of the city life: it was all rooted here in the South. Yeah, roots American music.

We just poked along in the Chevy wagon in no hurry to get anywhere now, still chuckling over the Holiday Inn fiasco. We had done a few great gigs proving that we had something that people really liked, we were all happy. Satisfied. We remained quiet, entranced by the mellow radio waves, lulled by the Southern darkness.

I'd never spent much time in the South before, there was something pretty attractive about it. The music, fried chicken, the warm nights, it almost seemed worth joining them, way down South in Dixie.

Before we left Florida we went to catch Jimmy Stafford playing an afternoon gig at a hotel in Winter Park, Florida. He was playing solo, sitting behind an electric piano with a Fender Strat on his lap. Gram waved and we went over to the bar. Jimmy was set up on a raised section of a dining area, surrounded by numerous potted plants, like a greenhouse. We ordered whiskeys and leaned on the bar. Jimmy was playing easy going background music. I realized that Jimmy Stafford could have been the guitar player who we would have been working with if he had made it up to the New York sessions last year.

Back in Cambridge, in October '65, we had jammed a couple times with Gram and rehearsed a few songs that he wanted to record in New York. The next time we got together, Gram was excited about having been in touch with one of his musician buddies from Florida.

"I called my friend Jimmy Stafford last night, we haven't spoken in awhile. He sounded good. Jimmy and I played together in a couple of bands in Florida, he's a great guitar player and I wanted to let him know what was going on," Gram told us.

"Oh yeah?"

"M-m, and he wants to come up and do the recording."

"Really?"

"Yeah. I had told him that if I got something happening up here, I'd let him know about it. We've been friends from way back. He's waiting to hear back from me about a date. So, I guess, I won't be needing you to do the session," he said to John.

"Really? I can't quite believe this is happening," John replied. I was surprised as well. We had only rehearsed a couple times and hadn't made any promises or signed anything but we had assumed that Gram had settled on the guys who would be doing the recording. We had been practising together, working things out and expected that we would go into a studio soon. John was a little dazed by the sudden change of plans. He shook his head and said, "Well this news has hit me like a keg of nails."

"Hey man, I'm sorry. I don't want to be a drag but I had always wanted Jimmy to do it if he could. I wanted to let you know as soon as I spoke to him." After Gram left, John was still surprised.

"This is really unexpected, it came right out of the blue."

"Yeah, it is. Gram never mentioned this guy to me either."

"I would really like to do this recording. I'm going to have to talk to him about it. Maybe you can mention it or find out what's going on."

"Well I can try. I remember Gram telling me about a band that he had played with but I thought it was a folk group or something like that. This guy, Jimmy, sounds as if he's more like a rock 'n' roll player. You know, Gram might be changing his mind about what he wants to do. I thought that what we have been doing here has been sounding good."

"I'm really disappointed about this."

"Yeah sure. Now I'm beginning to wonder if Gram's going to tell me that he's got a bass player coming as well. He could get a ride up from Florida with the other guy. Save time and money. Nothing's for sure. You just can't tell about anything."

"It looks like that is certainly the case."

Within a couple of days Gram was back in touch and told us that Jimmy Stafford had a few gigs or other commitments that made travelling all the way up to New York too difficult for him. John Nuese was back on board for the recording session.

After catching part of his hotel set and having a drink with Jimmy, Gram and I were walking back to the car when he said, "Jimmy's got so much talent. You only heard him playing that cocktail music, it's just background, he barely had the amp turned up. You ought to hear him when he lets go, he's fantastic. Trouble is, he's just got, sort of, stuck here, doing all of these local gigs. Some people just can't get out of their little hometown. They just get woven into it, stuck, like in a big spider web and they can't get free. Like, their wings fall off."

It's chilly here in Joshua Tree, not like those warm nights down South. That Florida tour seems like a long time ago even though it has only been a couple of years. I thought I knew where I was heading back then, now I'm only sure of where I've been. The stars in the desert night blaze and sing. They shine down with continuity. When I look up, I know where I'm at. I'm sitting right smack in the middle of NOW.

The two days at Joshua Tree had created a wider gulf between now and LA. The first long leg of the journey lay ahead, at least three hundred miles from Joshua Tree to Zion Canyon and a new campsite in Utah. We had an early start and, with luck and ten or fifteen gallons of gas, I could get there today. Parts of the drive would be on small roads. Going through the Mojave Desert, I'd do a bit of Route 66, always something that had a little magic about it. You couldn't help singing when you saw the road signs. 'Get your kicks on Route Sixty-six'.

This was going to be good, really rolling. New roads would lead to new horizons and places I'd never been before. What I see through the windshield is full of promise. The rhythm of the engine is becoming the cadence of my life. Time slows, laboring up long hills to the mountain passes, then flows, coasting down the other side. The VW four-cylinder clock is keeping count now.

The VW microbus is so old that the speedometer registers kilometers-per-hour and the high speeds indicated, eighty, ninety or one hundred, translate into dawdling miles-per-hour. I've learned to do a quick calculation for conversion. The vastness of the Western states and the distance between anything, or anywhere, is often daunting. The rarefied, clean, desert air increases the clarity of far away features and arriving at a landmark that appears to be only a few miles off seems to take ages. Huge flat valleys and salt lakes stretch on and on, convincing me that I'm only crawling along. There is no point in rushing, the Cinerama vistas are intoxicating. The dark tape of highway shrinks to a thread that pulls me into the future. The further I get from LA, the better. I want to wash myself in the dust of this desert, maybe disappear into that dry world and roll around in the arid ocean of the West. I want to be like a snake, shed my city skin and, sliding along in a new suit, absorb the peace and power in the canyons and mountains, while I'm spitting out all the venom.

The road is almost empty. Occasionally a car scorches by or a lone truck, creating air-wakes that rock the van and anger the dust into sneezing clouds. They roar past in the opposite lane, I close my window when one approaches. Winding through the Sheep Hole Mountains, the hills are a cinnamon dust. In Another few miles I reach Amboy, California and turn right on to Route 66, proof that I'm getting somewhere. A sign on the left points to Kelso and a dirt road runs off, north, toward mountains. A faded sign warns, DO NOT TURN OFF MAIN HIGHWAYS ON TO DESERT ROADS WITHOUT MAKING LOCAL INQUIRY. Why? What could be going on out here? Bandits? UFOs? Vaporizing cars? It almost sounds inviting. There could be something good going on out there, but there is no one around to ask.

There's more traffic on Route 66 than the road through the hills. I'm on one of the older sections, a single lane in each direction so traffic can only pass in a few stretches. The big trucks are followed by a caravan of cars that have to wait for a straight stretch to over-take. A motor cycle approaches. The rider is wearing a cut-off jean vest, his hair flapping, then, there is the Blap-blap-blap-blap-blap of a big Harley as he throbs by.

About a year ago, after the Submarine Band had done a couple of scenes for The Trip, I remember being at Peter Fonda's place. He and Dennis Hopper were talking about an idea they had for some sort of movie. They wanted to ride around America on motorcycles, shooting scenes with small movie cameras. They were both very excited about the idea of a film that showed the other side of the USA. Hopper was making suggestions about places they could go, what might happen there and he would get very spun-out saying, 'That would be so-o weird man!' The ideas sounded cool. Maybe they're doing it now and while I'm on Route 66 I should keep my eyes open for a couple of guys on bikes with cameras.

I was with Brandon that afternoon and after we left Peter Fonda's place Brandon had said that it sounded like they had a great theme for a movie and he would like to be in it. Brandon was looking for the right role or project to come along that he could dive into, something that would help to build a new identity and alter his child-star celebrity. Over the past couple of years he had a couple of attempts at modifying his career when he did some music and recording sessions. The Submarine Band had backed him on a session at the end of '65.

"You know, I can't really remember what happens in the middle of that song Brandon played for us last night."

"Well, it's just the middle." Gram laughed. "We'll fall right back into it. It'll just happen, relax. I got a feelin' this is going to fun. Take it easy. I mean if the songs turn out to be awful, Brandon's not going to get kicked out on the street or have his house repossessed or anything like that. He's experimenting. It'll be fine."

I had already forgotten what it was about the arrangement that bothered me, as the cab elbowed its way along 52nd street and I watched the sidewalk matinee rolling past. Gram and I had put our instruments in the trunk of the Checker cab and were on our way to meet the other guys at a studio. This was our second trip to New York in '65 to do some recording. We had come down to New York about two weeks before this to record a couple of Gram's songs, on this trip we were going into the studio to lay down two or three of Brandon's ideas. "We just have to remember to have a good time. Don't freak-out about anything, you know. We could be on our way to court or clockin'-in, to sit behind a desk all day, adding up balance sheets at an accountant's office, instead of going into a recording studio."

"Where you guys goin'?" The cab driver looked up into his rear-view mirror.

"The corner of 8th would be okay."

We found the building and pushed the doorbell. The small speaker squawked.

"Yes?"

"We're here to do some music with Mister DeWilde today, if his voice hasn't finally changed." Gram spoke into the grille.

"Fourth floor. Elevator's on the right." And the door buzzed open. As the elevator door was sliding shut, a big brown leather glove wedged in and pushed it open.

"Ah, we can just fit in." A guy wrapped in a big jacket and a fur hat, held the door for a woman wearing a long, dappled, fur coat and thick makeup. His jacket had a fur collar and she wore a Persian lamb hat.

It was like going to the zoo. They got out after the elevator bing-ed on the third floor.

"Man, I thought one of them might have started growling any minute. Gr-r-r-r. Back, Bruno, back!"

In studio number two, the guys were setting up. Brandon was strumming and tuning his acoustic.

"Hey. Here are the late arrivals." Brandon walked over and began talking non-stop. "Feeling bright and chirpy? I've got an idea for one of the songs, okay. Tom was warming up and he played something on the electric piano that I liked. Just a couple of chords. See, hear what he's playing now? That would work in the middle of 'All the things I Never Knew'. We'll try it in a minute."

"I'm going to have to hear that one again. Let me set up and then see what's goin' down, okay." I walked away as Brandon began telling Gram that he had re-written the chorus to one of his songs.

"I was doing it like this," he strummed the guitar, "to a G. Now I'm going to a D, like this, then to the G."

"Cool." Gram replied, "Sounds good." Brandon had been writing songs during the last few months, when there were gaps between acting work, it gave him a sense of direction. He was a Beatles fan, even more so after getting together with them in the Bahamas when Help! was being filmed and meeting Gram a few months ago had also been an influence on him.

"Okay, Brandon, I'm ready." I had the bass guitar.

"Can we play through a couple of them now? I need to see what's happenin'. Let's pull a couple of chairs over here." Brandon put on his glasses.

"I need to see the lyrics to this. I re-wrote some of them last night, where are they?" He searched the pockets of his corduroy jacket. When he unfolded the paper it vibrated in his hand, he was nervous. He took a deep breath and blew. "O-okay. Let's see. Like this." He strummed a few chords then said, "What about an intro to this? It needs one. Any ideas?"

"Maybe you could have the piano lead it off." Gram suggested. "Wha' do you think Tom? Can you do something here?"

Tom looked down at the keyboard and played around with the chord. The rolling tone of the Wurlitzer electric piano sounded cool. It spoke with a jazzy, blues voice. He looked up, squinted and settled into a two-chord figure. He looked over at Brandon questioningly and shrugged his shoulders.

Brandon bobbed his head, listening and liked it. "Yeah! That's it. If you keep doin' that, like four bars, then I'll come in."

"Okay."

"Cool." We ran through the intro, then the song, it seemed to work.

"You know what." Brandon said. "I think we shouldn't wait. We ought to record that one right now, before we forget it and lose that feeling."

We recorded two more songs. They were simple enough and, after a few takes the backing tracks were down. Brandon had booked four hours of time so we decided to move on to the vocals and overdubs so he would at least come away with a couple of finished recordings. Brandon had also brought-in the New York session musician Buddy Lucas, who was waiting to lay-down some harmonica. The song that hit us as being the strongest of the three was 'Begin With You', which he had written a couple of months ago. The electric piano had set a cool mood on that one.

"I wrote it when Susan was away, visiting England, and I knew I really loved my wife. You know how distance gives you a perspective on things. You can see what stands out, what's important and what's too insignificant to count." Brandon explained the background. "What if you sing the last line of the verses, ah, and part of the chorus with me?"

"Sure." Gram replied.

"What else shall we do? M-m. We've got enough instruments already. Maybe some percussion? Tambourine, or something? On the chorus?"

"Sure, fine. Two of us could put something on. Tambourine, car-crash and trampoline. We'll just play along on the play-back." We put the headphones on.

Brandon sang to the tracks to get a level and try out the harmonies with Gram.

"Yeah, that works okay, I think. Let's do it. Um, wait a sec. What was that sound, that tapping I heard?"

"Yeah, that was me, the French maid, down here in the boiler room." Mickey's voice came through on the headphones.

"That sounded good. What was it?"

"A pick box."

"A pick box?"

"Yep." Mickey had held a little plastic box, a one-inch cube, up close to the mic and had been tapping it with his finger. He had conjured-up a sound like a tiny beating heart. It worked. Turning ordinary objects into instruments was one of the tricks we had learned from the recordings we had done at Brandon's place. The pick box percussion had brought the casualness of the home recording into the studio.

Not long after the Harley had roared by on Route 66, there is a cop, California Highway Patrol. It is the first cop car I have seen for a few days. Southern California was loaded with cops. There were all sorts of them; LAPD, State Cops, Highway Patrol, Sheriffs and probably even more in the air, on the sea, in the forest and undercover. It seems like there are more and more cops all the time. They must have upped the recruitment numbers, doubled them. They are over-worked with all the demonstrations, love-ins and disruption on campus. Almost everyday there is something on the news about disturbances at the universities, clashes at colleges between cops and students, it has become a regular event, almost like sports. You can get the score; 14 police, 53 students injured in last night's game. The cops are still at the top of the league but their lead shows signs of narrowing, it could be a close-one as we get to the end of the season.

One of the first big confrontations was last fall at the University of Wisconsin. Dow Chemical Company reps were visiting the campus to recruit science undergraduates and offer them a bright career future. Dow is the biggest producer of Napalm, a product that recently has not been up there in the top-ten on the students' play list. Several hundred people had occupied a campus building in protest. The university Dean panicked and called the cops. They stormed in, swinging clubs at the kids who were holding their home-made peace signs, and injured over one hundred students. About seventy kids were hospitalized; the confrontation was shown on that night's news. That was it, like an unofficial declaration of war, a couple of million young people made a decision that evening about which side they were on.

The guys who were students were safe, maybe not from the skull busting cops, but as long as they were registered at school they wore a sort of bullet-proof armor; the student deferment classification, 2-S. Oh Yes! Unless everything went completely crazy, Vietnam was way, way, way over there and students could stay here, dancing at the campus party.

When I was in high school, there was a day when the recruiting officers came for a friendly talk with the boys in our senior class. I don't remember what branch of the services they were from, Army, Marines or Navy, just big guys in uniforms, caps, buttons and badges. My school was so small, I could not see why they had wasted their time coming here. There were only a dozen, or so, guys in our grade, the baby boom was a couple of years behind us. The officers reminded us that we had to start thinking about our futures. It was a federal law that, at 18, every young man was required to register for the Selective Service. Had we considered the wonderful opportunities that the military could offer? There was training in mechanics, electronics or catering. We could expect to travel, see the world and make great friendships with guys like ourselves. Driving jeeps, tanks, loading artillery, shooting guns and polishing boots were also offered to whet our appetites. Hey! Wow! Look at the uniforms and the hearty, he-man smiles. I was not sold on the idea.

A couple of the boys went up, after the presentation was over, shook hands and took a brochure that had, pictured on its cover, a young soldier, smiling, saluting and standing-square before the rippling Stars and Stripes. I guess some of my class mates could see the opportunities in Army catering or artillery that I had somehow missed. I knew right then that I had to get into university, I could do my tank driving there.

Later that year I was accepted at the Rhode Island School of Design, RISD. I started in September so, for awhile, they could not swear me in and put me in uniform. I lost my student 2-S status when I dropped-out at the end of '64. Since then I had been on the move and they had not caught up with me. What better place, for a guy on-the-run, than out here in the Mojave Desert.

It used to be a lot easier to get out of being drafted. People played all sorts of tricks to flunk the physical and the interview. When your number came up, you were notified and had to report to a local induction center, where you went through a physical examination. 'Step on the scales, read the numbers on the wall, do you wear glasses?

Stick out your tongue and say A-a-h-h.' They put on rubber gloves and asked you to take down you shorts, checked your dick, put a finger in under your balls, and said 'Cough please'. Long lines of guys, most all of them understandably nervous, were realizing that they were getting one step closer to the base camp at Lai Khe, Dha Nang or somewhere else that sounded like a dish on a Chinese take-out menu. Back then it was pretty easy to fool them but the Army medics eventually got wise to the game.

You didn't have to be too inventive back in '64 or '65 but by '66 you had to work harder, the examiners had seen a lot of the ruses. Now, the chances of getting out were getting even slimmer. You couldn't get away by wearing pink underpants, or going cock-eyed, lolling your tongue and answering 'What?' to anything they asked you.

During '64 when I was at art school and hanging around with the alternative crowd, there were some great draft board cons going on. A friend of mine, Alan, was a dancer and homosexual. He arrived at the induction center wearing a mink stole, and a bit of rouge. That was just about enough. The desk Sergeant looked at his papers, raised his pen to tick the rejected box and said, 'Well I'm afraid you're just not Army material, boy'. The Sarge felt sorry for him, assuming Alan would have to go back home, his tail between his legs, and tell Mom and Pop the awful news; 'Jeez dad, they turned me down. I guess I'm not man-enough for the Army. I don't know what I'll do now. Can we have macaroni-and-cheese for supper tonight Mom? Please, maybe it'll help me to feel better and get over this'. Later that night there was a big party. All of Alan's weird friends hung-out and one side of an unattended Little Richard album played, over and over again.

Randy went down to the center the next week and stood in line, appearing fairly normal. When asked to lower his pants, the medics were greeted by a huge load, stinking and sticking to the inside of his thighs. 'What the Hell! You get into to the men's room and clean yourself up, boy! For Christ's sake! What next!'. The toilet paper clean-up would not do much good as he had gobbled down three whole boxes of Ex-lax a couple of hours before his physical.

The guys would claim to hear voices, see purple skunks, sleep with their mothers or relate phobias, nightmares and homosexual tendencies during the psychiatric evaluations. Most of the time something like that would work. If you did not get the 1-Y disqualification, on grounds of mental instability, at least you might get a six-month deferment. 'We're going to want to see you again, later this year', they might say. But, it was another six months of freedom.

The draft was also a bit choosy back then. They wanted the healthiest, fittest, the cream of the crop. All the jocks, the guys who played sports in school, were premium stuff. Pitchers, catchers, quarter-backs, basketball aces, track stars and shot-putters, the whole varsity team were top grade sirloin. Yes Sir! Asthmatics, diabetics, anyone with heart murmurs, myopia, flat feet, migraine or more severe health problems, would be classified 4-F; physically unfit for today's modern Army. Usually that meant you were out of it, maybe crossed of the list. I bet they have lowered the standards recently, an awful lot of those high school sports stars are coming back home with one leg.

Gram's number came up in '66 about six months after he had dropped out of Harvard. It seems that all the institutions, authorities and organizations were working together to hound us down. Luckily, they gave you some warning and a few valuable weeks to come up with some evasive maneuvers. Gram sweated out the days as the date of his physical drew closer. He was in pretty good shape, maybe he could not sprint for a mile, bench-press two hundred pounds or do one hundred sit-ups, but the Army would be happy to rectify that.

Gram decided that the best thing he could do for the physical was to get pretty fucked-up. Four days before the date, he went out looking for some supplies. Later that evening he returned with a couple bottles of whiskey, two medicine bottles full of biphetamines and some LSD. Three days before the physical he started on the draft dodgin' diet with the black beauties. He stopped eating or sleeping, watched loads of TV and began to tremble, start and shake. The morning of the big day he took half a tab of acid. He had to find his way down there at least, no good taking it all. He drank the remaining half bottle of scotch. He was grubby, unshaven and his eyes looked like sunset in Acapulco.

"Well, see you, ah, later, huh." Squinting in the daylight, he stumbled on the front-door steps.

"W-oo-oops, didn't see that one comin'. Guess I'd better watch it." He chuckled.

"Hey, take it easy man."

Gram weaved away, down University Avenue.

"Don't you dare come back in a uniform, okay."

"No, I'm gonna be comin' back later with some Champagne."

When he woke up, over a day later, Gram could not recall anything much about what happened at his physical. He thought that he might have fallen down a lot. He was lucky that, even in New York, a good act could still be convincing.

A couple of weeks later, a buddy from my RISD days, who had also moved to New York, came to visit. He was driving an Army-green VW bus and it was loaded-up. He had heard that the physicals were getting tougher to fake. The military examiners were used to all the dodges and, by now, had seen just about every gimmick and ploy that the boys could dream up. Les knew of a couple of guys who had not been as lucky as Gram and were being sent to boot-camp for basic training, then off they'd go, to Vietnam. He had his van packed and tomorrow would be taking the thruway, north to Canada. It was a drive you could do in less than a day.

"That's it, man, I'm going."

"You're sure?"

"I have to get out of here, like now. My physical is supposed to be at the end of this week."

"You're not gonna try and fake it?"

"No, I don't want to risk that. Fuck! If I pass the physical, that's it. They load you right into a bus!"

"Yeah, really? Shit!" We were both getting agitated.

"Yes definitely. No waitin' around or 'see you tomorrow' stuff, man. That's it. You pass, you're gone."

"Too late then, huh?" He was beginning to creep me out.

"You said it. Screw it, I'm NOT going! I'll go over the border at Niagara Falls. I'm not gonna to stop 'til I can see the falls and the you-ess-of-ay, from the other side. They can have their stupid Vietnam!"

The Canadians were letting draft-dodgers stay and, if they were not AWOL, the American border patrol could not prevent people leaving.

"Wow. What are you going to do then?"

"Then?" Les exhaled, like he was relieved to reach this part of his plan. "I'm gonna have a nice, relaxed trip, all the way 'cross Canada. I'm heading for Vancouver."

"Wow. That's a haul, man. I did that trip the other way round once." He showed me the interior of his VW van. He had built a bunk, storage spaces and had a couple of little hi-fi speakers fixed in corners. When he closed the doors, it was like being in the cabin of a small boat, ready to sail. He decided to take me for a quick drive around the block.

"It's great isn't it?"

"Man, you are going to have one Hell of a good trip. Cool"

"I just wanted to say goodbye, I'll let you know where I am. When I get to where ever that is."

"Yeah, I could be heading up there myself, who knows."

"Hey, you sure you don't want to come along?"

"Um-m, well, sounds cool, but I'm workin', we've got gigs, you know. Good luck!"

"Later man. Don't let Uncle Sam sneak-up on you." I waved as he drove off, away from the Draft Board.

It had been the same in LA; lots of guys facing the Vietnam dilemma. Draft cards, physicals, induction or running to Mexico, Canada or Europe. You could be asked to produce your draft card by the police even if you were being given a parking ticket. It might not have been legal but it happened. The war was getting intense and LBJ was committing more troops, more planes and lots and lots of money to fight Ho Chi Min.

The TV news-hour seemed to show the same footage every night. B-52's emptying strings of bombs, rows of explosions blooming out of the jungle and American GIs tramping down muddy tracks with twigs and leaves stuck-on to their helmets. The news reels showed examples of successful bombing missions, Viet Cong attacks on South Vietnamese villages and defeated North Vietnamese communist troops. We saw the same images over and over again, that film must have been wearing out.

There were other reports in The LA Free Press, a newspaper that was sometimes shoved in your car window by hippie-kids waiting at the traffic lights. There was always a different story than what was shown on TV. The headlines read, 'Innocent Villages Bombed', or 'Burned' or 'Baked', 'American Troops Invade Cambodia, Laos', 'Hundreds of Square Miles Defoliated: Agent Orange' or, 'US Troops Killed by U.S. Artillery'. The paper showed a completely contrary picture, the other side of the story. And the photographs! Jesus! The piles of blackened bodies, the soldiers wrapped in blood-stained bandages, the guys on stretchers with their arms flopping over the sides as they were loaded on helicopters, Vietnamese kids missing arms and legs or with burns that covered half their bodies. And hundreds of poor bastards in their flag-draped coffins were being unloaded out of those huge C-103 transport planes. It makes you fucking cry.

A few years ago, before the public started getting hip to what was going on, people could accept the US troops being over there, helping out a poor little country defend itself from the Commie threat. Oh, those darn Reds, always making trouble in the Far East. Now, more and more people could see that we had become the invaders and ruthless killers that had no right to be there. Anyway, what were the Communists really going to do, what sort of threat to us are a bunch of people who wade around muddy fields growing rice and live in bamboo huts? They all look so weak and skinny, particularly the Vietcong in their black pajamas and bare feet.

Just before Needles I leave Route 66 and swing onto 95 heading toward Las Vegas, about one hundred miles north. There isn't any alternative, all the roads in this pointy, southern tip of Nevada lead to the city. I guess I'm gonna have to see Vegas. I've had it with cities, I dig this big wilderness where there is almost no evidence of settlement and the highway is the only corruption, just a string of intrusive concrete decorated with road side rubbish.

The detritus stands out against the backdrop of this desert road, my eyes are so attenuated to product recognition, I just can't help it. The brands and logos are all so familiar, scored into my consciousness from years of watching TV, hearing jingles, commercials and floundering in the American ocean of consumerism. 'It's the tobacco that counts', 'The pause that refreshes', 'A little dab 'll do ya', 'Breakfast of champions', 'A name you can trust', 'Chew your little troubles away'. The hundreds of slogans become a litany of advertising and space-age poetry. Lies, implanted deeper than The Lord's Prayer. My education.

I can't help recognizing the Marlboro-red-and-white of a flattened cigarette pack, the gold, squashed can of Miller High Life ('the Champagne of bottled beers') and a Coke bottle, so strong they don't seem to break. A flat, hip-pocket, whiskey bottle is intact, maybe it didn't shatter because when it got tossed out of a car they were weaving along too slowly to do any damage. The sun picks out shards, chips of glass, green and amber, that sparkle, delineating the road's edge. The cars and trucks have shed scraps of their metal skin and scales as they have whizzed by. Hub caps, windshield wipers, radio aerials, rear-view mirrors and black snakes of unwound tires, the highway's adornment.

Occasionally I see a car on the side of the road, with the engine hood raised, others are smashed-up or upside down. How did they manage to do that? It's hard to believe because the roads are so straight and flat. The drivers probably fell asleep at the wheel, dreaming of all that money they were going win at those Vegas slot machines.

Everywhere a road forges, the junk soon follows. Littering probably started with a horseshoe, thrown as the wagons headed West, then a boot, a broken axe handle, harness and crates. Those settlers were on the move and didn't look back on their sparse trail of rubbish. Now it's part of our way of life, heaving stuff out and covering America with junk, almost like it was written into the Constitution or the Bill of Rights. We're fulfilling our patriotic duty, from sea to shining sea.

During the year at Burrito Manor, a hybrid tree sprouted and grew out of the blacktop. The limbs climbed upward and eventually sprouted pizza-sized, chrome blossoms and strange fruit. The flood of traffic that cascaded like a river down Laurel Canyon Boulevard constantly left flotsam that washed-up on the roadside bank. In the rush to get up, over the hills and to be somewhere else, cars and trucks shed bumpers, hubcaps, headlights, doors and taillights, between Sunset Boulevard and Mulholland Drive. Mickey and I occasionally harvested these cast-offs. Urban beachcombing.

We wired several twisted bumpers together, creating a trunk. Tailpipes and chrome strips were grafted on to the column, these branches eventually sprouted and flowered with helitropic hubcaps and night-scented taillights. The tree did well in the arid LA climate, it loved sun and never wilted, demanding neither oil nor water. On the occasional gusty day some of the fruit might fall to the ground with a clang, that was okay, they were already bruised. We considered planting a grove of the Detroit trees until the landlord complained. Probably, after we left, he had to get some scrap-yard jacks to cut it down.

In the Bronx, while walking down University Avenue to the Fordham Road, I tripped over what looked like a log, lying on the sidewalk. It was a large slab of metal, a cylinder head from a straight-six engine. The balk of cast iron had a repetitive pattern of cavities, circles, the size of silver dollars and numerous holes. In the dusk the forms suggested faces or masks, a machine-age totem pole with six individual characters. A couple of the faces, that lacked valves, winked. A dark valve-stem port starred, the remaining valve, like a lid, closed over the other eye. I tried lifting it but that was impossible, I had to go back to the house and try to sell the salvaging idea to Mickey. We lugged it back, struggled up the stairs and set it down in my room to have a look at it in some light.

"It looks great. I'm going to clean it up. Maybe use some sand paper or polish it in places."

"Uhm-m. Yeah, it's good."

"A bit of shine would make each face look different." We pondered the metal.

"You could glue-on some screws or bolts to make teeth."

"Yeah, that would put more life into it."

"Machine-o-man, our forefathers' sacred piston god, motor- morpho." Mickey chanted.

"That's what I was seeing. I'm going to find some rags and start cleaning it up."

Gram leaned through the doorway. "Huh. I can see that you guys have been up to no good, around the neighborhood."

"Yeah, we found him wandering the streets and figured he needed a good home."

The house in the Bronx was large, a couple of rooms were never used and remained empty, their doors were rarely opened. We brought very little with us when we moved to the city, a few clothes, records and instruments. To fill the vacuum, more street salvage came through the front door. A car bumper, a school desk, a crate, vacuum cleaner hose and an iridescent stuffed fish, a tarpon, came in off the street. I fixed together a couple of old doors and some timber to make a cabinet for my comic books and records. On the door I painted an image of a dejected, introspective figure. He could have been a blues singer, passed-out, in a dark alley, or a sharecropper, exhausted and broke.

I began building a structure from empty, orange-and-black Minute Maid orange juice cans. Over the following months, it grew into a city skyline. Like a kid's building block game, the challenge was to see how high it might go without collapsing. Eventually, the structure incorporated buttresses and secondary stacks and reached to almost five feet. I painted the ceiling with broad, alternating, blue and salmon-pink bands, radiating from a white, full moon disk. Upstairs, Mickey was working on a dark mural. Sinuous bands of color wandered around shrouded figures and miscellaneous fragments of household objects. One of the painted figures wore a shirt that he had thumbtacked to the wall. Another figure shouted through a sardine can mouth. The Submarine house began to attract visitors. People we knew began bringing their friends to see what was becoming an expanding, unofficial, exhibition.

On a New York morning, in the afternoon, a couple of the guys from The Turtles came up to the house. I was doodling, drawing cartoons and overheard talking and laughter from another room.

"Hey. We just rolled one, out here." I heard Gram announce. "Anybody else want a poke, huh?" They were sitting around the dining room table having a smoke. The guys who had come to say hi did look a bit like turtles; Mark had a lot of wavy hair, was wearing large glasses and chuckled a lot. They were in the city promoting a single, doing some showcases, radio and TV. The Turtles had a couple of hit records that had that, ok-everybody-sing-along thing: Bah-h-h, bah-bah-bah, bah-h-h.

Mark talked about the tour. "Weird, man. We did a TV session last night. It's all just lip-sync. You feel like you're in the same place every time. You're sure that you got off a plane an' it said, like, Dallas or Philadelphia or Denver on the sign at the airport, but you always seem to be in the same studio, again. A guy's wearing earphones an' counting down, a couple of blondes are dancin' on stage and I'm even sure I've seen the same cameraman a couple of times. Weird, the same guy. It made me wonder, what's goin' on? Like, hey, where are we? Are we actually going anywhere? Did I get on the plane, they circle around for awhile, an' then, like, land at the same place! What's goin' on?" He pulled a dumbfounded face and scratched his head.

"Maybe one time the sign will say Italy, like Rome or somewhere and you'll know that you're not in Ohio again," Gram suggested, then began telling a story about a recent Submarine Band TV spot. "We did a thing for TV last week. The managers office called-up, ha, sayin', 'TV, great exposure. DJ is putting together a one-hour special.' Okay, cool. They said, 'It's out at Palisades Park, over the Hudson in Jersey, big amusement park. It'll be closed and they'll be filming.' Talk about lip-sync, right. I asked where we were going to play, they said, 'Oh you're not going to have to play. Maybe bring a guitar or something, you might not even need that. They'll over-dub your record later.' What the Hell, we went out there. There's the DJ in a shiny, sky-blue suit and a cameraman. They're lookin' around at the rides, talkin' about the Ferris wheel. The cameraman decides it's no good, an' some other rides spin around too fast for the shot. So, we end up on this kids ride! You know, some little Donald Duck, Porky Pig cars. We climb into those! The guy is saying, 'Yeah, looks great.' But I can't barely fit into Goofy's seat, my knees are up to my chin and I'm holdin' the guitar up, in front of my face! It just won't all fit. They say, 'We don't really need the guitar in there.' A funky lookin' wino, in a phone booth thing, pulls a lever and round-and-round-up-an-down we go, like Chubby Checker says. Lip-sync forget it! Too sophisticated. Ha."

"So, what have you been doing today?" He's noticed the black ink on my fingers.

"I've just been drawing some, like, cartoons."

"Yeah? Cool. Can we see them?" We troop into my room.

"Hm-m. Look at that." He gazed up at the painted ceiling for a moment then said, "Wow! Psychedelic!"

"Well, it doesn't keep me awake at night."

"Hey, look at that, man. Orange Juice City. Weird. Psychedelic!"

I opened the door of the cabinet, the interior was wallpapered with a collage of politicians, glistening toffee-colored roast turkeys, Supergirl and toys.

"Man! Psy-che-del-ic!"

I hadn't categorized the doodling, drawing, collecting junk and making things as psychedelic before. It was a hobby, goofing around and childish.

You have to have something for dealing with New York.

'WELCOME TO NEVADA' the big sign says. I'm out of California, into another state! I lean on the horn for a suitable fanfare of celebration and get a metallic croak out of the VW, it'll have to do. The speed limit goes up to 70 miles per hour, Nevada needs to whisk those suckers on their way. I doubt that I could get this thing to go that fast. Soon the big billboards appear; The Sands, Tony Bennett appearing nightly, Gold Nugget, Caesar's Palace, Silver Dollar Hotel and Casino, Desert-View, luxury apartments. A huge bow-legged cowboy wearing furry chaps spins his lariat over his head advertising the big jackpots at the Corral. Another place claims winners have walked away with millions from the casino. Maybe I could take my little bunch of fives and tens, my travelling money, swagger on into The Sands and slap my stake on the table and yell, 'Hit me again dealer' or 'I'm puttin' it all on seventeen red!'. 'Luck be a lady tonight! Roll 'em, yeah, come on sevens!'

Vegas just couldn't spin me around or tell a good enough lie to make me pull over and take advantage of all that free parking at the casinos. I leave that town with the same amount of cash as when I crossed the city limits. That's another place behind me now. I didn't bite. I didn't chomp on the hook hidden inside that promising, juicy worm. I had munched before.

A few miles beyond Las Vegas I pull over to get out for a stretch. Out of the city and back in the desert again. Everything suddenly becomes a screaming whoosh! Two Voodoo jets scorch by, low overhead. The sound turns into a rumbling blast, I can see the flames of their after-burners. They are flying low, their noise alone is like a weapon. I had seen on a map that a large area above Vegas was dotted in red, designated 'Las Vegas Bombing Range', it was about one-hundred-and-fifty miles long and a hundred miles wide. They had plenty of room. That's probably where they were adjusting the bombsights for raids on Hanoi. Looking back down the road to Vegas I can see a cruder sign, not as flashy as the casino billboards, it reads: WE WILL WIN IN VIETNAM, God Bless America.

A couple of hours later at Mesquite, I'm surprised to see a state border sign welcoming me to Arizona. I am only going to be cutting through the top corner, on the road to Utah. I come upon a large road sign that says; MY COUNTRY RIGHT OR WRONG. These guys in Arizona didn't even want to discuss it. War, peace, right or wrong, forget about it, doesn't matter, we're American, that's it!

A road sign says that Salt Lake City is three hundred-and-twenty miles. Salt Lake City is about the only town in Utah that anyone can name. It's way up there somewhere, I was never sure exactly where. A couple of months ago Gram had played me a recording he had done up there with the Byrds.

It was spring. I rang Gram, I had been up early and there was part of an afternoon ahead.
"Hey." He answered.
"Hi. How are ya this mornin'?"
"Well, I'm just getting' going. I'll be alright once I get some oxygen."
"What? Are you going to the 'Y' to swim some laps?"
"No, some coffee and a cigarette would work."

"That's probably what I need too." I agreed.

"Well you could come-on over, in a bit."

"Hey, I'm not begging, I wasn't trying to sound desperate."

"No, it's cool. Tell you what, I'll play you something I recorded with The Byrds."

I knew that Gram had been recording with them, cutting tracks for a new album, but I hadn't heard anything that they had done. Gram had told me they were working on some songs that had more of a country feel than you might expect to hear from The Byrds. Things had changed, Gram was working with them now and even though he was leaping from band to band, he wasn't throwing the country identity aside or hanging-up the sequinned shirt.

I drove down to his place.

"You feelin' more awake now?" he welcomed.

"Yeah, a few yawns later and I'm just about okay."

"I got some coffee right here. That ought to do it for ya."

"Okay, hit me." I took a sip, it was dark. "Where have you been lately? I saw you a couple of weeks ago, I guess."

"Yeah, I came up to Burrito Manor to see you guys. Come on."

"M-m, that's right. Time has a way of getting' a bit homogenised once and awhile."

"Are you guys still going to stay-on up there?"

"I guess so. As long as we can pay the rent. John's moving-out, going to a place on Ridpath with Corneal, I think." We both had a drink. "Ah-h, good. What about that recording? What have you got? Are you goin' to play it for me?"

"Oh-h, I was, wasn't I. It's something we recorded out of town, on the road."

"Yeah? Where have you been?"

"Well, we did a few dates in the West. Ah, Arizona, Utah." Gram switched-on a turntable and picked up a small disk, like a 45.

"What is it, a single?"

"Oh yeah, definitely a single. It's the only one." He showed me the record. 'Record-O-Disk'; red letters on an off-center label and, hand-written in pencil, 'Salt Lake City'. He dropped the needle on the edge. "Yeah, we cut this in a booth in Salt Lake City. Two minutes for three dollars," he chuckled.

Crackles, then a hiss, a thin voice began, 'Hello?, hey! it's working! Well, what do you Byrds think about being in Salt Lake City?' There was constant hissing and maybe a rumble of ghosting traffic but no response to Gram's opener. He continued, 'Yeah here we are in Salt Lake City, dum-de-dum, o-ow o-ow yeah.' Another voice, half-heartedly joined-in on the o-ows. 'Hey come-on guys, don't let me down here, we've still got forty-five seconds left. Ha-ha. An' I gotta send this to my Aunt Mildred up there, in Buffalo…she's hopin' that….TICK, TICK, Sh-h-h-h-h.

"I guess we should have rehearsed it and had some, ah, better lyrics." He laughed.

In the late afternoon, the road begins to climb into mountains, through trees and forest. I turn off the highway onto a small road that leads to the town of Hurricane and on to Zion National Park, now only twenty miles away. Driving through Hurricane, I spot the old Chevy van parked in the town's little main street. Briggs is outside, on the sidewalk, looking in the window of a shop selling hunting and camping gear. The display is like a shrine to the outdoor life. It has a stuffed racoon fixed onto a log, surrounded by adoring hatchets, fishing rods, kerosene lanterns and camouflage hats. A couple of stumps display big jack-knives, daggers and hunting knives stabbed into the wood making a fan pattern.

"Hey, ya gonna do some carving, need a Bowie knife?"

"Yeah, I'm plannin' on spending the night whittlin' away, under the stars. You have a good run?" Briggs asked.

"Yeah great, no trouble. I didn't stop anywhere much, 'cept for gas outside of Las Vegas. I just kept driving through, I didn't stop to play the slot machines. Yeah, everything's cool, the van went fine."

"It looks great around here, I like the trees, it's good to be out of the desert, it seems to go on and on forever. Barry's over 'cross the street at a butcher's, he thought he'd get something to cook. Maybe we'll be havin' a banquet tonight, barbecued racoon, who knows. I'm gonna grab some cold beers before we go."

"Yeah great, lemme give you some money, get me a couple, okay? I don't really care what, whatever they got, maybe a G I Q."

"Okay, I'll go see what I can find. They might have some sort of weird laws about booze here, never can tell, it's a different state, hope not. I'll see you in a bit."

The road winds along a valley at the base of steep mountains. The trees cling amongst boulders on the cliffs, a tunnel cuts through a massive twin-topped peak and brings us to the park entrance. A park ranger comes out of a booth wearing a Smokey the Bear wide brimmed hat, short sleeved khaki shirt with some insignia. He looks like a cross between military and boy scouts.

"Hi, welcome to Zion Canyon National Park. Here's some information and your guide. Are you going to be camping at the park? Okay, there's just the one entrance fee, two dollars, okay?; that's good for up to two weeks. Let me just get your tag numbers. Fine, okay, I'm going to put you guys in number eleven, in campground A. Okay? You'll see the signs for all the facilities and you can help yourself to campfire wood from the big pile down there. If you need any help with anything just ask one of the rangers or come in to our headquarters. I hope you enjoy your stay."

What a good deal; staying here in heaven for a dollar a week.

We park up, get a few things out and open a beer. I can see the mountainous woodpile that the ranger had mentioned and, after a couple of swigs, I walk over and carry a few logs back. Each site has a circle of stones for a campfire, a stone-built barbecue and a large, chunky picnic table. We get a fire going and Barry T starts carving some meat.

"It's breast of lamb, a real cheap cut. See, I've gotta slice it like this, trim out some of this layer of fat, there's a bone here. It's good. Will ya skin that onion, chop it up a bit, okay? I'm just gonna throw a bit a this off-cut in the pan and maybe I'll need a little oil, yeah that's better." The onions sizzle, Barry smacks his lips and winks, as he browns some of the lamb. "M-um, this is the start to a good stew."

"Okay Chef, I believe ya. I'm gonna bring a few more logs over."

I walk around the campsite area to check-out the new neighborhood. There are just a few other groups here. A couple of campers, a few vans and pick-ups, that's about it. The campfires are going and I can't help seeing some of the gear that other people have; cooler boxes, deck chairs, big transistor radios and bright propane lanterns on high stands that illuminate their campsite with a lime glow. A picnic table is set with matching orange plates and bowls, the orange striped glasses filled with something dark, maybe Pepsi? A plump woman wearing a frilly apron is ladling-out potato salad and a guy pokes at the barbecue with a long-handled fork. He smiles and waves with his other hand. These people are so organized and have such flashy stuff. Compared to the happy campers with their bright 'n' breezy, colorful outdoor accessories, our campsite is definitely from the Grapes of Wrath school of outdoor, recreational living.

We had collected all our camping gear at the big swap-meets in Downy. Frying pans for a quarter, odd knives and forks, old fashioned Army-green sleeping bags. We bought a load of blow-up air mattresses for about a dime each. The seller wouldn't guarantee that they didn't leak. We brought them home and blew up more than a dozen 'til we were ready to pass-out, hyperventilating, seeing stars and left the air mattresses leaning against a wall. Within an hour, half of them had slumped over, deflated like soldiers collapsing after trying to stand at attention all day in the sun.

In LA, messages and litter collect under the windshield wiper within minutes when parked on a city street. Dry cleaning -we deliver, Dom's Pizza, Boy Scout car wash -Saturday 9-1, City of Los Angeles-Traffic Citation. One day a small card appeared; 'Giant Swap Meet, 14711 Paramount Blvd, Downey, admission $1, or Free with pass'. Swap meet? I had to ask what it was and learned that it was a mammoth junk sale. Anything could turn-up there, absolutely anything. Sounded cool. Mickey and I decided to drive out there one Sunday.

The site was at a drive-in movie lot. Acres of cars and vans, parked in-between the speaker stands, fanned-out, radiating like ripples from the off-duty, image-less, concrete movie screen. There were hundreds of sellers. We walked into a labyrinth of tunnels and alleys created by the stalls. An Atomic age souk, stuffed with jetsam, detritus, over-spill and disposable, discontinued, superfluous, unwanted, useless or meaningless consumer goods. Yet, judging by the interested browsers, grazing through this plethora of excess, most of this mass of material was desired, wanted, coveted and absolutely compelling or necessary to someone. Cutlery, obsolete coffee percolators, mud flaps, Kate Smith Fan Club certificates, cowhorns, Army surplus, Mommy surplus, dentists' probes, post cards from Niagara Falls and Atlantic City, Davy Crockett hats, Cow-girl shirts, last year's TV guides, Studebaker grilles, Edsel hubcaps, Toreador pants, construction workers' alloy helmets, full-dress Marine uniforms, outmoded outboards, bald tires, a croquet set (one hoop short), coat hangers in boxes of a thousand, a stuffed moose head, a one-eyed owl and a sailfish were some of the things I didn't buy.

The next row offered a jeep, a Hopalong Cassidy lunch box, a wide brimmed black hat, like Zorro's, bicycle saddles and bells, frilly square-dance skirts, toasters and waffle makers that must have come from a warehouse fire, and a sixty-five seater, old, yellow school bus. It was all here, the life-blood and corpuscles of the USA. A bumper crop. Used to be, the corn was as high as an elephant's eye, now we're beginning to wade through an in-coming tide of second-hand expendables.

I noticed a card table covered with records, a stack of albums and a column of singles. I began flipping through the LPs. Christmas With Doris Day, The First Family by Vaughn Meader, Bert Kaempfert, Lawrence Welk, The Fireballs.

"I got more back here if you want to see 'em." I turned and mumbled 'okay' to a jowly guy in a short sleeve, aqua, shirt with a yellow fish-pattern, a small-brimmed straw hat, with golf tees stuck in the hat band, and a Coke in one hand. He was pointing to his car. In the open trunk of a Plymouth Savoy was an orange-crate and another box, full of 45s. I took a deep breath, sat side-saddle on the bumper and started fingering through. An orange Capitol label, next, RCA, Elvis; 'Wooden Heart'. Hugo

Winterhalter, Vic Damone and Tony Bennett; 'I left my Heart..' Excello Records, Slim
Harpo; 'Scratch My Back', Federal, Freddie King; 'San-Ho-Say'. I had hit a seam of blues.
King records, 'Try Me' by James Brown, 'Black Nights' by Lowell Fulsom. Then, 'Tom
Dooley'- Kingston Trio and 'The More I Want You'- Chris Montez. They got worse, the
'Green Leaves of Summer' by the Brothers Four, I quit, that was my run.

"Aw, gimme seventy-five cents, okay?" Four r'n'b disks, sure, thanks.

Past a table of plastic dog collars, dented caldrons and a stamp album, an astronaut
leans against a Ford van. A dummy wears a jet fighter pilot's suit and helmet. USAF
emblems on the chest and arms, a hose, stitched into the bronze-colored fabric, runs
up the arm and shoulder, other connections and wires are on the cuffs and chest.
The bubble facemask is impenetrable, only allowing a respirator and microphone in.
What an outfit, it looks great! I want it! I've caught the bug and have a bad case of
Ihavetohaveititis, the plague that is sweeping through America. It's a struggle for me to
keep my money in my pocket and, slowly, I back away from the jet pilot's suit. I bump
into a box of bicycle reflectors, like a plastic pirate's treasure chest full of enormous,
light loving rubies. Barbies, Cindies, Tiny Tears, Betsy Wetsy and Chatty Cathy who says,
'I Wuv You', when a pig-tailed girl, wearing a 'Hey, Hey, We're The Monkees' T-shirt,
pulls the string on the back of the doll's neck. A sapphire transistor radio trickles
'California Dreamin',

'I'd be safe and warm, if I was in LA,'

Old licence plates, each with the different state-colors, are laid on the ground like
a tiled terrace. They have curious mottoes, 'Live free or die', 'You've got a friend in
Pennsylvania': I don't think I do. I spot another stack of old records or maybe they've
seen me. We rendezvous. The labels are scuffed, some have stamp-sized stickers on
them, 'this record belongs to Carole Boyce'. The Dot label, Pat Boone - 'April Love',
Roulette, Buddy Knox - 'Party Doll', Jamie, Duane Eddy - 'Cannonball'. Yeah, a couple of
good ones there. Nothing wrong with having another copy of 'Cannonball', who knows
when I might need it. I keep shuffling through and see an odd-ball Atlantic 45, with a
yellow and black label. Wow! Never seen that before, Clyde McPhatter and The Drifters
- 'Lucille'. Man, that must be old, must be good. Thank you, a few more good ones. At
the end of another crescent, I spot Mickey who is trying-on an Indian head-dress, the
feathers fan-out like a tom turkey, beaded belts run down over his shoulders.

He nods his head and grins, "Cow-a-Bonga, I play war drums now."

The lure of the chase, tracking down the old recordings that were still running
wild, brought me back to more of the swap meets. I trapped dozens, hundreds of old
recordings, each one told more of the story and filled-in the gaps in early-fifties music.

Jimmy Wakely and Rocky Starr and His Happy Cowboys played western swing and silly songs, often using an accordion and a boogie rhythm. Tiny Bradshaw's honking sax blared with a morning-after, hangover echo on top of a jump beat. A Speedy West single was a gushing mix of old honky tonk and what sounded like a sound track for 'Attack of the flying saucers from planet X', crazy stuff. I found a wonderful single where B.B. King sings about dropping-out of society. The tax collector is hounding him, he goes to church for some spiritual uplifting but they try to screw money out of him as well. The only thing left for him he figures, the last option, is to move to the jungle, way-ay-ay out in the woods. That old 45 became one of my favorites, I had to play it to everyone.

During the times when the Submarine Band was hungry for old country music and gleaning what we could find, Gram and I homed-in on the melodramatic songs with the most bizarre lyrics. There were a lot of them, if you could see into it. Recently, within the band, that element of humor seemed to have taken a hike, gone AWOL. The record people and managers hadn't encouraged us and appeared to think that the unusual material we liked was, pretty much, poison. If we played too much of the Hick music live, the club audiences scattered like it was teargas.

In the summer of '67, when Barry T and Billy Briggs showed up, we began jamming on old '50s songs, rock 'n' roll, guitar boogie instrumentals, and shreds of doo-wop. We all needed to take a breather and get a laugh. As the '60s had rolled on, rock 'n' roll music seemed to be mutating into a more academic, scholastic form that said, 'bye-bye banality'. Psych-101 had stepped-up to the plate. Nervous Norvus had been replaced by J.D. Salinger.

At the swap meet, the occasional abused saxophone, limp-necked semi acoustic guitar, tarnished trumpet or half a clarinet would catch my eye.

Old amps with ragged grilles, punctured speakers and missing knobs hid under the tables, but we already had amps that were reliable. In their refugee tatters, the old amps whispered memories of our first bands, when two cheap guitars were torturing a 15-watt Silvertone with 'Rawhide'.

On another old record archaeological dig in the Fall of '67, I had found a few 78s; the 'Paper-Boy' by Bill Haley, 'Do You Want To Jump' by Big Joe Turner and 'Faded Love' by Bob Wills and The Texas Playboys. I had walked past jars of pickles and a Lionel train set and was knocked breathless by the pollen-colored glow of a venerable Telecaster. The guitar casually leaned-back, dozing in a guitar stand. Next to it, not wanting to be parted, sat a small amp. The infant amp had a tweed finish and the speaker cloth was the faded canvas color of a Grand Banks schooner's jib. The wear on the black pick guard and maple neck testified to years of action.

"It's a Fender guitar, sorta old, but it still works okay," the guy offered. I was trying to wipe the shock off of my face. "An' I got this here little amp too. It works." I picked up the Telecaster. They're not big but they are solid. "Probably needs new strings." The wear spots, from tens of thousands of finger tamps, revealed the rich wood of the fret board. I turned it over, there was a kidney shaped scuff, worn by years of contact with the musician during thousands of nights on the bandstand. Playing what? Probably rock 'n' roll, country? blues? maybe polka?

I wondered who it could have been. I looked at the serial number etched on the chrome plate at the base of the neck. Zero, zero, zero, zero, Jesus! Four, Seven!! Man! This baby's ancient. It must have been from way back, when Leo Fender started making Telecasters, like in the first year, maybe the first couple of months.

"How much do you want for this?" This thing was like a fucking Stradivarius!

"Well, you can have the guitar an' that lil amp for a hundred an seventy-five."

"Oh yeah. Hm-m." I can feel the guitar glowing, warming, vibrating. It's like the old records, they are loaded and ready to fire.

This guitar could have been played on some of the old records that I've become addicted to. I don't think I have the money, in my pocket, under my mattress, in the bank or in the future. I do have a couple of gigs next week but I don't know what they are paying. Something will work out. That's how it goes.

"I don't have that much on me today, but I'd like to buy it."

He frowns like I might suggest mowing his lawn for the rest of the year or some other primitive bartering. "How about if I give you, uh, let's see, uh, thirty bucks and I come back and give you the rest next week?" he rubbed his chin, sighed and scanned the sky for financial advice.

"Well I don't know. I woulda liked to of had all the money."

"You keep the guitar and the thirty dollars and I'll be back next week. I want to get it." I tried again. He looked at the few people drifting by and heard the sounds from tables that had begun to pack-up the unsold plates, car batteries and bicycles.

"Okay then. You seem alright to me." I guess I didn't look too down-in-the-alley today. "You want me to give you a receipt? I'll write one out."

"Yeah, thanks." I fold the paper and his business card, Economy Music, in my pocket and have another look at that beautiful Fender. "I'll see you next week."

Next week I didn't have the money. I had a design job in the pipeline, but it was for a band's album cover, so who knows. I brought him another fifty and promised I'd be back next time.

I went back to the swap meet with the money I owed for the old Telecaster on the next Sunday. The drive-in movie lot was again transformed into a limbo for items awaiting adoption and a new life. New owners revitalise junk, the tawdry and superfluous are transformed and rapidly appreciate when fondled by new hands. I looked around for the stall with the half-paid-for guitar but he wasn't where I left him. I scanned up and down the rank of sellers but the objects, people and tables blurred, individuals camouflaged in the jumbled-up jungle of material.

Several cigar boxes held a collection of seashells. Under taped-on glass, a card read 'Clearwater, Florida 1962'. Pairs of bivalves, ranked by size, spread like the unfurled wings of pocket-sized angels. Delicate honey colored stripes mimicked feathers but were overwhelmed by the flower-pattern wallpaper lining the bottom of the box, eradicating the appeal that the shells must have had when they glistened, lying on that creamy Florida beach. Several tables pushed together carried tools. Rows of pliers, deep in conversation, vice-grips like gaping pelicans and assorted wrenches, sang the Hallelujah Chorus through chrome jaws. There were drills, corkscrew bits, exhausted hammers and screwdrivers with lemon Jell-O handles. Voltage meters, gauges that monitored pressure, wattage or fuel, all registered zero. Opinionated, tu-tone clock-radios disagreed about the hour. A monochrome plastic garden sprouted car tail-lights. Bullets, cups, chrome-rimmed bowls, chevrons, almonds and domes of red lenses all wanted to say 'stop', again. I passed shell-shocked lawn mowers and projectors, burned-out by Mom and Pop's trip to the Grand Canyon. A shrunken parking lot held a traffic jam of pedal cars; fire engines, the Batmobile, slow motion racing cars and kindergarten jeeps. Next to a stall with ex-Army fatigues, I spotted the table with a few instruments and the Telecaster. He was relieved to see me. I had scraped the money together and was able to take that beautiful guitar home. Barry T liked that old Tele and played it on some Burrito's gigs, it was made for some of the songs we were doing.

In the spring of '68 I went to the swap meet with Brandon and entered the kingdom of U-need-it, again. Possibly, a lot of the stuff there was constantly circulating, spending a few weeks in a new location before returning to the lot to be sold again. I spotted a stack of records.

"I'm going to check these out. I'll catch-up with you."

"Okay. I'm going to wander around. Maybe I'll do some early-bird Christmas shopping."

I flipped through the stack of singles and decided that I could live without 'Perfidia' by the Ventures. Beyond a corral of sewing machines, I spotted Brandon by the fringed rawhide jacket he wore, the leather strings whipped as waved me over.

He pulled his head back and through a clench-toothed smile, hissed, "You're not going to believe what I just got." He turned his head and I followed his gaze which fell upon a large glittering object, like a Mexican altar, sparkling in the noon sun. A scaly skin of mirrors covered what looked like the summit of a '20s skyscraper. Brandon asked the guy to plug it in again.

"Wow! What is it?"

"Neat, huh? Watch this." On ledges and in alcoves, electric candles began to glow. "Wait a second, 'til it gets going." The numerous candles were small glass tubes filled with a colored liquid, tiny bubbles began streaming up in each straw. "Hah! Beautiful huh? It's a radio!"

It had the elements of a home-made jukebox with the streamlined, architectural features of the Chrysler building. The guy fiddled with a dial, turning it past hiss, static and whistles until he found a station playing the Perez Prado song, 'Pricilla'. The music Mamboed, red and yellow candles burbled and the diamond mirrors reflected fragments of our adoration. Interspersed amongst the hundreds of mirrors were small glass tiles touting card suits, mirrors and hearts, mirrors and spades.

Someone, out in their garage, workshop or down in the basement, had wanted to escape from a chilly marriage, the boredom of retirement or some other aspect of feeling useless and had hooked into the salvation of creating a monster. They had amused themselves for days or weeks constructing this kitsch sculpture, spawned by the culture of excess.

"I've got a place, ju-ust right for this, in my kitchen," Brandon nodded.

The last couple of trips to the swap meet were in search of practical things. The Burrito Brothers had fragmented, Barry, Briggs and I had decided to do the road trip. Instead of old Superman comic books, hula-girl thermometers and Red Ryder cowboy shirts, we were searching for barbecue forks, spare tires, tarpaulins and sleeping bags.

Barry T reminded me to look-out for a camping lantern, plastic food containers, a potato peeler and maybe a bucket.

We headed in different directions to scout, then he shouted, "And we're gonna need a couple of potholders too."

We found most of the gear we needed for campfire cooking and backwoods, outdoor living. The Army air mattresses were a deal, bundles of ten for a dollar. The impulse spending was out-of-season now, if I picked up a wrench or a hatchet, I'd heft it, weigh it up, and imagine tightening a loose nut or splitting wood. We weren't going to be playing old records during those chilly nights out there, in the mountains.

Man, that Barry T sure could cook. He enjoyed it, liked to sit back and watch things simmer, give 'em a stir and an occasional, judicious taste. Then, maybe, he'd add a bit more seasoning or decide to give it a little more time, take it off the heat, let it improve.

By the time we get into that campfire lamb stew it's dark outside.

"How about one of those beers?"

"Yeah. I've got a couple right here."

"Great." I take the bottle. "Hm-m what's this? Blatz beer?"

"Hey, it's wet. Tastes good to me. They were on sale."

"Funny, how you go into a different state and there are beers that you've never seen before."

"Yeah, when we moved up to Boston there were a bunch I never heard of, even in Connecticut. Carling, Narrragansett." Briggs said.

"I had never heard of Knickerbocker or Rheingold when I moved to New York." I remembered.

'My beer is Rheingold, the dry beer

Look for Rheingold, whenever you buy beer.'

Rheingold brewery was one of the major sponsors of the weekly Friday night free concerts in Central Park, during the summer of '66. Monte Kay management must have got that booking for the Submarine Band. The concert series featured a wide spectrum of music for New Yorkers; jazz, rock, and folk. Over the season many big names appeared in the park, Otis Redding, Peter Paul and Mary, Ramsey Lewis and others. We were booked to open-up for The Young Rascals.

The Rascals recently had several top-twenty singles. 'Good Lovin'' was a big one, then 'Mustang Sally' and 'You Better Run'. They were an excellent band, especially live. Some of them had been playing the New York clubs for years, working in Joey Dee's band The Starlighters. They must have been young guys, back then, when 'Live At The Peppermint Lounge' was recorded. That scene was pretty much dominated by guys from an Italian-American background, who seemed to have a lot of big-city-soul. We dug The Rascals, Felix and Eddie were good showmen, Dino and Gene were great musicians.

New York was the Rascals hometown and they had a massive following so a big crowd was just about guaranteed. New York was now also the Subs home base, where we had been actively gigging for the past half-year, and Central Park would be an important, high profile gig for us to play.

Car-less in New York, it wasn't that much of a problem. Cars in the city were a pain, judging by the half-full draw of parking tickets that Gram had accrued while he had a car there. He still had the tickets, but he wouldn't drive the car in the city any more, afraid of getting busted. Whenever the equipment had to go downtown for a gig we might rent a station wagon for a half-day to haul the gear. Other times, we'd get two taxis, stuff the drum kit and the drummer in one, the three amps, guitars and one guy in the other. The two of us remaining would have to hop on the D train, downtown. The Central Park concert was a rent-a-wagon gig.

In the eve we crammed into the overloaded wagon and drove down through the South Bronx over the bridge and down to Central Park. Looking for the stage area, we were flagged over by a cop standing next to a 'caterers, crew, stage' sign and red-and-white Rheingold banners.

"Where youse guys goin'?" He squinted, pulled the peak of his hat and decided that we looked enough like a band to be let through.

A cordon was dropped and we were waved-in and pointed towards the backstage loading platform.

New York dusk. A performance of sorts, setting up the gear, as there was no stage curtain. Columns of New Yorkers ooze into the park to join the hundreds inside, in deck chairs or lying on blankets with picnic baskets, bags and, probably, bottles of Rhinegold extra dry beer.

ER-R-R-RCH! SCH-H-H-HICK! The big speaker system jolted awake, after some high-voltage shock treatment. A turntable must have been piped-in, the Rascals LP faded in.

I said Doctor, Doctor, Mister M-D,

Tell me what it is, that's wrong with me.'

Backstage, we tried to tune-up but with solid-body electrics and loud music on the speakers, twisting the tuning-pegs was only an approximation, just fishing around.

"Let me hear your D."

…a faint….ting.

"Again."

"I guess that's close?"

"You guys better turn those amps up all the way, I'm going to be breaking sticks tonight."

"OK caveman, I'll whack it right on up."

"Play your D again."

Ting.

"Isn't that a bit flat?"

"John, don't worry about it. Sounds okay to me."

"We're going to be playin' so loud out there that it will sound like fuzz-tone anyway."

Summer night in the hot, Hot City. Still and sweaty. Now a lake of seething citizens. Heads, hats and shoulders undulate, ripples of flesh, body waves reverberate. A mass that is generating babbling blasts of greeting, seduction, digestion, coughs and courtesies, speaking in tongues and smoking cigarettes.

Ba-Thum, Ba-Thum, Da-Tum, on the Fender bass. The Ampeg B-15 is boiling-over.

Thwack-a-Bam, Thwack-a-Bam, drums.

Zha-r-r, Zhi-n-ng, Zha-r-r, guitar.

And the Telecaster, sounds as if it's down at the other end of a field. His singing returns, seeming to have been around the block, my harmony vocals run off, checking-out the neighborhood. Above, the arc of stage lights, wide-eyed as if startled, shower down and, except the first few rows, the thousands eating, drinking, embracing and talking are submerged in the dusk. Occasional flashes, reflections from glasses, foil, necklaces and lighters, sparkle from this sea, responding arrhythmically. Disembodied arms, shoulders, palms and heads sway, ebbing and flowing in sync. A hand breaks the surface and flutters for a moment before disappearing.

Hundreds of hands keep meeting.

"Hey! Thank you!, thank you. Yeah. Sure is a good night to be out and not sittin' home watching, uh,' the Price is Right." Gram's meandering warm-up greeting booms out. 'Here's one that's gonna be our new single, for the folks at Columbia records.

OK, John?' The Telecaster saws-out the intro to one of the Subs original songs, 'Sum Up Broke'.

'Do you hear me? Look my way,

Do you hear me, I gotta say.' Gram and I sing a double lead on this recently written song, we're both running on autopilot and trying to stick with the drums. The sound on stage is stormy, there's a big space out there, licking it up.

'Love's not there, the love's not there.'

Dee-you deet, dee-you deet-dah-h. Guitar solo. Gram begins jogging side-to-side, foot-to-foot, see-sawing his Rickenbacker, I join in, bobbing the bass neck up and down, turn my back as we edge closer, fencing, jousting. It's a big stage, we close,

Gram's guitar cord twangs taut, I have the springy, telephone-style cord, red and curly, that suddenly tugs the amp, pops out of the input and snake-strikes my leg, Twan-ng! The bass dies. We're still using small-club gear, inadequate for playing to a crowd of fifteen thousand. Fledglings flapping.

We end the set with the old rock 'n' roller, 'Rip it Up'. A few dozen people have got up to dance near to the stage. A Hispanic couple spin. Hot dancin', bellies jelly, ass pumping hot, bouncing boobs, pelvis throbbing, arms in the air armpits airing, moving, in celebration of the night, in the hot, Hot City.

'I'm a fool about my money, don't try to save.

My heart says Go!, Go!, have a time.

It's Saturday night, an' baby I'm feelin' fine!'

Breathless, backstage.

"Hey! How 'bout that!"

"We survived."

"Man, I'm drippin'-wet, should have been naked, phew."

"Anybody bring anything to smoke?" Mickey hopes, rubbing his hands together.

We are jittering, pumped full of adrenaline, panting. To unwind we walk tightening circles. Sweat burns my eyes. It's just gone up a few degrees more.

"Hey, you did great."

"Thanks." Gram answers. "Sure was hard to hear. You know I think your mic went off, close to the end of 'I Can Tell'. You almost knocked the thing over, what you got against mics Ian? Ha."

"Yeah, really? I whacked it with the bass neck when I turned around. Yeah, I though something sorta weird happened, shit."

"Hey, don't worry, it was just around the end, you looked good singing your heart out."

"You know, gigging outdoors, to a huge crowd, is a totally different ball game."

"Yeah, that's cool, we're tryin' to play it."

A few jabs at the organ, then a chord, held. Felix Cavaliere is firing-up the B-3, the cheering grows and keeps swelling.

'One, two, three, four! Good lovin', good lovin'

The Rascals fan the flames. The hot, Hot City is ready to ignite.

The campfire heightens the sensation of the night that surrounds our glowing circle. Nocturnal sounds grow stronger; 'Err-r-rt, err-r-rt, err-r-rt' and 'Woo-who-who', 'Ca-caw-w-w'. They are out there singing and squawking. Maybe talking, persuading or selling themselves; 'Hey, dig this', 'can I come over there and see you?', 'I know you've been out runnin' around with another bug/frog/bird, why d'you treat me so bad, baby?' Yeah, the wild things sometimes sound like they have the after-midnight blues and they need to pour it out, play it again and again.

Zion National Park covers an area of about three hundred square miles or more. Most of it is wilderness, forest, deeply eroded, sculpted valleys and canyons, mountains, hills and spectacular, bizarre rock formations. Immense fractured rock thrusts up to the sky, sheer cliffs rise hundreds of feet above the valley. The predominant colours, red-baked earth, dark green trees, bronze and sienna rocks and the bright blue sky, are vivid, intense.

According to the guidebook, the park has a couple of hundred miles of trails winding through the wilderness. Inside the Ranger headquarters are several large maps showing the park trail network. Each trail is ranked according to the length or severity on a one-to-ten scale. Along the big bruisers, the marathon hikes, are shelters where walkers can camp-out, that's the serious stuff. Hikers are required to sign-in before setting out, signing-off when they return, with their blistered feet and torn flesh. There are other notices about recognising poisonous snakes and what to do if you are struck by a rattlesnake. They are the same instructions that were in the old Boy Scout Handbook, with diagrams of cutting those X's in your arm above the wound, sucking the blood and, of course, spiting it out. You'd be screwed if the rattler got you on the back and you couldn't see where to make those precise incisions or suck-out the venom. Another poster addresses bear encounters; don't panic, back up slowly, repeat under your breath, 'take it easy, Smokey didn't mean any harm really, just, ah, passing through, see ya later.' Cougars, lynx, and porcupines, hornets in hollow logs, ticks dropping from trees; the posters make hiking sound like opening the cage door and walking into a zoo. They are probably intimidating enough to keep people down in the campsite area, safely locked in their cars, loading-up their .30-.30 rifles and reaching for their spray-cans of Raid. We decided that we'll take our chances, trust in fate and go out on one of the trails tomorrow, anyway.

Along a valley trail, through a dark fir wood, about a half-mile beyond the Rangers station we arrive at a trail head. The rustic wooden signs point in different directions to romantically named destinations; Northern Trails, that was probably one of the epic paths, Widow's Notch (8), Sleeping Stones (6), and Wishbone trail-loop and caves (5).

"Maybe we should aim low to start with Wishbone?"

"Looks about my speed. Sure."

We take it easy and walk out of the valley on the uphill trail and are soon able to look out onto huge rock formations and the mountains beyond. A massive cylindrical column pushes straight up out of a dome of land, the rock is crowned with a triangular peak and deep vertical scars run down the sheer face. It is dotted with small trees that have found tenuous footholds and have managed to grow. The Wishbone trail winds along the side of a mass of rock, offering more dramatic vistas as we move uphill. Under arches and vaults, past rugged spires, we come upon some small openings, caves.

One of the caves is wide with a huge crescent of an open mouth. The top lip of the aperture is about fifteen feet high. I look into the darkness and can hear dripping. As my eyes became accustomed to the dark, I see a large pool. We walk in, out of the sunlight. The water is clear, shallow, in a large oval bowl formation. The ceiling vaults up over a very large chamber. I begin to discern a back wall of rock formations that look figurative, suggesting icons, or statues. It's like entering a natural cathedral. Still, except for the echoing plip-plop of water.

"Hello-o, welcome to the sanctum-tum." The echoing spirit-like voice startles me. I search through the gloom trying to see who is in there. I finally see the group of people sitting by the edge of the pool about forty feet away. The speaker's face is wreathed in dark hair and they are all wrapped in blankets. Cavemen, troglodytes, four of them.

"Jeez! didn't see you there. Hi"

"Yeah, we've been keeping quiet, just listening," he says.

"Man, it's a beautiful place, amazing. It makes me want to whisper, I'll keep the yellin' down."

We introduce ourselves and talk back and forth, quietly. The two guys are musicians, play trumpet and percussion, working on the West Coast with the Don Ellis Big Band, jazz guys. They have been recording and gigging but have come out to Zion with their girlfriends for a break, getting away from the city. They tell us what they'd been doing.

"We've been listening to the frogs, there must be hundreds of them in here. They all get going, after one of them starts up. It needs one leader to begin the chorus and then they all take-up the song. First it'll be something like be-reep, be-reep and soon hundreds of them are singing be-reep. Then you'll hear somebody else start something new, a variation on the first song, like be-re-re-reep, be-re-re-reep and soon he'll get some of them to follow his new verse. It changes the rhythm, two competing choirs, but eventually they'll all change over and sing along to the new version."

"Yeah, really? Ya know, we always think that frogs just go croak, croak." These jazz guys had ears and were using them, beginning to adjust to the natural vibe, getting tuned-in to the sounds of the primeval world, erasing the constant background-din of the city that eventually deafens us.

"No, there's more to it than croaking, the frogs get some very complicated riffs going. After they've been doing a second song and they all seem settled into that, someone will introduce a third idea, re-be-re-be-reep, re-be-re-be-reep and that will eventually catch on. Takes awhile but they'll get into it. It's like they want something new, some novelty and development but gradually the crowd will accept it. Look at us, we're really not all that different, it's the same thing as the frogs, what we do with music. It keeps evolving, like from Dixieland jazz to Ornette Coleman or Bill Haley to Hendrix. It keeps going. Nobody wants to go with anything that's too freaky 'til they get used to it."

"Reep-reep-reep, reep-reep-reep." The two girls sing a bit of the frogs' latest song.

"How long have you been up here listenin' to frogs?"

"We've come back up here a few times now. It's cool in here isn't it? Yeah, it's a very special place, here at the frog concert. They don't do a lot of gigs and we've got great seats, right up front."

I sit down and join them, keeping quiet, hoping that the frogs might do another set.

I love Zion Canyon, one of the most beautiful places I've ever been to, it's up there near the top of the list. The rangers bring more firewood for us every couple of days and most of them seem to be happy, relaxed and enjoying their jobs. We have more great campfire cuisine. One evening Barry T makes a stock from beef bones that simmers for hours before the vegetables are added. We get out the guitars to play and sing or listen to the owls and see what they have to say. I do a few more hikes and begin to feel quite at home. It is a beautiful place that is breeding peace and manufacturing quiet. I decide to see if I could get a temporary job around the park, at the moment it feels right for me.

Up at the rangers' headquarters, I ask to see the park manager or someone in charge and am shown into a small office. The head ranger is a middle-aged guy with a graying flat-top. He greets me in a pleasant 'and-how-can-I-help-you-sir' manner, expecting I might be inquiring about a lost flashlight or wondering if the park had laundry facilities. He is interested when I ask about a job and offers me a seat by his desk.

"You know, we often hire-in a bit of casual help around this time of year. There's a lot to do gettin' ready for the summer. That's when we get a load of people on the site." That sounded encouraging.

"Yep, we could use a few boys like you who don't mind a bit a work. Some of the trails need clearing, trees come down durin' the winter, need cutting' up. Spring cleanin'. There's always something that needs doin'. But, I'm afraid I can't offer you anything, our budget's been cut. Federal funds are being reduced, they don't have the money for the Parks Department or recreation and leisure. Yeah, this Vietnam War is beginning to affect us now. They're spending so much over there, it's beginning to have an impact on everything, roads, education, environment and the parks. It's a damn shame, I don't know how long it'll go on, we might have to think about letting some of our staff go. Yeah, sorry son, too bad, but I can't help you."

Zion is so remote, with hardly any legible imprint of 1968, yet it seems Vietnam is making an impact here as well. We can't get away from this fucking war. We carry it around inside our heads. You wake up to a new day but, like a headache from the night before that painfully reminds you of what went on, Vietnam slowly creeps back into focus. Oh Christ! It's still here hounding, chasing us, even in the wilderness. You'd have to go deep into the woods or out in the mountains and cut yourself off, guard your thoughts and then, maybe it would go away. The frogs, rattlesnakes and bears are just carrying on like they've always done, peeping, slithering and eating berries, oblivious to being at war with a distant enemy. They don't watch the TV news. Their heads aren't full of all the bullshit that is being pumped into us about freedom and democracy.

We stay for about a week at Zion Canyon and are now ten days into a different life. Los Angeles is over five hundred miles behind. I'm readjusting to something else, free from schedules, telephones or rent. On the run, on a roll, on the road.

Heading south, past Knab, Utah, I follow along the thin, paved stripe. The land declines in a series of giant steps, a flight of plains and bluffs dropping down towards Arizona. As I look down the colossal stairs it seems as if all of southern Utah is spread-out before me and I could coast for miles and miles. Back in Zion the frog chorus was probably going full-blast in the cave pond, they'd be singing and peeping. Most of the frogs would be wondering whether to accept a new song. They would, as long as they kept hearing it over and over again, but the one or two frogs that come up with a new tune must be getting burned-out trying to sell it to the rest of them.

Chapter 4
ARIZONA HIGHS
AND LOWS
MAY 1968

ZION NAT'L PARK

LAKE POWELL

UTAH

O KANAB

ARIZONA

JACOB LAKE

MARBLE CANYON

RT 89

NAVAJO RESERVATION

GRAND CANYON NAT'N'L MON.

PAINTED DESERT

Colorado River

O TUBA CITY

N

GRAND CANYON

RT. 64

O CAMERON

W E

S

0 10 20 50

Suburbia on wheels.
780 Miles from L.A.

South from Kanab Utah, through arid plains heading toward the state boarder in the north of Arizona, I'm on the way to the Grand Canyon.

We thought that it might be a busy place. The Grand Canyon is probably up there with the Statue of Liberty and the Empire State Building as one of America's most well known landmarks. There might be a better chance of finding some work and earning some bread. Maybe they need some guys to clear fallen rocks off the trails that lead to the canyon floor. A few bucks would help us out.

As I get closer to Arizona, on the high plateau in southern Utah, vultures wheel above columns of cloud, so high that the big birds appear like insects. How can they see anything, a half-mile, a mile, up there? They are looking over the curvature of the earth, seeing what is over the hill or 'round the bend. They have more knowledge of my immediate future than I do. I only glimpse the occasional road sign informing me that a town is eighteen miles away, they have an over-all picture. The soaring birds can see that town, the dust or rain blowing up ahead. They seem miles aloft. Two, four, six, eight miles high. A Byrds' song.

I met David Crosby a couple of times soon after arriving in L.A. He was a friend of a friend and shared the same personal manager as several people I knew. At an informal get together at manager Larry Spector's place, David had invited a couple of us over to his house.

"After this, whenever that is," he said, "why don't you come over to my place, I've got something very special I want to play for you, an' you're going to flip-out."

"Oh yeah? Sure, that would be great. What have you got?"

"Ah, we'll leave that 'til we get there," Crosby replied, adding to the mystery with an intriguing smile of complicity.

"Ha, Okay. I guess we'll have to wait an' see. You finished with Larry?"

"Yeah all done. It's never really done though, is it? Managers, phew." He rolled his eyes. "You know where I live? You could just follow me over, it's not that far."

His house was L.A./Spanish in style. We went in and through a living room, sombre after the bright afternoon sun. A large rustic Mexican mirror monitored our passing. A studio room adjoining was a like a white box with a trestle table that carried a tape recorder and stereo system with black, expensive, speakers.

David opened a small incense box, removed some Zig-Zags and began to roll a joint.

"Let's try some of this shit."

A lighter flared. I took the grass and had a deep toke, locking-down, holding it in and passed the joint to Crosby, who regarded it, licked a finger and dabbed the paper to keep an even burn. He took a big drag, squinting, closed one eye, then topped-up with another little hit. He turned, picked up a flat box on the table and removed a reel-to-reel tape, held it out, waggling it slightly, and in a squeaky rasp, releasing a minimum of breath, squeezed out, "This is something McCartney just sent me. You just wait." There was a cloud of smoke as he expelled a lung-full, his lips slightly flapping. Taking a few short restorative gasps, he threaded the tape, pushed Play, and the leader coursed through to the empty spool. "Hardly anyone has heard this yet." The pot was strong. Crosby stepped back, through a shaft of sunlight, his shirt glowed, gold-leafed.

A hiss, then piano. The singer had heard the news today, oh boy. The distant vocal, echoing from a cavern, sang about blowing his mind. Drum fills, playing on the outside of the beat. The voice wanted to turn us on. A growing din of instruments swelled, ascending to a roar. The lyrics were about combing hair and the music jumped into a different groove, double-time of the first verses. The Beatles sang about going into a dream. Another change, followed by a reverberating celestial choir, joined by a howling orchestra, hitting accents to bring the song back to the original tempo. Then, more lyrics about turning on. The track built, louder with all sorts of instruments; trombones, strings, guitars and horns blaring and playing out of tune. Voices joined in, tribal chanting, a tidal wave of cacophony mounted and grew into a crest that thundered down, hitting an accent and then… a wash of slowly receding sustain. Debris of sound floated listlessly in and out of the fade.

We were stunned by this powerful, orchestral, operatic recording, it was a slightly frightening experience. There were so many instruments, chanting and references to smoking pot. A monumental, textured work, it seemed about ten minutes long. It didn't sound anything like the Beatles of a few years ago, with their catchy but slightly corny songs and tinny guitar sounds. This was a whole other form of music.

"Man! The Beatles! Crosby said with some reverence. What do you think of that?"

"Is that going to be a record?" I was still slightly agog.

"McCartney said they want to put it out as a single."

"Jesus! Really. Do you think anyone will play it? It seems so long for radio plays. No one has done anything like that before."

"They're incredible! They just keep coming up with weirder shit, all the time."

"How could they ever play, stuff like that, live?"

"I guess they could if they wanted to but I don't think that will happen. They didn't tour this year, I think they just want to spend their time in the studio coming up with more weird music." David turned the knob to rewind, "You want to hear that again?"

The second time we listened to 'A Day In The Life', I was prepared for the textures, layers and the assaults, but the music was still astounding. The Beatles were an exception, they were huge, but if this was where rock groups might be going, by comparison, the Submarine Band was headed, one-eighty, in the opposite direction, wandering-off into country, distancing ourselves from psychedelic music, mammoth productions and the music biz. By becoming acolytes of hillbilly singers, down-home sentiments and broken hearts we were going to end up lost in a desert of rhinestones and grits. I was beginning to wonder how long we could keep beating this path to nowhere. It could take too much out of your system, going the wrong way, like those early explorers trying to get to the North Pole. First they'd shoot a seal, then they'd have to eat the dogs, next they started eyeing each other up, but they all froze to death in the end. How could we stay warm, singing 'Together Again', in Los Angeles?

On Route 67 in Arizona, I drive through a small place, Jacob Lake. I wonder if there is a Jacob's Ladder? Jacob fell asleep in his coat of many colors and dreamed about a huge stairway with angels moving up and down. I don't know why they didn't fly or use the elevator, well, it was his dream, not mine. I remember a picture from when I was a kid, in an illustrated Bible or a coloring book at church. He is lying there in his stripy coat and the angels are bustling up and down the stairs like rush hour at Grand Central Station. Jacob eventually made a good living out of having all those dreams. He got himself on the Pharaoh's payroll by predicting years of bumper crops and famine in Egypt. He could see when the crash might be coming, Jacob was a useful guy to have around.

I'm having more dreams now, probably because I'm not so zonked-out all the time, like I have been during the last couple of years. I would like to get more messages from the other side and see if I'm going to cross that river to the promised land or have seven years of famine.

I remember when we used to screw around with the Ouija board trying to get messages from the other side.

'Lips, put a smile, on my face,
and eyes, don't let her see you,
shed a tear.'
Buck Owens and Don Rich sang, running through a medley of ballads, on their Live at Carnegie Hall LP. Gram, Mickey and I were at Brandon's house in Topanga Canyon.

The Buck Owens album was one of our favorite records because it had been recorded in New York and suggested that country music was beginning to break through into the mainstream, instead of remaining a strange flaw of the Deep South.

"Wow! Listen to Don, how he can always stay right on top of the harmonies, even when Buck is bending the vocal all over the place," Gram admired.

"Man. They're so soulful. They've just about got it off, like perfection," I agreed.

"Maybe, if you guys got some of those flashy suits, you'd just slip right on into that sound," Brandon suggested. "Maybe the suits are a bigger part of it than you think. Why don't you rent some, see if it changes everything."

"So, is that your professional opinion, as a man of stage and screen?"

"Ha. Sure. That's it." Brandon raised his finger like an old professor about to make a rhetorical point. "Yes. An-nd, I know what to turn to if you need more advice." Brandon got up from the table.

"What is it, the horoscope?"

Brandon returned to the kitchen carrying a flat box, like a pizza delivery guy and put it down in the middle of the table.

"The Ouija board. If you want the ultimate answer, it could be here. We'll ask the spirits." Brandon unfolded the board. The ornate letters of the alphabet were fanned out around the board, in the lower corners were, 'yes' and 'no'. "Let's get this set up. You have to move down to this end of the table, we all have to be able to reach the board." He picked up the pointer and flicked it, like a nurse shaking down a thermometer. "We don't want any leftovers, from stale, old spirits, in there. O-okay, put the pointer in the middle, everybody touch it, just one finger of both hands. Can we all fit? Yeah. There." He got up. "Wait a minute, let me shut off the bright light. We don't want to scare 'em off. They probably don't have electricity in spirit land."

"Isn't Thomas Edison dead?" Mickey suggested that they might be all connected now, up there.

"Okay, ready?" Brandon glanced around the table.

"Yeah, okay pilot."

"Are there any spirits here?" Brandon addressed the room, in an exaggerated stage voice. "Does the spirit world wish to communicate?" There was no noticeable response from the Other Side.

"Are all of you spirits having the day off, or something?" Gram queried.

"Don't piss them off already, before we've even started."

"Hey, it just moved, I felt something."

"Is there a spirit, coming in, for a landing?" Brandon asked the board.

"The flight deck is clear, spirits." The pointer moved making the track of a lazy 'S'.

"Are you pushing it?"

"No. It wasn't me." The pointer moved again, with more conviction, and headed straight to 'No'.

"Hah. No. The spirits don't want to commit themselves. Maybe we've got a joker here."

"An ironic spirit?" Gram thought.

"Why don't you want to talk to us?" The room was silent, the board was still.

"I guess 'No' was their final answer."

"No, look, it's moving again." The pointer crept over the board and stopped on the letter L, then began to move to the right, halting over I. Quickly it moved across to the letter T and ceased.

"L, I, T. Lit?"

"Little?"

"No. Maybe it's 'lit', like lights. There's still too much light in the room," Mickey figured.

"We've got a fussy one huh? Okay, lets see, I'm going to turn the wall light off and light this candle. We want to make that spirit comfy." Brandon touched his lighter to the wick.

"Should we ask it if it wants a drink?" The pointer moved again, down to 'No'. "Okay, the bar is closed."

"Now. What should we ask it? Come on." Brandon encouraged.

"Are you a friendly spirit?" There was a slight movement but it faltered. We watched the board for a moment.

"Who do you think it is, Casper the fuckin' ghost?"

"It could be a little kid or something."

"Why would a kid necessarily be friendly? Like, he was out riding his tricycle one day, just pedalling along and, bam!, gets hit by a car or he died of tuberculosis or some other horrible disease. I mean, he'd be sort of pissed-off at the living wouldn't he?" The pointer moved upward, circled and came to a rest on 'No'.

"Hey well, that's encouraging. They're not pissed-off. It's all 'no regrets', upstairs in spirit land. Jack Kennedy could be saying, 'Hey, Lee Harvey Oswald was just doin' his thing. I really enjoyed Dallas, ha, ha, I'll get back down there again, sometime, when I can schedule it."

"Okay, wait a minute. How about this; Does the spirit have a name?" There was no movement.

"Yeah, see, they're sort of cagey. They don't want to give too much away." The pointer began to slide upward, toward the middle of the alphabet, to M, to the left, going all the way over to A, moved away, then did a u-turn to D and inched over to the E.

"M, A, D, E. Made? That's not a name. How about, Maddie?"

"What about 'Ma'? Ma Dee."

"That's it. Hey Brandon. It's your Grandmother! Ma DeWilde."

"Hi-ya Granny."

"There you go Brandon, you've got a connection."

"Okay. U-m, lets see, ah. What should I ask?" The pointer started to move. "Hold on, I didn't ask you anything yet." Brandon said to Ma Dee.

"Are you pushing it? I can feel it."

"No, I'm not," I said.

"Neither am I." It continued to move, to the letter U, then G, a short hop to E and across to T, more rapidly over to C, then O and L.

"U, G, E, T, C, O, L? You, get, col?"

"Hm-m. Let's see. What about, ah, you, get, m-m. What's 'col'?"

"Call! Maybe? You get call." Brandon interpreted.

"So the phone is going to ring?"

"Hah, the spirits are getting too lazy to bother with the Ouija board now."

"Well, it is slow, and, you have to be able to spell."

"O-okay. We're waiting. It's not ringing."

"Let's ask it; Who, is the call, for?" The pointer moved and snaked over to the letter G.

"Gram! They like you tonight."

"Um-m. I bet it will be a collect call, too," Gram said and smiled.

"Gram. You ask it who's calling."

"Okay spirit; Who is that, callin' up, at this time of night, when decent Christian folks are supposed to be in bed?" There was no movement, the pointer sat still.

"You keep insulting them. Wait, here it goes. It's moving again." This time we got, D, A, an L and back to the A. "Dala? That mean anything?"

"Dollar?" Mickey suggested.

"Dala?" Gram bit his lip. "Hm-m, Dala. Dah la? No. I don't know. Maybe the message is for someone else."

Brandon asked the Ouija board, "Okay, Dala, do you have a message for Gram. Make it fast, he's beginning to yawn." The pointer moved, jerkily, to 'Yes'. "Oh man, keep it short, okay." The pointer moved and rested over D, then on to A.

"Looks like it's still stuck on Dala. Ah, excuse me spirit, but we got that already," Mickey reminded the ethereal messenger.

"Oh boy, oh boy. You're not going to believe this," Gram whispered, looking shocked. "Wait, I'll tell you in a minute, when we've got this word." The pointer travelled on, to N, J, a bit more to the right, for O then stopped over R.

"Hm-m. D, A, N, J, O, R. What's that supposed to be?"

"I don't know."

"Okay," Brandon asked Gram, "what were you going to tell us, Lulu?"

"Well. It might have been back in Georgia, when I was a kid. An' we had this colored maid, called something like Dayla. Maybe her name was Dahlia, like a flower, I don't know. Bu-ut, she was a maid. Right? The board spelled, 'made'. I was a little kid and if I was going out, to play or something, she'd take a jacket off a hook in the kitchen and say, 'You better wear this, you get cold.' You know, them black folks, always feelin' cold. And, that's what the board spelled, 'you get col'. That's what she always said."

"Aw come on. You must have been pushing the pointer around."

"No, I wasn't. Really. I was just holdin' on."

Brandon said, "We were all pushing it around, that's what happens. It's like, some sort of a collective consciousness thing, that takes over."

"And maybe, Dayla was pushing it as well."

"So what's the Dan Jor bit?" I asked.

Gram shook his head. "I don't know. Dan Jor? Don't know the guy."

Winding through dry hills in North Arizona I fiddle with the radio.

The station fades in and out, it was coming from a long way off.

The DJ had just played 'Jim Dandy' by Laverne Baker and it was eroding into static, I didn't bother to turn the dial, the hiss and whistling was okay. Another oldie slowly materialized out the noise, 'Tears on My Pillow'. I remember catching their act in LA. It was over a year ago, I guess.

'Tears on my pillow'

'Pain in my heart'

'Over you-oo-oo, oow-oo-oo-oow.'

Brandon, Mickey and I sat at a table sippin' on our second brandy-and-soda. Little Anthony and The Imperials were on stage, four singers with a small back-up band. They wore cabaret outfits; bow ties the size of flapping crows, ruffled shirts and yellow suits, the lapels, cuffs and outside-leg edged with black piping. The wardrobe might have been zingy in Reno but on Sunset strip, that get-up made them look a bit too much like clowns.

We had gone out earlier that night to catch some music and have a drink. After sticking our heads inside the Troubadour, where a young band was grinding-out Rolling Stones' songs, we went back outside and ambled down Sunset Strip. Groups of people bubbled along the sidewalk. Reflections and flashes glinted pink, blue or yellow off the hair of the beyond-blondes, as they walked beneath bright signs and club lights. A convertible with several college guys on board, ogling the chicks, was blasting out Tommy James and The Shondells': 'I think we're alone now'. On the corner, a young hippie guy was holding newspapers. He approached us, his nose and glasses sticking out of a mop of hair, holding out a paper; LA Free Press. The Marquee of the Whisky a Go Go had, 'Little Anthony and The Imperials' billed. A classic act. We went in.

Little Anthony sang a couple of songs from the doo-wop era, 'Whisperin' Bells', 'In The Still Of The Night' and his hit, 'Tears On My Pillow'.

"You know, Nancy used to work here," Brandon said. "She was a dancer, a go go girl."

"Was she?"

"Yep. She used to be up on one of those platforms, waving her arms in the air and shakin' that beautiful ass of hers."

"Hm-m. I bet she looked good. No dancing girls tonight."

"Yeah, too bad Nancy's not here. I think that this was where David Crosby spotted her. 'Course then Gram spotted her, or she spotted him."

Little Anthony sort of lost it when they sang 'Yesterday', with an awful lot of oow's. They should have stuck with the old stuff, doo-wop was their thing.

Half way through their buttery version of 'I Left My Heart In San Francisco', Brandon muttered, "Oh Jesus," and began singing, "Ol' man riber-r-r." He wasn't yelling, but it was loud enough to attract the attention of a guy, sitting at the next table, who looked over. I was thinking, 'Brandon, cool it!' I recognized the guy, it was Arthur Lee, from Love. We had done a gig with them awhile ago. But Arthur was also shaking his head and blipped his eyes upward, like he was disappointed by the way Anthony had adopted the old black man song-and-dance thing. At least they hadn't started doing a tap-dance routine but they were acting-out a role that reinforced the old stereotype, one that rubbed Arthur the wrong way.

We have to drive a big loop to get to the south rim of the Grand Canyon on Route

89, through hills and forest then down into dry flatlands of rock and dust. There is no bridge over the canyon, you have to go around it. The road edges in and out of a Navajo reservation on the way to a place called Tuba City. About fifty yards off, I see a couple of guys walking in the scrub and sagebrush carrying a rifle. They could be out looking for jackrabbits, hunting for something to eat. They are wearing jeans, tattered short sleeved shirts and sweat stained, dusty cowboy hats. They have black, shaggy hair and dark chiselled features. They definitely live here and must be Navajos. They don't seem to be wearing any bright patterned clothes, fringed buckskin jackets, or beaded headbands. The 'Indian look' is something for concerts and love-ins, it hasn't caught-on yet down on the reservation.

I had been invited to Griffith Park a couple of times before I finally went over to check it out. Almost every Sunday there was an outdoor party in the hills and they were calling it a love-in. I had heard that the love-ins were a San Francisco thing that had spread to LA and by the spring of '67 a couple of thousand might show up to picnic, hang out or play music. Probably the reason was to meet people who also wanted to smoke pot and take LSD. It could have been called a smoke-in.

Griffith Park, east of LA, encompassed rolling hills and small areas of woods, interspersed between open, sloping fields. The hippies scattered themselves over the landscape. Some were in large groups, settled on enormous patchworks of blankets. One bunch seemed like a beginner's guitar class. About a dozen of them strummed acoustics, accompanied by several others tapping tambourines and bongos, their lolling heads swaying. The whole group sat shoulder-to-shoulder performing the same slow weaving movement. Other people were perched in trees, legs dangling, straddling the limbs. A mustard-colored kite, the shape of a star, hovered against the blue sky and trailed yellow ribbons.

A lot of the love-in crowd were dressed for a party, with ribbons, beads and feathers woven in their hair. Sombreros, a couple of black top hats, a turban, with peacock feather antennae, sprouted from a bunch of heads. A tall woman moved along with a twirling walk, arms raised, head tilted back. With each spin her light skirt flared like a saucer, revealing fine pink scarves that wrapped her calves. A lot of the people here seemed young, like teenagers. There was a complete absence of grandmas and pops and average American families. Other than the Flower-Power fashion, it could have been any warm Sunday in a city park, if the entry was restricted to 'young, beautiful people only'. I had noticed several police cars in the parking lot but there didn't seem to be any cops around. Of course there was always talk of plainclothes cops ready to make a bust. Plenty of talk.

I was walking through a gap that led into a field and noticed a group sitting or sprawling on a bank. As I looked up at them, I recognized David Crosby reclining on the grassy knoll. He was wearing a loose, green velvet shirt and a big strand of beads the size of marbles. He resembled Henry VIII, early on in his reign, back at wife number one or two. He raised a hand and smiled through his droopy moustache and the hair that framed his round face. I smiled back as he raised his hand to take a drag on a huge joint. He extended his arm toward me, raising his eyebrows and saying in a clenched-breath, 'Mellow Yellow', not hash, not pot, he wasn't taking any chances. I took the joint, shrugged my shoulders and took a drag. It smelled like damp, smouldering leaves and tasted like rubber bands.

I had heard about the Mellow Yellow craze, there were several myths and rumors floating around. Some claimed it was a mild hallucinogenic, yet some people I knew, who had prepared a batch, said it didn't do jack-shit for them. They had bought forty-five pounds of bananas, ate a couple of them, put some in the freezer and heaved the rest. The scrapings from the inside of the peels were placed on racks in the oven at a low temperature, overnight and the dried remains were grated. They wondered if they had got the instructions mixed up, since after smoking pipe after pipe-full, they only succeeded in barbecuing their throats. Maybe it was the peels that were supposed to be discarded.

Several supermarkets had instituted a policy of, 'bananas for domestic consumption only', either turning away the kid pushing two banana laden trolleys to the till or limiting customers to one dozen bananas, per family, only. Desperate Mellow Yellow shoppers would have to make several stops. Another story was, the FBI were doing exhaustive lab research to determine if bananas should be categorized as a dangerous drug and the big fruit companies were panicking and preparing to bribe senators. The word was going around that Del Monte had already paid Donovan fifty-thousand dollars to put the song out. I smiled and passed the joint back. Mellow Yellow served the purpose of allowing pot-heads to play that they were smoking dope openly.

A couple of stalls attracted some hippie shoppers. A big red-headed woman was selling incense. Alongside, tie-dye T-shirts were hung on a washing line strung between two trees. A breeze stirred the shirts, a couple of them flapped and elicited a small chorus of 'Oh wow'. I turned to see several people sitting on the ground awaiting the next puff of wind to ruffle the T-shirts.

"Hey-y, you want to drop?" a guy with Harpo Marx hair had sidled up next to me. "This stuff is like nothin' else, man."

"What?"

"Acid, man. You want to drop some? 'Cinderella'. It'll take you beyond the other side."
I had never heard of that one before. There were so many names now. The latest model
could also be a con, a sugar cube with a splash of iodine, aspirin painted pink. I shook
my head.

"No, not today. Okay."

"Okay, you're missing a great ride." He flashed the peace sign and walked off.

Another band had set up and began to play. The small stage was about a hundred
yards away and most of their sound evaporated into the open-air park but the music
had an impact closer to the stage, where people began moving. Some of the lyrics and
drums wafted across the field.

'Take me there-ere-ere-rare-rare-rare-rare'.

An attractive girl, near to me, began swaying. She had long dark hair and was wearing
what looked like a Spanish dress; she should have had a fan fluttering below her dark
eyes. She noticed me checking her out and returned an enchanting smile.

"Hi. Do you like this band?" I asked.

"Well, we're a bit far away to really hear them. How are you, on this beautiful day?"

"Oh, good. I'm enjoying being here and looking at everything that's goin' on. And,
the people; it's like a four-ring circus."

"Do you like music, like this?"

"Well, I guess it's not my favorite type."

"Oh? Are you a musician?"

"Yeah. I'm in a band."

"Really. Are you going to play today?"

"No, no." I laughed and shook my head. It sort of cracked me up.

"What band are you in? Do you play?" she asked.

"Yeah, I do. It's called The International Submarine Band and we've played a bunch of
the big clubs around L.A."

"I like the name. What sort of music do you play?"

"Ah, country, sort of, country music."

She was a little puzzled. "You mean like old, traditional music."

"No, not stuff like that. I mean country, like country and western."

"Really? God, you don't look like a country and western singer. That squawky stuff.
They all have greasy slicked-up hair and wear suits that look like bullfighters. Yodel-ay-
dee-oh."

"Yeah. That's just about what everyone thinks, it doesn't have to be like that though.
Hey I like those suits, I think they're cool."

"I can see why you're not playing here, huh?"

"Hey, come on, don't let that scare you away."

The Grand Canyon campground is vast. Zion was like a private club by comparison. Grand Canyon is the grand daddy of the national parks. There are campers, trailers and vans from all over the US, the dozens of different licence plates verify that. The big campers are the size of busses, with boats, motorcycles, TV antennas, awnings and flower boxes. Their rears are plastered with stickers and decals that boast of all the places they have been. Along side of them, our vehicles stand out and draw attention as if we are an exhibition about how it used to be done before sun-loungers, generators and on-board showers. It's a weird neighborhood, like suburbia on wheels.

Barry T is unrolling his olive drab army surplus tent and wondering if he can hammer the tent pegs into the stony ground. The tent is old and might have been from World War II. I remember a very different new tent that I had helped Gram to put up, a couple of months ago.

"Hey man. I'm in trouble. Can you help me out?" Gram was on the phone. "I'm up at Lake Isabella and the van's broken down, I can't get it in-gear."

"Oh yeah? I think I know what that is. It's a linkage thing, it's happened to me before. I know how to fix it. Where did you say you were?"

"Well, it's up, sort of, near Bakersfield, in the hills. I was going camping. Why don't you come up, it's only a couple hours from Topanga."

"Okay, I'm pretty sure I can fix that van. Yeah and I'd like to see you."

I drove up in the VW bus, the first trip I'd done since getting the engine rebuilt. It was a beautiful spring day. I hadn't seen Gram for awhile, he'd been recording and touring with the Byrds during that spring of '68.

I found the road to Lake Isabella State Park and came upon the stranded Dodge van. Gram and Nancy were sitting inside with baby Polly who was now a few months old.

"Hell-lo-o-o Ian, glad to see you. Hel-l-lp!" Gram greeted. I wriggled under the van and looked up at the transmission.

"Yeah, here it is. It's just fallen off. Lemme show you, in case it happens again. See this thing on the end of the cable? Ya just click it back on this arm thing, here, stickin' out. There, that's it."

"Gee! That all it was. Thanks. We were getting worried about getting' stuck out here with Polly."

"You're the knight in shining armour Ian." Nancy kissed me.

"No sweetheart, more like a desperate bass-player in ripped jeans. A-a-a-t your service. Hey, in a way, you've rescued me. Got me out of LA. Even though being out in Topanga isn't really like LA, it's good to get out in the sticks."

"Great, now we can stay." Gram was relieved when we drove into the camping area. "Lets have a beer first then I'm going to set-up that tent."

I looked into the back of their van and saw cardboard boxes filled with food, plates and paper napkins. A pile of bedding, pillows and blankets were dumped in the back. It looked like a rapid evacuation, with the sort of stuff people grab before fleeing from a hurricane. Gram began erecting a new igloo tent so there would be someplace where Polly could be comfortable.

"Oh shit!" I looked around at Gram. He was on his knees, hunched over and holding his hands together as if in prayer. "I just stabbed my hand!" He had been forcing two of the bendy metal support rods together and one had slipped puncturing his palm. "Man, this tent is out to get me. What have I ever done to you, tent?" We got Gram bandaged up and together erected the vicious tent. When it was finally standing we climbed inside like cub scouts to enjoy the novelty. Gram suggested we christen it and started rolling a joint of grass and hash.

"Yeah, us Byrds got great drugs," he winked.

We had a smoke and began catching-up, talking about what had gone down since we last met. He had been active, recording and touring.

"We cut some things in Nashville awhile ago with Lloyd Green on steel."

"Yeah really." Green played pedal steel and was a renowned session musician.

"Man, Lloyd played some beautiful stuff, he really dug it."

"Was that for Columbia?"

"Yeah. For an album, maybe comin' out this summer. We're goin' in the studio again next week."

"Christ, Columbia! I hope it was better than when we were there the last time."

"Ha! Yeah. Columbia didn't give us much of a chance in New York, did they? It's a lot different than back then. It's The Byrds, not The International Submarine Band, so they're gonna listen. You tell 'em what you're gonna do and do it." Gram had dreamed about that for a long time, he wanted to record in Nashville and be taken seriously. "Yeah, and we played the Opry."

"Wow! That's amazing."

"We gave 'em a set of solid country music but they didn't like it at first. I was singin' a Merle Haggard song and they were booing me!"

"No shit?"

"Yeah, an' then a few days later, we're doing a gig somewhere else an' The Byrds fans are yellin' 'Play Mr Tambourine Man!' and booing the country stuff! Hey, you can't win."

"Man, there are still such clear-cut dividing lines in music."

"Yeah, people can be so closed an' narrow minded, hung up on what they think their identity is. Like they're afraid of strayin' off that straight an' narrow path."

"What could happen then? Oh my God, you might catch a disease if you listen to Tammy Wynette!" I said.

"Watch out, it could be contagious, it might pollute your rock-music head!"

"Yeah, conformity comes in all sorts of disguises."

Gram picked up the flow. "And it's available at a convenient outlet in your neighborhood folks, so what are you waiting for? Hurry on down while stocks last, don't be disappointed."

"The disappointment you save might be your own. Just take our conformity home, share it with family and loved ones. We'll give you a thirty-day trial, absolutely free," we ping-ponged.

"And if you're not happy with our complete conformity package, just bring it back and our friendly representatives will give you a total refund."

"How can you lose? Try conformity today at no cost what-so-ever to you."

"Ha, ha, ha."

"Man, it's good to see ya."

There was a cry from the tent and Nancy brought Polly out. We took turns jiggling her around, trying to soothe her. She began to cool-out after we sang a couple of songs to her. We gave up on the Supremes' 'Where Did Our Love Go' as we ran out of lyrics and moved on to the unseasonable carol 'Silent night, holy night, all is calm all is bright,' but started mangling the lyrics. 'Holy infant so tender and wild...screech in tent-erly peace.'

"So what's goin' on with the Johns and the ISB? I haven't seen them for awhile," I asked

"Oh man, I don't know. The record company is on my ass. Lee Hazlewood is makin' noises that I'm still signed to them. I'm lettin' the lawyers wrangle it out. It seems like a long time ago. I don't know if they finished mixing it." This was the second deal that Gram had decided to rip up in just over a year.

"Steve spoke to me over a month ago, said they might need a bass player if they went out on the road. He said somethin' about a tour with The Turtles," I said.

"They ought to do it. I don't know if they'll get it together. Ya know, the ISB thing started off okay but it ended-up being a hassle, I couldn't deal with 'em anymore."

"Hey, I know what you mean. Get this! Steve also said something about a tour in Vietnam! Jesus! Can you believe that? I can't see how they'd get any bands to go over there."

"Well, they've got Bob Hope and Nancy Sinatra, let them take care of the troops."

"Yeah. I said, What? Are you kiddin'! I burned my draft card, I'd be scared shitless! Seemed nuts."

"Everythin's like peanut butter; a mixture of nuts and oil, to keep it slidin' along. You add a bit of this, divide by a bit of that an' then multiply by sixteen an' that's your answer." Gram theorized.

"I'm enjoying a break from bands, that's my answer to the equation."

"You guys aren't giggin', what are you gonna do?"

"No, we haven't done any for a few weeks now. We've been getting' the vans ready to go on a trip, drivin' around the West. We'll probably go right across to the East Coast, Barry and Briggs want to check-out things back there. Maybe we'll get something going."

"Where? New York?"

"I don't know, I'll just be happy to get out of LA. I've had enough of it for awhile. The weather's great, it makes it easier when you're up-to-your-neck in bullshit but I'm sick of wallowing around in this deluxe swimming pool full of marshmallow-fluff and bubble gum."

"Yeah deluxe. I've been out of here, touring. Ya know, just travel, play music and get stoned. Don't know how long it will last with The Byrds. Have to see how it goes, I don't want to get stuck playin' Byrds hits all the time. The country stuff is sounding great. You'll have to hear it sometime. I'll play you something."

"Sure, if I'm around by then. I want to see somethin' else, I don't know what I'm lookin' for but I know I've had it with LA. The great pyramid of sleaze and all them sinners dancin' around the base, waitin' their turn to climb the steps and be sacrificed to the city of sin."

"Ha. We better pray for us all. Lord protect us, send down your silver angels an' shield us from ol' Satan before he takes over the whole place."

"Yeah, send down those radiant chariots, loaded-up with miracles and anything else you've got for earthquakes and smog," I agreed.

After some more tales, gossip and instant philosophy, I settled down in the bus for the night. I thought about Gram sleeping in the tent with his new family. Everything seemed to be working-out for him, so many aspects of his life were going well. It looked as if he was enjoying a sense of security. Polly was offering him a chance to have a family of his own. He had revealed to me, during the times we had spent together over drinks, joints and long drives, that his childhood and family life were a wild mixture of painful trauma and wealthy security. His mother had died a couple of years ago and it seemed that he had a difficult relationship with his stepfather. A woman like Nancy and little baby Polly might supersede or erase all the unhappiness of his past.

He had finally really made-it in the music business and was working with one of the biggest bands in the world. The Byrds were huge and were probably going to use some of his songs on their next album. It would be a hundred times easier to push the country music, surfing on the strength of an established band than struggling against the tide in an undiscovered, obscure group. We had tried that and it had been, mostly, discouraging and even destructive. Gram wanted to be accepted. I guess he really needed it more desperately than I had realized when we were playing together. He seemed to express a carefree, easygoing attitude to everything. He addressed things, with his laid back, casual manner but maybe that was a front. I could remember a couple of times when I saw his panic.

Nothing had happened with the tapes we had done for RCA and in early '66 Gram's manager had lined-up a demo session for another major label record company, Epic or Decca. It was only a couple of years ago but we did so many sessions in New York that they've begun to blur. The studio was in mid-town Manhattan and we only had to bring instruments, the drums and the music in our heads. The studio was small and business like. Fold-up metal chairs were stacked in the corner, a piano, music stands, amps and mic stands were positioned in orderly intervals around the room. We had been told we could use the studio amps, there were two Ampegs and a Fender Reverb. We set up and plugged in but couldn't turn them on. We couldn't find the usual off/on switch. All the amps had locks. They needed a key, like a car door. When we asked the engineer if he had the amp keys in the control room he looked perplexed then told us we were supposed to have our own keys. They were New York Musicians Union amps and all members had keys. We hadn't joined the union yet, so no union cards and no keys. He suggested that we look in the adjacent studio to see if there were other amps. Maybe he thought that there might be some illegal, strike-breaker amps hiding in a closet. It seemed unlikely but we were new to the scene.

When I returned from a fruitless amp hunt Gram was sitting, facing the wall and strumming his guitar. It made a flat, un-electrified sound. As I got closer I could see he was shaking and looking down. When he raised his head I saw his tears, he was crying. The amp-key thing was too much for him, he felt defeated and frustrated. He was dejected, he lost it. The session, the songs and getting a deal were steps that he needed to take, climbing to somewhere. He had begun writing a new chapter that needed to keep moving, now, immediately. He couldn't wait around for locked-up amplifiers or any other trivial obstacles.

Angel Bright Trail weaves and twists along the ledges on the sheer canyon walls and eventually, after almost ten miles, descends to the floor and the river. The trail passes beneath arches, around boulders and columns as it undulates down along the cliff profile. A bend in the trail, around a rock formation, opens up yet another knock-out vista. I have moved into the sun and sit down on a ledge at the side of the trail. It is quiet, silent, less than sound. The canyon is so huge that it sucks sound away, vacuums it out of the air. I see a couple big dark birds flying below me but there is no Caw-caw-ing. The soundtrack is missing. I've never been near to anything that has such an immense identity. Joshua Tree would fit inside the Grand Canyon's wallet. I'm only a spec of dust, or smaller. This is Forever's signature. Eternity's phone number.

On the opposite side of the canyon is a landscape that could be from a huge planet like Jupiter. It's beyond comprehension. The canyon runs for a couple of hundred miles across Arizona toward Nevada. Other massive valleys split off from the canyon. Rock formations at the intersections are monumental. Across from me is a formation that looks like the Sphinx in triplicate. The canyon walls that catch the sun are glowing. Layers of rock and minerals have been eroded to form distinct horizontal bands of color. Yellow, pink, red and orange stripes follow the profile of the cliffs.

Receding and projecting, they keep the striped pattern as if they were painted or woven. The more I stare, the more vibrant they become. The stripes are loud, they are the soundtrack. They remind me of a bright, striped sweater I bought at a Sunset Strip boutique.

"If you like the look of it, go ahead and try it on. You have to see how it fits. They're very strong colors but you could wear it well." The French salesman held my shirt as I pulled the sweater on. I was with Larry Spector at a boutique on Sunset Boulevard, picking out some snappy looking clothes. He suggested bright and bold. He wanted The Submarine Band to look sharp and stand out in the scenes we would be doing in Peter Fonda's movie. "Ah, yes, yes. You see for yourself." He gently steered me toward a floor length mirror edged with lights. "There. You look good." The bands of blue, gold and white beamed back at me and I smiled. "Very good, don't you think? Now, I think we had better look for some slacks, those blue jeans you have on look like something somebody would be wearing on a construction site. Let's see what's over here." The salesman was standing at the end of a rack, he swept his arm with a gesture of invitation to choose.

Gram had pulled the sleeve of a red silk shirt from a rack and was contemplating it.

"I don't know about this color, maybe a bit too fire-truck?"

"We have zat one in burgundy." The salesman pulled a folded shirt off the shelf and held it up for appraisal. I began looking through a rack, pushing hangers across, like thumbing through a book. I paused at a pair of pants with broad steel-blue-and-cream stripes.

"No, no, too many stripes, just too much, with that top that you have picked. No." I pulled a few more across and stopped at a pair the color of mustard-bronze, with a faint white grid. "Nice color, it goes well with the top. Yes, good choice, I like it," Larry confirmed. We settled on our choices.

Larry invited me to lunch and we walked down Sunset to a restaurant and took a small table on the patio. Julio glided over fanning menus.

"Ah, good afternoon Meester Lawrence."

"Well hello Julio. Do you have something wonderful for us today?"

"Si, si, we have thee most tender veal, a poached salmon with dill hollandaise and Omeletta d' Espana."

"M-m-m. Thank you, give as a moment to choose please, Julio." The restaurant had a Mediterranean theme, a grape arbour and terracotta tiles. It was busy with shoppers taking a break from spending and entertainment industry people grabbing a quick lunch meeting. The patio simmered with banter and smiles, the waiters retrieved plates of barely sampled food and replaced them with ashtrays.

After finishing my sirloin, someone said, "Excuse me." I looked up at a guy wearing a suit and tie. "Aren't you Ian?" I was a bit slow to admit I was, I had no idea who was addressing me. I smiled. "I thought it was you. I interviewed you when I was doing an article for Life magazine about Gram, at Harvard and being in a band; last year, maybe. Cambridge?"

"Oh sure, now I remember. You know, I don't remember ever seeing that article."

"Well, that's how it goes, typical of journalism. Seems like only about half of what I cover ever gets to print. It was a shame, I think it was an interesting story. What are you doing now, are you still in that band with Gram?"

"Yeah, we're still going. We've had a couple of records and we're out here in LA now."

"Good I'm glad. I just wanted to say hello, I have to run. Give my regards to Gram. Goodbye."

I explained to Larry. "Man, I didn't really know who he was at first. He was with a photographer, at least a year ago, and they took a lot of pictures around Harvard. I remember he came over to the apartment where I was living and his eyes just about fell out of his skull. There were big murals and paintings on all the walls and ceilings; he just kept looking at them with his mouth open. He couldn't understand what we were saying. I think I said something like, I live here with my ol' lady and he said, 'oh your mother is here?' I had to laugh and explain, no man, my ol' lady, my girlfriend."

Later that afternoon, I decided I'd better fold up the new clothes to keep them clean for the movie set. They were expensive and smelled like it. New clothes for a new gig. I suddenly remembered one of Thoreau's mottos; 'Beware of ventures that require new clothes'.

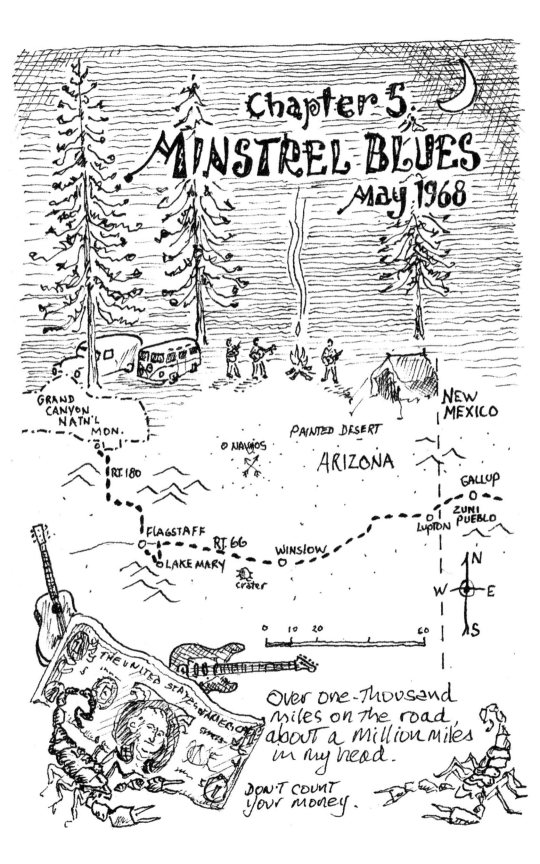

South of the Grand Canyon, close to Flagstaff, Arizona, there is a roadside sign. A goofy Mexican riding a burro welcomes you to La Fiesta Café, serving Tex-Mex food; tacos, enchiladas, chilli and burritos. There it is again, our name in lights. A year ago in LA, the band name had been born and delivered in the emergency room of a funky Mexican café in the Valley, during the summer of '67.

In Encino, at a low-end Mexican café, we take the wobbly table and chairs on the cracked concrete patio. Next door is a crazed parking lot with several sad, dusty cars. Opposite is a car upholstery workshop. The four of us look over at the scrawled menu board, deciding between frijoles, tacos, enchiladas or burritos. They don't serve any beer. Barry and Briggs have been staying with us for awhile and we had a yearning to go out and hunt for some authentic Mexican food. Barry T likes sniffing-out places that serve regional food.

"It's been a long time since I've had any real Mexican food. It might not have been since we were out here at the end of the tour." He means The Beatles tour, about a year ago. Since then The Remains hadn't really done much. That tour was a pinnacle still looming above the trail behind them. They flew too close to the sun and melted down. Not long after the tour another one of the original band members, Verne, split leaving just the two of them.

"Buenas Tardes. You want something to eat?" The guy had just suddenly appeared wearing a stained apron that looked like it had been chucked-out at a slaughterhouse. We order a mix of the café's offerings.

"We gonna jam again later?" suggested Briggs.

"What the Hell, it's better than sittin' around, waiting for nothing to happen." Mickey replied.

"Hey, I'm diggin' it. I've had it with waiting around." All of us had begun to feel that we were drifting in the Doldrums. The Remains had parted with their management and the album that had been released by Epic Records was floating out there, somewhere, with less and less interest from the label. The radio in the back kitchen was bursting with jumpy Norté accordion music that was beginning to overwhelm the smell of burning corn oil.

"What do think is going on with you guys?" Briggs meant the Submarine Band's management, recording and other options.

"Huh!" A sarcastic snort from Mickey.

"Well, you know, the usual fog. It's hard to tell when things go hot an' cold." I was not sure if the band was really still afloat and shrugged my shoulders. "We're still signed to Monte Kay in New York but, I mean, really, I don't think he has a lot of pull in LA. We don't seem to be in touch, lately. He handles a lot of TV people there, and now New York seems like a long way away. Too far away."

"Maybe it's in the past," Mickey agreed.

"John was talking the other day about seriously considering going back to New York. I really don't know. We might be able to swing another single out of Columbia. But that isn't much, if you consider that they didn't do Jack-shit with the last one." I summed it up.

"Gram doesn't want to go back to New York. No wa-ay, he's out here for good," Mickey advised.

A dark complexioned, squat woman with Indian features came bustling out of the kitchen balancing the food and then clanked tin plates down on our table.

"Wow! That looks good. Thank you." She brought over a large bottle of Tabasco sauce.

"Salsa es muy picante. E-es Hot!" she warned.

"O-okay, Thanks"

She beamed a wide smile and time slowed down. I became mesmerised by her black eyes, the alternate gold and enamel pattern of her large teeth, framed by the dark skin and sparking-coal hair.

"M-m-m, fuckin' great taco!" Mickey had a bite.

"Yeah man!"

"South of dee border, down Mexico way…"

"I was hungry, I might have to order another one of these."

"Hey, uh what is this weird glop?"

"That's those re-fried beans; I don't know how many times they re-fry them."

"There's something I like about this café on this crusty street, the people in the kitchen and this food. I couldn't live on it, but you got an idea what you're going to get. It's honest, they do what they do. They're doing the right thing and it sticks out a mile. There is so much crap goin' down! You just don't know who's tellin' the truth. I've had it with all the bullshit, up to here." I praised the café.

"Uhm, white man speak with forked tongue, tell-um big lie for many moons, send-um all braves to reservation, steal-um all wampum and squaws."

At that moment we were in agreement that we had fallen under the evil spell of the guys-in-suits who had made too many promises that didn't pan-out. We'd been duped into believing them, like the old time side-shows at a travelling circus, where the barker would stand outside the open tent flap hustling passers-by, enticing them inside with exaggerated promises. 'Hey-ya, hey-ya, see the world's most egg-xotic, most be-you-teeful, na-a-ked ladies! Right this way, right this way, only one thin dollar, you got to see 'em, nothing like you've ever seen before, come on in, see the naked ladies!' After the dollar, behind the faded velvet curtain, awaits disappointment in a sequined bra.

"God! That sauce is making me see stars. Phew! Have you tried it? Man, what did they put in that stuff!"

"Pass it over."

"Woah! Don't put too much on, take it easy with that. You'll explode."

An overloaded dump truck trundles past stirring curbside scraps, litter and dust, adding the authenticity of Tijuana to the meal.

"Damn! I just want to go out and play again." Mickey shook his head, he didn't like sitting on his ass, being idle.

"You know, I swear I was makin' more bread when I was out playing in high school. Just a kid."

"Yeah, me too," I agreed. "I'm getting fed-up hanging around, only playing to guys from a record company who come out once and awhile and then won't answer your phone calls."

"It's been getting a bit too long a-time now. The days are turnin' into weeks"

"A-a-men!"

"Hey how about this?" I chewed and swallowed my mouthful, "Maybe The Submarine Band will get another deal, who knows. But in the meantime, we almost have a couple of sets already, if you counted up all the stuff we've been jamming on over the past few days. We all need to get out and do some gigs and shove the fuckin' music business in the freezer! Let's put a band together. We can call it, ah..." the rough neighborhood and the jumpy Mexican food melded and conjured-up, 'The Flying, ah, Burrito Brothers! We can all play, we've been doing it for years there's no reason why we can't go out and earn some cash. What do you think?"

"Sure, man!"

"Yeah, I'm up for it. We've got all the gear and equipment we'd need. Why not."

"Yep! I been waiting on Hollywood to arrive for too long now."

'Ay-Yi-Yi-Yi', agreed the greasy kitchen radio.

By the time we roll in to Flagstaff, Arizona, our wallets are a bit on the thin side and we decide to look around to see if we could earn some cash.

"We're only going to make it through another couple of states before the gas gauge hits empty for the last time," Briggs estimated. We don't want to face the reality of how fast money vanishes even when you're living in a tent and cookin'-up bone stew.

"Maybe we can get a gig and play here, somewhere."

"It's worth trying, I guess."

Briggs is looking across the street. "I'm going over to that gas station and see if they need someone to pump gas." He heads off toward the Texaco sign.

"We could make more money if we could play somewhere."

"We don't have any drums."

"Still have piano, bass and guitar. We could use one of the big cabinets as a PA," Barry suggests.

"Yeah. I guess the weekend's comin' up," I agreed.

"There's a college or a university in town. I saw a sign for it, at an intersection, back up a bit." Briggs returns to the parking where we are leaning against the van.

"There's nothing there, but the guy told me about another place down the street. I'm going to drive down there to check it out."

"Well maybe we could go out to that college and see if there's anything happening there." Barry thought.

"Yeah. That would be good. It would be perfect if we could fix ourselves up with a gig." We agree to meet up at this drug store parking lot later.

We had tried busking in the campgrounds of the state parks. One evening Barry T had been strumming an acoustic and we started singing 'Bye-Bye-Love', sitting around the campfire. A couple, taking an evening stroll, stopped to listen. They politely applauded and said, 'Well, that was real nice boys. Thank you.'

After they had moved off Barry said, "Maybe we ought to play, try to get a few people gathered round, and then, pass the hat." Barry had done some playing on the streets when he was travelling in France, during a summer, before he went to university. "We want to do a few songs first, try and get them going, then I'll say, 'here comes my friend Buffalo Bob' and you go round with the hat." We experimented with a few boxes and pans to see if we could find some sort of percussion, all the instruments we had were electric, no good for playing in the woods. We decided to give it a whirl and walked over to a central position in the campsite next to a large pile of firewood. Barry started strumming and announced, "Hey everybody, music. Over here." The campsite was pretty large and there weren't a lot of people. Some of them were inside their campers, one or two peeked out from behind a trailer. We sang but no crowd gathered. We tried it again, "It's music night at Zion, folks." After the next song we were still the only ones standing out there.

"Oh well, this is a waste of time."

"Maybe we just have to get in closer," Barry T suggested, not wanting to quit yet. We walked along the camp road as he strummed the guitar. A couple was sitting at a picnic table near the edge of the track.

"Oh, we thought we heard music," she said. Barry sang 'Party Doll' and we did 'Bye-Bye-Love', again. They tapped their fingers on the plank tabletop.

"Well here comes my friend Buffalo Bob." My signal, I took off my baseball cap and approached the table. They were perplexed, looked at the hat, then each other. Soliciting, in state and federal parks, was probably illegal and I began to feel like a dork, holding the hat out so I put it back on.

"Are you boys musicians then?" she asked.

"Yes, we are, working our way back east."

"I wanted to be a musician. My sister and I used to sing together at church. People always said we should be professionals. We liked to sing McGuire Sisters' songs. But my sister got married right after high school, so that was the end of our dreams. Do you know any McGuire Sisters' songs?"

"No sorry, we mostly play rock music and blues."

"Well, we sure did enjoy listening to you."

Barry T gave it one last try, "Well say good-bye to my friend Buffalo Bob," and nodded to me. Oh shit, not again, I thought, as I took off my hat. This time the guy reached around for his wallet and dropped a couple of bucks in the hat. I didn't know if I should respond with an oink-oink or yee-haw. That was hard work, we agreed as we shuffled back to our campsite.

In the university neighborhood, Barry and I cruise down a street flanked by large fraternity houses with classical facades, wide steps and columns. There are big Greek letters above the doors. Δ π Σ. We notice a guy on the lawn in front of a frat house.

"He looks like a likely customer." Barry T smiles. "He could be our man." We stop the VW and walk up the path.

"Hi. How ya doin'?" He is hunched down, holding a golf club, polishing up his putting technique. He has sandy blonde hair, a square face and flashes a big smile, white against his tan. He is wearing a lightweight cream sweater, with one of those little green alligators over his heart, faded Madras slacks and brown loafers. He swings the putter up and lays it casually across his shoulder.

"What's up guys?"

"Well, we thought we'd ask if you guys are having any parties here."

He grins and shakes his head, "We sure do have parties at Delta Pi. We had some that started on Friday and lasted all weekend. They had to get a truck to take away all of the empties."

"Sounds like some party."

"Oh yeah! There were still people lying in those bushes, over there, on Monday afternoon."

"Wow."

"That was a party for the record books." He nods proudly.

"Have you guys got anything cookin' for this weekend? We have a band and are looking around to see if there might be a gig somewhere."

"Really. A band, huh? That could be interesting." This university playboy might be just what we are looking for.

"Are you guys in town for long? Do you have a phone number?"

"No. No phone. We're just passing through."

"Oh. That's too bad. I was thinking we could talk sometime in September. You see, the house has been on academic probation since spring break. The Dean thought we were getting a bit wild and he's got us on his black list, but that gets lifted in the fall and we could have a big blow-out to celebrate."

"Oh."

"Most of the brothers are gone now anyway. The year is o-over. I'm about the only one left. Just killing time. Waiting to go on the yacht next week, out of Savannah."

We drive back to the parking lot to hook-up with Briggs, who is waiting in the old van.

"How'd it go over there. Any action?"

"No the playboy frat-house has been shut down for bad behavior and the campus is closing down for summer."

"Oh, well. I hoped that something might have happened. I struck out, except for a place that offered shit money." Traffic moves away from a stoplight. An old Buick with a blown muffler roars past.

"I don't like it here anyway."

"Let's get on the road and stop somewhere, where we can think."

"Let me get a map out. We'll have a look at it, see what we can do." I grab the state road map from the VW.

"Okay here's Flagstaff. Route 66."

"Hey look at this, on another road. There's a national park campground, just a few miles out of Flagstaff. Coconino Forest. See, right here."

"Oh yeah. It looks close."

"Maybe about ten miles. Lake Mary campground."

"Man, that looks just about right, we could be there in a half- hour."

"If we're going to do that, I'm going to look for a butcher, if we pass one. We should stop and get something for a big stew," Barry says.

"Yeah, cool. What else do we need?"

"M-m you know, stew stuff."

"Okay I'll look for a vegetable stand. If we lose each other, I'll meet you at Lake Mary. That'll be perfect. Catch you later."

I pass the park Ranger station and a sign that says; Coconino National Forest. Lake Mary: 4 miles, Elevation 7,000 feet. The road winds uphill through stands of huge pines. The hills begin to look like I am in Switzerland or the northern California Sierras. Some of the trees are giants. The Lake Mary campground is empty. No campers, rangers or picnickers. I drive on the campsite road and choose a site with a table and a stone fireplace under an enormous Ponderosa pine. I sit at the picnic table and appraise it, like looking at a new apartment. I like it, I could move in. As I take a couple things out of the VW, the old white van rolls in.

"Okay? Man, that was easy huh? From the city to the mountains in a few minutes." It was extreme, just over a half-hour ago we were on a noisy city street now it was silent. I could hear some birds caw-ing, spreading the word that people had arrived. "It'll be light for hours but I'm going to go over there," I point in the direction of dense trees, "see if I can grab some wood."

"Sure. We'll get set up."

The fire is going and Barry T has a big pot over the flames and is sitting at the table pondering his small sketchbook. He breaks off his concentration and looks up, perplexed, shaking his head slightly and asks me.

"Where was that place we played? We drove way out to Ventura or somewhere like that an' Mickey got sick. Do you remember? I'm trying to make a list of all the places where we played. There were so many Burritos gigs that I can't even remember some of them now."

We had played dozens of bars and clubs during the last, what was it, eight, ten months? It had become a blur of songs, dimly-lit interiors and a drunken parade of faces.

"Um-m, was it that place the Sidecar or the Glass Slipper?" I suggest.

"Yeah. The Si-ilver Slipper, it was called. That's another one. Maybe the place I'm lookin' for was the Sidecar. I think that could be it. Phew, I forgot about the Silver Slipper. Man. I can't remember anything about that night. Can you?" I tried to form a picture, recollecting anything I could from that gig but just kept getting a blank. That night was buried, down there beneath a hundred other gigs.

I remember an early one, maybe at the end of the summer of '67. It might have been one of The Burrito's first. I can't remember how we got the gig; it was before we had an agent. It was at some club out in the Valley on Lankershim Boulevard. and could have been one of the gigs that we booked ourselves. A couple of us, when driving by the place, saw a list of bands on the sign out front. We stopped and went in to ask about a gig. A guy with red hair and a moustache, wearing a sports coat, was just hanging-up the phone. He heard us come through the door.

"We're not open yet guys, just nights," he said.

"Okay, we just want to talk. We saw the sign out front and wanted to find out about playing here."

He pursed his mouth, rubbed his cheek and squinted back. "You guys any good? I can't just take anybody off the street, can I?"

"Yeah we're good, been playing for years. We do rock 'n' roll, rhythm 'n' blues, good dance music."

"Yeah really?" He studied us again then looked at his watch. "Well, as a matter of fact, I just had some guys cancel on me for Thursday night. That's the trouble with getting' in people I don't know."

"We're reliable."

"Yeah? Well, what about this Thursday then?"

"We're okay for Thursday. We could do it."

"H-m-m, I don't know." He grimaced, "Well, these other guys left me hangin', so I'll just have to take a gamble on you guys and hope you're good." Seemed it was settled, without an audition or anything.

"How much will you pay us?"

"I don't know what you're like. How many of you in the band?"

"It's a four-piece."

"Okay, I'll guarantee you eighty. Best I can do."

"Well that's a bit thin but, okay. I guess it'll have to do. What are the hours?"

"We want the band, nine-thirty to one. You can take a few breaks, but not more than ten minutes."

"Sure. Thanks. Okay, see you Thursday night."

"Well, I've heard that line before. I'm takin' a gamble on you guys. I usually don't do this." He nodded like a judge. We got in the Dodge van and headed back, out of the Valley.

"Man you got balls, the way you pushed that guy."

"No, he was sort of desperate," Briggs replied

"Three hours, that's a long time. We don't have that many songs worked up."

"Hey, we'll do long solos, a couple of blues-riff instrumentals. Any old stuff, to fill-in a bit. No sweat."

The next day we ran over some more songs and made a set list, adding, pretty much, anything we could agree on.

"'Before You Accuse Me', a-and, you could do 'Mojo.'" Barry T suggested.

"We want to do the up-tempo stuff."

"'Louie-Louie'?"

"M-m-m? I don't know about that one," I said.

"Well, in case we're really desperate and it's twelve-thirty."

"Yeah, you're right."

During the Burrito's rehearsal, Gram walked in, carrying his guitar case and smiling at the action."

"Hey Guys! Thought I'd just come by and see what you're up to today."

"Hey man. Hi. We're just puttin' together a set."

"We've got a gig tomorrow night and we need to figure out a few more songs."

"Yeah, really? That's cool." Gram set his case down and sat on the couch.

"We're going to be relying on a few blasts from the past. It's a long gig," said Barry T.

"Ha. So you're polishing up the ol' Chuck Berry songs huh?"

"Yeah, you got the idea."

"It's lookin' that way. Hey, do you want to play a bit? Come on get that guitar out o' the box."

Gram tuned-up the Gibson acoustic and strummed chords. "What about this one?" he strummed again. "In G."

"Yeah? What one?"

"A Merle Haggard thing, 'Somebody Else You've Known.'" We jammed along on the song. I knew the chorus and sang. We played a couple more, 'Truck Drivin' Man' and 'Blue Eyes'. They were all songs that we used to do in The Submarine Band and they sounded good with Briggs playing the electric piano.

"Hey, Yeah."

"Ha! Alright!"

"Yeah. Well, I ought to let you guys get back to work huh?" Gram was putting his guitar back in the case. "You got a show to do, an' everythin'."

"Well, we've got a few dozen songs down on the list, we're getting' close."

"Great. Do it!" He encouraged. I began to feel that Gram probably missed getting up and playing. It had been at least a month or longer since The Submarine Band had done any gigs, apart from playing to a couple of producers who had come to the house. He had been writing, playing at home with a few different people and had done some recording sessions with Barry Goldberg but he hadn't been up on stage for awhile.

"Hey, what do you guys think," I decided to suggest, "Why don't you come down to this gig and sit in with us? We could do those songs we just played. They could work and it would take the pressure off of Barry, having to sing most of the vocals. Huh?"

"Sure."

"Okay." No one objected, it could be fun.

'Swee-ee-t, dre-ee-ams, baby
'Swee-ee-t, dre-ee-ams, ba-ay-by.

Barry T was singing our version of the Orbison song. We had set up and started on the dot of nine-thirty. Played, 'Philly Dog', 'Get Outta My Life Woman' and a Fats Domino song, 'Poor Me'. There was a line of people leaning on the bar, a few tables were full and several couples were dancing. Red, the manager, walked past, nodded and smiled, he was relieved that we hadn't turned out to be a hippie psychedelic band or just really awful. We took a break at about ten-twenty, got bottles of beer and Mickey lit-up a Kool.

"Hey. How's it goin'?" It was Gram.

"Pretty good, so far. How you doin', you still going to get up and do a few?"

"Yeah sure. I brought my guitar. I'll just go over an' get a little drink. Be back in a second."

We started the second set with a Booker T. song, 'Be My Lady' and a few couples boogalooed. 'Ok, you want to come up now', I signalled to Gram. He stepped on to the crowded bandstand and picked up his guitar that had been leaning against one of the amps and threw the strap over his back. He was wearing the jacket from the Submarine Nudie suit and blue jeans.

"Yeah, okay." Strum, strum. "Wait a second the D's a little, ah."

He tuned it up a bit. "Okay. In G." We did one of the songs we played with him yesterday afternoon and a few people started dancing. A chubby woman wiggled and laughed as she spun under the arm of her guy who had a slicked-back DA hairstyle. Another couple did the Twist.

'Yeah I must be somebody else

You've known.'

The dancers clapped. We went right into an up-tempo 'Truck Drivin' Man', like fast. The chubby girl and DA jigged around for a minute then danced-off, back to the bar.

'I'll put a nickel in the jukebox

And play-ay the truck drivin' man.'

A guy sitting at a table near the front, flapped his hand with a get-outta-here gesture. Just as we wrapped it, Red came bustling up to the front and hissed.

"Hey! No country an' western here!" We all looked back blankly, surprised by his reaction. "If you wanna play that stuff, go down to the Palomino. Not here."

"Ah, yeah, okay."

"Whoops. I guess I better split, an' let you guys alone." Gram giggled.

"Shit. Sorry man." I offered.

"That's cool. I'll stick around for the rest of your set."

We launched right into 'The Letter', a song that was in the charts. People got back on the dance floor. The response we had to playing 'Truck Drivin' Man' was the typical country music syndrome, some people couldn't stand it. It freaked them, for some reason, and prompted the get-that-stuff-outta-here reaction.

"Hey, there you go again." I said to Gram on our second break. "Country music, huh? It's dangerous stuff."

"Yep, that's how it goes sometimes."

"Hey what did he say about that Pal-o'-Mine place? I didn't catch it."

"I just asked a guy at the bar. It's a club or a bar called the Palomino, like a horse. You know, like cou-u-n-ntry-y," Gram wiggled his head and stuck out his tongue. "It's a place out here, about a half-a-mile down the road."

"Yeah?"

"I think I'll have to go down there an' check-out what's happening."

A week later Gram went to The Palomino and found that it was a country and western club. People who went there wore western shirts, boots and jeans and the jukebox was strictly country. A redneck joint, sort of entrenched in the old-country, cowboy thing. The resident band was Red Rhodes and The Detours and, one night a week, they had 'amateur night' when anyone could grab their guitar and get up and sing. Gram decided to go down there and do it. The first couple of times when he got up to play, he was booed and some of them yelled, 'Get outta here, ya hippie!'

We are sitting around the campsite table under the sky-high pines in the mountains of

Arizona remembering some of the gigs we had done and musicians we had known in LA.

"Yeah, it's hard to believe, let alone remember, how many gigs we did."

"I think our record was twenty-eight days straight."

"Huh. Was it, really?"

"Well, I think it was. There was a time maybe in November, we did six nights for three weeks in a row at Peacock Alley, a week at another place, The Laurel Club, I think it was called and we played every Sunday at the Prelude gig. That's twenty-eight days."

"Phew. What a marathon."

"Yeah, I'm sure about that. A month without a night off." I had my figures right.

"The other thing I was trying remember was some of the people who sat-in with us. There were a lot of them. Like Indian Ed and that drummer, Levon Helm." Barry starts counting.

"Taj Mahal. Didn't he get up with a couple of the Okies one night?" I remember.

"Yeah I think so, he came down with Jimmy Karstein."

"And Duck Dunn. He sat-in at The Prelude."

"Who was that sax player?"

"Which one?"

"A real tall black guy."

"I don't know who he was."

"There were a bunch. It's hard to remember one night from another."

I get up to find a sweatshirt in my van, it's getting chilly as the sun goes behind the trees. I move around a couple of boxes and see the speaker grille of a Fender Dual Showman amp. It was a big amp, powerful. I didn't need to use it when we were playing at smaller venues, it was easier to carry a small amp and not bust my ass. It had been parked against the living room wall at Burrito Manor for weeks sometimes. I pull on the sweatshirt and go back and sit on a stump by the campfire.

"I wonder if those guys down the road, in Laurel Canyon, ever got anything going? What were they called?" I ask.

"Who do you mean?"

"Remember, one time, we were jamming with them at Burrito Manor in the garage. I don't know why we were out there, maybe all the gear was in the van and we didn't feel like bringing it inside the house. There were seven or eight of us, all playing at once."

"Oh yeah, that time. I think they called themselves The Rockets. What a noise, two bands. Man."

"Oh God, I know. We were playing 'I'll Go Crazy' and that guy came running up the driveway, in pyjamas or a bathrobe or something, waving his arms like his house caught fire. It was in the middle of the day but he was furious."

"No wonder, I bet it was loud. I don't think I ever saw any of those guys again."

"I think I saw the bass player, somewhere, again. I can't remember what he was called." I searched, but couldn't come up with a name. Barry lifted the lid on the big pan and stuck a fork into the potatoes. "You remember that other guy?" I mused, "Ah, what was he called, Bob, Rob? He looked like a scarecrow, or some tormented character out of an Edgar Allen Poe story."

"Yeah," Barry T thought for a moment, "He was weird."

"I remember getting up one morning and he was sitting in the living room smoking a cigarette. I just said hi and walked into the kitchen. I figured someone else was around and had let him in, but none of you guys were up. I thought, what the hell? Was he here last night and then passed out in a corner or slept on the couch?"

"It's funny, because I had thought he was a friend of yours."

"Yeah, that's what was so weird, I thought he was a friend of Steve's. He kept coming over, like that Basset Hound that used to scratch at the front door and, I guess, no one really knew who he was. I had some idea that he played piano but I never saw the guy play anything."

"He did look a bit shady with that gaunt face and baggy suit. Um-m, it might not have been a suit. Maybe a dark, rumpled, sports coat, he wore the same thing all the time."

"Yeah, and that old, like, '40s hat. He looked like a sleazy used car salesman from Disasterville or somewhere. And everyone thought he was somebody else's friend, ha."

"What happened to him? He stopped coming over."

"Well, I think, it was one morning, when I rolled out of bed and as I went into the living room I saw him ducking in through the porch window. One of his spider legs was, like, already inside and he just slid right in. It creeped me, I lost it and blurted out somethin' like, 'wha' the fuck are you doin'? I mean, he was like a burglar. It just hit me the wrong way and I reacted, over reacted," I admitted.

"Oh. Well, he suddenly stopped hanging around."

"You know, I thought that he was a friend of Gram's," Briggs adds to the mystery.

"Did you, why?"

"Well, I thought he had said something like, someone had told him we were putting a band together and might be looking for a piano player."

"What? You were the piano player."

"Yeah, that's something that doesn't quite fit. Anyway, I thought, he said it was Gram who told him that."

"Hm-m. Maybe so. It could have been something that Gram might have said, sort of casually. Could be. The thing about Gram, sometimes, is he likes makin' connections, and sometimes he'll just about say anything to make people happy. Like he can't help it, he just doesn't think. It could be, 'yeah, sure' or 'hey, great' to anything. The response he's getting is more important than the reality.'"

"Well that only works if you're lucky. He seems to have plenty of bread to patch it up, if it goes wrong."

"Yeah maybe, but I don't think it's just that. I think the thing is, it's so important for him to feel that people like him and he has to keep finding more people to keep that feeling alive."

"Well, these ol' potatoes are just about done." Barry T is about ready to dish it out.

During the Burrito Manor period, a large number of people came by to rehearse, play and jam. Some of the sessions were subdued; others were loud, cacophonic and attracted angry neighbors. There was a line of amps in the living room. A couple Fender Dual-Showmans, an Ampeg, a Twin Reverb, a big Sun cabinet, an old Fender Concert, a Vox Super Beatle and two big Altec theater speakers were all jammed against the walls. There was also an upright piano, electric piano and drums.

Numerous musicians played at the Manor. Besides the residents, (Nuese, Gauvin, Tashian, Briggs and me), Gram, Brandon, Chris Ethridge, Jr. Markham, Bobby Keys, The Rockets, Bloomfield's new band The Electric Flag, Big Black, a percussionist and others played. There were dozens of them who came over to jam, rehearse, hang out or listen to some of the vast library of old 45's.

Chris Ethridge had knocked me out with his style of bass playing. Instead of slinging the guitar strap over his shoulder in the usual way, he routed the strap over his right shoulder, snaked it around his back and fastened it to the nub, from his left side, holding the Fender Precision in a vertical position, like an up-right bass. He was a killer player. He grinned, a wide mouth in the midst of goatee brush, bobbed his head, shaking a mane of dark hair as his left hand spidered up and down the neck.

"Yeah, ah always played it like this," he said, explaining the odd way he held the electric bass, in his Mississippi accent. He was from Meridian but had been out in LA for a bit. "I been doing some tracks for the Mamas 'n' Papas," he said.

Harvey Brooks was another bass player who had done a lot of recording in New York and played on some of the Bob Dylan sessions. He was at Burrito Manor rehearsing with Mike Bloomfield's new band The Electric Flag. Harvey asked what sort of a bass I had and I showed him the '59 Precision that I had recently found in LA. He liked the look of it and wanted to try it out. He picked it up and, unlike Chris Ethridge, Harvey adjusted the strap so the bass sat high up against his rib cage.

"M-m-m. I like it." He attacked the strings, rattling-off some extended, continuous scales climbing up the neck. My jaw dropped. "Man, this is a good one. A real beaut." He walked a bass line up and down and conscious of me watching he threw in a couple of exhibition trills. "Yeah, you were lucky to pick this one up." So many great musicians and intimidating bass players.

The Electric Flag were using the Burrito Manor rehearsal room to knock their set together, it was all bluesy stuff. They ran through a few B.B. King songs and a couple of other old blues standards, a Freddy King tune and a jumped-up version of 'Drinkin' Wine Spo-dee-O-dee'. The Electric Flag was a big band; Elvin Bishop, Mike Bloomfield, Harvey Brooks, Barry Goldberg playing a C-3 organ, Nick Gravenitis singing some of the vocals and big Buddy Miles on drums, grimacing as he whacked the hell out of them. Once after an Electric Flag rehearsal I picked up several small nuts and washers that were lying on the carpet, knocked loose from the bass drum by Buddy's beating.

Jon Corneal, a drummer and songwriter from the South had also stayed briefly at Burrito Manor. I remember once when Jon was sitting in the living room playing an acoustic. He sang a few of his tunes and also did a couple of the most doomy Roy Orbison songs like 'Cryin''. Someone said it sounded like the top-ten chart of desolation songs.

"I wonder if Corneal got anything together with The Submarine Band album?" Barry asked.

"I don't know. The last I heard was it had sort of fizzled-out. They didn't get a band together or do any gigs. I know Corneal was hot to do something, even after Gram quit, but it was probably too much of an up-hill struggle. You know, country music seems like a losing battle. People just don't want to know."

During the week that The Electric Flag were rehearsing at Burrito Manor, The Submarine Band had been jamming on a few country numbers; a Merle Haggard song, 'Somebody Else You've Known' and new one, 'Mental Revenge'. Bloomfield was sitting-in, playing along.

'Surely I must be somebody e-else you've known', we're singing. Gram backs up from the mic,

"Okay, guitar solo." The two guys playing electrics are hesitant, each giving way to the other. John Nuese extends an open palm to Bloomfield who flicks the pickup switch on the gold Les Paul he's using today and takes off on a run of blues licks, Humbuckered-up to the top.

After the song he shook his head slightly.

"I don't know man... country music?" says Bloomfield, "I still can't see it. I don't get it."

"Hey, it's not all that different from B.B. King," counters Gram.

"Well, m-m. I don't know, it's just so... white."

"Yeah, well, so are we."

"Okay, but it's those whiney voices, always stuck into the same, hokey things."

"They're just singing about the same thing as Jimmy Reed. You know, this city sure is tough, my baby left me, I'm bustin' my ass makin' no money and I sure could use a drink to get me through this mess. Same story. The white mans' blues. White mans' soul."

"Yeah, well maybe so. I'll have to listen to a bit more of it sometime."

Gram leans towards Bloomfield, raises one eyebrow slightly, like a guy who's got a hot tip on a horse. "I've got a great George Jones album I'll lend you."

"Hm-m."

The morning is chilly. We're at high altitude. I wait for the sun to get up over the hills before I climb out of the van. Barry T is wearing a big army jacket and he pokes a stick into the ashes.

"I'm thinking about some coffee. There's still a bit of life in the embers." He throws in a handful of rust colored pine needles and they begin to smoke. "Yeah, a few sticks and we'll have lift off."

"Yeah, looks good. I could murder a cup of burning hot coffee."

The pile of firewood that seemed like a big stash last night is almost gone. "I'll go up there into the woods and see if I can scrape up some more wood."

"We could do up some toast as well."

In the shadows of the trees it is chilly and damp. I have to walk further in as we had dragged out the nearest dead wood yesterday. Several thick branches stick up out of a large fallen tree. I grab one and lean back to snap it off the trunk. The limb breaks with a crack. I stumble back and trip over a rock and have a soft landing on the carpet of pine needles.

The underside of the big trunk is crumbling with rot. A troop of small mushrooms sprouts from the decaying wood. They are the color of jaundiced flesh, probably not the right kind of mushroom to use in an omelette. Toadstools. They might make you sick. Maybe they are the psychedelic ones. I don't know. I've only seen the magic mushrooms dried, in little plastic bags, looking like mummified monkey ears. People often puked after they had taken them. Gram and I thought we might be sick when we took some sort of mushrooms in New York.

Gram had found some psychedelic thing that was supposed to be synthesized magic mushrooms, some sort of psylocibyn.

"Look what I just got hold of," Gram said, taking a small vial from his shirt pocket. It was about the size of lipstick or a shotgun shell and held about a couple of teaspoons of a liquid, the color and viscosity of honey. "It's like magic mushrooms, supposed to be great."

"Hm-m, looks like we could just about spread it on a piece of toast."

"The breakfast of champions. Could be a way to take it. Um-m, maybe not," he thought, "sometimes those mushrooms can make you a bit sick, 'til you absorb 'em. Hey folks! It's the latest, it's the greatest. Everybody's talkin' 'bout psyl-oh-cy-bin," he rattled-off, in the style of a detergent ad on TV. "Now you can enjoy the adventures of magic mushrooms in the comfort of your own home. Take advantage of this amazing offer, today!" he giggled. "You want to try some of this with me?"

The trippy syrup tasted oily. Maybe there were only a few drops of the chemical mixed with corn oil. The dose only just coated the inside of my mouth. We decided to wash it down with a sip of water. In Gram's dark bedroom, we sat back in anticipation, not knowing if we'd be suddenly propelled, like, WHAM, crashing through the ceiling as we were sucked into the wallpapered funnel of a floral tornado. We might start shaking and juddering, like astronauts, in the films that showed their faces being distorted by the G-force of a rocket launch. A few minutes later, after no sudden reactions, we relaxed.

"Hm-m. I'm not feeling anything yet."

"No. Neither am I."

"Well, he said it was supposed to be enough for a couple of trips, or, a couple of people."

"Yeah? Or, maybe, half a trip for four people."

"Or a tribe of pygmies. Well, I'm very relaxed. Hope I just don't fall asleep."

"Maybe this stuff is like opium, you conk-out and have huge, five dimensional dreams."

As we sat in the dark room, I began to perceive a rumble and, after a moment it seemed to have gained in strength. I heard a distant growl and a muffled boom, like a jungle drum, from the far side of a mountain in the Andes. The sound became louder and I saw a pulsating orange glow illuminating the window, then a hiss-ss, a clang-ng and a shout. I imagined a ceremonial procession. Sweating priests, wearing gold head-dresses, held flaming torches aloft, and were followed by eight warriors who strained under a yoke that carried a huge drum, made of jaguar skin and was beaten, in long, slow strokes, with a femur bone from a previous human sacrifice.

"Hey-y, it's the garbage truck. They never sleep, in New York." Gram chuckled.

"Oh man! Wow, I thought it was a bunch of Aztecs. Huh. I guess this stuff needs a lot of, ah, imagination, for something to happen."

"You know what? I knew that you were going to say that. Wow. Like exactly what you said. Like, I could almost see it, see the words, just before you were saying them. I'm beginning to see, ah, little, lights. Sort of like neon. Like a fire fly, writing out words."

"I just saw, ah, like, a little bird. It's gone into some leaves. There's a tree?" I began to see stems and a profusion of blade-shaped leaves, spreading and growing. Some began sprouting blooms, little scarlet faces with petal ears. Creamy gold, button flowers opened, like stars blooming, as night fills the sky. I was in a flower garden. The ceiling was dripping with small, green, tongue leaves, waggling. La, la, la, la, la, la. A silent breeze, in syncopation with my breathing, moved the leaves. I gathered a cloud of blossoms to my face. They regarded me with amber eyes. A wall was covered with shining ivy, I looked up as long bodied, jungle animal, like a lemur, delicately tip-toed along the top of the wall. It sat, lazily, and its orange-ringed tail uncoiled, reaching the floor. It turned its head and questioned me with the same amber eyes of the flowers. On its chest was a pulsating heart. Be-gin, be-gin, be-gin, it beat. The animal yawned, its tongue protruded and pointed toward a bird, fizzing with silver sparks that rained and pooled on the floor.

"There's too much more than circles," Gram had decided. That did sum it up, I guess. Theology, physics, relationships. I guess so.

"All the knowledge and science, it's all geometric, that's how they see it, like a straight line of history. Like, hey, there's the caveman, oops, there goes Columbus, we just passed George Washington, straight ahead of him is Hitler and Kennedy. But it's not a railroad track, all of this stuff is liquid, sloshing around. If you pee in a swimming pool, that little yellow patch doesn't stay in one place. It's all in motion, all the time, like an ocean. We're drifting in it right now, we're not really at this address, or in New York. Really we're in a sort of orbit. Swirling. No fixed address. Vagrants." I couldn't argue with that.

"Are you alright?" he asked.

Am I alright? I opened my palm and looked at the strange mass of wriggling meat before me. Was it me or history or evolution?

"I'm an ape." I informed him. I felt my face to see if I was covered with hair. I couldn't feel any pelt.

"Water," he said. "I gotta get a drink." He seemed to fly out of the room. I heard his footsteps recede down the hall and die away. I attempted to speak in English, uncertain if I was stuck in chimpanzee-ese.

"Here I am," I just about managed. There was a thudding and Gram came back into the room.

"I couldn't go down the stairs, they just don't, connect to, the house, anymore. So steep. Oh. I see. Man this stuff is powerful. Are you alright?"

Why does he keep asking me if I'm alright? How do I know. Some part of me managed to reply, "Ah, yes," as I wandered deeper into the jungle.

I walk on a Forestry road that follows the shore of Lake Mary. The lake is long and narrow, a basin in the Arizona mountains. There are still no other campers or vehicles, maybe the weekends were busier when people came out to fish or have picnics. The campground was probably under ten feet of snow in the winter. When I return to the campsite Barry T is sitting on a stump with his sketchbook.

"Hey. What are you up to?" I walk over.

"Just a little painting of the campsite. I want to remember this." He has done a miniature watercolor painting of the view over the lake to the distant dark green hills.

"That's cool."

He laughs slightly apologetically. "Well maybe one day I'll get the hang of it. My father is an artist, I'm just a doodler."

"Yeah but it's cool. If you do a sketch or something of where you are, it's like you only begin to really see what's around you. I remember in the Bronx, sitting out on a balcony and doing a drawing of the street. Like the house opposite, trees and telephone poles, just what was there. And I was amazed when I realized I hadn't really seen most of the stuff I was drawing, even though I had been living there for half a year."

"You can't see everything. Usually there is too much happening at once." He closed the book. "I'm going to mosey down over there and get a bit more wood, so we'll have a big stack for the night."

He walks off. I look out at the lake. The breeze has kicked up small waves that sparkle like chrome. A large bird swoops down over the lake. I dismiss it as a seagull after it disappears behind the dark trees.

The bird flies in low again and splashes on the water. It flaps up carrying a wriggling fish in its talons. It isn't a seagull.

"Woah! Man! Wow!" I hear a yell and look over. Barry T is backing away from a log. "Holy shit." He approaches shaking his head. "Man, I was picking up a bit of wood and there was a scorpion underneath it! My hand was only a couple of inches away from it when I saw it. It was about the same color as the pine needles. Phew!"

"Well, your luck's still holdin'"

As we are talking, a green pick-up comes along the road and pulls into the campsite. There is an emblem on the door and the guy who gets out is wearing a khaki uniform.

"Hi. How are you?" He is a Forest Ranger. "Are you planning on staying long? This isn't actually a long-term campsite. Really, it's just for day use." He is friendly, just letting us know.

"We didn't see any signs. We were just going to stay another night, maybe."

"Well, actually, the main site up the road is temporarily closed. They're doing some maintenance work. So I could bend the rules and let you stay here."

"Good. Thanks a lot."

"Really I should charge you two dollars."

"Oh. You know, we're sort of low on money."

"Well, I was going to say, since it's not the main site with all the facilities, I'm not going to ask you for anything."

"Hey, thanks a lot."

"Well have a good time. Enjoy yourselves. The Ranger station is four miles back down the road." He waves as he drives off.

"Too bad we didn't have some sort of National Park free pass," Barry thought. "Two bucks here two bucks there. It adds up."

"Yeah, money. Where does it go, huh? I don't know what's in my wallet." I take it out of my pocket. "Well, look at that, I've still got some cash. I don't think I'll count it." I flip through the plastic windows that hold cards or photos.

"Hey there's one from Manny's Music." Barry recognizes the business card.

"Yeah. Lets see what else we've got here. McConkey Booking Agency."

"Huh," he chuckles. "Gail McConkey was a good ol' gal. She got us gigs."

"New York Musicians Union Local Eight-O-Two."

"Well, that could still be useful."

One of the cards I didn't have was my draft card. Another was a New York Cabaret Card.

The management deal for The Submarine Band with Monte Kay in New York, yielded gigs, TV spots, a couple of record deals and a lot of paperwork. Management took us out of the shadows and headed us on a course to being legal. New York had very structured systems, there seemed to be unions for everything. Garbage men, sign painters, algebra teachers, tarot card readers, and piano movers all had unions. In order to record, or perform at some venues, we had to join the musicians union, local 802. Being accepted into the 802 brotherhood was simple and orchestrated by our management. They provided affidavits, sponsors and witnesses, a few signatures and numbers, and we were given our cards.

Another hurdle was obtaining a permit that might have been exclusive to New York, a Cabaret card. According to the law, performers had to be registered before they could work at clubs, bars, theatres, or sing in the chorus at the opera. The Cabaret card could have been something that was a remnant of the Prohibition era, when clubs, crime, musicians and illegal substances were considered to be hand-in-hand. Today it's slightly different. The card requirements seemed to have been dreamed up by the FBI. It demanded, name, address, another ID, a mug shot and fingerprints. None of us liked the sound of that much. I remember discussing the prospects;

"What right do they have, to take your fingerprints."

"Fuckin' Fascists."

"It's like out of the days of The Cotton Club, with Dutch Shultz runnin' around, spraying bullets with a Tommy gun, man, they just can't get over that."

"What are they afraid of now? Too many protest songs?"

"Just more people tryin' to spy on you, I don't like it."

We wondered if they would ask for an up-to-date draft card; that was something to avoid. The Night Owl and other small clubs in the village didn't care about Cabaret cards. Registering for the Cabaret cards kept sliding off the unwritten list of things to do. At one club, when the manager brought out a notebook to enter our Cabaret card numbers, we told him that they had been delayed, maybe they could be in the mail, who knows; we didn't. He sort of breathed a sigh of relief, like it was all a needless pain in the ass and closed the book.

The New York Musicians Union sent a monthly newspaper called, something like, The Allegro. The paper featured shots of people from Broadway musicals or orchestras, getting awards, or Barbra Streisand posing in a mink coat. One issue had an article that stood out, there was a column headed; 'Sinatra to Oppose Cabaret Cards'. Frank had a campaign going, to get rid of those cards, he had a couple of lawyers on the job and they were challenging it. He had the right idea, we didn't need the city or the cops to have our fingerprints on file. It seemed unconstitutional and an unnecessary persecution of poor harmless singers, jugglers and trombone players. So what, if they want a drink or have a smoke or a taste of something else: you want entertainment or not? Get off-a our backs! This new anti-card lobby made registering even less important, in our eyes. A month later, the Cabaret card was history, so we never made it to the fingerprinting session. Ol' Blue Eyes must have turned-on the charm, or donated to someone's retirement fund or twisted a few arms. Maybe a buddy of Frank's needed his fingerprints erased. Thanks Frank, for keepin' my fingers clean.

That night, sitting by the campfire under the Arizona stars, we decide that we would hit the road tomorrow and head toward New Mexico. We would be back on Route 66, heading east.

On Route 66 going through Winslow, Arizona I see a road sign to Gallup, New Mexico, one of the towns that cited in the song. Gallup is one hundred-and-fifty miles away. I pass a do-nut shop that has a giant golden brown do-nut sign mounted on the roof. Under the burning sun, the paint has flaked revealing the cement underneath. Past a big Texaco truck stop, out side of Winslow, there is a drive-in movie theater. Tonight they are showing Speedway with Elvis and Nancy Sinatra. On Friday night they are having Horror Night with Astro Zombies. The teenagers will be looking forward to that. You can't beat a good low-budget horror flick.

When we were on the set, filming for The Trip, I had recognized the faces of a couple of the minor actors. Their names would probably only appear near the bottom end of the credits. I was sure that I remembered the guy, who was playing the role of the bartender, from an old horror movie made in the early '60s. His face was familiar, it had to be him. The movie that I remembered was A Bucket of Blood. Along with 8½, The Wild One and Hell-za-Poppin'; Bucket was one of my favorite flicks. A Bucket of Blood had a Bohemian theme, like a beatnik horror movie. The scenes set in art studios were ridiculous, the actors, with goatees and berets, threw buckets of paint on wall-sized canvases and followed that explosive creativity with affirmations of 'Oh yeah, man! Cool daddy-o!' The movie had a few coffee house, poetry reading scenes where the poet melodramatically read poems that were a cue-card version of Beat poetry, they were trying to sound like Ferlinghetti. I remember a line like; 'The artist is, an obscure hobo, hitching a ride, on the omnibus of art.' Maybe it was profound? It's still there, in my head. I also remember how all my friends who had come to watch A Bucket of Blood on TV that night, had cracked-up with laughter, amazed by the fantastic banality of the film. The same actor, from Bucket, who had murdered people to turn the victims into sculpture, after coating the bodies with plaster of Paris, had also been in The Little Shop of Horrors, another low-budget, trashy horror flick. By the mid-60s, Shop of Horrors had become a 'classic' in the arty, underground scene. I found out that the director of the Trip, Roger Corman, had made both of these wonderful, crass horror movies.

Yeah great. I couldn't believe my luck. Corman had produced loads of low-budget horror movies. I had seen a lot of them on late night TV shows, where two or three movies would be shown in succession. The appealing thing about them was, they were almost amateur. The movies were only slightly beyond what anyone could do at home, with basic equipment, a couple of empty rooms and a floodlight. Corman's movies had just a few themes; alien invasions, hot rod zombies, or a terrible lurking, mutant creature, running around in the dark, who was obviously someone with a blanket pulled over his head and wearing a toilet seat around the neck. The mutant eyes on stalks were two eggcups, taped to the blanket.

The company that made these masterpieces was called American-International and when that title appeared, my friends and I would chorus 'Hubcap movie, yeah!' The inevitable, low budget, car chase scene always featured a close-up shot of a spinning hubcap, the same shot seemed to have been used again and again. We often recognized the locations from other A-I movies. The square, suburban house used extensively in The Man With the X-ray Eyes, might appear in the following movie on the same night. The house could have belonged to one of the film crew, maybe it was the home of that wacky guy in A Bucket of Blood.

I told Mickey about spotting the bartender and recognizing him from the horror flicks. He agreed that this was another achievement for us, in the bizarre world of trivia.

"Maybe Brandon knows who the guy is. Fonda would probably know. Ask him," Mickey suggested.

"Man, if I was sure that it was him, I would have gone up to him with a piece of toilet paper and asked for his autograph. That would have been cool."

"Yeah. Like getting Soupy Sales' fingerprints or a lock from Gypsy Boots' beard. I still have that pencil I took off Zacherley's desk, when we did his TV show."

"You know that other guy who is in The Trip? Dennis? We met him at Fonda's, ah, Dennis Hopper. He was in some of those horror movies too. I don't know if it was Bucket of Blood, or another one? One of 'em. We'll probably see him again. I'm gonna ask him about it. Hey, we've really made it into the small-time, huh?"

"Oh yeah, we're right down there, in the bottom."

Funny, about the continuing journey, deeper into the realm of trashy low life, I liked it. It was part of the Pop Art culture that I had picked up at art school, an attitude of rejecting established culture, replacing it with the ordinary and being entranced by lowlife. Maybe, it was acknowledging the richness that exists within vulgarity. A culture of comic books and chrome. The Submarine Band, particularly for our own enjoyment, had played a lot of songs about life, scraping-along at street level. The band kept getting more out-of-step with what was going on. We hadn't been singing songs about wearing flowers in your hair, our favorites seemed to be about murder, depression, alienation and alcoholism. Yeah, definitely lowlife stuff. On the music scene, we had become like a bullet-riddled stop-sign, stuck, out of place, in the middle of a field of sunflowers.

Getting close to New Mexico, the hills and mountains challenge the old bus and it struggles along Route 66 with a handicap of being overloaded. The amps and big speaker cabs add up to be almost more that the egg beater VW engine can stand. I have to take it easy, shift down a gear and keep crawling ahead. I didn't seem to have a lot of possessions when I left LA, just a lot of items, but when they are rounded-up, herded together, jammed into boxes and squeezed into the van they add up to bulk, not little things anymore.

The records alone probably weigh-in at more than I do, all those slim 45's, hundreds of them, only a few ounces each, with their few minutes of passion, originality or banality captured in another place and time. Messages in a bottle. Some of them are new but most of them are used, collected at junk stores and swap meets for a dime each. Low price, high value. Take the weight, divide it by the enjoyment, sum it all up, it's worth going up-hill a bit slower.

After all the different recording sessions, there are only two ISB 45's in the boxes with the others. There should have been, at least, a couple more but some of the sessions somehow were lost in double-talk, kidnapped or side-tracked and never got pressed. Sum it up, that's it.

'Sum Up Broke' made it to the presses. It was an original song, hinging around an odd guitar riff that John had construed. The figure slid around on the bottom three strings of the guitar, in John's case, in keeping with his eccentricity, they were the top strings. He played the guitar upside-down. The riff had a shade of The Kinks, it looped in a novel way, suggesting an odd tempo and it was catchy. Gram had worked with the riff, scribbling ideas and lyrics that wound around the guitar idea. Tinkering on a keyboard, he developed another theme, with a lighter touch, that worked as a bridge. The clavinet he was using spoke in a Baroque voice, that suggested the homonym, broke. Sum up Broke.

We cut the song at the Columbia studios in New York at the end of the summer of '66. We had been in studios several times that year but never for long enough to feel relaxed. Some sessions were better than others but it always seemed like a rush job.

"We'll have the drummer set-up in the both, back there. The bass, goes behind this screen. Put the guitar amp over there, behind the baffles. We'll get your backing tracks down first, add the vocals later." The studio technician uncoiled leads and cords, screwed mics to the stands and adjusted the booms.

"No, don't touch that. I'll do it. We'll wait to check the signal with the control room. Here's a headphone set for you. There's already a set for the drummer. Put them on so you can hear the engineer." I slid the headphones over my ear and the lead fell across the bass strings. The metal chair already seemed uncomfortable. Why were we sitting down?

"Guitar player!" The headphone blasts. I take them off.

"Can you turn these down, please."

"Just hold on. We'll get to you in a minute." The technician hovers around John, moving the mic stand. "Put your head set back on," he says to me.

With the headphones on, it is hard to identify who is saying what. All the voices and comments sound like a long-distance operator.

"Bass player?" The headphone speaks.

"Hi."

"Can you hear me?"

"Yes, it's blasting me out."

"Okay, we can fix that. Bass player. Is that better?"

"I guess so, yes."

"Good. Now, play a bit, please."

"Okay." I play a line. It sounds metallic, a lot of fret rattle, sounds bad. I add a bit more bass on the Ampeg amplifier. That gets rid of the clanky tone.

"Bass player. Turn down your volume by about twenty percent, please." I play. It sounds distant. "Bass player. Hold on, please. Yes, there's a hum." Over a speaker, in the room, there's an announcement. "Mike. Check the bass for earth, thanks." While the technician is looking at my amp, there is an explosion in my headphones.

BAM! WHAM! BAM!

"Drummer. Hold it, please." I hear Mickey mutter, under his breath. I get the thumbs-up from the technician.

"Drummer."

"YEAH!" Mickey's voice booms out.

"Drummer. You don't have to shout into the mic. Play the bass drum, please."

BAM, BAM, BAM, BAM.

"Okay. Thank you."

BAM, BAM

"Drummer. Thanks."

BAM, BAM, BAM.

"Drummer. Hold it."

BAM, BAM.

"Drummer, have you got your headset on? Will someone check his head set."

"Hu-r-rum, um." Someone clears their throat.

"Okay band. Let's try a run through," says the engineer.

"Are you ready?"

"Hold on, my headphones are dead. There. Now they're working."

"Yeah."

"Okay."

"I'll count it."

"Wait a second. The headphones are too loose."

"You can adjust them."

"I've tried that."

BAM, BAM, BAM.

"Could you turn the guitar up, please."

"We'll do that in a minute. I need a run through, please."

"Hold on, just a second."

I hear drumsticks clicking. "One, two, three, four."

We go into the song. The guitar stops abruptly.

"Just keep playing, band, thank you." I begin to play harder and hit a bum note. I turn up the volume.

"Chorus," Mickey yells. He's counting, the rest of us are just about staying on top of the chords. We blow the ending.

"Sorry. I missed that."

"Band, I want you to remember not to talk, until you see the light go out."

"The drums are too loud."

"I can't hear myself."

"They're not that loud."

"Who said that?"

Chink-chink. A guitar lick.

"Wasn't that a bit fast?"

"I'd like it, if I could hear some lyrics."

"Maybe."

"I couldn't hear the piano."

"Band. One at a time, please. Drummer, can you hear the bass?"

"No."

"Maybe I wasn't playing loud enough. I'll turn up."

"No. We'll control it in here. Bass player. Play, please."

Bum, Bum, Bum.

"Drummer. How's that?"

"I can hear it now but nobody else is playing. I'm not playing."

"It should be better now."

"What?"

Chank. A guitar chord.

"I need to hear a bit more of my guitar, please."

"Try that."

"That might be better."

Gram is playing a Boogie-Woogie lick on the electric piano.

"Okay. Thank you, band. We'll have another run through."

BAM, BAM, Bash-sh-sh.

"Drummer. Are you going to use the crash cymbal?"

"Yeah. Maybe."

"Play it again, please."

Bash-sh-sh.

"Thank you. Could you use a lighter stick on the cymbal?"

"No."

Boom, Boom, Boom.

Dah, Dah, Dah.

"Can't we have any vocal? It would make it easier."

"No. We want to get clean backing tracks."

"What if I say, first verse, second verse."

"Okay."

Z-Z-Z-R-R-R-K!

"Jesus! What was that?"

"Don't unplug the instruments!"

"Sorry."

"Hey, come on. Let's go."

"Wait a sec."

"Band. Are you ready?"

"Um, Okay."

"No."

"I just changed my volume."

"Who said that?"

"Said what?"

"Hello?"

"Ready?"

"Can you hear me?"

"Is this thing still on?"

After run-throughs, abortions and a few live takes, we put the vocals down onto a version that was more tame than earlier takes. The tracks hadn't gone into the red and met with the approval of the stern engineer, who adhered to science lab specifications. We had worked quickly, probably feeling prodded and, wanting to add a bit more, Gram put down an acoustic guitar track. We hadn't ever used a flat-top on the song before but we were in the studio, so what the Hell, why not, you never knew how long it might be before we might be back, it could be awhile.

We were never invited back to the mixing session by Jack, our producer, or Columbia, presumably we weren't considered worthy of an opinion. A week or so later, the management phoned telling us they had a test pressing at the office and we zipped down-town to collect the ten-inch acetate.

We were zapped to hear ourselves on something that sounded like a rock single, that would be released on a big label. The B-side, 'One Day Week', rocked along with a touch of country rolled inside. We were excited, couldn't help feeling that we had climbed that first big hill and were ready to start picking up speed. The following day, listening to 'Sum Up Broke' a few more times, the aura of novelty had dulled revealing some irritating aspects of the mix.

"He's mixed the acoustic guitar too far forward, listen," John noticed. "It's fine in this part, but here...it's too much." I heard what he was saying, the rhythm guitar was flapping right across the beat and making the rhythm section seem out of time. It diluted the electric, rock feel. "Come on GP, listen. The acoustic is all over the place and right on top of the Telecaster. Why did he mix it like that?"

"Um-m. Well, yeah. I see what you mean, but I don't know if it makes that big a difference?"

"It's changed the whole feeling of the song," John maintained. "The lead guitar should be more in front, it has to cut through. We've got to do something about this."

"Well, OK. What should we do?"

"We have to call Jack and tell him. Either we've got to re-record it, or they've got to re-mix it and pull the acoustic down, completely out in places, and jack up the Telecaster.

All they have to do is change the levels. It's not that much."

"Well maybe, but it might be more important not to hold this up so they get the record out as soon as they can. Columbia is a big label. We've been shootin' at this for awhile now." Gram was always interested in moving on, John was into details.

After one or two of the 'He's not in the office now, I'll tell him you called' exchanges, Gram spoke with Jack about our opinions and reservations about the existing mix. The next day the word came that it was already too late, the masters had gone for pressing. That was it, no second chance.

"Hey, we've just got to think positive."

It felt a bit too much like being a patient, hospitalised and waiting, while people in institutional, white lab-coats instructed 'Sit here, raise your knee, say ah-a-a, play the drum. No, not that loud! Softly. There, that's better. Fine. Okay, that's it. Thankyou boys, we'll let you know when we get your results and have a look at them. Bye.' We had a couple of songs, they had the sound equipment, the engineers, the marketing structure and a procedure that involved a complicated ritualistic dance of inter-office politics and pecking orders. We had simply accepted the producer, no questions asked, unaware of anything he had done or what credits he might have had to his name. He had mentioned doing something with John Sebastian but that might have been a deal in the pipeline, it was laid-out in the dialect of fast-talk; a language laced with superlatives, enticements and show-biz slick. In less than a year after the Columbia session, I began to get the word that bands were signing agreements guaranteeing the right to have some control over their releases. I had also begun to meet musicians who were independently recording and producing their music.

Gram didn't like getting bogged down in tedious details. I could understand that, neither did I, what the Hell. Moving-on was more important than wasting all that time reading the fine print, that wasn't our thing. By the time The Submarine Band dove for the last time, several managers, producers, record companies and contracts had walked the plank and were bobbing in our wake.

On Route 66, I cross the state border into New Mexico just after Lupton. New Mexico is the fifth state so far. A cluster of sheds and shacks up ahead have big signs; Blankets, Moccasins, Jewellery Made by Indians. There are also Live Rattlesnakes. I haven't seen a rattler lately so pull off to look at the stands. The snakes are hiding under rocks in the snake pit and aren't putting on any show.

I start walking down a small road, I need to stretch my legs. The sign says the road leads to a reservation and the Zuni Indian pueblo. The earth and the hills around me are the color of a rich brick-red. Dark green plants and bushes dot the landscape in a regular pattern. Back from the road barbwire is strung between fence posts made of branches and planks. Each one is different and they lean at odd angles. Some of the smaller plants look like a sort of cactus, low on the ground. I wonder if peyote grows here. I could be in Peyote Pass or the Peyote Hills. Maybe the Zunis take peyote at ceremonies, at mid-summer, in the month of the antelope, weddings or birthdays. They might save it, only for special occasions. If they collect it out in the hills at least they know what they are getting. Like pulling a carrot out of a vegetable patch, wiping the soil off and eating it raw, without freezing, preservatives or added ingredients. They would know what they are putting into their systems and would have an idea of what sort of a trip they were going on. It's not like that with acid or chemicals, these days you could be taking just about anything.

Acid was unpredictable at the best of times but there was so much shit floating around. Often it was brewed-up by amateurs and chemistry degree drop-outs. They worked in so-called labs that were bathrooms, empty warehouses, sleazy hotel rooms or mobile homes. There was no manufacturer's guarantee of a sterile processes or a, so-called, brand name you can trust. You never could be sure what you might be shoving into your system to frazzle your brain. More and more people I knew had decided that acid was getting too weird and wouldn't touch it any more. An easily broken promise, I can't remember anyone actually signing the pledge.

One of the last couple of trips I had taken was disappointing and irritating, a poison ivy, mosquitoes and measles experience. I doubt if the pill I had taken was LSD. I had climbed through brush and tropical plants up the hill that wrapped Willow Glen Boulevard, attempting to find a more natural scene and get a good view of LA.

Spread before me, the hills, buildings and grid of streets, were vague and obscured beneath a pall of pollen-hued smog. A frozen dust storm incubated the city, a miasmic hen brooding on her nest of mutants, soon to peck free of their shells. Sitting on the arid hilltop, I could hear a subdued swoosh of vehicles going up and over Laurel Canyon Boulevard. Ant traffic crept silently along their meandering highway, an insect bend looped near to my foot. The ovoid, turquoise mirrors of empty swimming pools below me shimmered with mixed messages. A jangled sensation of a dozen late night coffees seeped through me. Dissatisfaction, intolerance and a headache bloomed confirming that I was being driven by a bastard breed of chemicals I had taken. A Trojan Chihuahua had cajoled its way through the main gate to start yapping. Another parasitic charlatan, churned-out for the burgeoning commerce of hippie culture.

A blizzard of drugs was drifting across the country and you needed a shovel to find anything genuine. Casually bought highs were a powder bullet, Russian roulette. Acapulco Gold could be used in spaghetti sauce, considering the amount of oregano it could be cut with. Pills and powders could be a round-up of white strays; chalk, Alka Seltzer, Ajax, Drano and a miscellany of pharmaceutical concoctions. It's just a frontier town free-for-all, rustlin' and hustlin' the tenderfoots, who are lining up to buy something to get stoned, anything. Yee-haw!

I remember when Gram took some awful acid.

He arrived at Burrito Manor; I don't know how he got there. He had been having a bad trip and wanted to get out of it, pull the plug and bail out. He had taken Thorazine, to counter the acid and bring himself down. I guess he had been having a rough time and didn't want to be alone. He needed a change of scene or the reassurance of being at home with the guys who he had tripped with over the past couple of years. A pile of rubble, crashed on the living room couch, he sprawled full length, his arm across his face, layin' low and emitting a cadence of long sighs.

Mike Bloomfield happened to be hanging-out that day. He began spouting-off about acid, pontificating on trips. Tripping 101.

"If you're going to do it, you've got to do it. You've got to go with it, where ever it takes you and face up to it. I can't stand these people who take it, like they don't know what it is or what the Hell it's going to do to them and then freak and want to bail out. It's a total cop-out. I mean they shouldn't be fuckin' around with it in the first place."

I didn't know what the purpose of this was, or if Mike was aware of GP lying there or not, maybe so. In a way he was right, it's not a light-weight thing. Too many people are just screwing around. I noticed that Gram couldn't shut the conversation out and unable to ignore Bloomfield, slowly raised his hand, like saying; Okay yeah, count me, I'm one of those people, today. Shut up, Gram.

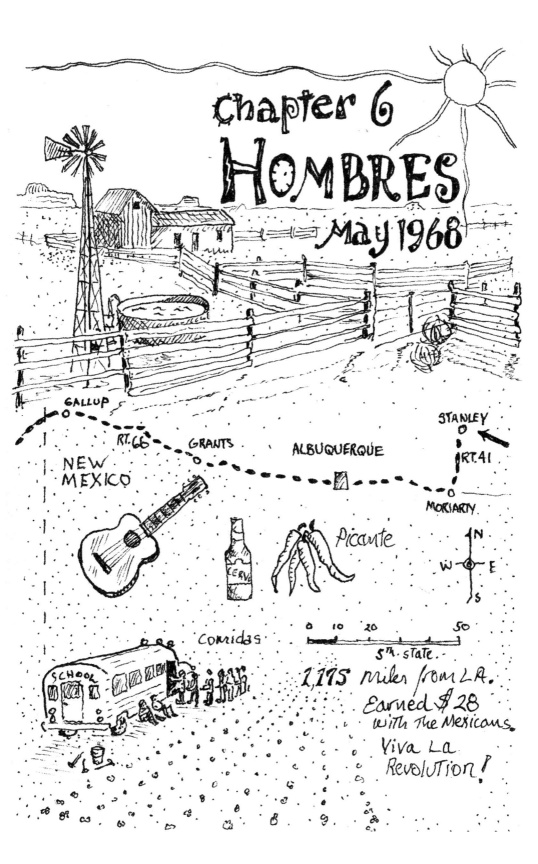

Eleven hundred miles, two and a half weeks behind and LA still chants, where are you going? But that question has died to a whisper here in New Mexico and can't compete with the powerful silence that surrounds the ranch thirty miles south of Santa Fe. Our last campsite was in eastern Arizona and nursing the old vans along Route 66 has been a trek. I had been relieved to recognize the cross roads at Moriarty, the left turn to Stanley and finally the long barbwire-flanked track leading up to the adobe ranch house.

After the drumming engines were cut, crackling and ting-ing with relief, we sit in silence on the edge of a water trough under the windmill. I paddle my hand in the cool water, swish it around then wipe it across my face. The corral, wooden barn, pens and cattle-crush are all from the old days. I remember helping to herd cattle in here for branding, de-horning and shots. This evening the place looks dilapidated, fence rails missing from weary posts. There is no one around. No sign of life on the ranch.

My Uncle's family homesteaded the land in the early twentieth century. The Fishers traveled west from Kansas to claim a quarter section, a hundred and sixty acres, when another area of New Mexico was opened up for settlement. To obtain ownership of the land they had to remain on it for a year. It's no Eden, a barren handout, not much of a prize so they must have had a tough year. The land is inhospitable, the rainfall and fertility are so low that the stocking rate is one head per hundred acres. Once, my Aunt had shown me a photograph of their ancestors striding west, a group of people ahead of a team of horses pulling a covered wagon, shovels, pickaxes, and farm tools lashed to the side. The women wore long heavy skirts and bonnets, one of them held a baby to her chest; my Uncle's father. They were young, ambitious, and I read the determination on the face of the guy leading his family. How could the photo, taken only about sixty years earlier than the first space launch, be any part of the twentieth century? The Fishers struggled, survived and now my cousin is the fourth generation of ranchers settled out here. Isolation, drought, dust storms and cattle that sometimes freeze to death in the winter, are part of his life. The nearest neighbor is a rattlesnake, other homes are specks on the horizon.

I've been to the ranch several times, enough to know some parts of the fifty thousand acres. When I was fourteen, I camped with my cousin in the scrub hills, a couple of miles north of the old adobe home. We saw vultures and buzzards wheeling above and, at dusk, a cougar, who turned his head for a quick glance at the boys trespassing on the boundary of his home. We chased the antelope, springing across the plain with gravity-defying leaps, mocking our 1954 Ford pick-up and the .30-.30 rifle.

I rode Champ, a quarter horse, a veteran of hundreds of roundups, an old hand who knew the routine of herding strays so well that he acted independently, ignoring my greenhorn riding, lack of commands, spurs or balance. My Uncle Leroy was a cowboy. He had the bandy legs of a range rider and had often won prize money at rodeos for roping cattle and riding broncos. I had held onto the parched, dust-beaten rail-planks of the corral while my cousin Louis caromed inside the enclosure, breaking a horse, its snorts and bucking not enough to throw him. Now the pick-up trucks have replaced the horses.

The last time I had visited the ranch was early in '67. I was with two of the guys from The Submarine Band, the guitar player and the drummer, we were driving from New York out to Los Angeles. We had been in New York for more than a year, and the City had thrown down a few crumbs and a couple of singles deals. We were on our way up, young guns heading west, LA was gleaming. A year and a half later, LA and its shine behind me, the ranch seemed to be an oasis of peace with its thick beneficent silence.

"Wow, it's so perfectly still, I bet the acoustics are amazing," Barry T says. He has noticed an electric outlet on an upright timber of the windmill and has walked over to his van and carries a guitar case and the battered Fender Concert, one of the old brown tweed amps from the '50s. The amp's top is scarred with amber burns from dying cigarettes; lit between numbers, they smouldered while we played. The amplifier had been used as an ashtray during long nights at a nightclub in LA, where we slogged through what seemed like a marathon of sets. The comb of burns, is a cuneiform-like tattoo, a prison-wall tally of the nights spent living the blues. Barry slings the strap of the Epiphone semi-acoustic over his shoulder and starts playing simple rhythmic chords that drift out over the prairie, flavoring the evening with a strangely suitable soundtrack, gently animating the tired buildings and ranch yard. The tattered amp is playing to a very different audience.

"Let's try a bit of Tremolo here, now." Chunga, chung, ka, chunga, Chung, chung. The sunset dances.

We are down to a few dollars. I had hoped we might be able to scare-up some work around Stanley. My uncle was a part of the community and he might have been able fix something up for us but his absence makes finding work a different story. We agree that we'll have to look around tomorrow.

We have a campfire burning. The tumbleweed and sagebrush stems crackle and flame under the simmering pinto bean and frankfurter stew. It gets chilly out on the high prairie after sunset, I have to put on another layer but I can still feel the cold on my back as we settle around the fire with our spoons, bowls and glowing faces. A campfire as a daily routine has been an element that separates this new life on the road from our city-slicker past. Fire has been the humans' ally throughout history, it comforts us. A fire is much better than TV, you can watch it and talk, or just shut-up and gaze. The snap of wood burning in the waltzing flames fills any lapse in conversation. Poking around in the bed of coals with sticks, opens a conversation with the fire itself, that responds with cracks, buoyant sparks and smoke signals, an ascending monologue of answers. The lonesome cowboy's oracle.

The morning sun illuminates the space and solitude. With my sketchbook, I wander around the yard, settle down and do several drawings. The stark silhouette of the old windmill is skeletal, its tail folded back against the blades, motionless. The stables are empty. Disheveled corrugated tin sheets must thunder and flap in the dust storms that sweep across the range and herd the tumble weed, piling it against the defeated fences and gates. I drive over to the dusty village of Stanley, to sit and sketch. There is an old hotel, leaning, exasperated. The entrance had swinging doors, one has fallen now, the other frozen on rusted hinges. Inside it is dim but I can see some warped floor boards in the areas that are not covered with dust or tumble weed. Until the '50s, the railroad came through and loads of cattle were shipped out. When the old doors were still swinging there must have been a rowdy babble of railroad hands and cowpokes drinking at the hotel bar, this morning all I can hear is the wind. Empty, with a few traces of lingering ghosts. I remember the ex-movie star's Hollywood mansion and how it had hinted at a vivid past.

On the way to score some pot, we were heading out somewhere toward Studio City. Briggs was driving the Dodge van, he was one of those guys who liked to do the driving.

"It's somewhere, up here," he scanned up ahead. We drove past a high wall and several elaborate gates that advertised big houses within. "I was out here a couple of weeks ago. I got turned-on to this guy by someone I knew from Boston who's living in LA now." Further along the Boulevard Briggs put on the blinker. "Yeah, this is it." We slowed and turned in. The big, stone gateposts were topped by a pair of sculpted eagles, one of the wrought iron gates had collapsed and saplings grew through the bars. The drive went through a front yard the size of a small park, with ornamental palms and tiled pathways.

"They're kinda weird here, but we don't have to stay long."

The rutted, gravel driveway lead to a big house built in the Spanish Colonial style, with a few Gothic flourishes. It could have been home to one of the big movie stars in the old days of Hollywood, someone like George Raft, Peter Lorre or Bogart? There might have been a chain of those big, long-nosed old cars, lined-up, bumper-to-bumper, for cocktail parties, back in the '30s. The dance band could have been set up out here, blaring out 'Tiger Rag' as girls shimmied; wearing thin, lustrous, straight dresses and some of the guys competed to see who might have the moustache that most closely resembled a single stroke of black ink. The large fountain that gushed and splashed back then is dry today.

A young woman who had been sitting on a large, overturned flowerpot stood up as we slid out of the van. She was slight, with bronzed hair, large sunglasses and was swaddled with a purple and violet, Indian bedspread.

She spoke with the energy of an overtired owl. "Hi-i-i-i."

"Hello, how ya doin'. I wanted to see Kel about something."

"Oh-h. Yeah." A breeze ruffled her sheet but, other than that, there wasn't much more of a response.

"Ah, is he in? I spoke to him on the phone about an hour ago."

"Um-m, yeah, he's here," she vaguely confirmed. "Let's go inside." We moved out of the sun into a large hallway. The floor was patterned with faded-poppy-pink and pistachio ice cream-green tiles, a ceramic carpet in the otherwise empty space. Her Indian sandals slapped the tiles as we followed her. "Why don't you wait in this room an' I'll tell him you're here, okay?" She made an apologetic smile as she diminished. The large room was almost empty except for a mattress, covered with a dusty-yellow and royal blue bedspread, a folk guitar that leaned in the corner and flaking paint on the ceiling. Several large, red cushions lay on the floor.

"I guess these are the seats, take a pew." Through the curtain-less French windows, I heard approaching light footsteps. A thin guy in jeans and tie-dye shirt moved past the aperture. Briggs whispered, half to himself, "Come-on-n-n. I don't want to sit here all day." In the distance was the chuck-chuck-chuck of a helicopter. Our little hostess surreptitiously materialised, framed in the dark doorway, like Scotty had beamed her up.

"Kel says, he'll be down, he's just finishing something."

"Okay, we're not goin' anywhere."

"Yeah, right. You're in a band?" she asked.

"Yeah. We play around." Briggs was brief, I had become speechless, the emptiness of the house had seeped-in.

"We've been making mor-re new-w-w songs," she announced. They're more like journeys than songs, each one would fill, like, the whole side of an album. They are such a trip, so, so dee-eep."

"Hm-m."

"The last show we did was a-may-ay-zing. We were up by Santa Cruz. Really, really beautiful. The music was beautiful too. It went on and on and, like, it was almost like it might never, ever end. It was so-o-o groovy. We played just before sunset and that might have been a sign. It was like totally, wow-w. We were playing one of the new songs about these, like, really hip, like, magic animals, who live in this beautiful golden world and they, like, tell people, help them to see, how they can get to that same groovy place. It was amay-ay-zing." Briggs and I had the expressions of tourists, lost in Yokohama, being given directions in unintelligible Japanese. "So, when Sunshine is really getting into this, like, raga guitar thing, up in the sky, coming through the clouds, I saw this huge hand, getting bigger and bigger, reaching down, like it was going to, just, pick us up. Wow! It was, just, like, amazing."

"Well, ah, maybe, you'll get another gig, um, if they, ah, liked you so much."

Rapid footsteps echoed in the tiled hall. A guy wearing only black underpants and a flapping, burgundy bathrobe zoomed through doorway. "Hey, wow. How ya doin'? I was right in the middle of something when Rosie told me you were here. You know how it is." Rosie beamed up at Kel, who bounced slightly, as if he was tuned-in to a Supremes song that was playing somewhere else. He kept up this ducking motion, like riding a very, very gentle horse, his long, dark hair springing in tempo. "Okay, look." He dug into the bathrobe pocket and produced an envelope. "Here you go, amigos. You had some of this before? It's the same stuff. Here, have a peek." Briggs looked into the packet.

"Well, I'd like to taste it, first."

"Okay, sure. It's the same as I had last time." He reached back into the pocket like Captain Kangaroo and handed over a little pipe. "See for yourself. Good stuff. Yeah, so you're in a band right? How's it going?"

"Yeah, okay. Earnin' a living, just about."

"Hey, that's great. I'll have to catch you sometime. Playing at The Troubadour or anywhere?" He asks.

"No, we haven't got anything lined-up there," I replied.

Briggs nodded, after a couple of tokes. "Yeah, okay."

"Yeah, it's the same stuff. I got it from the same guy. Same as last time. Twenty-five, yeah?" The money went into the pocket along with the pipe and lighter. "Hey, I

INTERNATIONAL SUBMARINE BAND

Personal M
Monte
200 West 57th

The International Submarine Band during a busy period of recording and
performing while living in New York. Spring 1966.
Left to right: Mickey Gauvin, Ian Dunlop, Gram Parsons and John Nuese

International Submarine Band around the time of the release of their first single 'The Russians are Coming' (inset). The B-side Truck Drivin' Man was their first country music recording

Far left: John Zacherley – surreal New York horror-show host. The ISB appeared live on his disco-teen tv show in 1966. Left: early '60s chart star Freddy Cannon. The band backed Freddy during a tour of Florida in early '66

Gram Parsons and Ian Dunlop during their time in Laurel Canyon,
the dormitory of rock music, in the spring of 1967

Gas was cheap, with 10.8 gallons costing just $3.80

The author's 1953 Volkswagen microbus which achieved 'dawdling miles-per-hour,' pictured at Lake Mary, Arizona – another campsite on the trip heading away from LA in May 1968

Above: Ian and Gram in New York in 1966 before leaving for Los Angeles. Right: David Crosby was flying with the Byrds. He shared both management and friendship with the International Submarine Band and introduced the author to a preview of a startling new song by The Beatles in 1967

Actor Brandon deWilde was a close friend of Gram and the band

The geodesic domes at the Drop City commune near Trinidad, Colorado were between 25 and 30 feet high

Top: The ISB had a cameo performance in the psychedelic-exploitation film 'The Trip' by Roger Corman that starred Peter Fonda and Dennis Hopper. Above: Stanley, New Mexico, Barry Tashian plays electric guitar plugged-in to a windmill. Left: ISB drummer Mickey Gauvin in Death Valley, California. Right: International Submarine Band publicity shot around the release of the band's second single, 'Sum Up Broke' in the of summer 1966. From left: Gram, Ian, Mickey and John

When drummer Mickey Gauvin and Ian Dunlop recalled one of the Little Rascals 1950s tv shows and Dunlop remembered the name of the show's comedy orchestra he shortened the cumbersome name and Ian, Gram, John and Mickey (left to right) became The International Submarine Band got something goin' on, so-o, see you again, huh. Where did you say you guys were playing?"

"Oh, around. Mostly one-nighters we get from an agent. Usually don't know too far ahead. Yeah. Thanks. We'll see ya."

"Maybe catch you sometime." He said as he backed away, down the hall.

We drove back down the driveway, away from the house, toward the old gates.

"Wow! What a weird place. That chick, is nuts!"

"What's that guy's story? Man, he was jumpy."

"He says he's a record producer but I think he's mostly a dealer."

"Only record he's gonna have is a police record. I think he was a bit of a speed merchant. Man, what a bunch!"

"Yeah. Cal-eye-for-nigh-ay, huh?"

I remember the family who runs the post office and general store in Stanley, New Mexico. I go in to say hello and to ask around about some work. They have already heard that there is a stranger in town with a pencil and paper, doing drawings of trucks and the well drilling rig. I might have been the first artist they had seen in Stanley who was interested in a landscape of collapsing buildings, battered trucks and junk, piled against a background of barbwire and mountains. They are pleased to see me at the post office, remembering me from the time when Granny and old Joe were still around.

They have heard there is some work and if I drive down to Jeff King's place he might need more people for a field gang. It would be worth asking. His place is a mile down the road and I'm able to speak to him. He could use just a few more workers, if we want to show up tomorrow morning at six-thirty.

An intense blue sky and plenty of sun at six-fifteen; a couple dozen Mexican workers wearing sweat-stained straw hats, T-shirts, sleeveless sweatshirts and pants that are torn or patched, lounge under a few stunted trees and regard us with curiosity. We are at the end of a track, running alongside a vast flat field that glows tender-green with young plants; lettuce seedlings, millions of them, needing to be hoed. The Mexicans begin taking tools from the back of a pick-up as the foreman explains the routine to us gringos.

"Ya need to hoe 'em out, leaving about six inches between the plants so they've got room to grow. You get fifty cents a row. We're gonna be goin' 'til late afternoon."

Well, there are a lot of rows, so lots of dollars. The hoes he hands to us are sawn-off, the handles are only about a foot long, designed for the Seven Dwarfs.

The Mexicans have already begun working their way along the rows, the herd of bent backs move like grazing chimps as they chop at the plants. After a few yards into my row I feel that I am several feet too tall. I keep going, guessing and estimating; five inches, six inches, okay, oops, cut the wrong one, hm-m, six inches, chop, a bit too close to the last one. When I look up again the Mexicans are about fifty yards away, they don't seem to be sticking to the six-inch rule. I wonder how long the rows are as I can't really see the far side of the field. The rows are long. I take at least another half-hour to see the end of my row. The foreman has driven around the field, to keep his eye on the six-inch interval, I see his pick-up awaiting us. In the back of the truck there is a milk churn full of orangeade and a box of Dixie Cups, the guys are getting a drink. He leans against the side of the red Ford, his jeans are dark, new-blue. A western shirt with pearlescent snaps, tucked inside his tooled leather belt, reveals a pack of Marlboros in the pocket, his hat shows only the slightest sweat stain.

"Well, how do you like it boys?" he chuckles as we down our drinks, notch-up our first half dollar and notice with despair that most of the Mexicans are already a quarter of the way back across the field.

"I'll see you guys back over the other side," he winks. It is already beginning to get hot and it's not nine yet. I take off my T-shirt. I might have to try tying it around my head soon, Arab style. Soon, the Mexicans gabble as they pass us going the other way and I notice that they are hoeing two or three rows at once. Shit! No one told us that was the way to go. They've got it figured out by now after miles of rows.

What seems like many hours later, I see that an old yellow school bus has arrived. The gang has stopped working, it must be a lunch break. At the end of the row we head to my van for a snack, a Snickers bar and a packet of Red Seal chili potato chips, illustrated in yellow, red and green; a sombrero and a cockerel give the pack the fiesta look. My back already hurts. We'll be lucky to make ten bucks each if we can make it through the afternoon. Both my buddies are dusty, sweat trickles off us.

"Shit, man. How do you feel?" I ask.

"I'm trying not to think about how slowly the money is rollin' in."

"Hombre, hombre. Comida. Ven aca." One of the Mexicans, a short man with Indian features, was smiling and gesturing to us to come and join them. Another guy, Juan Angelo, spoke English.

"Hey, come on over". We rise from the rocky seats and shyly amble over, surprised by their generosity. "Comida." We are each given a battered tin plate and fork and line up with the gang at the front door of the old bus. When my turn comes the tubby, whiskered chef ladles-out rice and beans from two huge blackened pots, dumping them on my plate.

"Muy buen, arroz, frijoles y tortias." He is running with sweat, and beams at me from under a red bandanna; his smile broadens revealing gold teeth and gaps underneath his broom moustache.

"Gracias Señor." The Mexicans are forking down the meal but some of them catch my eye, smile and nod affirming our comradeship. I wonder how many crazy, ex-university boys had joined them for a meal in this setting, right out of Steinbeck, probably not many, it's a novelty for all of us.

One or two of the crew have kept their eyes on us, I guess they are waiting for our hearty approval of the grub. I smile back and go for a fork full. HOLY SHIT! It's like eating a napalm bomb, this stuff is pure fire, where's a drink? Quick! How can these guys work, bent over under this scorching sun, earning fifty cents a row and eat this stuff for consolation? It could be medicinal, to numb the back pain, make the arduous work and heat seem less oppressive, or it's magic, just an essential part of the ritual. Maybe we're eating peyote, or something.

I have succeeded in plummeting from a Hollywood hills life-style to bending my back as a field worker in less time than it takes to say, you fuckin' idiot. Last month I was lounging around by the swimming pool at Brandon DeWilde's house in Topanga or sitting on the beach at Malibu with a movie star's beautiful English wife. Now I was glad to be offered this rough meal, I had fallen from glittering with the stars to rubbing shoulders with wetbacks.

I am just beginning to understand the meaning of all those Jimmy Reed blues shuffles; all that stuff about hard work and toil, the 'Big Boss Man', the chain gang and pickin' cotton. Yes sir, this is really the blues, making a guest appearance in my life today. Here he comes like it or not. One, two, three, four, the whole twelve bars over and over and over again, making sure you've done your home work, and you've rehearsed it enough times and got it down. Each row is another hard-times verse, sung more convincingly than in any club in LA. Anyone can pick up a guitar and bang out the blues; in a penthouse, in the comfort of your living room or kitchen, in the security of suburbia, or sophisticated cities thousands of miles away from the Delta. Here, in the field, like where it all came from, you don't need to worry about buying that guitar. Save your money you're going to need it, the crop won't last forever.

My beat-up tin plate has a patch of rust where the enamel is chipped. I'm sitting on the ground eating scorching chili and drop my bent fork. I reach down for it and wipe it off on the edge of my sneakers. I laugh to myself. Yeah, this is cool. I'm glad I'm here today. I love it. I love the soil, the sweat, the Mexicans and the chili. You can keep your empty Hollywood swimming pools.

Larry Spector, a personal manager, had suggested a contract to me at an appointment in his Beverly Hills office. I had trouble finding the door, along the darkened-glass and stainless steel office façade, I just kept pushing different sections until one finally opened. His regular clients had learned the way in. I waited on a long charcoal leather-and-steel couch that was out of place in what seemed to be a tropical aviary. The room was forested with large jungle plants but there were no toucans or red parrots, just a slender, young, straight-haired blonde with heavy, dark eye shadow sitting behind a desk. Larry finished his meeting, a guy walked out carrying a brief case. He was no one I knew. Could have been an accountant, tax man, a business type. Larry leaned out of the doorway and invited me in. His inner office was a glass enclosure, much like an aquarium, the potted plants, were like seaweed. An expansive cream and chocolate-colored rug, woven by Berbers, who could never have imagined this, covered most of the floor. Larry sat behind a large teak desk, the size of a banquet table, its surface slick and clear except for a diary and a small clock with no numerals. In this office time was too valuable for low numbers.

Larry handled a lot of my friends and acquaintances in LA. A few months ago he had secured The International Submarine Band an appearance in Roger Corman's movie The Trip, with Peter Fonda and Dennis Hopper and recently had put some TV-extra work my way. He had a knack for juggling careers, mortgages and contracts among his clients. If there was an opening, a slot or an opportunity, he'd always try to fill it with one of his guys. It was personal management, entailing complex leap-frogging maneuvers involving cars, properties and, in some cases, relationships. The manipulations appeared to elevate everyone another notch further up. Larry handled some of The Byrds' affairs, he also acted as Gram's personal manager and Gram was now in The Byrds. It worked, just perfectly, for everyone.

Larry wanted to get me on the Hollywood escalator somewhere. He knew that I had left The Submarine Band and might be looking for something else.

"Do you really think that being in a band is the right thing for you? I see you more as an individual," he suggested. "Maybe we could move things along in that direction if you're interested. You're a good-looking guy, don't you realize that? I could arrange some meetings, a photo shoot and screen tests and get you some parts. Why don't you just think it over and we can meet again, to get things rolling. By the way, does your father have a receding hairline?"

I had been offered a place at Hollywood's big banqueting table, the ultra feast, where the courses kept coming, overindulgence was admired and most diners gorged on the riches until they burst. Often the guests' table manners were disgusting. Food, being primarily for entertainment, was ranked fairly low on the priorities, people filled up on prescription uppers and downers. Something stopped me from making that next appointment with Larry. I figured it was about time to get out of the Hollywood pool and think about going for a swim in Walden Pond. Maybe my banquet was destined to be this chili in the battered enamel dish.

The chili must have worked, helping us to hoe our way through the rest of the baking, sun-cured afternoon, increasing our speed back and forth across that vast lettuce field. By the end of the day we'd get a bit more money to get us on the road again. We would be gone soon but the Mexicans would still be here for days, or weeks. This is their Hollywood dream, they will go down through Ciudad Juarez and back home with a load of dollars and a big sense of achievement.

After finishing, while we are saying our shuffling good-byes, one of the gang, Juan Angelo, invites us back to the bunkhouse for a drink. I decide to take their offer and follow the old school bus' dust cloud for several miles through the prairie to a timber shed that is the field gangs' bunkhouse. The interior is mostly wall-to-wall bunk beds, army-green metal frames, shiny under the bare bulbs hanging from a timber roof. A warren of beds, packed so close together that it must take acrobatic agility to settle-in for the night without trampling your neighbor. The room smells spicy and fried. In a lean-to kitchen at the other end of the shed, the radio is tuned-in to a Spanish station playing accordion music. Juan Angelo opens the rusty fridge, reaches in for bottles from the crate of beer, pops a few open and hands me one.

"Cerveza, amigo?"

"Gracias, Señor." I take a swig and the radio sweats out lively Musica del Norte.

"De nada."

I begin to feel like we are in old Mexico, on some little ranchero, in..somewhere.. Chihuahua? I look out through the open door into the evening, where that powerful New Mexican sun is settling itself, getting in position for a searing sunset. Already streaks of gold are banding the western sky heralding a wild finale to a sun-ruled day and I'm glad to say 'bye to that vicious fire God. The sun droops to meet a range of hills, gold clouds mimic the mountains.

Other music has joined the radio in the bunkhouse. One of the field gang is strumming on a battered, abused guitar. One of the strings is knotted down below the sound hole. He plays a few chords, the radio goes dead. A few of the guys clap as he picks out a melody that develops into more flayed chords and flourishes. God! This guy could play! And sing! He starts into a lamentful ballad, I can't catch any of the meaning, it doesn't really matter if I comprehend; it sounds great. I understand the feeling, it makes complete sense. It might be that the hot, passionate food I shared with them is doing the translating. Now, I have Mexico in my stomach.

There's no need for a Marshall stack or wah-wah pedals, this guy and his guitar is the bottom line of expression. A couple of the others, lying on their bunks, join in on a chorus or the parts they know, blending with those sweet, sweet close harmonies, their eyes closed. Spellbinding. Magic. They have me convinced.

"Ole! Ole! Viva la Revolution!! Yeah!" I applaud.

The guitarist smiles, nods. One of the guys says something and the guitarist offers me the guitar. I shrug, but then camaraderie takes over and I reach for it. What the Hell.

"Si, Si, cantas, cantas!' I strum a bit, I'm a terrible guitar player, but I can sing. I give them a bit of the Merle Haggard song,

'I got swingin' doors,

a jukebox and a bar-ar-stool.

My new ho-o-me's got a flashin' neon si-i-ign.'

I manage to get a few laughs anyway. It's a thrill. Oh Yeah! Jamming with the wetbacks, crossing the divide. Amigos. Hermanos.

"Hey, good, amigo." Juan Angelo laughs.

The old man who is helping the cook, looks over at me from under his caterpillar eyebrows. He's got a big nose, a furrowed brow, he tosses his head slightly.

"Trabja mañana?" he asks.

"What'd he say?" I ask Juan Angelo.

"Tio, he wants to know eef you weell work tomorrow." I can see that some of the others guys are waiting to hear my verdict.

"Yeah. I need the money. I gotta go further up the road, a long way to go yet."

"El necessita dinero para vijar." Juan Angelo announces to the room.

"A dondé va?" asks Tio.

"Where you go to?" translates Juan Angelo. I shrug my shoulders, I can't come up with a destination. Tio shakes his head, again.

"A dondé esta su espos y sus niños?" asks Tio.

"Where ees your wife, cheeldren?"

"I don't have a wife or children."

"Nada"

"Otra más de los perdidos," mutters Tio, nodding sagely.

"A-nother one of thee lost."

"Si Tio. Yeah, I'm a bit perdido, I guess."

I swig the last of my beer.

"Mañana amigos. Gracias. Thanks for the beer Juan, I'll see you." Tio waves to me.

"Dios, a los ciegos tú siempre iluminate."

"What did he say?" I ask Juan.

"Dios, He always illuminates thee blind."

"Okay, I hope he does. I'm waiting. Buenas noches. See you guys mañana, huh. "

It's very dark outside the bunkhouse. still. In the distance I hear a diesel, faintly, probably a cattle truck. Yeah, maybe this is illumination.

That night I dream about Mattapoisett, near Cape Cod. Buzzards Bay is sparkling before me under a warm, southwest, summer breeze. Dry seaweed crunches under my bare feet. A large silvery, sparkling bass snakes through the clear shallow water. The beach is almost covered by huge starfish, their arms glow with neon letters forming words; 'BOX, FRIO, UBU, DUST, LIE DOWN, BY, THE'... a wave washes in covering the starfish and undeciphered text.

Two days of field work has given me enough bread for several tanks of gas and the freedom to keep rolling. There are only two directions to go from the ranch, north or east, both good enough for me. There is no sense in backtracking, I'm not feeling pangs or yearning for what I have left behind in LA. Weaving through the Wild West is where I am going. So, let's make it northeast, up through Santa Fe and then Colorado, I have never been up there before and at the moment new places are exactly the right medicine for me.

The old VW has taken me the first thousand miles and, since it is a geriatric, in van years, it should have a health check-up, change the oil, look at the transmission level, fan belts and hope it can do another thousand, or more. For the time being the bus is my home.

I have picked up a few souvenirs during the last couple of days. A large cow skull, bleached white by the sun and a piece of metal, maybe part of an agricultural implement and a tool or ironwork from an old wagon. Its design, with several holes and a twisted finger, is sculptural, I like it. I want to take these artifacts of the range with me and pack them along with the musical instruments, boxes of records, sketch books, clothes and stage outfits that make up my possessions.

I have left lots of things behind, over the Band era, moving from Boston to New York to LA. A ceramic, 50s-design, fondu set for four and an architects drawing desk had been left in Boston. Some furniture, several of my large sculpture-assemblages, a stuffed and mounted seven foot-long blue marlin and a decorative Benelli motor cycle that had occupied my room and stayed in New York. More junk-sculpture, garage sale kitsch curiosities and paintings remained in LA. Collecting and constructing unusual things is my other job but all that stuff seems as easy to forget as it was to acquire. The act of accumulating or creating, piecing together and working in the now was what must have mattered, rather than ownership.

We agree to meet at Raton Pass, a summit in the Sangre de Cristo Mountains on the Colorado state line about two-hundred-and-fifty miles northeast. It could take most of the day, as the roads pass through a mountainous region and these old vans would have to struggle.

"Catch you later." I wave as Barry and Briggs pull away in the old van, creating a wake, then cloud of dust on the dry road leading out to Stanley. Their van is only a speck when it turns right, onto the black top and starts crawling north on Highway 41. I'm looking forward to getting behind the wheel again.

Chapter 7
TRIBES
May 1968

COLORADO

TRINIDAD   DROP
            O CITY

RATON
PASS

NEW
MEXICO

EAGLE
NEST

CIMARRON

TAOS   Palo Flechado
        Pass 9102'

Rt. 64

N
W   E
S
SO

0   10   20

SANTA FE

1,405 miles
Colorado is the 6th
State on the trip.
gas 29¢/gal.

O STANLEY

Santa Fe was one of the colonial outposts of old Mexico and has a small city center of old adobe buildings. Over the years supermarkets, gift shops and restaurants have appeared masquerading in the rough-timber and adobe style. Driving through the colonial-look main street, the sidewalks are busy with tourists, most of them appearing very mid-Western and browsing the shop windows. Everyone seems to be wearing Western-style outfits; cowboy and cowgirl shirts, hats, boots, string ties, and waistcoats. Sunglasses, Bermuda shorts, cameras and a couple of little poodles on leads are also on the scene. I'm heading out to the Pueblo to see the dances and hope that the costumes will be a lot more interesting than the tourist attire.

Rectangular adobe structures radiate baked sienna. The Santa Fe pueblo has grown in a modular fashion, one structure added on to another, extending itself by architectural cell division, to create a cohesive community; cubes, building blocks, multiplying to make a whole. The round end-sections of trees used for the rafters protrude from the top of the walls and the off-cut branches are used to make the rough ladders up to the flat roofs with other rooms and little huts. A rug covering a doorway parts, a woman appears and throws some scraps to her hens in a little pen, the community building houses a few different species.

There are a few sightseers milling around the various stalls selling crafts and gifts. A small woman stands by some rugs draped over a fence of sticks. The rugs and blankets are vibrant, even vibrating. Red, black and white saw-toothed stripes dance around the field of the blanket, zigzagging their way towards a central diamond that struggles to contain jostling yellow and black squares that create a vortex of color. The longer I look, the more engaging it becomes. The rhythm of the blanket wraps me in its dazzle.

"One hundred dollars," she quotes. Hum, a hundred bucks. It looks great, it could be a good, warm companion. A hundred is not too bad for a vehicle to infinity.

Jewelry is spread over a rough tabletop. Rings, bracelets, necklaces, earrings and pins glow silver and turquoise like stars, little constellations, the Pleiades. The stall-holder is wearing a necklace made from chunks of turquoise, it probably weighs a few pounds. I pick up a small ring; very simple, four round bits of turquoise set into silver in perfectly balanced geometry.

"The Zuni people make them. It's the four elements. You like it?" Yeah, I like it. This was our world in microcosm, reduced to fit on my finger. The next stall is bright and beaded. Pin-head-sized beads, threaded in thousands to headbands and bracelets. Chevrons and diamonds race along the length of a belt and collide with a tin buckle, stamped with a Texas longhorn that seems more of a cowboy design than Indian. I pick up a medallion necklace, the beads shaping concentric circles with a pentagram in the center. It is stitched on to a soft leather backing, I turn it over, revealing 'Made in China'.

A crackling little PA announces the ceremonial dance is about to start and soon drumming begins. Several performers have entered a roped-off area and I move closer to get a look. Two guys in jeans are playing hand drums, delivering a steady back-up beat. The older of the two, beating a bigger drum with a bent stick is smoking a cigarette. The dancers are dressed in leather breaches, like chaps, moccasins and feathered headdresses. They shuffle along, bare-chested, in a line. Bracelet and anklet bells jingle, adding to the rhythm. Circling, the dancers chant a repetitive group chorus like gargling. At the end of several verses one of the singers cries out, and really lays it down in a high wavering voice. He's definitely the lead vocalist and manages to get everyone's attention with his passionate outburst. They finish their first number with a shout and a drum flourish, the pattering applause seems too thin for a reward.

'And now the pueblo dancers will do the Eagle dance'. The drummers get into a more up-tempo beat, ba-ba-ba-do-bi-do-bur-r-r-rt, ba-ba-ba-do-bi-do-bur-r-r-rt, on the hand drums as the dancers enter the ring again. A guy is wearing a mask with big eyes and a long red beak, a cape of feathers trails down his back to the ground as he squats. His outstretched arms are inside a framework covered with big feathers, he flaps his wings, stands up and, soars around the dance area, weaving in between the other strutting men. Around me is the cricket clicking of Kodak Instamatics. This is a bit more like it, what the tourists had expected from these dancing Indians, something from the Wild West, too bad they couldn't have fitted-in a tipi somewhere, that would have made a great shot.

After the dancing the announcer informs us that the next dance would be at twelve o'clock. These guys are working a pretty tight schedule, hardly enough time to get in a couple of drinks between sets but I'm sure they would. I knew what it could be like, knocking out the same material night after night but at least, in their case, they were covering the songs of the Gods.

The dancers are going through the crowd and I say to one of them, "Hey man, that was great."

He puts out his hand for a tip.

I walk back past one of the stalls and notice little hand drums, some are baby sized with a fluffy white feather attached. Would that look groovy hanging from my rear view mirror? No, maybe not. I don't want to look too hippie, driving around middle America, no sir. I scan the postcards. Pictures of the pueblo dancers in costume, dark cactus profiled against an exploding sunset, the red and black patterned Gila monster, rattlesnakes and somber portraits of famous Indian chiefs. One caught me, he looks out, right at me, with his stern eyes, no headdress just long gray braided hair, a turquoise necklace and a faded jean work shirt. He looks like he must have been about one-hundred-and-fifty years old, worn, torn and lean but healthy. I pick up the postcard, turn it over, it says, The Medicine Man. This guy definitely looks like he knew something that I didn't. I have found a guru, he's riding with me.

"Hey, how much is this card?"

I head the old bus north out of Santa Fe, on to Route 85 and get ready to slot back into the highway groove, the rhythm of the road and white line fever. Just about time for some of that truck driving music. I switch the radio on and twiddle the knob trying to find a country station.

'I'd like to settle down but they won't let me,

a fugitive must be a rolling stone'. Yeah, Merle Haggard, that'll do.

After moving to New York, The Submarine Band had begun to learn some of the old truck driving standards and by early '66 were using them on our live gigs. We managed to sneak 'Truck Drivin' Man' onto the B-side of a single for Ascot Records, when no one was paying much attention. We often played 'Six Days On The Road', 'Widow Maker' ('Were the words so big, painted on the bumper of a shiny rig'), 'Roll Truck Roll' and other classics that succeeded in confusing our urban audiences and alienating us from the music industry. They might have wondered what we were singing about. Jamming gears, Georgia rigs and all-night truck-stops in west Texas, with juke boxes that only seem to contain records about trucks? We just kept going on and on, doing it. We were hogging the passing lane, highballing down that road to obscurity like sixty, sort of driving on the wrong side of the road at night with no lights. Some people liked us just for that. Gram and I agreed that ridiculous gestures, romantic meandering and jousting with windmills was more important than winning first price at the talent contest.

I'm heading for Route 64 which winds alongside the Rio Grande up towards Taos. I want to cross the route that Jack Kerouac took in the '50s and make my gesture of homage to the wild man Beat poet. I had read bits of Kerouac's On the Road when I was a teenager and his writing had taken me out of my small town and small brain. He had criss-crossed America many times on the old highways and always seemed to be travelling on an eight dollar budget. Now, for me, he has become sanctified.

Kerouac was never on my High school American lit reading list. We had Mark Twain, Washington Irving, maybe James Fenimore Cooper, representing earlier American writing. We looked at a few twentieth century writers like Fitzgerald and Hemmingway but on the English syllabus, in small town New England, the Underground was pretty well buried. Maybe they were not even aware of it.

Eventually the news always leaks out and I had heard about the Beatniks. They lived in New York City, always wore sunglasses, day or night, black clothes and berets. The guys had goatees and listened to weird jazz all the time. They used some of the same language as Elvis and Gene Vincent. All their friends were 'cats' and were 'crazy, man.' They were always digging things, particularly huge splattery paintings, poetry that didn't rhyme, make any sense or had to be read while someone played a flute or bongo drums and lots of other stuff that sounded improbable or impossible. Yeah man, crazy, I dug it.

Some of my friends in high school had heard about a Beatnik coffee house in Boston. One Saturday morning, when we weren't at school, one of the guys borrowed his father's Ford station wagon and we drove into the city to see the Beatniks. At ten a.m. we pulled up outside of the Turk's Head and were disappointed that the place was still locked and the Beatniks hadn't shown-up for breakfast. We waited around for another half-hour but still never got to see them.

The bus coasts down a long hill, out of the Espanola hills toward a valley, I can see the river and a road sign. Taos is forty-five miles. In about an hour I'll cross Kerouac's cold trail and pay respects to one of my tribe's elders. The Godfathers of the underground, the alternative society, are becoming more important to me as I feel increasing alienation with mainstream American society and its elected leaders. I'm from a privileged class; a white boy on the road, even if I was slightly on the run as well. It was almost impossible for me to know how those Indians at the pueblo must have felt about living in Lyndon Johnson's 'Great Society'.

Last week, on Route 160, up near the Black Mesa in northwest Arizona, I had driven through Tuba City, a dry, dusty shambles of a place. I can't remember even if there was a speed limit, it was so insignificant. Approaching, I slowed down to have a look at the little desert village. There were a couple of featureless, low, concrete block buildings with bars across the windows like a military barracks or jail. A few old, very beat-up pick-ups were parked randomly along the side of the road, the dust and mud splatters made them a uniform color matching a couple of cars that were even more trashed. Figures, shapes were strewn against the walls. They were people, sitting, huddled or leaning against the buildings, squatting, even lying on the sidewalk. No one was walking or standing. I could see a few cowboy hats and baseball caps on the heads that were hunched down between their shoulders. Some were wrapped in blankets or big coats; I couldn't tell if they were men or women.

There were no shops, no window displays, nothing for sale. No TVs, record players, refrigerators, sports coats, freezers, toasters, waffle irons or Jefferson Airplane LPs. Nothing proclaimed 'SALE NOW!! 25% OFF!! ON EVERYTHING!!' No tennis or golfing items. There was no sound. The only movements were dogs, a couple were tracking me another was sniffing the back tire of a truck and a scrawny brown bitch was taking a pee but the rest of them were crashed-out like their masters. A pick-up came from the other direction, a few people in the cab, more sitting in the back with a couple of dusty, camel-colored sheep. I drove past a semblance of a church, Christ the.. something or other. What must have been planned as a sports facility, a weed invaded blacktop patch, had a listing pole with a basketball hoop and glistened with broken glass. Another couple of wrecked cars later and I had rolled past the limits of Tuba City. I was going slowly now and saw the sign on the other side of the road; TUBA CITY, Navajo Reservation, Dept. of Indian Affairs. What a place! What a mess, what the Hell have we done! What did these people do to deserve this?

Tuba City didn't look like the USA that I knew. Not a sign of the land of opportunity, with freedom and justice for all, it seemed like I had landed in a refugee camp. The American Indians were the originals, the landlords of the whole vast country. Until about a hundred years ago they still ruled the West. In Massachusetts, where I grew up, a majority of the places and towns had Indian names; Achusnett, Naragansett, Weeweeantic, Sconticut, Mattapoisett, loads of them. There must have been a vast history but I never knew anything much about the people who lived there, except that some of the Massachusetts coastal tribes were the Pequot.

Massasoit, a chief, leader, or maybe just a compassionate good hearted guy, bailed the pilgrims out of trouble when they were about to starve to death during their first winter at the Plymouth colony. They must have been pretty hopeless, considering all the mussels, clams, quahogs, crabs, lobsters, bass, scup, bluefish and flounders that filled the bays and clustered around beaches in those days. I remember a large bronze statue of Massasoit in Boston, out in front of the Shawmut Bank. He was memorialized astride his horse, arching back, arms outstretched, face raised upward as if addressing his God. He was probably saying, 'What the fuck have I done! I should have let them starve.' His grandson tried to lead a rebellion but by then it was way too late.

Did the government expect that Indian residents of Tuba City, who could be drafted, would be willing to proudly serve their country in Vietnam? They had already been dealt such a bad hand, for generations. I bet any young guy who was given his draft papers would hoof it, off into the hills and hide out.

As I head up the road, the surrounding country looks bleak and empty except for the occasional shack or tarpaper and tin-roofed hut and a couple of wrecked vans. There is no green. No grass, corn fields, pumpkin patches, orchards, animals or agriculture and there isn't a golf course in sight. This was desolate, a society in ruins but without the pyramids. Maybe I was just getting a glimpse, a stilted view, I just happened to come by at the wrong time. I might have just missed the good days when there were festivities, parades, chicken barbecues and pool parties. When there were people gathered around tables laid out with cakes, pies, strawberry ice cream, trifle, lobsters and pork chops and they had hired a guy with a PA and all the kids were dancing around to songs by The Turtles. Maybe it was just a bad day in Tuba City.

I fiddle with the radio, 'Last night police clashed with demonstrators at an anti-war rally at the University of Colorado. Police authorities reported several injuries and eighty-five people were arrested. In Washington, a spokesman for the Secretary of Defense gave details of another successful bombing mission on Hanoi. And the outlook for the listening area for this afternoon; it will remain dry with highs in the upper seventies, tonight; clear with a low of fifty-five'. Now is the time for the whole family to pay a visit to Bronco Toyota and see those BEAUTIFL sixty-eight Coronas. We've got the cars, we've got the LOW, LOW prices, so come on out and make yourself a deal, free balloons for all the kids, that's Bronco Toyota, 33 60 West Boca Gordo Avenue; Los Alamos; come and RIDE the Bronco'.

Route 64 winds along the valley, sometimes with large hills and mountains on each side. The old VW is pretty slow in the hills and never has the guts to pass the smoking semis. I have learned to settle in with the trucks, shift down into third gear, give it a bit more gas and maybe edge past if they are really crawling. The VW's supposed thirty-six horsepower seemed to be an over estimate.

Taos is spread over a couple of rolling hills and looks luxuriant with adobe houses, some green trees in between and that rich, red New Mexican soil. At the edge of town there are a few potteries with studio ceramics and sculptures displayed outside. In front of one house is a sculpture, like a totem pole, a pillar of heads and faces. Mythological creatures, animals and birds, beaks, wings and tails protrude from the tree trunk-sized pile with bright, shining glazes. A pinto horse stands in a small corral next door. A few people are sitting on a porch, the sign in front says, Out West Art Gallery. On display are a couple of large, exploding abstract paintings. A group of hippie kids walking along the roadside wear tie-dye T-shirts, Indian headbands, ragged jeans and are barefoot. A large peace sign banner is draped on the street-facing wall of another place. In the driveway is a blue Ford Eco-o-line van with a paint job, huge white daisies with yellow smiling centers. Anna's Café advertises vegetarian meals and the adjoining bakery has home baked wholemeal bread, date and walnut cake, sunflower and pumpkin seed muffins. A guy with a long beard rides on his bicycle. He has wire-framed sunglasses and looks like Alan Ginsberg. Taos appears like a town that had been zoned; arty and alternative.

I stop at a small gas station to fill up. In the windows are posters announcing; 'Stop the War, Dance, Friday, the Rainbow Café, with Rattlesnake Blues and guests'. Hand written signs offer; 'Yoga classes (Monday nights at the elementary school)'. 'For Sale Martin guitar $275. English Bike 26" $30'. 'Tarot card readings by Karla'. "62 VW beetle new brakes $400'. 'Lost female tabby cat, answers to 'Tripper', $5 reward". Playpen, free'. 'Aura readings'. 'Bass player/singer wanted, must be willing to go to the other side'. Hum, maybe I could get a gig here, but I guess I have already spent enough time on the other side.

I don't see a hell of a lot of Cadillacs, lawyers, accountants or men in gray suits, it's not that sort of place. Taos seems like a town that is going against the grain of modern America and nonconformity had become the norm, where a majority of the citizens are eating brown rice during their breaks from yoga, tarot cards and guitar lessons. Maybe it is a reversal in conformity and it could be difficult if you didn't take your aura readings seriously enough. Taos sure seems a lot healthier than LA and more positive than Tuba City. You could probably always find a banjo player for your bluegrass band, a healthy meal and even the gas station sells several brands of rolling papers. Taos was known as an artists' colony way back in the '50s when Kerouac visited and I wondered if it was more eccentric then. I bet the local bar has a jukebox that would play Peter, Paul and Mary and Joan Baez.

I have to stay on Route 64 out of Taos, that will take me northwest through some high mountains. Palo Flechedo pass is up ahead and the altitude is over nine thousand feet, it's going to be a slow trip to Raton Pass and the Colorado boarder. Probably Barry is a few hours ahead of me. There is no way that I can just goose it and catch up, I'll just have to settle back and enjoy the few hours of daylight I have left.

I always have a good view when driving the old VW bus. The seat is right over the front wheels, quite upright and eye level is about the same as standing. It has taken some time to get used to the frightening feeling of the road rushing towards me, since there is no long, flat engine hood like most cars that offers a sense of protection. It feels a bit like being right up in the bow of a boat. You really want to avoid crashing into

trees, on-coming trucks or even a daffodil, when you're driving one of these things.
Just about an eighth-of-an-inch of steel is all that shields me, only a bit more than a
Vespa motor scooter. A bluegrass band, Jim and Jesse, did a novelty song about VWs;

'There's a diesel on my tail
doing ninety miles an hour,
my reflection in the mirror is mighty pale,
can this compact take the impact
of the diesel on my tail'.

I have 'The Medicine Man' postcard that I bought in Santa Fe pueblo pinned to the
sun visor and hope that he will be watching over me.

The Burritos had worked with a couple of guys who were Indians, or part Indian
blood. They were from Oklahoma, around Tulsa. They might have been Shawnee, or
Chickasha or who knows. They were great western blues musicians. Junior (Jimmy)
Markham had a dusty, parched voice, played dirty, down in the alley harmonica, and
a bit of trumpet. He had cut a bunch of tracks with 'Indian' Ed Davis. When we went
out as a six-piece, Junior sometimes played trumpet along with Bobby Keys on tenor
sax making a classic soul band sound. Junior could sing all those Otis Redding things.
I particularly liked doing 'I've been Loving You Too Long'. It took a lot of control to get
that one right, but when we did… yeah man! You had to play it very sparsely, give it
space, the modulations and especially the coda, were cool.

'No I just can't stop now. Please, please, no, no, don't let me stop now'. Yeah, Jimmy
was surely one hell of a great soulful singer.

Indian Ed had long, straight black hair, dark eyes and sharp, strong features. He
always seemed to wear blue jeans, cowboy boots, a checkered shirt and brown leather
jacket. We first met at an audition for a gig at the Topanga Corral in the fall of '67. The
Burritos were looking for the gig and so was Junior's gang of Okies. Leon Russell, Billy
Boatman, Jimmy Karstein and Indian Ed were in a group that Junior had put together
for the audition. Some of them were part of Junior's shifting line-ups of the Main
Street Blues Band. They were good, like really good. I could tell that as soon as they
started playing 'Man Or Mouse'. It wasn't going to be easy getting this gig. Could be
a bit of a battle. Indian Ed was very cool, he didn't jump around on stage, just stayed
locked into his Fender Telecaster, looking down, his eyes narrowed and smiling or
grimacing as he tossed out those amazing licks. He played with a small slide on his
little finger and jumped back and forth between picking notes and sliding. He had a
cool, distinctive style. I remember looking across our beers on the table at Barry T and

both of us rolled our eyes, I mouthed 'Wow'.

The Okies played a few more blues songs at the audition and we applauded them all. When they finished their set we went over to say hi. I wanted to meet them. I could feel the talent a mile away. We got up to do a short set, knowing that this was a challenge and threw in a couple of numbers that might impress the other guys; The old Ray Charles tune 'Maryanne', that had a nice time change in the bridge and Albert King's 'You Upsets Me Baby', with its accented, ascending-scale intro. We threw in a couple of pop numbers that got the bar staff dancing and we got the gig.

We started doing a few gigs with Junior and that's how I met Bobby Keys. Bobby was from Lubbock, Texas and he actually knew Buddy Holly. He told me about the first time he'd met Holly, who was driving a brand new Buick convertible. When Bobby came over to the car to say hi, he saw a case of beer on the back seat. 'Man they were just driving around, opening one beer after another,' Bobby had told me. That must have been the seminal moment in young Bobby's life. That booze, that car, rock 'n' roll, he was converted. He fell down on his knees, right there and then, raised his hands up towards heaven and cried, 'Yeah Lord, gimme a load of that!'

"Kicks! Hell, I'll tell you about kicks!" Bobby Keys shouted out of the side of his square face. Most of Bobby's comments or observations were announced in a burst of fired-up Texas drawl at the distorted level of a police megaphone. "Hell! We used to take LSD, go out to the fairground, get on that damn roller coaster, have a slug of whiskey and when we got up the hill, Hell, we'd snap one of them amyl-nitrates! Just as we go over the top, we'd stand up in the damn car! God damn it, I'll tell ya, that's kicks! Hell, man. That is kicks!"

Bobby raised a beer to lubricate his larynx. He stood with a wide stance, leaning back slightly, compensating for the weight of the tenor sax that hung from a strap around his neck. We weren't having a competition about who could come up with the best kicks story. We were supposed to be running through songs, working out parts for some new material, now that The Burrito Brothers had expanded to include Bobby, his sax and his shouting. If it had been a kicks play-off, I guess he would have walked away with the prize under his arm. It beat Mickey's tale about a band he had been in. They had overslept, awoke in the swamp of a hangover, to remember that they had a gig in South Carolina later that day. Their car barely dipped under a hundred when they hit the road but it didn't quite make-it round a bend and went ploughing through a tobacco field, somewhere south of Charlotte. Bobby's acid experiences made my trips, sitting on the bank of the River Charles, watching ripples, seem spinelessly placid, even though, at the time, I felt as though I was riding a roller coaster.

We were rehearsing some numbers that were up-tempo, good for dancing and featured the sax. Otis Redding's version of 'Shake' was on the list.When asked if he knew the tune, Bobby yelled, 'Why, Hell yeah, I can play the God damned song with one hand tied behind me! Heh, heh, heh. Loose as a goose. What key you want it in? Aw Hell, just count it off.' Bobby frequently added a bit of a nursery rhyme to a count-in, drunk or sober he'd chant 'buckle ma shoe', after the 'one, two'. Bobby fit-in with us just fine, he knew all the old '50s rock 'n' roll, blues and soul music. He might have seemed like he couldn't give a shit and just wanted to coast along with one hand tied behind his back but where there was a challenge, a difficult part to learn, he'd tackle it. Bobby would scrunch-up his face, clamp his eyes shut and blow. 'Just lemme hear that again, one time. I gotta get that together.' He didn't have to keep his eyes open, we never used any sheet music; only occasionally did anyone need to write out chords.

Some of the clubs where we played found that having Bobby in the band was a good investment. He played great, rocking sax, no doubt about that but if a club was a bit empty Bobby could immediately improve the ambience by filling the room with echoing 'Haw-haw-haws' and would get the bar rolling for the night, calling out, 'Okay, how 'bout a bit of service down here? Hell, I'm just about dried-up here waitin' on a drink. Is anybody workin' at this place?' On some of the long nights at clubs, Bobby would revive the sluggish bar staff by making the cash register play 'Jingle Bells'. Several times, on pay day, or pay night, when we settled-up after working a club for a week, Bobby managed to finish the week owing. Because of his heavy bar tab, on one of his whiskey weeks, the alcohol he had knocked back had exceeded his pay. 'What! That cain't be right!' he would argue, but it was. On one late Saturday night Bobby insisted, 'You add that up a'gin!' When the barman relented and got out his pencil, it turned out that he had made an error and Bobby was even deeper in the hole. But sometimes, by the end of the second set, with a couple more hours still to play, the rest of the band would have come around to Bobby's point of view and wanted some fast bar service but we lagged behind in decibels.

At the end of one gig, Bobby, sitting in the back of the van, was bellowing out suggestions of what we should do next, or directions for getting to an impossible, three a.m. destination. 'Hell, ah know there's a party goin' on somewhere. Where was it? Damn! I can't remember. Why don't you just try takin' a left up here. Come-on man. There must be something goin' on. Hell, what's the matter with you guys? Shit, I'm jest gettin' goin' now.' Some of us were dozing off on the ride home but Bobby would be looking for some action. 'Aw, let's go find us some whores! Man, that's what I need, haw. Come-on we're in the right neighborhood, just stop, if you can see anyone. Ask 'em where we can find us some whores. Hell man, I sure could use some of that black cherry pie, tonight.' Sometimes, Bobby's blaring sounded like his rasping sax, it was the same song.

The saxophone had been banished from the music scene as the '50s music faded. The horn had been one of the loudest voices of jump, r 'n' b, blues and doo-wop, shouting, screeching and crying out, Go-Go- Go! The last white bands that used a sax all the time were Duane Eddy and The Rebels, Johnny and The Hurricanes, The Champs, The Royal Tones and a few other instrumental bands. Early '60s surf music was all guitars and reverb. The Beatles, The Rolling Stones and other English bands didn't use a horn. The poor old sax had been sentenced to exile, back to the ghetto, in the hands of the black guys who blew it in multiples. The old warrior, scarred from so many victories, was being retired, no longer suitable for pop music that wanted guitars, guitars, guitars.

The sax was too difficult, a bit too funky, something that had to go, if you wanted to clean-up the neighborhood, like getting the beggars and hoodlums off the streets. There was too much of the ranting crazy guy or the incoherent wino in the sax's voice. As folk began to fuse with rock the sax was elbowed out, it never made it up on the stage at the Newport Folk Festival. The sax sang with just a bit too much of a lowlife sound for the college folkies, too primitive, I guess. After hundreds of gigs with The Refugees I had put my sax in the case when I started playing bass in '64.

The Burritos wanted some of that old sax sound. We had an inclination, like The Submarine Band, to play old-fashioned American music. It was reactionary, moving away from the happening thing in rock music. We were listening to Fats Domino not Sgt. Pepper and Bobby Keys knew the music and played it with the voice of the Dust Bowl.

Bobby was a joker, laughed a lot, christened people with silly nick names and often came to the craziest conclusions, laying them down in his west Texas drawl. One night, after floating himself into a transcendental, dimension-free consciousness, Bobby decided to 'phone up Mezz Mezrow, the hepcat jazz trumpeter and author of Really The Blues. Mezz had died awhile ago but Bobby wouldn't take a 'no' from the operator when she couldn't find a listing for Mezz in the Chicago phonebook. He wouldn't give up, 'Well, Hell, operator, try St. Louis then!' He was determined to get through to Mezz, it was no good trying to stop him, he believed he could get there.

Bobby could play sax in that New Orleans rock 'n' roll style and he had a great Bill Doggett, sleazy lounge tone when he wanted to pull that one out. He would close his eyes, chomp down on the mouth piece, his face would crease up, his neck would swell as he blew a cloud that contained the essence of ashtrays, spilt drinks, broken promises, bad deals, old cars and big talk out of the bell of his horn.

He was a great ally on stage, even more valuable when we were playing some of those LA dives, making his entertaining, satirical comments about people in the crowd or the bar staff and coaxing appropriately goofy sounds out of his sax. When we'd rush to the bar after the first set he'd say, 'Wale boys, o-o-o-only three more hours to go', knocking back his whiskey, slamming the glass down, 'Hit me again dealer'.

For a while it seemed we were indentured to Peacock Alley and were there for weeks. To relieve the tedium we'd occasionally all swap instruments to finish the set. We called it 'Musical Instruments'; play one song then pass the guitar or horn on to the next guy or sit down at the piano or drums and have some fun. Right opposite, on a wall above the bar was a clock reflecting back each minute, a torturous location, as it sometimes seemed to get stuck at twelve-forty-five, I finally trained myself not to see it.

Outside of Peacock Alley, around midnight, a bit further down the street away from the club entrance where the light was dim, we leaned against a wall, back in the shadows, passing along a joint. I spotted a couple of black guys coming along the sidewalk. You never knew what was up. One guy leaned in and in a velvety voice asked,

"Whacha boys got goin' here, huh?"

"A little bit of Colombian, you want a hit?"

"Yeah, al-l-lright. Pf-f-f-f-f-f-f-f-f-f-ft. um."

He passed it over to his buddy and exhaled,

"Ah-h-h-h-h, yeah." The other guy did the same and passed it back.

"Yeah."

"Okay, Yeah."

"Later, man, later."

We could have passed it on over to Mezz Mezrow, he would have dug it.

We would usually finish playing there at two a.m. and if we were ravenous, might swing through Watts to one of the late night soul food joints. A favorite was The Golden Bird, for their fried chicken, sweet potatoes and collard greens, oh yes indeed! or The Rib Pit for barbecue and cornbread. Occasionally we'd get razzed a bit, a few hostile glares, but mostly it was a pretty mellow night time scene, just a few hungry night owls, black or white. We never really got any hassle, maybe we were lucky. Maybe the Muslims or the Panthers just didn't dig that old fashioned Southern food.

After late food, driving home and, like a school bus, dropping-off guys in the band at different locations we often wouldn't get back to Burrito Manor 'til three a.m. or later. I usually stayed up late, maybe conking out about dawn and sleeping into the afternoon. For awhile I was on regular breakfast of Jell-O and Gallo wine that seemed just about appropriate to get a good start for another day in the Hollywood hills. It was an easy meal to throw together if I remembered to get it in the fridge the night before and it had the added appeal of being so bright and decorative, raspberry red, lime green or lemon yellow. I sometimes dropped little items into the gel when it was partially set; Grapes, cherries, M&Ms, and sometimes pharmaceuticals, black beauties or Seconal always looked good. Now, I'm getting used to the daytime, early bird routines, sleeping at night when you're supposed to and enjoying the sun.

Thin rows of clouds, like strung beads, are glowing gold in the last light of a pumpkin sunset. The snow-capped peaks of the Sangre de Christo Mountains reflect the warm rays as I grind uphill towards Raton Pass, at last, only a few minutes away. It's just about dark when the old bus finally makes the summit. I pull into the rest area and cruise through the parking lot, past cars, the truck-lot to a section where motor homes, campers and vans are lined up. There is the old white van. Barry and Briggs had found a picnic table site and have the camping stove going. It feels like home, I guess home can be anyplace where there is a meal coming together.

"Hey how ya doin'? It took me a bit longer than I thought, I stopped in Santa Fe and Taos."

"Yeah, we just drove right through Santa Fe, it was full of tourists. We've only been here for awhile, had a bit a trouble with the van. It over-heated when we got into these mountains, there might be a radiator hose that's cracked, I'm going to look at it in the daylight, I can't bother with that shit now," Briggs explained. He was good with cars and engines. He used to have a hot rod in high school and belonged to a gang of hot rod heads, The Downshifters. Since then he has ridden bikes; motor cycles. Before leaving LA he had dismantled his B.S.A. 650, the motor and other bits were in their van and the frame was roped onto roof rack of my VW. Both vans were loaded down. It was a bit of a wagon train, plodding along, but heading east, a direction that could be considered as the wrong way.

"I was thinking about Bobby and Junior awhile ago, I wondered if Junior did that crazy gig in Alaska?"

"Man, they're welcome to it if they want to keep doing shit like going to Alaska to do a week at an Air Force base and playing the lousiest LA clubs," said Briggs. "Screw that."

After the months of playing dives, bars and weird clubs around LA, The Burritos had started pulling some better gigs. We had our act together, the band was tight, we had played some big clubs and showcase venues. We had settled down into a groove. The band's name hit people the right way and they liked the old jump/blues/rock'n'roll style that we could pump out. We had been offered a slot in a big festival that was being put together for the summer of '68 and that had led to disagreement about what sort of line-up would be best and who might not fit in. Band politics, kangaroo court. At about the same time, Junior got offered a gig by some plaid-suited agent: 'A week at a military base in Alaska, not great money and ya gotta get back to me by eight tonight'.

We had come to a cross road and were faced with a decision of whether to scrape by doing loads of lousy gigs that would pay the rent, climb back onto the music biz ladder or go and live in a treehouse. It was a choice that we had kept avoiding. Being outsiders with no ambitions had been a relief after the disappointments of major label record deals, tours and expensive mismanagement. The Flying Burrito Brothers had been our dropout flophouse. A couple of months ago Barry, Briggs and I had been walking on Sunset Boulevard when a few teenagers drove by in a convertible, one of them pointed and shouted to the others, 'Hey, it's The Flying Burrito Brothers!' we were actually shocked by being recognized.

"Yeah, I guess Junior is one of those people who are on that 'I- want-to-BE-the-blues' trip. I had enough of Peacock Alley, man, I couldn't have done another night down there. Honky-tonked to death. That fucking clock on the wall, over the bar; the club owner with his toupee and his mascara moustache."

"You think that's what it was? I always thought that moustache looked weird. It was hard to take him seriously, with the worn-out tux jacket and red cummerbund."

"'When are you boys gonna learn some new songs? You're still playing that Fats Domino stuff,'" Briggs mimicked. "Well I'm not doing anymore of those gigs. We're going to get back on the college circuit." Barry lifts the pot lid and stirs the red bean stew.

A big tape recorder was whizzing round. Dozens of cables and leads draped over the edge of a table, snaked across the floor and up to a console. A guy with shoulder length hair and a beard was pushing a fader up, just a little bit at a time. The speakers were pushing out a punchy, sort of, gospel-blues shuffle. He jabbed a button on the console and an electric, slide guitar cut in over the rhythm track with a rusty, distorted sound. Man, they had a groove going on. We were at Leon Russell's house on Skyhill Drive to cut some tracks with Junior Markham.

I had met Leon once before at the Topanga Corral one afternoon when several bands were auditioning for a gig. Junior knew Leon from back in Oklahoma where they used to play together in the early '60s. Through Bobby Keys and Junior we had got to know some of the Okies who were in LA doing gigs and we sat-in or hung out with some of them. Junior had done some recordings and had a couple of records out. The blues singles he had cut had something different and original about them. The music was blues but it had something else, a Western feel somewhere inside of it. I remember liking the name Junior used on the singles, The Tulsa Rhythm Review.

With the track playing, Leon spoke slowly "Well, I'm tryin' out this guitar part in the chorus." He listened for a moment. "Yeah. I like it. Think we're gonna go with it. We had another guitar, it wasn't so trashy. I like this one better."

"Damn! It's nasty," agreed Junior. Leon was recording an album and doing it all in his own house. The studio was small, the house wasn't very big. All the recording equipment was stacked on tables and chairs in the crowded control room. Out in the living room/studio, wires trailed across the floor to mic stands, headphones and amps. There were a couple of easy chairs against the wall and a stack of magazines.

"We're shakin' it now. Got more down in the last couple of days," Leon remarked. I was amazed to see this set up and that someone could do their recordings at home. Even though we had done a lot of messing with tape recorders, the ISB had never tried recording at home. Recording seemed to involve a lot of fancy mics and expensive equipment. It suddenly became obvious that this was how you did it. You didn't have to go to some strange place and rush through songs, working with people who acted like science lab technicians.

While we were setting up, Ed Davis came into the studio and greeted Junior

"You all met Ed?" Junior patted him on the back, "He's going to get a bit o' guitar goin' on."

Leon came out of the control room. "What you lookin' for here?" he asked Junior.

"Well, Just straight ahead and snaky, I 'spose."

"We'll go on an' see what it's soundin' like, live. We can always put some harp on later if you're gonna want it. He looked around the room. "We gonna put the drums in the broom closet. You plug-in the bass and use that amp inside that baffle wall there. Yeah. All the mics are pretty much set."

We had played through the song Junior wanted to cut, 'Divin' Duck', at Burrito Manor, so had a bit of a handle on it. The bass and guitar played a line together that was like a slower version of 'Lucille'. When everyone was set up or plugged-in, we had a run through to get some levels. The song had a cut-off, choked ending that had to be clean.

Barry T and Indian Ed were going over the licks, figuring out who would play what. We had a run through the changes.

Junior shook his head, "We gotta tighten this up. We got to get it right in the pocket, it's not in that pocket yet." Junior leaned over to me,

"Ian. I need you to get a bit more poke in that bass." He smiled, "Put some more lard in the fryin' pan." We went for a take. Junior wasn't satisfied. "Damn! We gotta get a bit more rattlesnake goin' on. Can you get a bit more fire under that snare drum? Okay." The tape was rewound for another pass. "Okay, don't lose it. It's right here." Junior bobbed his head and snapped his fingers. "I got it, right here, one-two, one-two."

The next take sounded good. Someone lit a cigarette.

"You all mind not smokin' in the studio." Several of us stepped outside for a break.

"I think that sounds good, man." I said to Junior.

"Well, we can't take all day. Leon's doin' me a favor. We'll see how it sounds. We can't take much more o' his time. I don't want to get too far in the doghouse." We went in to hear a play back. The rhythm sounded together. Ed Davis had played some glistening slide licks on his Telecaster.

"Well. I think you got what you got," Leon summed up laconically.

"I might want to sing it again."

"Well, Junior, you could do that if you want." Junior didn't immediately say 'yes'. "Well, I believe you gonna have to sleep on it then."

"I don't know, Leon. Will it make my dreams a whole lot better?"

At Raton Pass, we decide that we would go to visit Drop City, a commune that is somewhere near Trinidad, Colorado, an hour or so from here. Brandon had told me about Drop City and had shown me some film that he had shot there with his Super-8 movie camera. He had been there about a half-a-year ago so they might still have the community going. Drop City was a place where people were living outside of American society and building these strange dome houses. The short film that I had seen looked interesting, the houses were like big kaleidoscope patterned igloos. I'd like to see it and check out what they were doing there.

It didn't take long to reach Trinidad, Colorado, only about thirty miles, most of it down hill from high mountains at Raton Pass into the rolling foothills. Outside of Trinidad, there was a choice of roads. There weren't any big signs saying, 'Only Two More Miles To DROP CITY, Fun for all the family. Visit our gift shop'. It wasn't Disneyland, these people were trying to get away from it all. I knew my hunch about taking the road due east was right when I saw the cluster of round shapes. Across the range ahead a track from the state road winds towards the settlement and ends at a wooden perimeter fence.

There aren't any cars inside the fence except on old Mercury station wagon that looks half buried, one of the earlier settlers' vehicles that only just made it here and expired. There are a few people around.

"Hi. Is it okay if we come in?" I call over to a woman. She waves us over.

"How are you doing?" she says, when we are closer.

"Yeah, fine, okay. What a wild place."

"Yeah, we like it. A bit windy sometimes though."

We introduce ourselves as, by now, a few more have gathered to check out the visitors, they probably have had a few and want to make an assessment of us. Briggs asks if anyone would like to smoke a joint, he has something hidden in the van.

"Yeah okay, that would be great", a guy with a long pony-tail replies, "but, we've just got to step off of the property to do that. We can't have any dope inside." They aren't against it, maybe they have rules to protect themselves and don't want to risk getting busted. I bet the local cops could give them some grief, but maybe they've been here long enough and people have got use to them. The West did seem to have its share of desert rats. I'd seen all sorts of odd settlements in the Mojave or out towards Joshua Tree - shacks, old trailers, Quonset huts.

We sat down in a group on the warm dry ground. Briggs rolls a couple and they get passed around. From a distance I can see about eight domes. A couple of others are under construction, just the skeletal framework and there are a few other small cabins or sheds. They are geodesic domes based on the Buckminster Fuller design, a theoretically perfect shape. A couple of them are big, maybe twenty-five or thirty feet high and at least forty feet across, at the base. The outside skin is not really round and is actually a lot of triangular sections that fit together to make pentagonal and hexagonal sections. They seem, to my eye, to keep disagreeing or changing and rearranging from one geometric shape to the other and I haven't even had a hit on that joint.

There are several little kids around the place and the community has their own school system, or teaching methods worked out. One of the women, Kate, has a degree from U.C.L.A. and has done a few years teaching in San Francisco. She is the official teacher but they worked on the principle that everyone has something individual or special that is worth passing on.

"Cooking, playing music, telling stories, nature, your own family history or travel. Just about anything is education, the regular schools out there are just too closed minded, they shut people off, instead of turning them on. They don't really care what harm they're doing to kids." Yeah, I could see that.

Another guy has dropped out of medical school and is studying alternative medicine. He talks about medicinal herbs, roots, plants and the Chinese and Indian methods that involve applying pressure to specific points on the body, Homeopathy and other practices.

"The doctors, the hospitals, they've stopped seeing the whole person, all they look at is the isolated manifestation of the problem. If you've got an ulcer they give you medicine, they don't say 'stop eating all those hamburgers'. If you can't sleep and you're anxious they don't say 'hey, change your life you're on the road to a heart attack'. They'll just give Librium or Tofranil and say, 'now you'll be fine, 'bye.' A lot of the remedies are here, they were discovered centuries ago, they just don't fit in with today's medical industry'.

One of the domes is Siamesed, connected to its duplicate by a passage. Each of the twin domes is a hemisphere but appears to be a jumble of squares, triangles and pentangles. Mismatched windows are fitted into the roof following the odd angles and it's a patchwork of colors. On top of each dome is square box structure, maybe vents or chimneys. This place probably would get pretty hot in the summer and could get plenty of snow in winter. I see a porch area under the eaves of the irregular roof.

"Hey, if there's anything left on that roach pass it over this way." Luke, radiating a halo of curly hair, had been in a Bay Area band, Ninth Earth, but he has dropped out of the psychedelic music scene up there. He must miss the grass, it's probably not so easy to get out here. "We opened up for Quicksilver at the Avalon, played at a couple of places in Mill Valley, Sausalito, you know. We started recording an album but then the record company shut us down, said we were taking too much time, shit, we wanted to do something really different but hey, they don't know which ways is up." He goes on with his take on the music scene. "Then one of the guys took some bad acid or something and got locked up in the loony bin; a really bad scene. Somebody broke into our rehearsal room and stole all of our equipment."

"Wow what a drag."

"Screw that scene, my girlfriend's brother Jamie was out here, so we left 'Frisco a couple of months ago."

"You don't want to go back?" I ask.

"No way, glad to get out of there. Everybody's doing way too many drugs. They don't even know what they're taking any more, could be speed cut with Ajax."

"Yeah, it's nuts."

"We're building that dome over there on the end. We're going to get it covered-over by the end of summer. You want to have a look, I'll show you around."

"Okay, see you in a bit."

"Thanks for the smoke, yeah. Now I'm just about set up to bang in some nails."

The smoke session breaks up and we walk towards the domes. The structures really look like a set for a science fiction movie, like the planet Zong, or where ever it was that Buck Rogers or Commander Cody and the Lost Planet Airmen used to go, in those old black and white films. Maybe it looks a bit like Mars, with the mountains and the dusty red soil. If we all were wearing metallic jumpsuits, bubble helmets and air tanks it would be very convincing.

"Do you want a drink of water?" Kate asks as we near the twin dome that must have been her place. "Here, I'll get you some."

I peer through the doorway, my eyes adjust to the shade.

"Oh, would you like to see inside?" and she motions me in with a sweep of her hand.

"Yeah sure, I've never seen one of these before." It seems dark at first but daylight comes through the diamond shaped windows to illuminate most of the downstairs living area. The walls are covered with fabrics, batik, and Indian bedspreads with all those tiny mirrors. There is a poster of an Indian God, with blue skin and rows of arms, and he is sitting in a huge white flower. She fills a couple of glasses at the sink.

"There was a well and tank in the old farm and we ran pipes underground. They're going to dig a trench, running to Luke and Anna's new place. We've got electricity here but Adam is working on a system that will run on a windmill, a generator. He's going to hook up a load of truck batteries, and then he can use lights from cars, you can get all that from a junkyard."

"Wow, that's a great idea." I tell her. These people are getting it all worked out, using materials that you could get for almost nothing. There aren't any stores around here anyway.

"Adam is going to try to get completely away from money and monthly bills from the electric company. He won't be able to have toasters or dishwashers or TV working on the windmill system but he's already got a Hi Fi with a bunch of car radio speakers running off a battery. He's really an inventor in disguise."

There is a chunky, steep, wooden staircase leading up to a loft that covers about half of the open space above us. The flue pipe from the potbelly wood stove goes straight up through it. I can see the nail heads that fix the stair treads in place. The kitchen counter and cupboards have been knocked together from planks that had to be sawn to fit the odd angles of the dome's interior. They were carpenters as well, doing everything for themselves.

"The other dome is the bedroom, it can get a bit chilly in the winter but it's not too bad. After awhile you just get used to it, you know, it's got everything we need. I've been here for about a year and a half. Last July I went back to Oakland and did a summer school job and that took care of our bills for a while."

I wondered what they did with money around here, if it is a commune, if they have to share everything. That was one of the problems that arose when you lived a co-op, or tribal life style. When The Submarine Band shared a house in New York, the money from gigs always seemed to have to go towards the rent and the next priority was getting hold of some high class dope. New York necessities, I guess. There was never much cash left over after that.

I am enjoying the gypsy life, travelling with my buddies but being alone a lot is a change. Living day after day, rehearsing and gigging with the same people, began to get to me after two-and-a-half years in that routine. There were more people here in Drop City, than in a band, so they might not have had the same problems, squabbles or taking sides. I had heard of an art colony that existed near Woodstock, New York, Byrdcliffe. Founded in the early twentieth century, it was big, a hundred people, maybe more, who were all doing arts and crafts work. They had studios, a farm for their own food and tried to live a simple life away from the wound-up, frantic city and concentrated on their art. But Byrdcliffe failed. Another Utopia down the drain, like Animal Farm. Maybe the most successful commune was The Munsters.

Outside, I look across the dry rolling plain, the foothills and beyond to the snow capped mountain peaks. There is almost nothing else in sight, except a small group of farm buildings, over a mile away. The slash of road leading back to Trinidad is empty. A magpie croaks and then flashes black-white-black-white-black-white as it flies. It is quiet out here.

Bam, bam, bam, bam. Metallic drumming thunders, behind me.

I turn and see a figure, bent over on top of the largest dome. Wham, bam he starts hammering again. I walk towards the dome, scaled with white, sky blue, red and black triangles. The geometric pattern seems to shuffle, an optical illusion, the meeting points of the triangles become stars. I reach out and touch the skin, it is metal, the colors are from the car paint. The sections are welded together along the seams. I step back, call up to the guy on the roof:

"Is this made completely out of cars?"

"Yeah. Hoods, roofs, doors, trunks, anything, as long as it's pretty flat. The best thing is the side of a van, they're easier to handle."

There must have been a dozen car bodies incorporated into this dome. No big problem, since there could be millions of cars in junk yards all over America and they were still rolling off the assembly line in Detroit twenty-four hours a day. More and more and more all the time. If a space ship flew over, the aliens would probably think that the car was the dominant species on Earth.

"Where are you from?" he asks, as he straddles the top of his metal planet.

"I just left LA a few weeks ago, heading back to New England", I keep my story simple. "I wanted to come by here to see what was happening, a friend of mine told me about you guys, it looks great."

"I'd never go back to LA, that place is screwed, the smog and fumes. The traffic on the freeways! And now riots again, what a mess. Pretty soon no one's going to want to stay in LA, they better get their asses out of there, before the next earthquake." He knows the score on Los Angeles.

"Yeah I was glad to get out of there. It was okay for a while but it just got too weird for me as well. You know, most of them love it, they all think they died and went to heaven, you couldn't drag them away. The weather was pretty good," I remembered, "That's one thing about LA, but, I don't know, there's got to be something else."

"There's more and more people who want to come out here. I heard from a couple of friends of mine the other day, they've had enough of all that pollution and crap in LA, they're going to drive out soon, they'll love it. Look at the sky! The color, crystal clear, always is. At night, the stars are so bright it's almost like moonlight, you can hardly see stars in LA with all the millions of lights that are on all the time. They could probably run all of Africa on how much electricity they waste in one night in Southern California."

He's probably right. I can remember looking down from Mulholland Drive. The big, flat LA grid of lights, stretching away on one side, Encino and the Valley on the other, all the Avenues blazing. Typical of LA, trying to outshine the heavens, boasting, 'All the stars are right down here!'

I hadn't noticed the guy who is standing, slightly behind me and has been listening to our conversation. He wasn't around earlier. He is small, has short hair, wears wire-rimmed glasses and is generally more clean-cut than the other guys.

"Hi, how you doing?" I greet him. "This dome is fantastic."

"Yes, it's the largest one in the community. How did you hear about us, were you just passing by?"

"No, I was interested in seeing this place. A friend of mine told me about Drop City, he came by here last year. He showed me some film he'd shot with a little movie camera, it looked good. We just came through New Mexico and were near so, thought we'd have a look."

"Who was your friend, what was his name?" He's making a bit of an inquiry out of this.

"Brandon. He was with another guy, maybe in September or October, last year. Do you remember him?"

"Oh yeah", he replies. "You know the CIA came around later looking for him."

"What!? Are you kidding, are you sure?" This is ridiculous. He must be puttin' me on. There was no way the CIA would be chasing around after Brandon, like he was a KGB spy, come on. This guy must be reading too many James Bond novels, or he's imagining things, seeing spooks, the Bogey man in his closet, the headless horseman at the end of the bridge, afraid of his own shadow. Maybe it's paranoia, there's a lot of it around lately. Stoned-out people getting all sorts of messages from UFO's, Nostrodamos, the I Ching or Indian predictions.

"Hey, well, I hope the CIA don't hassle you anymore, huh."

I turn back to the guy on the roof.

"Did this cost you much to build?"

"No, not much money, just time. It's mostly all been used and is waiting around to be salvaged. Everybody throws too much away, things are obsolete before you know it, at least that's what they try to tell us, trying to sell us on the idea that you're nothing unless you have more and more possessions."

"Yeah. Spend, spend, spend."

"The dumps are filling up, they're taking all sorts of toxic stuff out to sea and heaving it over the side, even radioactive stuff. Man, I bet pollution is going to get us before the Russians do."

"Yeah, it's all big business, advertising, consumerism, money, money, money," I chorus.

"Those are the sins today, I don't know when people will finally get the message through their thick skulls, you can't just keep treating the Earth like an ashtray," he sums up, "sooner or later something's got to give."

"Yeah, it's pretty scary. Hey, we're going to hit the road. Good talking to you, I hope everything goes okay, maybe see you again. Next time, huh?"

"Sure. I hope you have a good trip and find a place you want to be in. "Bye." He gives me a big arching wave from on top of the dome.

"Bye." I like him. I agree with what he's saying, how the USA is heading down a dead end road of pollution. He is making a stand, against the world's biggest economy, the land of squandering, the Kingdom of Waste.

They might not of had much land, they were building their domes quite close to each other, yet there was so much space around them. The emptiness of the West might be something that intimidates people who have come from the city, making them feel that they have to huddle together for companionship and warmth. Dependence might be one way to define a community. Drop City wasn't a ghetto, with people all piled on top of each other like an ant colony, but it was clustered. That's probably what they wanted. I'd like a bit more space if I were going to live out West, you might as well get some of that wide-open trip, if that's what is on offer.

I wave 'bye to a couple of people as I wander back to the van.

We look at the road map deciding on our route.

"Looks like 160 east, maybe about a hundred-and-fifty miles to the Kansas boarder," suggests Briggs. "Depends if we want to do some miles or not. How 'bout we meet-up outside of Ulysses, Kansas? See what we feel like then. Okay?"

I get back on the road, the land is flattening out and I can still see the tops of the domes several miles away. They shine in the mid-day sun, maybe it's that car paint that makes the flashes, like a lighthouse. Beacons in the middle of nowhere.

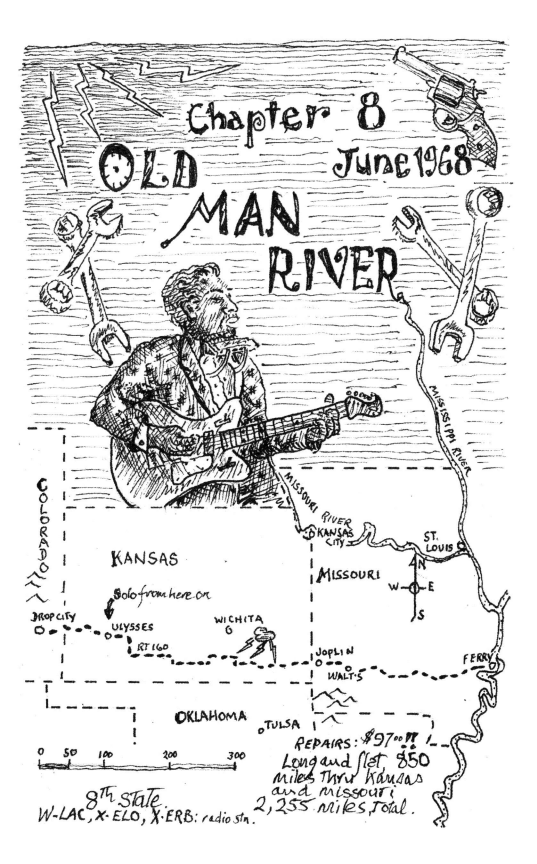

Drop City had a lot of good qualities and ideas kicking around. It was a village of inventions, they were building a community out of dreams and junk. They were throwing away the rulebook and living outside of the constraints and standards of mainstream America, laying down their own laws. Maybe some of them had moved to Drop City out of fear that the world was about to end. There seem to be a lot of those apocalyptic predictions that come and go.

I remember a little End of the World party at Brandon's place in Topanga a few months ago. There was a rumor going 'round that an ancient Hopi Indian prophet had predicted the final curtain, or end of a cycle, in February of '68. When that day rolled around we had decided to see the old world out, sitting on a roof terrace, taking the opportunity to get a bit of a last minute tan. Drinking Cinzano-and-soda and smoking Acapulco Gold, we reminisced about the good times we had shared during the last few years and things we had not done or experienced. Everything becomes more important when you think you might have missed your last chance.

"Man, I sure would have liked to have fucked Chris' wife, she was nice. I liked her little English ass," Brandon confessed.

"Well, I won't have to go to that dentist appointment on Wednesday."

"Too bad we won't be able to watch Star Trek later tonight." Gram was on tour with The Byrds. It was a shame he wouldn't be with his old buddies when the big switch was thrown and we all got shut off. We raised our glasses to Gram, wherever he was. We passed an acoustic guitar around and sang a few songs. One of them, a George Jones tune about being born out of darkness and, appropriately, 'It's Over' by Orbison. It was a beautiful sunset, a couple of hours after the moment of oblivion had passed us by.

What I think of as The West, out-West or the Wild West is almost behind me now. There are so many characteristics of the West that I like; the vastness, the monumental, dramatic deserts, mountains, canyons and the colors. Man! All so overpowering, yet still. You can get lost in space and silence out there if that's what you want. I don't know how long I could live out there like a hermit, feeling like a flea in that gigantic atmosphere. In the van I'm a gypsy moving through it, just having a taste of everything; the dust, wind and sun in my eyes, the boulders, mountains and sand under my feet.

Rolling east, away from the Rocky mountain chain, the old VW putters along through the foothills of eastern Colorado towards Kansas and the great central plain of the USA. It's a dramatic change of scene. The bus will have an easier time on the hundreds of miles of flat roads ahead; it's almost like surfing, catching a wave across the plains to the Mississippi Valley. There are no more mountains to cross and the roads are so straight I barely have to turn the steering wheel.

In western Kansas I pass a crude sign, 'Last gas for Fifty miles'. I somehow recognize it. I've seen the scrawled blue letters and the hunched stick figure, carrying a red gas-can somewhere else. I've never been on this road before or in this part of Kansas. Is the sign from a dream highway or is it déjà vu? Weird. It seems familiar. Then I remember seeing it in one of Brandon's road trip films. He had shot rolls of Super-8 film in the fall of '67, during a drive from New York to LA. He had stopped at Drop City on that journey. Brandon must have been on the same road, but was heading the other way. I remember sitting in a small room in his house in Topanga where Brandon had a projector set up. We had watched the images of winding roads, hitchhikers, roadside signs and hobos that he had filmed while hanging out of the car window holding the camera.

As we watched, Brandon gave a film editing monologue; "Yeah, I'll cut that bit with the 'Welcome to the land of opportunity' sign and splice it in, just before the section with the old hobo sitting on a truck tire holding an empty bottle. That would be great." Brandon wanted to edit the dozen or more reels down to about ten minutes. He had an idea for a short film presenting a candid portrait of the middle of America.

Brandon had some footage of the Submarine Band rehearsing and hanging out when we were in Vermont and he had also brought the camera to a couple of our gigs in New York. He had home movies that he had shot when he was working on the sets of some the major league movies he had appeared in. We once watched some film from '65, when they were shooting In Harms Way. The movie had a big cast; John Wayne, Kirk Douglas, Henry Fonda, Burgess Meridith, Larry Hagman, etc. Harms Way was set in World War II. Brandon played a young Navy officer about to go into action.

"Okay, watch this," Brandon had chuckled as the film started. On the screen was a harbor. A launch is alongside a wharf where cameras, soundmen, flood lights, technicians are ready to shoot. A guy slams the clapper board and Kirk Douglas jumps into the boat. "Okay, look at him," Brandon narrates, "watch." Kirk Douglas puts his foot up on the engine box, drapes his arm over his knee, crouches forward and sets his face to determination, narrowing his eyes at the horizon. "Who does he think he's supposed to be? Christopher Columbus, Leif Erickson, George Washington crossing the Delaware?" Brandon's shot tracks the launch as it pulls away then swings back over to the dock where a few of the film crew are bent over laughing at the hammy seafarer characterization.

There was more footage of John Wayne, trying to light a cigarette and mouthing swears as each match was blown out by the wind, Henry Fonda waving, then trying to hide his face as Brandon moved in.

"I remember that was a bad day. Otto Preminger was in a lousy mood. We could always tell the days when he didn't get a blow-job that morning. He could be nasty then." A guy exploded into a huge toothy grin and winked, Brandon laughed. "Larry Hagman and I would get so stoned sometimes. One day we were really zonked. We were finished and had smoked some DMT. The room was whirling around and someone knocked on the door saying they needed Larry for one more shot. He couldn't walk. We didn't want to open the door, you know how much that stuff stinks. We said, 'Wait a minute, okay, Larry's not feeling well.' They said, 'Oh, shall I get a doctor?' We were saying, 'No, no, he's feeling better already.' We were stalling, waiting to come down."

Brandon also had some film of a trip to the Bahamas where he met The Beatles. The bit of film looked like some of the scenes out of 'Help!' They were working on that movie at the time. The screen showed some of The Beatles sitting on a terrace ringed by a stacked wall of coral. Palm trees, waved like windmills, against a bright blue sky. A black waiter is bringing over a tray of drinks and George Harrison jumps up, grabs hold of the edge of the tray as if it were piled up with concrete blocks.

Brandon said "I wish I had shot more of them but I felt self conscious. I mean that's all everybody does with the Beatles, they must get sick of cameras. I really wanted to talk to them a bit more."

One of the clips I enjoyed most from Brandon's home movies was a sequence he had shot in Vermont. We were sitting in a car and Brandon spotted two nuns on the other side of the street as they approached us. Brandon grabbed the camera and decided to shoot them in slow motion. The nuns were chubby and soft, their black habits rippled and swayed like some dark seaweed, deep underwater. Passing through patches of sunlight, their fleshy cheeks and double chins kept the slow rhythm of their retarded pace as they moved gently up and down, rising and falling like a carousel. The film was an amazing image of motion.

In New York we often used to hang out with Brandon and spent many good times talking, joking and getting stoned. The later the hour the deeper the conversations would sink into strange territory delving into politics, music and culture.

Gram, Brandon and I had been sitting at the kitchen table in the house in the Bronx. We had smoked something and had been listening to Ray Charles and then Buck Owens. Brandon was talking about a John Mayall record he had bought.

"Another blues band. It was all blues. Good, I guess, but you know how it sounds a bit like the last blues band you heard."

"Yeah, everybody is trying so hard to sound black. Playin' the blues. But they're not bothering to black-up, like Al Jolson or the old minstrel acts. You know, they might as well. They'd believe themselves even more, every time they looked in the mirror. 'Yeah, man, lookit me, I'm a bluesman.'" Gram giggled.

"Shee-it, I wuz pickin' cotton wit mah pappy, down on de Delta, 'afore ah wents to school. Yas suh," Brandon drawled.

"So what are we going do if we're playin' country 'n' western?" I wondered. "I guess we gonna have to white-up. M-m. How do we do that? Smear on a layer of toothpaste, white shoe polish, cold cream? Get a ten-gallon hat, cowboy chaps and drag a big cactus on stage."

"Well, we're already part of the way there, we're white, that'll save time and money on make-up."

"It is sort of funny, if you give a white kid a guitar and watch which way he goes, like, what he's gonna choose, he'll probably start tryin' to play like Muddy Waters, or B.B. King. As if no white guys ever did anything. Forget Elvis, Jerry lee, Link Wray, Carl Perkins or, ah, Lonnie Mack," Gram suggested.

"Or Hank Williams, Jimmy Rogers. In a way, that's what's good about The Beatles, it's English. They played a Chuck Berry song on one of their first records, but mostly they are just being what they are, English."

"Same with The Beach Boys; California, surf, cars, high school, they play and sing about what they are. Like they're surfers from Malibu, or where ever and they're not pretending they're from Chicago or Detroit," I said.

"It takes a while to see, that even though you can sing r 'n' b, it's fun, it's music, I mean, it's great music," Gram paused. "But, in the morning, when you're washin' your face or brushin' your teeth, standing in front of the bathroom mirror, it's hard not to notice that you are white. It shouldn't come as a surprise."

"E-ee-k! Las' night, I swear I was playin' 'Stormy Monday', this moanin', holy shit!" Brandon acted being astounded, "I'm white! My roots are showin'! But you know, you can slip into this thing about being white, like being embarrassed because you're white."

"What do you mean?"

"Because of the hundreds of years of stupid presidents, fat bankers, tycoons, generals and slave owners and all of the Wild West heroes who, mostly, just went around exterminating Indians and buffalo. Jesus, with all of that history it's pretty hard, going around being white."

"Well, there must be enough cool white guys to balance out all the complete assholes?" I hope.

"In history?" asked Brandon

"Well yeah, or anytime. It looks like we're a bit desperate here. We need to have a tally to see how it adds up."

"Okay. Aristotle.."

"No, no, not ancient Greece, were talkin' about America."

"Okay, let's see. Mark Twain, W.C. Fields, James Dean, ah, Buster Keaton, Marlon Brando, Tennessee Williams, um.." Brandon gets in a few actors.

"Elmer Gantry, Bruce Wayne, Batman..," Gram adds.

"Hey, come-on. Only real people count."

"Ralph Waldo Emerson, Melville, ah, Spike Jones, Jerry Lee Lewis, Jack Kerouac..," Gram cited.

"Is this cool? Or crazy?"

"Well, they're sort of a blend. It's better that way."

"Orson Wells and the guy who does the cartoon voices, Mel Blanc. Um-m, Stan Lee, Stan Kenton, William Burroughs, definitely, Mose Alison. And artists; Jackson Pollack, Edward Hopper, de Kooning, Jasper Johns, Winslow Homer, Bruce Conner..," I suggest

"Then there's a load of musicians. Bill Evans, Gerry Mulligan, Brubeck, Carl Perkins, Gene Vincent, ah, Elvis, can't leave him out."

"Jimmy Clanton." I offer.

"Jimmy Clanton?"

"Yeah. I think he was cool."

"Well, that's better. There are quite a few of 'em, settin' a good example. But, in a way, they are all sort of obscure. Musicians, writers, artists. If you asked somebody in the street, in Ohio, or just about anywhere, who Jasper Johns or Mose Alison is, I bet ninety-nine percent of them never would have heard of either one of those guys. They'd say, 'Who?' Wouldn't have any idea who you were talking about."

"M-m, probably not. Are there any statues in Central Park of Spike Jones or Tennessee Williams? Hell, no. It's gonna be Ulysses S. Grant, J. Edgar Hoover, one of the Rockefellers, maybe Roosevelt, I guess. You know, Gene Vincent isn't on the five dollar bill."

"Be-bob-a-five-buck," Gram sang.

"Imagine a dollar bill that was designed by Jackson Pollack or with that Marilyn Monroe, by Andy Warhol on the back, in yellow and purple."

"Yeah, when you think about it, the whole US government needs to go to a Madison Avenue agency to get their image updated," Brandon suggested. "The whole thing needs to start over again. There are just too many years of crap, fat guys wearing suits and civil war beards. No wonder being white is so embarrassing, sometimes."

"Makes you feel like going around with a big button or a sign, around your neck that says, 'Hey don't blame me, I didn't make this society.'"

"We're white and country is, sort of, the white mans' form of blues. All that music pretty much comes from the same place, the South, it's just that the different neighborhoods came up with a different take on things," Gram said.

"Well, we've been listening to black and white music all our lives," I said. "When I was about ten, I first started hearing records that my friends' older brothers and sisters were playing. There were all those black vocal groups. The Gee-Clefs, The Orioles, The Cadillacs, Frankie Lymon as well as Ray Charles, Fats Domino, Jackie Wilson, hundreds of 'em. Chuck Berry, Bo Diddley. And, there was Elvis and all the white guys. When you think about it, there was a lot of country and the rock 'n' roll was, just about, half country anyway."

"A lot of that stuff got wiped-out when Frankie Avalon and people like that took over. Suddenly music was coming out of Philadelphia. A lot of the black music was about new dances, The Twist, The Pony, Mashed Potatoes. That's all the lyrics were about, the message was, grab your partner and do the new dance steps."

"Wha-a-a, wha-wha-tutsi," Brandon chipped in.

"The black and white music, from about ten years ago, was a lot closer together than people think. It got divided up and separated by people stickin' the word 'race' on it," Gram said.

"When we did those radio interviews, in Florida, last spring, a guy at one of the stations gave me a whole stack of gospel 45s," I remember. "Incredible stuff. He told me, 'We get a ton of records like these, they send 'em out to all the stations, but you can only play those on a Negro station.'"

"I bet they've got another garbage can full of country records and they'd say they could only play 'em on a Hillbilly station."

"Hey, man, I'd take 'em all off their hands. It's almost worth doin' another trip down South. We heard some fuckin' great music down there didn't we?"

"Yeah fantastic," Gram agreed. "When you found the stations that were playin country and r 'n' b, no corny pop music, just all real American, Southern stuff. Yeah, a knock out."

"Well Whitey, you-all want to smoke some of this?"

"Sure Pelbert, lets have a puff."

"We don't want you getting' any whiter."

"Hey, too late now," Gram shrugged his shoulders. "This is what we are. Might as well go along with it. We're stuck with it. You gotta just accept yourself for what you are. Like, I'm white, I sound white, I sing white. Doesn't mean I can't sing or don't have anything to say."

That was one of those late nights with Pelbert J. Long and Lulu Round; my two friends' pseudonyms.

In the fall of '65 Gram had introduced me to his buddy, Brandon DeWilde. They had bumped into each other earlier that year while shopping for drugs. Both of them had been introduced to an exclusive uptown dealer, known for his line in high-quality hashish. A lot of his clientele were established jazz musicians and the deals were quantity, no nickel and dime stuff. He could cater for a whole band, getting ready to go on tour.

In the summer of '65 Gram had moved to New York and was living in an apartment in the West Village. He hung-out, meeting new faces on the music scene and began playing at the Village clubs and cafes. Gram was writing songs and trying them on for size anywhere he could perform.

Brandon had begun to write songs as, being an actor, he had time-off between gigs, movie shoots or TV. His early roles had elevated him to child-star status. His part, in the Broadway adaptation of Carson McCullers' A Member of the Wedding, was highly acclaimed and, at about seven years old, he was hailed as a natural. He went to Hollywood, to do a movie version of A Member of the Wedding, and won a golden globe.

Brandon came from a theatrical family, his mother was an actress and his father was a stage manager. Soon after playing the Wedding, Brandon had a lead role in the Oscar-winning Western, Shane. Marlon Brando might be remembered by one of his lines in 'The Wild One'; when asked, 'Johnny, what are you rebelling against?' Brando snaps back with, 'Wha d'ya got?' DeWilde had trouble escaping from his famous line; 'Shane, Shane, come back!' Show-biz wanted to keep Brandon perpetually nine years old, blonde and innocent.

In '66, Shane was showing in a mid-town New York theatre and the Subs and Brandon had gone down to see it. Master DeWilde flashed up on the screen, peeking-out from behind a bush at the stranger who just rode into the homestead. The image promoted giggles, from us.

In stage whisper Brandon demanded, "Okay, I'm a kid. Just get used to it. Quit the giggling or I'm not going to be able to stay here."

I could see that Brandon was concentrating, more interested in what happened off-camera and what might be evoked to provide some clues for dealing with child-star syndrome.

Music was new turf for Brandon to plough, there was no type casting in a zone where he was free from the template of his acting career. He could use his voice rather than a face from the past. Brandon and Gram hung-out during the summer they first met, playing, singing and shopping for that uptown hash.

Brandon and his wife Susan had bought a small farm near White River Junction, in the hills of Vermont. They went up to the little white farmhouse to get out of the city for a taste of the New England countryside and escape the smell of a New York heat wave. Along a gravel road, tucked between the hills, the farmhouse had a big stone fireplace, creaky floorboards and an old-style kitchen. Brandon often visited the old mills, smithys and barns that had been converted to antique shops looking for curiosities, old hats and tintype photos. Enamelled signs offered or stated; Cream of Wheat, Boots repaired 5¢, Gentlemen Only. He picked up an old autograph book from the early twentieth century, flipped it open and read the flowery dedications written in an elaborate cursive hand, and laughed. He brought the little book back to New York.

Gram and Brandon were siting at the old pine table in the small kitchen of Brandon's 10th Avenue apartment. The dinner plates, pushed aside, gave way to ashtrays and elbows. Brandon lit an Old Gold and showed Gram the autograph book. Gram glanced over a couple of pages, concentrating to unravel the faded messages. The stilted sentimentality moved on to an ironic stage when delivered by a contemporary voice.

'When e-e-evenings are dark, and y-y-y-ou-ou feel alone,

the ones who clear y-y-ou-r-r shadows,

are right in y-y-ou-r-r swee-ee-t home.' Gram and Brandon got into it, taking turns reading and characterizing the maxims, dramatizing the proverbs and mangling the platitudes.

'When shadows fall, a-a-a-nd memories call…Hello? Hello?'

The autographs and the roses-are-red-violets-are-blue verses seemed to have been penned primarily by two writers. As they turned over the pages, the same names appeared repeatedly. Most of the book was a two-way correspondence between two characters with names that could have been dreamt-up by the Loony Tunes animation department; Pelbert J. Long and Lulu Round. Gram and Brandon played with the characters;

'Oh Pelbert, how do you contrive such romantic delusions?'

'Well Lulu, I always wear a straw hat that is three sizes too small, that is how we stimulate the brain, up here in Rutland.'

Brandon and Gram decided that opening the vault to release these two playful spirits was the most important event of that day and appropriated the pseudonyms. Over the years the nicknames from the Vermont autograph book stuck and, within our circle, Gram was known as Lulu Round and Brandon was Pelbert J. Long. These alter egos would emerge during home-recording sessions, late-night poker games and acid trips. I can't remember Lulu or Pelbert showing-up recently, they could have been a remnant from different times, before things started going a bit crazy in LA.

The flat plains enable the old vans to cover more distance in less time and as planned we rendezvous outside of Ulysses, Kansas. The old Chevy van is parked where I could see it, on the side of the road by a gas station and café. The screen door bangs shut behind me. Barry and Briggs are sitting down at the end of the counter with cups of coffee, looking at a road map.

"Hi. Looks like I'm just in time."

"Hey. I guess you were only a few miles behind us. Grab a stool and have a coffee."

"Yeah, I could use one, maybe a sandwich or something as well. Hey that was a good run, pretty quick. I thought we'd be longer getting here."

"No hills, you can really cover some ground when you can do sixty all the time. All those mountains in New Mexico, man, were we slow back there," Briggs remembers.

A trucker sitting further down the counter is slurping a big bowl of soup. It looks good and I order a split pea and ham soup.

"I don't know where to aim for next?" I say idly. "Never thought much about being in Kansas before."

"Well, I don't know. We've been talkin' about the route on the way here, we're not sure what to do."

"What do you mean?"

"Well, we still have a lo-o-ong way to go and we're seeing our money disappearing, getting sucked into the gas tank. The van uses a lot more gas than your VW."

"We're wondering if the best thing for us to do, might be lookin' for the most direct route back east. It's still a long haul," Barry T adds.

"Yeah?"

"If we have a breakdown or have to buy parts, we're gonna be screwed. We could, just about, make it back with the bread we've got, if we just keep goin' and don't make any more detours."

"Gee. I don't know if I want to do that. It would take a couple of days, or more, from here, even goin' straight through. I'd have to stop to sleep," I figured.

"At least fifteen hundred miles. But, the two of us, could just keep swappin' over, doing the driving, and keep going. If we wander around and keep stopping all over the place, like we've been doing, we're gonna run outta cash."

The counter waitress pours us another cup of coffee. I sip and think it over. I'm enjoying this meandering journey, more than enjoying, I need it, there is so much more to see. Right now this is it, what I'm living, the degree I'm earning, the trail I'm following or creating or dreaming-up. It's a bit of both, the highways are there, they exist, but I'm choosing different roads like strands to weave into the fabric, making a random pattern. I don't want to get on a white-line marathon, driving straight-through, back to the East Coast. That's what all those truck drivin' songs are about; get back to the wife, drink gallons of coffee, push, push, push! To what? I don't have a wife and kids to get back to, I don't really have a home anymore. Seems like I only just left California. There has been so much that I've seen and done between there and now, but it still is not enough. I don't know what I'm lookin' for. I don't know if I'd recognise it if I crashed into it. Anyway, it's too late, I'm hooked. The road, the steering wheel and the big country is my diet.

"Well, I don't know man. I don't think I'm ready to head back yet. I guess I'll get there, but I wanna to spend more time. I'm only beginning to get LA flushed outta my system."

"Hey this is a great trip, but we just don't know about the van. How far will it go before somethin' blows? It's burning about as much oil as gas," Briggs said.

"Yeah, I've seen huge clouds of blue smoke when I've been following you."

"I know it, and the steering's fucked, you have to turn the wheel half-way round before anything happens. We're just hopin' we can make it back. What are we gonna do if the van dies on the road? We've got all the amps and instruments. We really gotta think about going straight back."

"You're sure, huh?" I'm hoping that they still might be wavering.

"Yeah, it really looks like it. I think so."

I sip more coffee and let the proposition sink in.

"Well. I don't think I'm ready. I want to keep wanderin' around for a bit longer. I like it. I'm beginning to feel good, a lot healthier, you know. I guess I'm not quite ready for the next thing yet."

"Hey, you should do what you want but we can't see any other way right now, other than heading straight back."

"Yeah, I guess so."

We drain our coffees, walk back outside and lean back against the van. Highway 160 is trickling with a few cars, not many.

"Hey man, I can see what you mean. Driving straight back is probably the most practical thing to do, yeah. I'm just not into that yet, I wanna look around for a bit longer."

The soup-slurping trucker ambles out, gets into a pick-up and drives away breaking the silence.

"So you're sure you're goin'? I ask again. The romance of the road might overpower their sense of logic if the flat, Kansas highway started singing the Sirens' song that would lure them back into folly.

"Yeah, we've got to. Can't see any other choice."

"Oh well," I have to give-in to the new situation. "What are you gonna do, where y' headin'?"

"Maybe up to Wichita, get on the big highway up to Topeka, then just stay on the main roads, east. It'll be faster an' use less gas.'

"Ah shit. It'll be weird. But, I can dig what you're sayin'."

"Yeah, I know, but I think we gotta go," Barry reaffirms. We are silent again. Our minds are made up, we'll be heading in different directions, separate paths.

"Hey, can I get that kerosene camp-stove out of the van, if you're not gonna use it on the highways?"

"Yeah sure. What about any other stuff? There's some pinto beans and some vegetables."

"Ok, they might come in handy."

Barry gives me some of the camping food.

"I hope you have a few more camp fires, Ian."

"Yeah, me too. Look, I'll phone you when I'm getting' closer to Connecticut. We'll meet-up. We have to unload some of your stuff that's in the bus. Maybe we can hang-out before I go up to Massachusetts. Wow, it'll be weird bein' back on the East Coast." I hug both of my buddies, wish them good luck and bon voyage. They climb in, start the old van and wave as they pull back on to the road. There are blue puffs of smoke from the tail pipe as they shift gears, it is burning oil. Their van gets smaller as I stand there, watching them move further away every second. I feel a tug, an urge that I should jump in the bus, try to catch up and not be left here, standing on the side of the road in Kansas. I remember Roy Rogers and Dale Evans, dressed in their Hollywood cowboy outfits, at the end of their TV show, singing as the credits rolled;

'Happy trails to you, until we meet again.
Happy trails to you, keep smilin' until then'.
  "Catch you later guys," I say to the afternoon.
A truck lumbers by with a blast of noise and wind. I probably look like a hitchhiker standing on the side of the road, too befuddled to stick out his thumb.

I climb into the bus, sit back in the seat and sigh. Wow. I feel quite alone already, pared away from yet more of my close buddies. I sit there a bit longer and give the smoky van time to take Barry and Briggs further along the road, sort of sealing the deal. The impact of peeling away from so many of my friends during such a short time is sobering, scary.
  It has been just a few months short of three years now, that I have had a life with the guys in the band. Years of it: sharing houses, hotel rooms, gigging for weeks and weeks every night. Fuck, it could drive you crazy. That's probably why we were so stoned all the time. We were going nuts, climbing the walls. It's really quite amazing that none of us had killed each other. I can remember a few bad scenes, a bit of shouting and screaming but there really weren't all that many of them. It never got so violent that you had to stop two guys from tearing each other apart. I had to hand it the Submarine Band and the Burritos, we had managed to coexist peacefully, mostly. There may have been periods of black silence but there never were any broken noses or brawls. I can't remember walking into the kitchen and seeing fragments and shards of broken dishes covering the floor, or jumping out of the way, as tables were tipped over. I never saw any fist-sized holes punched through the walls. We kept a fine balance by being both busy and sedated, at least enough to keep from erupting.
  You can't expect a bunch of guys to live in a place together and subscribe to the sterling examples set by Father Knows Best, My Three Sons or Ozzie and Harriet. Even David and Ricky Nelson had a few lightweight squabbles. The Cartwrights, out there on the ranch in Bonanza, had those three rowdy boys; Hoss, Li'l Joe and Adam but they must have burned-off all of their youthful rage by ridin' the range and shootin' outlaws. Ozzie and Harriet didn't seem to have any deep personality flaws, the toast never got burned and their clothes never got dirty. Nothing like those Tennessee Williams plays, full of unbalanced characters straining at the leash, conspiring, hiding dark secrets and trying to keep the lid on their demons. They would have to explode eventually, smashing dishes, tearing down the curtains and slamming doors. They would pound their fists on their pillows, tables, the dashboard of the car or whoever was around to take their rage. Bottles would fly, smashing against the wall of the motel room or into the fireplace. Dreaded, shameful secrets would come screaming out causing everyone present to wither or faint.

Bands have been portrayed by the fun-loving Monkees and those jovial Beatles in A Hard Days Night. They must have edited out all the 'Why can't you clean out the fucking bath after you've used it!' or 'Can't any of you bastards ever wash the dishes!' or 'You always play the intro to that song too fucking slow! When are you gonna get it fucking right!'

I remember that there were a few opportunities when things could have gone the wrong way. It's not always obvious or easy to recognize the preamble or the warning signs before an explosion. Maybe it's hard for people to think of anything dramatically original to express their anger or frustration and we all choose from a very limited pallet or repertoire to use for our outbursts. It takes creativity to come up with gestures that are dynamic enough to make a big impact and convince other people to drop what they are doing and listen.

In New York we had a few hi-fi's and record players around the house, we listened to a lot of music. Gram had a portable record player, one of those compact units made by Acoustic Research labs; a little sound system (a turntable and two speakers) that was designed for travel. The speakers fit to the sides of the turntable, you'd clip them on, close-down the lid, snap the catches, grab the handle, load it in your car and off you go, to college, moving in with your new girlfriend or taking it with you for the weekend. It had a good sound and the AR player got moved around the house, sometimes into the kitchen to play a record announcing, with a bit of Buck Owens, that coffee had been made.

One morning, instead of an aroma of fresh-ground coffee brewing, I awoke to an acrid taint of burning, like a dump, the smell of plastic and tires. Gram was rubbing his eyes and walking around the house.

"God what's that awful smell?" we looked out the windows expecting to see a fire or an accident on the street.

"I don't know, I could smell it as soon as I woke up."

"Hey look! In the kitchen."

The sun was shining in through a window and in the shaft of light we could see a haze of gray smoke. We went into the kitchen and could not see anything burning, but the stink was awful.

"Look, the oven's on," Gram noticed.

I opened the oven and coughed as more smoke and a gagging stench poured out.

"What the hell is it?" Looking in the oven we tried to make-out what the mess inside could be.

"Christ! It's my stereo!" Gram spluttered and coughed. It was a bit like a dream as we peered in at the melted mechanical mess. There on the lower shelf, the one you'd use if you were baking a fifteen-pound Thanksgiving turkey, was the record player.

It fumed, lopsided and warped, with copper wires protruding through the gaping mouths of the melted casing, the needle-end of the arm fused into a black pool of a semi-liquid LP. The singed label said 'George Jones- Country Hits'. We were speechless for a moment.

"What the fuck!"

"Man, I don't know."

We stood up, shut the oven door, turned it off and opened the kitchen windows.

"My stereo?" Gram muttered. "Jesus, what?"

"What the hell do ya think happened?" We couldn't make sense of it, wondering if a prowler had broken in and done this, nothing else was missing or disturbed. Later that morning Mick told us that last night at four a.m. he had decided to casserole the innocent stereo.

"It was broken. It looks great now." He explained.

"Man, it only needed a new cartridge!" Gram argued, defending the roasted record player.

Really, there was something interesting and engaging about how the stereo looked in its melted metamorphosis. The oozing statement behind the roasting might have been, that Mick was beginning to go a bit nuts. Maybe he was having a hard time living in one place after years of being on the road. Maybe drummers are like that. Maybe it was from playing too much country music. He had chosen a George Jones record for the meltdown.

The never-ending straight roads finally defeat me, I can't keep on steering the perfect course after so many curve-less hours. I stop on a bare patch of land just off the road, lean forward on the steering wheel and hold my head in my hands. Man, what a long haul. That's what you do in Kansas, drive, drive, drive. I get out and walk around the van and look up at the stars. They are cool and refreshing. I could drive for another couple of hours if I switch on the radio to keep me company.

Out in the interior of America is where all the good radio stations are, the big boys that beam out across the vast states with maximum wattage. Their signals cover a few hundred, sometimes, a thousand miles. They play the best music. I guess they figure that, with such a big spread, they're covering a whole lot of rural America, farms, small towns, small people. They stick with that down-home sound, country, rhythm 'n' blues and gospel. On X-ELO, W-LAC they don't play Jefferson Airplane, The Byrds or Rolling Stones, their multi millions of listeners aren't going to hear 'Lucy In The Sky With Diamonds'. And, man, does it sound good, one killer song after another. When I'm tuned into a good one, I don't want the night to end.

The big X stations are over the boarder in Mexico, where they don't have to stay within the FCC regulations, and their huge transmitters have triple the wattage of the legal limit in the USA. X-ERB, just south of Tijuana, can be picked-up, on the dial, in Alaska. Even W-LAC, with fifty thousand watts, can be heard in eight or ten big Southern states.

I've just heard four or five good songs in a row. I recognized a couple of the names, people who had a record that got played, then seemed to have disappeared from big-city radio stations. William Bell, Arthur Conley, Johnny Taylor. I've heard them before and they are still doing beautiful, soul music. Hank Crawford and Ted Taylor are new, to me. We've been cut off from most of the rootsy music in LA. Los Angeles is too much of a big-time place, everything has to be a million-seller or a gold record to be played there. All five of the records I just heard, the 'Weekend Party Pack', could be mine for three dollars and fifty-nine cents, from the Record Roost, Box one-eighty-eight, El Paso, Texas. The night time DJ claims, if I send a money order, the discs will be dispatched in time for the weekend. Too bad I don't have an address. He plays a groovin' instrumental that I have heard a couple of times, 'The Horse' by Cliff Nobles, it has great horn lines.

I stop for gas at a small shack of a place. Inside, the radio is tuned to the same station, I recognize the DJ's voice. A few miles down the road, I pick up a different show, now it is country music. They're playing a very soulful song. The vocal seems familiar but I can't place him. He's singing about a heavy drinking couple. The guy was the one who dragged her around, into all those bars, when he was such a lush and she was just trying to stick with him.

'Well I know I'm to blame,

I made her, the image of me.'

It's Conway Twitty. He had disappeared, for years, after all the hits he had. Funny, now that I think of them, I remember how country he sounded, really country. He got into the charts because he had a DA and sideburns and looked like a rocker. He was another one of the guys with country roots, who crossed over into the charts that used to include them. What's the deal? rock 'n' roll got so cleaned-up, that the country music became unpalatable, it had too much rock-a-billy in it. Then there was the English sound; could blame it on them as well. Now, country has a bad name, like it's garbage, a threat to health, everybody, except the hicks, seems to hate it.

All of this great music that I have heard tonight is so simple, lean, cut right down to the bone, no fat, no London Symphony Orchestra or choirs and dozens of overdubs. It comes down to good singers and great grooves. Basic American music is too stark for urban people, it doesn't have enough decoration or it's not wearing enough make-up to be glamorous. The music contains a core of truth that holds soul. I believe in it and, within the radius of the radio signal, I'm keeping the faith. I'd like to live within the broadcast range of these stations, life might be better. There is consolation coming out of the radio speaker tonight. Maybe in the morning the signal would be gone, I'd turn the dial back and forth and find hiss and squeals, but, by dark, the radio would be loud and clear, the fountain would be flowing again. It's giving the country people comfort, in the face of floods, drought, cotton weevil, trichinosis and The New Yorker, not much else can do that, except sex and drinking, maybe. Of course sex and drinking are incorporated into most of the songs, one way or another.

I'm heading toward the Northeast, a region where the least amount of country music is played and the closest thing to soul is Motown. That thought is enough to make me take my foot off the gas pedal, pull over, and shut the engine off. I'll listen to the radio, climb into the back of the van and lay down, why not. The radio plays and I drift between twangy guitars, tumbling over cataracts until I'm floating, face-down, in a pool of fiddle.

The angel, said she'd take me,

To heaven, one more time.

An' she changed, my water,

Into wine.

There is a sharp crack of static on the radio. I open my eyes, and an instant later, see a burst of light, illuminating the sky, a cloud of electricity splashes onto a sea of ink. Another crackle and a bright flash, no zig-zag lightening, just an enormous celestial fart. Maybe global energies are jousting, there's a big dispute going on up there that we are unaware of, something unrelated to politics or news coverage, is being settled. Those eternal rivals, devils and angels, are making threatening overtures prior to a skirmish in the skies over empty Kansas. They're out here because they don't want to be observed. Maybe I'm the only witness and will have to slink away before I'm discovered. The DJ reads a pitch for high protein pig feed, guaranteed to keep hogs happy, down on the farm. Yeah, down to earth.

I sleep in the van, just about comfortably fitting in the bed-space, a sleeping bag on top of two big bass cabinets. I lay looking through the windshield at the intense stars in an inky sky.

I dream that I was at a dairy ice cream stand. All of the different colored ice creams are set out in long racks, holding the cones. I couldn't tell what flavors they are, can't make up my mind to choose.

"What do you want?" a soldier asks me, speaking in Latin. There are two iridescent pheasants at each end of the display. 'They have just flown the ice cream from Brazil, they're very rare. The orange ones are free but this green one is reserved for you.' He picks it up and as he passes it over to me it grows, increasing in size so much that when I reach out for the cone it is as big as me, I have to hug it to keep it from falling over.

"I can't eat this", I complain.

"You're not supposed to," a woman behind me whispers. "Just look after it, be careful." The others waiting in line begin humming, then make clacking sounds, snapping like dogs and growling, louder, until they're roaring. I awake to a blaze of morning sun as a diesel trailer-truck speeds past.

I swing open the side doors and breathe in the morning, already warm on the treeless plain. It had been a late night, I need a cup of coffee. Maybe there is a diner somewhere down the road. Where the hell am I? I can't remember where I was when I stopped and saw the lightening last night. Unlike Dorothy and Toto, I'm in Kansas, but to me it's as weird as Oz. This state should have been named Square-us or Rectangula; all the roads are so precisely straight, running north-to-south or east-to-west, nothing in between, ever. I remember going through a little place, Sedan, before I gave up last night. The map shows that I'm about twenty miles west of a little town, appropriately enough, called Coffeyville and twenty-five miles south of Cherryvale and that is near to a place called Parsons. I climb into the cab and start the engine, it bum-bum-bums into life but the rhythmic beat is accompanied by an intermittent screech. I open the rear engine flap and look in at the dark vibrating guts. An air cowling panel is loose, a bolt must have fallen out and the belt is rubbing. I'll have to find a VW doctor.

After coffee and toast at a diner, I'm poking along, taking it easy on Route 166 when I spot the round VW, Volkswagen trade mark on a road side sign; McDonough Volkswagen, Joplin Missouri. Joplin is only fifteen miles away. I roll into the service station at eleven.

"We'll have a look and see," Al says and calls a guy in a mechanics outfit over, his breast pocket badge says 'Arnie'.

"Um. The rear cowlings loose, see, here. An' it looks like the fan belt's pretty worn. We could do it in a couple of hours, okay? Come back after lunch. We should have it ready for you then."

I walk along the road and find a place to have a sandwich.

They had to do a couple of other things, and replaced the generator pulley, but I'm lucky, it only comes to seventeen dollars and fifty cents. Arnie is out in the lot looking at a VW Beetle.

"Hey. When I parked your van out here and shut the engine off I could hear it firin' through the valves, makes a sort of sputt, sputt noise. You could have a burnt valve. Don't know how far you're goin'? you might wanna get that looked at," he advises.

"Well how bad is it?"

"Trouble is ya can never tell, but if the valve stem burns out, it'll fall into the cylinder and then you're screwed. It will put a hole in the piston."

"Oh shit. I don't need that."

"We're pretty busy here, next couple a days, you probably don't want to wait around. There's a guy down by Stutts who works on foreign cars, 'bout fifty miles. You'll see his place, 'Walt's', it's right on the road, he might help you out."

"Hey, thanks for tellin' me. I don't want the whole thing blowin' up. Bye."

On the road out of Joplin a Corvette blares past me. I'm probably dawdling, nursing the van along, worrying about the valves that have been diagnosed as chronic. The Corvette recedes, they're fast. They're not so good on the curves though. I remember seeing them spinning off the track at Sebring, when we were in Florida doing gigs a couple of years ago and went to the race.

Gram was never quite clear about his step-father's various business ventures. Bob Parsons seemed to have worked for a company with an enigmatic name, Universal Imports or International Exports, something like that. The company had a name similar to the one that James Bond used as his cover when signing into a Swiss Hotel or gaining access to the executive offices of an electrical components company that was actually constructing a world dominating, orbital death ray. Imports, Exports, it had the right ring to it, vague but impressive.

Some people that Bob had dealt with in the past seemed to have had an interest in Cuba. They might have wanted to develop some business potential down there or just add a bit of a spark to that dreary Castro regime, maybe get some of those primo Cuban cigars back on the shelves at the right price and open up the casinos again. The vanguard sales team for this entrepreneurial venture came out for training sessions in the backwoods of the Snively estate, that was owned by Gram's family. Out amongst the scrub oaks and palmetto, the trainees drove jeeps, crawled around in camouflage uniforms and cracked-off a few rounds on their M-16 rifles for target practice.

Bob was a personable guy, beefy with a big handshake.

Wearing a check, brass button blazer he was comfortably at home at the country club, the 19th hole and the dinner dance parties in the central Florida area. Gram, always remaining a bit in the dark about Bob's business contacts, would smile and say, 'well, I've never been really sure about what he does…hey, that's Bob'.

As Florida is a Mecca for recreation, Bob made a few suggestions about things to do for some unwinding and relaxation while we were down there doing gigs.

"Do you guys like to water ski? We should get some steaks and have a barbecue." He also mentioned the Sebring Road Race that would be running on the weekend. Sebring was one of the few European-style races that ran in the US, a twelve-hour race around a twisting circuit of S bends and straightaways that began in the afternoon and ran late into the dark of night.

Early in the afternoon the car race fans arrived in flashy convertibles, sports cars, campers, pick-ups pulling trailers and soon were unloading their cases of beer. We drove into the race track in a stoic Chevy station wagon and hadn't thought ahead about bringing any Budweiser or Fritos like most of the race fans had. Beach chairs, card tables, crockery and plastic forks materialised, radios disagreed as hotdogs sizzled on the quickly erected grilles to a background drone of revving engines.

A herd of sleek sports cars crowded nearer to the start line, edging forward with bloodhound anticipation. Ford GTs, Cobras, Jaguars, Corvettes, Ferraris, and pack of aerodynamic Porsche displayed their racing numerals with dyslexic randomness. The engines built up a thunderous crescendo and climaxed with a war cry. The race-watching crowd roared in sympathy as the cars wound-up the revs and moved out of the burnt-tire pall towards the first corner, a half-mile away. Each circuit took about five minutes, the roar died away as the cars went through the backstretch and into another series of bends in the distance. By the end of the first lap, the original mass had thinned to a parade as they flashed passed and gunned down the main stretch. After another couple of laps some of the fans began drifting back to the barbecues and campers, as there was another eleven-and-a-half hours yet to go. Mickey and Gram caught my eye and nodded towards our wagon, I got the message.

"How 'bout a little poke to get that burning-oil smell out of your nose?" Gram winked theatrically.

"Yeah, I'll try one of those on for size."

"Well, I think that this'll fit you just about right."

We passed around a little pipe taking a couple of whopper hits each and the car filled with that warm Middle-East camel blanket-and-honey fog.

"Wo-a-ah boy!"

"M-m-m."

Someone flipped on the radio. The Stones, were doing 'Nineteenth Nervous Breakdown'. On the racetrack, a big bass roar growled past, then its twin, followed by an angrier baritone snarl.

"That one sounded like a Mack truck. How did he get in the race?"

"There's a few crazy Florida playboys out there just itching to blow their new Corvettes. Some guy Bob knows from Orlando is swerving around on the track showing off," said Gram. "There's not a Hell of lot of excitement down here in central Florida, I'll tell you that. You gotta take what you can get, there ain't no-o-o ice but you gotta skate."

"Well, anybody going to watch that race?"

"Phew, man, I don't know if can walk now."

"Well, see if you can crawl over to the fence…. and stick your fingers in your ears."

The straight-line Florida horizon was ready to gape a toothless mouth and swallow the barbecue sun. Dinosaur bees buzzing. V-8s argued and challenged, shouting insults and throwing down gauntlets with souped-up bravado. Cars streaked past, roaring open-throated territorial claims like giant canines. A pack of multi-cylinder wolves pursued their lumbering, bellowing prey as it weakened, leaving a trail spurting black blood.

Tortured tires screamed the hopeless agony of the victim until they were replaced in a flurry of arms and tools with fresh, innocent, virgin rubber. The cars, frustrated by interruptis, seethed with panting impatience, sweating and smoking as they strained to get back to the chase. The dead, bald tires stank.

Plum dusk. The color-drained night sky sprouts the first few seeds of lonely jewels that are shyly joined by their friends who, at first, can only delineate the extents of simple triangles. As it darkens, they soon spell out leaning letter messages and eventually erect mythological animals, heroes and infinite predictions. The night racers' headlights loom and sweep on the circuit's elbows like lighthouses on the Florida pampas.

Bee-e-e-e Wha-a-a-a, a big-engined car rushes past proving the Doppler Effect. Another, wounded, with only one headlight, rips by. Several vehicles lay dead on the side of the track and other casualties are towed into to the pits.

"Wow! Look at this one!"

A mighty Cobra-Ford, braying past, spurts flames from its belly, mechanical dyspepsia. A cheer goes up from a group of oversize guys standing further along.

"They taste blood."

"Yeah, that's what people are coming here for."

"Not really much of a race without a few good crashes."

"Yeah man, they're all hoping for that gladiatorial action. Got to have the blood, the thumbs up, thumbs down thing."

"Some people are in love with speed."

"I sure am glad to have made it through high school with out being in a bad car crash," I said. "It got pretty close a couple of times."

"Yeah, a few guys in my school said good-bye after going off some back road doin' a hundred in their mom's Buick."

"That's all we cared about then. Hot cars, new cars, you know. You'd think, wow! I wish I had a T-bird, then everything would be just fuckin' gr-r-reat."

"That's the whole car-gimmick bullshit, that people get sucked into. You look in a magazine at the ads and there's always a beautiful chick sittin', mashed-up-close to that guy drivin' his new Oldsmobile convertible."

"Oh baby, ya just can't lose with the stuff I use."

"Screw that, I don't know if I even want a car, I haven't had one for a few years. You don't need 'em in the city, anyway."

"Well Detroit ain't going to like your attitude much. Cars are part of the American way," Gram reminded us. "Isn't it written in the constitution that every citizen is supposed to own a car?"

"Oh yeah, that's true, I 'member learning that in my eleventh grade Civics class. Yeah."

"Who's winning this race anyway? I can't tell any more."

"Yeah, m-m-m, just seems like cars going round and round and round."

"It's a metaphor."

I head down past Sarcoxie and Aurora, Missouri, driving the time-bomb van, hoping that the next hill won't trigger-off the immanent explosion that could finish this trip or leave me stranded in the middle of America. If there was a big bang or maybe only a whimpering klunk, klunk, klunk, I'd have too much time to think about what a stupid idea this was. Staring at the smoking engine and the black, life-blood oil, pooling under the bus, would be a pathetic end to an exodus from the land of Hollywood. This is a lonely Goddamn road. I sure don't have any friends in Missouri, unless Barry and Briggs are somewhere on the road, who knows where. Most everyone I've been involved with over the past few years are about one-and-a-half thousands miles behind and over the past few weeks have moved-off into their own futures. Yeah, this road gets lonelier every mile.

'Walter's Automotive Service, foreign and domestic repairs.' The sign was painted on the gable-end of a large wooden shed, several cars and wrecks surrounded the building. Under a couple of suspended pool table lights, Walt is bent over the engine of a Peugeot. He rubs his head as I explain my situation, like he's very worried or has a headache. He doesn't answer right away, he sighs, as if he's reluctant.

"Yeah, I got some a them vee-double-ya valves. Always keep 'em, they're always goin' wrong. You're a lucky man. I could get right on it, jus' finished-up this one."

Nailed to the wall, near the big open barn doors are several signs; 'CASH ONLY, All Work Must Be Paid For', 'No Tools Loaned Out', 'No Smoking', 'NO CREDIT', 'JESUS SAVES'.

"What's it gonna cost me, you think?"

"Well, 'bout a days work, uh, depends what else. Probably needs all new exhaust valves, usually do. 'Round eighty, hundred, I guess." He rubs his head a bit more.

"Yeah, really?"

"Do it all the time. Ya got the money?"

"Yeah, just about." It's going to knock a big hole in my kitty.

"Like the sign says, no money, no work." I hadn't noticed that one yet.

"No, it's okay, I got a hundred," I assure him. I'll have to count it and see if I really do.

"Well, I'll get her up on the hydraulic, pull the engine 'fore supper. Might be able ta git the heads offa it tonight."

I sleep in the van that night. Walt really rubbed his head a lot over that suggestion, worried that this stranger might run off with the jack, sparkplugs and all the socket wrenches I could carry. He showed me a dark oil-smeared sink and toilet I could use, if I needed to in the night, because he was gonna have to lock the place up, couldn't take any chances.

I'm lonely. I wish there was someone in bed with me. But who the hell would want to be sleeping with me on top of a couple of bass amps, in an old van locked in a greasy barn in Missouri. I've been moving through or living in weird places. Sharing a house with a bunch of guys isn't the right environment for a love nest. Having a regular girlfriend doesn't fit in with playing gigs every night and travelling. Girls have been temporary, they briefly come and go.

From under her bangs her dark eyes giggled when she told me her name was Mimi, spoken in the voice of a squeaky toy, a rubber duck or baby doll. She appeared almost fragile, with thin white arms and twig legs that stuck out from her mini-skirt. She didn't seem to be from anywhere, she was just breezing through. She said she moved around and liked to travel, when she first came to stay with me at Burrito Manor. She brought nothing more than a tapestry shoulder bag. She couldn't have had more than a partial change of clothes, some makeup and an address book. Talk about a free spirit, she was as unencumbered as a swallow. Mimi was pretty closed about her history, other than she had been staying at the Buffalo Springfield's house in Malibu last week. Like a swallow, Mimi circled a couple of times before swooping down out of the blue, had a quick glance around and decided to stay with me.

She wasn't a doper, after a drag of pot she'd wrinkle her nose and sing 'Uh-uhh' or wave away the passing joint with a jingle of her silver bracelets. Sleeping was one of her qualities. She could sleep in a car, on a chair or folded in the arm of a sofa, with such captivating grace. She always looked fashionable when dozing, her head sharply turned, chin on shoulder, arm jutting over the end of a sofa, with a limp hand, dangling, as if the big silver rings were dragging it down. When Mimi dozed it was time to grab a camera.

She told fantastic stories or parables. They could be childish, like nursery rhymes but she had the ability to stitch images and characters together, never faltering as she expanded and developed a fable. Mimi would be the ideal fellow occupant in a lifeboat, an elevator, stuck between floors or a bomb-shelter. When awake, she was an enchantress, when asleep, she was truly ornamental.

She told me one day that she had invited a friend and, later that day a chick with long blonde ringlets, looking a lot like the Vermont Maid on the maple syrup jars, showed up. No car, just walked in the door with her sapphire eyes and an enigmatic smile. After a barely perceptible introduction, she took an album out of her Indian bag, walked over to the record player and dropped the needle on the first track. It was the Jimi Hendrix record, Are You Experienced. Mimi and Vermont Maid danced. They danced for days, just kept turning over the record and dancing. Other people came and went. One of the guys in the house grimaced, slammed his door and disappeared for days. The girls danced to 'Purple Haze'. Their dancing was sometimes gentle and spectral with closed eyes, hands tracing arabesque forms above. Occasionally they looked as if they were playing charades, miming ceiling painting and changing light bulbs. 'We love Jimi, he's what's happening', they said.

In candlelight, Mimi asked me where I wanted to go. She wondered what road I was on, where it was leading and when I might get there. I shrugged and replied that I had become more concerned about paying the rent than chasing rainbows only to find that the pots of gold, waiting at the end, were filled with Kelloggs Corn Flakes.

The new band wanted grocery money not promises. The Burritos had begun with a big cornerstone of cynicism embedded in the foundation. She said that the trouble with material things was that they kept you shackled, tied down and enslaved until you couldn't fly-off to a place that offered the freedom to be who you really were. That was the only trip, life was for spreading wings, she thought. She asked me if I wanted to fly, her bracelets clinked against my ears as she gathered my head toward her, gently puffed three times in my face and slid her tongue into my mouth to give me more advice. In the morning I did a small painting of china-white Mimi, as she carelessly slept in a bed with striped sheets, her head resting on a delicate arm that extended across the pillow and leaned against the wall. She was temporarily nesting and in no hurry that morning.

One day Mimi sat in bed and flipped through her address book, a loose page fell out and she inserted it inside the back cover. She said she wanted to call someone. Later she went out, saying she didn't need a ride, Mimi had some sort of magic carpet. In the evening she returned, picked up her bag, had a quick ruffle through it and smiled. She told me she was going to London. Jimi Hendrix was going back there and Mimi was flying. How long did Mimi stay with me, I can't remember if it was a few days or a few weeks. She just flew in and then, just as suddenly, flew off. She didn't leave any footprints behind.

It's strange when I wake in the night, glance out the window and can't see anything, no land, trees or sky. A warm whiff of grease reminds me that I'm locked in Walt's garage. It's weird and lonely. A few hours later, the barn doors grate open and wake me, Walt likes an early start.

"You could go down to Colleen's, they do a breakfast. It's just along there a bit, about half-a-mile. Can take your time, I'm not gonna be finished much before two or three this afternoon."

That still sounds good. This afternoon; better than being here for days. I'll be on the road again, great.

Colleen's is the little town's all day diner. I park myself, sitting in a back booth for a couple of hours and have a coffee refill every time the waitress asks if I'd like anything else. Coffee and a lessening fear of being marooned in Missouri perk me up. I read the paper. The Joplin Independent has an article about a couple of guys coming back to their small towns in Missouri from a hitch in Vietnam. The paper used formal portraits, showing them wearing their full-dress uniforms, probably taken before they were shipped out. I wonder how those same guys look today. There is another article about the Veterans Administration programmes, then, on the next page, pictures of a bar, a

GI's hang out, that has been bombed in Saigon, dozens of people have been obliterated or wounded. The paper doesn't have pictures of them.

Walt is doing well with the van repairs, he hadn't found any other problems with the engine, just the valves, but it will still be another couple of hours. I go to a grocery store and get a few things to eat in case I decide to drive late into the night. I also pick up a couple of cold beers. I offer one to Walt as he is replacing the rocker box. His eyes narrow at the invitation.

"I never use the stuff," he says. I feel embarrassed, but it isn't like I'm offering him cocaine or something.

The radio that has been playing a jaunty Herb Alpert and The Tijuana Brass song announces that they are going over to the newsroom for an important bulletin.

'News has just come in that Robert Kennedy, the front runner for the Democratic party nomination, has been shot at a rally in Los Angeles. The Senator had been addressing a crowd at the Intercontinental Hotel when the single gunman attacked, shooting Kennedy at point blank range.'

Walt puts down his wrench and a shakes his head, looking down at the oily floor.

"Lord sakes. What ever is goin' on, I just don't know, just don't know."

"I can't believe it!" I agree, "Seems like we only just got over President Kennedy. Man! I can't, just can't believe it."

"Tell ya the truth, neither one of 'em was my favorite, but this.. I just don't know."

"Man! I CAN'T believe it."

Walt and I aren't really talking to each other, it isn't a discussion about this new tragedy, we are both just vocalising, reacting to the blow and can't stop repeating ourselves. We are united in our shock.

"Lord, sakes."

"What is goin' on?" At the risk of infringing Walt's un-stated temperance dictum, I take a big swig of my Miller, he doesn't have a NO DRINKING sign on the wall.

A few minutes later the radio newsroom announces;

'Official sources have stated that Senator Robert Kennedy was pronounced dead on arrival at the hospital this afternoon. Police are holding the suspected gunman in custody. President Lyndon Johnson has proclaimed a day of mourning. The Senators body will be flown to Boston where funeral arrangements are being made. We're going over to local radio station K-RLA for an eyewitness report...'

Walt works and mutters. I go outside and lean against the door of the shed and mutter. Later I hand over the cash and Walt acts a bit warmer. When you share in a shocking event it brings strangers closer together. He gives me back my keys, I get back on the road heading east, wanting to put some miles and today behind me.

The Ozarks roll and the road is sleepy. It is an easy going afternoon in this soft country as I pass the occasional farm with some cattle in the fields or a green John Deere tractor harrowing rich brown land. Visually it's a scene epitomising rural peace and quiet. If I put the radio on the illusion is smashed by today's news. I still can't believe it; Bobby Kennedy is dead, as well. I guess it happens. Politicians are always in public, shaking hands with everybody, meeting the people at factories, schools, kissing babies, judging pie baking competitions, smiling and promising that things will be better if you vote.

It's a risky job, getting up in front of people, there are always hecklers or wise guys, drunks, people who don't like what you're saying, what you're playing or what the message is. Most groups of people, crowds or audiences have a limit to what they will accept; it can be a narrow band.

Somebody must be after those Kennedys. Couldn't be the Black Panthers, Kennedy was behind all the civil rights stuff. Maybe it was some Ku Klux Klan militia, segregationists or The John Birch Society. The Birchers even wanted to impeach Johnson. I remember seeing big signs on the road in Arizona; 'Impeach Johnson, Save America'. The Birchers were ultra conservative, they would drop an atomic bomb on Hanoi; Bobby Kennedy was talking about getting out of Vietnam.

Jesus! Bobby Kennedy seemed like the only hope for this screwed-up country. He could have won the election and, maybe, would have done something to turn things around. He could see what a mess this place is in today. His assassination is another step down the road to more riots and demonstrations as people get the message that nobody is going to hear them, no matter how loud they scream. It could just keep on getting worse, Vietnam might mushroom into a bigger war with China and when someone gets up to speak out against it they get shot. What's the point of walking around carrying peace signs, it doesn't make any difference, it doesn't change anything, they just send in more cops, the National Guard and tear gas. We're getting closer and closer to civil war. Fuck! I don't know if I can stay here.

The land in eastern Missouri flattens out as I leave the Ozarks behind. I've done about two hundred miles and it's getting dark. I want the sun to set on today, it needs to be over, finished. I look at the map; Poplar Bluff, Dexter, the Mississippi River is about seventy-five miles away. I'm going to get there tonight, then I'll think about stopping. I want to cross the Mississippi in the daylight. I want to see it, the mighty Missis-sip, it is the division between East and West. The river is a bit like crossing the equator; sailors have a ceremony and initiate the first-timers when they cross. An old hand dresses up as Neptune and the novices are hazed, painted with engine oil or fish guts to humiliate them, it's an old fashioned ritual, a part of the passage into the other hemisphere. What would be appropriate for crossing the Mississippi? Singing 'Ol' Man River'?

He don't plant tatters, don't plant cotton,
'n them that plants 'em are soon forgotten,
Ol' man river, he jus' keeps rollin', jus' keeps rollin' along.'

Yeah. Worry, decisions, assassinations, anxiety, Vietnam and exhaust valves are all temporary, soon forgotten, compared to the rolling Mississippi, rolling, rolling, rolling. I'm going to have to sit down on that riverbank and see. See what the Ol' Man has to say. See if I can understand his gurgling and if there is a message waiting me from the Mississippi oracle.

Out past Sikeston I get on state Route 80 and, past Corner, I see a sign; Belmont Ferry 5 miles. That's for me, that's the place. I want to cross the big river by boat. Neptune probably won't be aboard but that's okay. The last couple of times I had crossed the Mississippi was on the big old bridge, out of Memphis. It had a metal-grid road that made the tires sing and wail, ah-wa-ah-ah-ah-ah, interrupted by occasional cross beams, unk-unk-ah-wa-ah-ah-ah-ah, unk-unk. The Memphis Bridge Blues, a continuous mechanical melody, challenging the old river's song.

At the end of the rutted road I cross some railroad tracks and in the headlight beams I can see a wooden dock, pilings, the rusty wheelhouse of a boat and beyond, the rolling dark water. A crooked sign says 'Snap and Julie's Ferry'. It is closed for the night. The first crossing is at 7 a.m. Cars $1.50, Trucks $3, passengers $.75. I hear a clanking, chank, chank, chank and look upriver toward the sound. Under lights, a metal escalator thing is loading gravel or coal on to a rusty barge from several open railroad wagons parked in the siding. I can see a few lights across the river in Kentucky. I walk over to the edge of the dock and look down at the muddy river. It's moving along, quickly. The water sloshes through the pilings pushing the ferryboat against the dock that groans and protests. I move the van to the side of the yard and park under a tree away from the dock.

I have travelled just over two thousand miles, weaving through the West, from Topanga to the Mississippi River bank. It has been a long day since Kennedy's assassination. I have lost contact with my buddies, it would be a million-to-one chance that I see them again between here and New England. The barge loader clanks faintly after I pull myself into the sleeping bag.

I dream I am in Massachusetts. My high school girlfriend and I have been painting an empty swimming pool and we're spattered with sapphire paint. She is tanned, her nose is peeling and her teeth are snow white. I hear cattle bellowing.

"They're Brahma bulls, over there," she turns and points. We move toward a meadow surrounded by chestnut trees, next to our Latin teacher's house.

"Which one do you want?" she asks. "I like Claudius, the one with the crown."

I approach a huge piebald, rich mahogany-hued bull with a head like a buffalo. He breaths with the depth of breaking surf and looks into my eyes. I reach up, grasp one of his splayed horns and slide-up on to his warm back. The bulls carry us and amble towards a pond, picking-up their pace as we near the water until they are loping along. They begin galloping.

"I forgot something!" I shout as the bull springs up, leaping into the air.

"You trophy, he is over there." The bull says in an Italian accent, rich with sagacity. The water is much wider than a meadow pond and, as we rise, I look down upon a vast river. We pass through and then over clouds, into a silence. All motion freezes. The silence breathes in my ear, 'Bee, twee, nah. Bee twee nah.' We begin descending towards a city, a mass of buildings and pretzel twist roads. Sirens and horns blare as the mighty bulls smash through the roof into the television studios of WBZ TV. 'Big Brother', Bob Emery is just doing his 'toast to the president' routine. I pick up a large glass of milk and hold it up in salute to Eisenhower's framed portrait. Ike glares at me and commands:

"Do something about those children, stop thinking about yourself!" A baby is howling and wriggling on the icy floor, I bend down, pick it up and hold it to my heart. The infant's scalp is covered with a fine down, its crown is pulsating and forms colored patterns, little continents and oceans, like the earth seen from orbit. Blue and purple on the scalp begin to shape an M, an A, then N and a Y. The baby raises its face to me, smiles and nods. I understand.

I'm awoken by a couple of cars driving into the ferry dock. The river is wide, the far bank indistinct as I look into a morning haze of low sun. The ferry is a listing, rusty scow with a small tugboat attached by a big pivoting hinge and only has room for a dozen cars. A man unfastens a chain across the scow and heaves-up several planks making a ramp.

"Hi. Can I get across?"

"Yep, I don't see why not. You can drive right on now, an' put your parkin' brake on," the skipper replies.

The tug's engine revs and pulls us out into the river where the skipper manoeuvres the tug around to start pushing across. There are patches of disturbed water, mud banks or shallows creating curling rapids. The branches of a large tree, that protrude through the surface, have collected drifting twigs, weeds and a few plastic bags. A group of ducks paddle in the shallows. I climb over onto the deck of the tug and into the wheelhouse. The skipper has the wheel lashed with rope and is drinking coffee from a thermos cup. There is engine noise and the windows are rattling.

"How ya doin'? I thought I'd pay you now."

"Yep, that's fine, dollar-fifty."

"I've never been across by boat before. How wide is it?"

"'Bout a mile an' quarter over ta Columbus Landin', but we gotta head up a bit 'cause a the run, an' come down inside a the other flats ovah there. Back 'n forth all day long."

"There's enough traffic to keep you goin' all the time?"

"Yep, just about. Fifteen miles up to the bridge at Cairo, we can save folks a long trip up there 'n back. Always run, rain sleet or snow, like the US mail."

I look back over the churning wake of sandy water at the receding Missouri bank. There are dusty clouds billowing around the loading barges. I can see the road that I had used in the dark last night, it comes to an abrupt end at the river like the last chapter of a book. It had brought me here, one road linking to the next all the way back to the Pacific Ocean. We are nearing the middle of the Mississippi, East meets West and 'Ol' Man River' hasn't said anything to me yet about turning back.

In the morning sun of Western Kentucky I head north east on Route 60 towards Paducah. I begin to sense a familiar feel to the country I'm driving through. It is the East. I forgot how green everything can be. After living in the arid climate of Southern California, getting used to the semi-tropical plants, the deserts and long periods without rain, the lush pastures and deciduous trees shout-out GREEN! No more palms, cactus or tumble weed. Instead of barren mounts of rock, the hills are covered with green growth. Trees are in the full-leaf of summer. Rolling hills and fields, silos, barns and woods make a softer texture compared to the West where every feature is monumental and extreme. Kentucky is a big farm, a bit like New England.

On a knoll beside the road a large sign has been painted on the side of a barn: 'Chew Mailpouch Tobacco' it suggests. Funny, I've never ever tried that, even with all the years of getting into country music there are a lot of boundaries that I have not crossed. Many aspects of the 'down home' culture remain a mystery. I should pull into a diner, order up a large plate of grits, with a side of pork belly, a large glass of buttermilk and finish it off with a big chaw of Mailpouch.

In January of '67 The Submarine Band had rolled into Nashville darkness that shrouded any excitement. Our Pontiac gently cruised past the brick warehouses, dark side streets, the occasional wide, fanning stone steps and columns on the facades of municipal buildings. A few neon signs flashed PAWN SHOP or BAR. The figures on the night street weren't in any hurry or rushing to the after-theater party. I couldn't spot any signs that said 'Recording Studio' and didn't catch a glimpse of Porter Wagoner, Webb Pierce or Floyd Kramer as they left a session; we could have been in the wrong part of the city.

We were blurry from the long drive from New York and looking for a hotel. We pulled up in front of an old style place that had the name of an unmemorable president; Garfield, Rutherford B. Hayes, Taft or Sheridan -was he a president? A glass fronted, dimly lit lobby revealed a lonely scene, like a Hopper painting. A desk clerk, leaned over the heavy wooden counter, attentive to the recollections of an older guy sitting back in a plush armchair, a standard lamp cast shadows over the story.

"I guess this could be it, let's check it out." We were stiff from the hours in the car and had to stretch after we wobbled out onto the street. The car door clunk had interrupted the raconteur and the two faces inside swivelled towards us as we approached. The old man's countenance changed to a disapproving grimace as we entered, as if we were wearing Halloween costumes or had pulled bandanas up over our faces, for a hold-up.

"Hello, we're looking for a room." The desk clerk didn't respond, just squinted. A wall clock tic-tocked, several times. 'Do you have anything here tonight?" It was like pulling teeth.

"Well," replied the desk clerk, not giving anything away. Were they keeping something secret? Was it a whore house, an illegal gambling joint and they were waiting for us to use the right code word?

"Just for tonight," prompting him, again, for a reply.

"Well. I guess we got somethin'."

"Good. How much are the rooms?"

"Well, it depends."

"Okay. Ah, what do you have?"

"You boys from outta town aren't ya." He was right on that one.

"Yes, New York."

"Ne-ew York, I figured so. M-m. You want a suite, or what?"

"Hey we'll take whatever you got, it's been a long day."

"Hm-m." He opened the big register, flipped through a couple of pages. "Yes-s, I got two rooms here, on the fifth floor. One's two beds, other's a single." He smiled slightly, offering this tough conundrum for us to puzzle over. The wall clock clicked and bonged, quarter-past-twelve.

"Hey I don't care where I sleep, I'm shot, let's get the rooms."

The old guy, still a gargoyle, frowned with determination at the Yankee hippies, maybe thinking that the best thing these boys could do was to march right down to a barbershop and get a haircut!

The night owls had no idea that we were pilgrims who had travelled all the way to Mecca, Tennessee and were getting this chilly reception. We had been drinking-in Nashville and listening to country music. We could reel-off the session musicians who had played on this or that record, Christ, we could play them a medley of Hank Williams, Lefty Frizzell and Ray Price if we had to. That could have been a better way to get a room and break through this no-room-at-the-inn thing.

"Well, that'll be eight dollars for the one and six for the single." We forked over two tens and he examined them, turning one of them over, before stowing the cash in a draw. He laid the change and two keys on the counter. "New York," he popped his lips, barely shook his head.

"No, I wouldn't care to go up there."

Outside of Paducah I get on to Highway 62 heading east past Smithland, Eddyville and Charleston. Apart from a couple of Indian names, most of the places sound English, no more old Spanish, like out in the West. No Los, Las, Buena, or Santas. I turn on the radio, sure enough, they're playing bluegrass music. Just past Greenville, Kentucky, I come upon an old wooden building on the right, with a hand painted sign out front that reads; 'Old Records for Sale'. Boi-oi-oi-oi-oi-oing! I can't control the reaction that is going to make me pull in there, that same string has dragged me into all sorts of places hunting for records. Searching for great music has been a job or a crusade for quite a few years. It has taken me into some scary junk stores and record shops in Roxsbury, Harlem and Watts, in the black neighborhoods, looking for blues and soul stuff and there had been a couple of weird times looking for country music. Sometimes things can get a bit strange when you're not shopping at the mainstream outlets.

On that trip to Nashville in '67 a guy in a record shop did not like the idea of Yankee hippies looking through the discs, even though we wore big smiles. We kept telling him how much we liked country music and that it was so hard to get up North.

"Lemme play you-all one, see if ya like it," he had said with a challenging leer. He put a single on his turntable. It was a racist record by a singer calling himself 'Johnny Reb'.

'Ya ever been down to the dark side of town,

an' ya see an ol' shack,

an' outside 's parked a Cadillac,

an inside there's fifteen niggers,

all crowded 'round one can a beans.'

And, the chorus went;

'They're lookin' for a hand-out, from you an' me,

they're lookin' for a hand-out just wait and see.

And with the consent of the President,

they're gonna get their way.'

To add to that warm Southern welcome he got out a bullwhip and started cracking it.

"Now, you-all wanna buy that record boys?"

As I walk up to the open door of the old Kentucky shed, I can hear voices and I go into the dim interior. There are a couple of guys in the corner, one of them turns his head toward me.

"Howdy. You come-on in." He is paunchy, wearing a white short sleeved shirt and a small-brimmed straw hat. The tables and shelves are stacked with records, there are boxes full of them on the floor and more tables further back in the dark, hundreds, thousands. This is heaven!

"Wow! Where did all these come from?" I don't think I'd ever seen so many discs before, even in a record store. He chuckles slowly.

"Jukeboxes, we owned lots a jukeboxes. All ovah the county, we had to put new records in 'em pretty often, ya know, keepin' up with the hit parade. The style keeps on changin', cain't do nothin' 'bout that."

I couldn't help thinking, what? The Kentucky charts? Having to deliver a new Bill Monroe single once and awhile?

"Can I look around?"

"Sure, help yo'self, we're aimin' to sell 'em," he replied.

I look down at the table next to me. Jesus! They are all 78s!! I start going through a stack. Holy shit! Look at this. The radiating yellow, gold beams and the crowing rooster of an old Sun record glimmered: 'Matchbox' by Carl Perkins, 261, Vocal, Memphis Tennessee. WOW! The next record had the maroon and silver Swing Time label, with a conductor holding a baton in a cloud of silver notes: Lowell Fulsom sings 'Backhome Blues', with orchestra, Los Angeles, Calif. Then, the dark blue and white hemispheres with a knight and bishop: Chess Record Corp. 'SCHOOL DAY' (Ring, ring, goes the bell), Chuck Berry, 1653, Chicago, Ill. On the other side, 'Deep Feeling', that great easy-going blues where Chuck plays, using a slide. I hold the big 78 in both hands, my eyes fixed on the colorful label and begin to feel the vibration of 1957 as it slowly travels up through my arms.

MGM, yellow with a black band and the lions head, is the label for Arthur (Guitar Boogie) Smith, doing 'Three D Boogie with his Cracker-jacks'. Man! Stacks and stacks of them.

All of this dynamite '50s stuff! The source, the fountainhead, the goldmine, the Ten Commandments! I had found the fabled elephant's graveyard of old records. She-ee-ee-it! For the past few years all of the people that I had played with shared the same respect for the roots music of the '50s, an unpretentious era full of spontaneity and excitement. All of the different styles, country, rock 'n' roll, rhythm 'n' blues contained something very special, an unadulterated vibrancy that grew fainter and had just about disappeared by the early '60s.

All of the '50s greats, Jerry Lee, Elvis, Fats Domino, Hank Williams, Little Richard and hundreds of others had been overwhelmed by the new, smooth, manicured acts. Suddenly it was the Clean-Teens; Bobby Rydell, Tommy Sands, Frankie Avalon, Fabian or Lesley Gore, Annette Funicello and The Ventures. Gene Vincent was probably working at a gas station now, Be-bop-a Texaco.

Now in '68, I had stopped even wanting to hear new records. The Beatles and the Rolling Stones had completely lost it, their first few albums were good but Sgt. Pepper sounded like a Broadway musical, like 'Oklahoma'. And that last Rolling Stones thing, whatever it was called, was rubbish. They were just selling flashy album covers that had probably cost more money to print than Bo Diddley had ever earned during his entire career. All of the old stuff was cut in a few minutes. They were recording in somebody's garage or upstairs over a butcher's and they would cut six songs in an hour for ten dollars, nothing like the big productions now. Most everything today seems to be so over recorded, just too much.

I flip down further through the stack of old records. The Crown label, 'Rocky Starr and The Happy Cowboys, Hollywood Calif', probably western swing. The record is made of 'crown-o-flex, non-breakable under normal use'. Specialty, in yellow script on a black and white background, 'Get to Gettin' by Mercy Dee and Lady Fox'. Then that red and black Atlantic label, 'I Want To Know by Ray Charles His Orchestra and Chorus': I guess that meant The Raylettes. Another Atlantic, 'Feelin' Happy: Joe Turner and His Blues Kings'. Oh Yeah! I turn to the jukebox guys.

"How much are you asking for these?"

"Oh, twenny-five cents a piece."

"Okay, I'm gonna have a few." I can see that some of the money left after the valve job was going to go on records, not gas. I wish I had more money and a truck!

'Hook, Line & Sinker, Bill Haley and His Comets (fox trot and vocal by Bill Haley and His ensemble)'. 'The Wallflower by Etta James and the peaches, Modern Records, Hollywood'. And, on the purple and silver Capitol label, 'Be-Bop-A-Lula by Gene Vincent and His Bluecaps'. The other side is that frantic, breathy, 'Woman Love', Uh, hey, uh-hey-uh-hey-hey. Oh,wow! I've got to have this one, 'Wreck on the Highway, vocal with string band acc; Roy Acuff and His Smokey Mountain Boys'. It could be bad luck but what the hell. Barry T would have flipped if he were here. It's too good to be true but I have to draw a limit on old records here, wow, it's tough. I pick out about fifty.

"Where ya headin' now?"

I explain that I'm driving around seeing our great country, highlighting the geographical wonders of the USA, not touching any social or political topics.

"I left Los Angeles about, m-m, three weeks ago."

"Well. Some awful thing there yesterday. We sure are livin' through some strange times." He removes his hat and mops his brow. "That Bobby Kennedy there, getting' shot like his brother. Ah don' know, things aren't quite right. That there Veetnam war, my God, po' bastards gettin' all shot-up over there, 'scuse ma language. So many of 'em dying, ah don't know."

Kennedy was only yesterday, seems awhile ago now, like I have left that hundreds of miles behind, back in Missouri. I haven't spoken to anyone much since Walt's garage.

"No, it's not good is it? I don't like it, seems like it's getting' worse all the time, so much violence. They should bring the troops back home. I mean we don't even know why we're over there anymore."

I don't want to get too deep into the subject but I can see that Bobby Kennedy's assassination was a shock that is converting more people into sceptics. Like the jukebox guy, they weren't so sure if they could go along with this anymore. I pay him $12.50 for the records.

"Well, I'd like to buy more records but I'm going to have to jam this box into the van. Wow, it weighs a ton, these things are heavy."

"Hah. Don't we know it, bin carryin' 'em 'round fer years."

This is a beautiful road. I like the way it undulates through the countryside and small towns, past feed merchants, agricultural machinery dealers, with rows of new and used equipment parked alongside the road; tractors, balers, spreaders, wagons and mowers. The John Deeres are green, the Allis-Chalmers orange and the McCormicks are red. There seem to be more tractors in Kentucky than cars. Route 62 is quiet. Most of the traffic is ambling pick-ups with haybales in the back. I putt along taking my time, looking left and right enjoying the scene. The towns look as if they are under a spell that is preserving them, forever in the fifties. Dairy Queen, A & P stores, Woolworths five and dime, Ligget & Rexall drug stores, the Little League field with its tiny diamond and bleachers, like my old home town when I was in sixth grade.

I could stay on this road all the way up toward Lexington. A glance in the rear view mirror shows there is no one behind me, I begin driving slowly. I like it here. I might even be able to go into some of these homes and play the old records that I have just picked-up, there are probably still 78 players in their living rooms. Some people around here might not even know what stereo is, after all, this is the home of bluegrass. Simple music, just the act of getting together and playing. I can dig that, getting the right balance, enjoying it.

The last recording session I did with Gram and the other guys in The Submarine Band was an easy-going and uncomplicated night during the early summer of '67 when we laid down some nice grooves. We weren't aiming at anything specific, it was more like picking up pebbles off a beach and throwing them in the sea just to see the splash. Our focus had become blurred after a few months in Hollywood but we managed to hit the edge of the target with our eyes closed that night.

None of the record company execs that we had met with had offered anything more than platitudes. Not one of them had reached inside their sports jacket, whipped-out a contract and passed over a gold fountain pen while saying, 'Great stuff, I want you boys to sign right here, a-and here.' They were all scared of the country sound, which was the essence of what we were doing, our statement and identity. We were speaking in a dialect or a language that was unintelligible to most of them. No deal, just rejection with a well-groomed smile. We didn't fit into the mainstream music business, too hippie for Nashville and, just too country for LA.

We hadn't played a gig for a few weeks and were beginning to succumb to the deflated feeling that LA was just another leap to nowhere, only an extension on our path to obscurity. To kick-up the smouldering fire, regenerate and have some fun, we decided to book a session, record some different material and see what happened. We went down to the Goldstar Studio one evening with an open-minded attitude, no producer, no record company and no food.

Goldstar was a funky studio. Unlike our last session in New York, there was none of the cold, antiseptic, science lab atmosphere that had filled the Columbia studio. The ambience was improved by a bit of litter, a few old paper coffee cups and an empty beer bottle lying in the corner. I could smell cigarettes, a bar room, the morning after, odour. The place was scuffed, worn and had been well used. I later found out that a lot of classic LA rhythm 'n' blues had been cut there. The engineer was loose, casual, smoking a cigarette.

"How ya doin' guys, okay? Ya got everythin' inside now? I just wanna lock the door, don't want to be disturbed when we get rollin'. You expectin' anyone else?"

"No we're fine, that's cool."

We looked around, acclimatising while setting up. The studio was cluttered and dim. Beige sound baffles, tweed material draped over the walls, nicotine stained acoustic tiles, toffee-and-camel-toned carpets with spilled-coffee stains created an over-all brown theme. The organ, piano and a couple of old amps kept to the color co-ordination. Columbia had gone for the various shades-of-gray look, straightforward and serious colors.

Gram walked over and sat down at the Hammond B-3 organ and started diddling around the keyboard. He held a chord and tried pulling out the different stops, playing with the variations.

"Yeah, that's nice, yeah."

"Hey, Booker T." Gram had started goofing around on 'Green Onions', bobbing his head to the sound. More adjustments to the stops produced sympathetic body movements and poses, reflecting the B-3's different voices. He waggled his head and clowned, characterizing the act of playing cool organ riffs.

"Um-m, I like this. Why don't I play the Hammond for a bit, huh?" he raised his eyebrows and smiled over at me.

"Yeah Gram, it sounds real fine. I'm going to plug in, keep in that groove." The drums were set up and knocked-out a beat.

"Yes indeed," Mickey approved, as Gram pumped-out some jazzy phrases then tentatively tried the bass manual, Thum thum thum thum. I shouldered the bass, turned on the amp and began walking a bass scale, joining the swing-blues that the guys were jamming on. A few minutes later the studio monitor crackled:

"Yeah guys, sounds good. I've got some levels in here. Ah, you want to do somethin'?" That was fast, this guy knew what he was doing.

"Yeah, sure, let's go."

"Ok, lemme come out and set up a vocal mic, hold on."

It sounded like he was encouraging us to just go ahead and do some stuff live, all down at once. Maybe that's how he liked to work, spontaneously, going with the groove. Hey, why not. We only had this one session booked, we're paying for it, there's no record company involved tonight. We hadn't decided what we were going to record.

"What about that Little Milton thing we've been listening to?" suggested Gram, wanting to stay with the blues feel and keep playing on the B-3.

"Yeah sure, man. What key's good? What's that G?"

Gram moved the boom mic a bit closer and tried a few lyrics,

'Fee-el so bad, feel like a baw-all game on a rainy day.'

"You can come in a bit closer on the vocals out there. Ah, does the drummer want some earphones? Or, I could put some of the vocals back into the room, it'd be Okay, if it's live," the engineer suggested. He did like the live sound.

"Sure, give it a whirl."

"Okay guys, just go ahead. We're rollin'."

We went right into it, relaxed, like we were playing at home, jamming, throwing-in another chorus or solo and arrived at an ending, conjured out of nods and winks. Even though it was very casual, it felt like it could have been a decent take. The organ and the r 'n' b feel was refreshing, exciting and breaking-up the band's recent log jam of frustration. It was fun, playing together and different than trying to sell the band. This was play, like a game, like kids running around and playing tag.

"Wow. That wasn't bad."

"Man, the Hammond really pulls it together."

The engineer's speaker crackled, "That sounded good guys. Sounded good in here. Yeah. You wanna try something else?"

Christ! The guy was happy with one take and we thought it sounded pretty good too.

"Yeah, let's roll!" Mick affirmed.

"Ian, why don't you do that one, 'Hooked'," Gram suggested.

"Yeah, okay. That would sound good if we used the Hammond again. You okay with that?"

"Ha ha ha, yeah. I love it. I forgot how great they are. I wanna keep sittin' right here all night long."

"Okay. Lemme have that mic, I'm gonna si-i-ing that song wit' Mista Gee Pee grindin' his organ. Oh yeah."

"Uh-huh, you go on an' do it boy, 'n don't hold back on me, you hear?"

After a false start, we put down 'Hooked', another straight-up r 'n' b song. We kept the energy level going and drove it through with another good groove on the second take.

"I'd sort of like to hear what they're sounding like."

"Yeah. Maybe we're getting the wrong idea. It sounds good, in this room."

"Okay, I can hear you, guys," said the engineer. "Why don't you come into the control room for a play-back, then you'll get a better idea."

"Good idea, thanks."

"I'm just gonna roll back that last one. That'll give you a taste of it, okay?" He hit play, the track rolled.

'I been up all night, 'cause I can't sleep.'

"M-m. I don't like the sound of my voice," I criticized.

"That was only the first line."

The engineer said, "I haven't really done anything much with vocals yet. Look, I'll patch it through and give it a touch of echo. There, see? Not too much, just a touch."

"Yeah, that sounds better." The play back sounded good, we were pretty happy with it.

"I don't know exactly what you guys are tryin' to do, but, keepin' it simple is workin' out for you, tonight."

"Yeah, it sounds pretty good."

"You know I've done a lot of sessions here, been a few years now, and some of the best ones have been real simple. Some of the real good ones have been when they came into the studio and didn't even know the songs. One time an r 'n' b guy came in here, I'm not going to mention his name, but he's had some big records, okay. He had a big band, maybe eight, ten guys and he didn't want to shell-out a load of dough.

So, before they start he's already laying into them saying; 'Listen, if you niggas can't put this down in less than an hour, I'm gonna kick yo' black ass outta here. You got it?' He goes up to the drummer, I can hear him over the mic, and he says, 'Motherfucker, yo' lucky to be here tonight and yo' better keep it together.' Well those guys were so scared of screwing anything up that they all laid right back, and hardly played anything. The drummer only used a couple of fills, the guys playin' horns kept it down to a few notes. They wanted to get it over with. And, it was great. A killer groove."

"Well, we don't have a gun pointed at us. This is our nickel."

"I like the way it's goin'. Let's try something else. We might be able to do one more."

"Okay then, the floor is yours, guys."

Goldstar seemed to be the antidote to the stiff, uptight sessions of the past. We were just sliding right along and we put down a few tracks during that magic night. Yeah. Great feel. What was the secret? No inept producer interfering? An engineer who had a casual way of working? No fixed objective? The alignment of the heavenly bodies? Who knows, sometimes things just go that way and fall the right-way-up.

Late that night, we listened to the playback in the control room, as the engineer ran-off a copy onto quarter-inch tape. There were a couple of loose bits, all of us flubbed something, but they weren't important, compared with the flow and the feel.

"I don't like the beginning of that guitar solo," John remarked about the third track.

"Hey, no, it's okay, it's good. It was laid back and there's a good feel on the track. No, it's okay."

"That sounded fine to me."

"Relax."

It was a good session, no stress, no mess, good fun, great feel.

I'd like to hear that session again. I wonder what happened to those tapes.

In a little village in West Virginia, I stop out front of a gas station and store. The small general store's shelves are sparsely stocked with tin cans of soup, pork 'n' beans, flour, corn meal, soda and all sorts of tobacco. There are cigarettes, cigars, cheroots, and snuff, in tins and pouches, chewing tobacco and pipe tobacco. A lot of candy, cupcakes, devil dogs, cookies, life savers and gum for the non-smokers.

The store has an adjoining bar and I walk on through. The young woman who was behind the store counter and cash register comes through a doorway connecting the two service areas and becomes the barmaid.

"What kin ah git ya?"

There are strange labels and beer signs along with some of the regulars.

"How about a bottle of that Appalachian beer, I'll try that."

She reaches down, opens the lid of a Coke machine and fishes amongst the chiming bottles, catching my choice. The cap clinks into a bucket underneath the bottle opener on the back of the bar.

"There ya go. That's fiftah-fahv cents."

I take a swig on the bottle, it was nice and cold.

"Wha do ya thank a that beer?" asks a guy sitting at a table in the room. He's about my age and there are several empties in front of him.

"It's good 'n' cold." He could tell from my accent that I was a stranger, just passing through, on the road.

"We cull it West Virgin-ya water, hah."

"Yeah, how come?"

"There ain't hardly no alcohol in it. State law only allows two p'cent. Near beer." He reaches into his shirt pocket and pulls out a pouch of tobacco, extracts a bunch of dark brown leaf and kneads it into a prune that he shoves into the side of his mouth. He offers the pouch over to me.

"Ya want a chaw?" His cheek bulges and he works his lower jaw then tongues the tobacco into its usual spot. The chewing tobacco packet says Red Man in big red letters. An Indian with prominent cheekbones and a feather head-dress has an expression of surprise or bored acceptance at being caught within the white circle of the illustration. I take a tiny pinch and hesitantly put it in my mouth like an aspirin.

"Ya gotta have more an' that! Hell, you ain't gonna taste nothin'." The tobacco was already singeing my tongue. He laughs at my caution, which confirms to him what a bunch of pussies Yankees are.

The jukebox plays, 'Yummy, yummy, yummy, I got love in my tummy' and the music draws three little girls into the room who dance in front of the Seeburg box. Records always sound so good in jukeboxes. What comes out of a jukebox is random; someone else has put in a dime and made a choice. The music jumps out unannounced; there is an element of surprise not choice. The jukebox always seems to enhance the catchy bits, the intro, the themes or chorus. Del Shannon's song 'Runaway' with that,' I won-won-won-won won-nder' falsetto and the screechy organ solo, will always burst out of the speakers and persuade me to like it. That song gets people miming the organ solo, their fingers dancing on a table top or the car dashboard as they sing along with the 'Why-why-why-why why-yi-yi' bits. That just doesn't happen with 'The Times They Are A-Changin''. Dylan won't get the ten-year-olds dancing.

Outside in the warm evening, I can hear music. Piano and some vocals, it sounds a bit like Jerry Lee Lewis. The sound is drifting over from a wooden building, a shed or a hall. It's not a radio, someone is playing live, maybe a bluegrass or country band rehearsing. I walk toward the sound and as I get closer I can see through the open door. A few people are on a stage. A singer is rearing back, belting out a song with a couple of guys playing acoustic guitars. It must be a gig, there are a few people inside watching.

"Come-on along in, we jus' gettin' started," says a lanky guy standing inside the open door. A sign next to the door says,

The Lamb of God Congregation. It's a church, I put my brakes on. I had enough of going to church when I was younger, enough to last me several lifetimes. I've had to sit through too many long church services, prayer meetings and Bible study. I remember Junior Missionary Volunteers nights when a dozen kids were huddled on a couple of pews, watching a movie about how the heathen natives in Borneo, or somewhere, had given up worshipping their idols. They had turned away from the evil witch doctors who were all agents of the devil, covered up their bare breasts, got off their cannibal diet, listened to the missionary's message of truth and accepted our saviour, Jesus Christ into their black hearts.

"Ya like the music? Come on in, they gonna do some fine songs."

I relented, drawn-in by the soulful gospel group. They were playing high-energy music and, now inside, I could hear clapping, the tambourines, and the piano that all added to a room full of rhythm. The singer was drawing out the coda, getting more passionate with his vocals and a trio of back-up singers were answering to his testifying.

'He-e-e-e-s ma lord.'

'He's my lord.'

'O-o-oh ye-es he ee-es.'

'Yes he is.'

'Ah-h-h call on he-e-em.'

'Call on him.'

'Sa-a-aved bah thee blood.'

'By-y the blood.'

'His ho-o-oly blood.'

'Ho-oly blood.'

'Blood of-ah da lamb.'

'O-of the lamb.'

He stuck with that simple gospel music formula; draw it out, stay on the two chords, keep it going, work the crowd up, improvise, show the passion of your belief and let the Holy Spirit do the talking for you.

The singer began addressing the crowd.

"Oh yes-s-s Je-e-sus! I believe! Believe in the blood, the blood of the lamb. Yes! An' ah know hee-ya ta-night, we gonna feel his Ho-lah Spirit! Oh yes we are. Here ta-night we gonna see his Holy light! Revealed in his Holy word. Amen! The wor-r-rd of God almighty! Were gonna hear the word of God! Are you ready fo' the Holy word of God! It's right here. I got it all right here. Do ya wondah bout the ee-vents takin' place round us every day? Are ya troubled? The answers are all right here!" He holds up his Bible and displays it, slowly, sweeping the black book in front of him like the scan of a radar dish.

"Yas we a livin' in mighty troubled times ma dear brothas 'n' sistahs. We wonder, what is goin' on? Well I'm a-gonna tell ya to-night. It's all right here, in the Holy Bible." He pauses and scans the room.

"Wars, tem-pests, dee-bauchery and fornication. Sound familiar to y-all." Some people nod in agreement and mutter Amen.

"Thas right, we know it all too well don't we," he nods knowingly. "Signs of thee times, surely we are in the la-a-ast days, the time of thee end. A-a-men!"

"Amen," more agree.

"Only the righteous can be saved. Only those who have bin washed in the blood of the lamb will, one day, dress in them radiant raiments an' be taken up into the kingdom a God! But befo' that happens, the earth shall be wracked by wars, plagues, pollution and shall be despoiled! Yes, polluted and despoiled! It all right here. I'm a-gonna show you."

He opens the Bible, holds it in his outstretched arm and elevates the book above his eye level with a dramatic gesture.

"I'm a-readin' it right here, E-Ezekiel, chapter thirty-three. 'Thus saith the lord God, they that are in the wastes shall fall by the sword and him that is in the open field will I give to the beasts to be devoured and they that be in forts and in the caves shall die, of pestilence!'" He pauses, stares, giving the text time to sink-in.

"Tha's right! Even in your mighty fortress, high up on a hill, behind them thick concrete walls, you shall not escape the pollution and despoliation. An' Ezekiel says, 'For I will lay the land most desolate and the pomp of her strength shall cease.' Tha's right, the land will be desolate, owing to our abominations."

"Now you good people might want to warn your friends and naybuhs about wha's comin'. They might laugh at ya. Sayin', wha' you so worried 'bout? Everythin's just fine 'n' dandy. But let's see what the apostle Peter gotta say 'bout it, shall we? Chapter three,

'There shall come in the last days scoffers, walking after their own lust.'" He shakes his head in disgust. "That's right, scoffers! They're gonna be laughin' an' laughin'. You're gonna tell them, ree-pent, an' save your self! But no, they gonna keep-on laughin'. They don' know what's in-store, they haven't heard 'bout the wastin' and pollutin' that's a-commin'. Oh and it is a-comin'! Listen hear. Rev-el-ations chapter six; 'I beheld a pale horse and his name, that sat on him, was Death and Hell followed with him. And power was into them to kill with the sword and with hunger and death.' And there's more, they ain't finished their awful work yet. 'And I beheld when he opened the sixth seal there was a great earthquake and the sun became black...for the great day of his wrath is come!' We best believe it! Amen!"

"Amen," I was beginning to agree. Yeah, man!

The preacher pulled an apologetic smile as he reached for a handkerchief and mopped his glistening face. He had done several songs before he started in on his sermon.

"The Bible tells us more about how the earth is gonna be ruined. 'There arose a smoke and the sun and the air were darkened.' Yes sir! Dark days ahead, worse than any smog we already got! Chapter eighteen, John prophesies, 'The angel cried mightily, with a strong voice saying, Babylon the great is fallen and is become the habitation of devils and the hold for every foul spirit.' Yes sir, Babylon the mighty kingdom is a-gonna fall, takin' all a them dancin' fools down with her. An' he tells us who they are, 'For a-a-all the nations have drunk of the wine of her fornication and the merchants of the earth are waxed ri-i-ich through the abundance of her delicacies.' He's pleadin' with us, warnin' us, 'Come out of her that ye not be partakers of her sins.' Lord help us, help us here to-night. Yes, you-all stick to that road of righteousness, illuminated by his Holy light and stay away from the darkness of Babylon, and her shadows of death. Amen!"

"AMEN!" the enlightened souls chorused.

I took the warning, got up and left the church meeting. According to the preacher and the prophets, we all better stop doing the Tango, the Twist or the Boogaloo with Babylon. I wonder if the guys out in Drop City realize how far ahead of the game they are. I guess they must have been on the phone to the old Bible prophets already. Amen! Have mercy!

As I home-in on the East Coast, LA is wa-ay over the horizon and has been relegated to, back there, the past. Here, there, then, when, if, could be, was. Being on the road is always, Now. Living in motion, the Gypsy Dimension, even better at the plodding warp-speed I have been keeping. Man, it's the closest you get to freedom. No rent, bills in the mail, telephones or granite foundations, just rubber-rollin' on a million miles of tar-trail. I don't want to come down.

The remnants of The Burrito Brothers are hoping that, back on the East Coast, we might find a drummer, a horn player and get it together. We would play that mix of soul, jump, rock 'n' roll, western swing, and a touch of country that was the Burrito's thing. It could work, with some of The Remains' songs added to the play list. Maybe. But who knows what might be happening on the college circuit or if it is still the gold mine it used to be.

I wondered what Mickey, Brandon and some of the other guys back in LA might be up to. I hadn't spoken with any of them for about a month or more. It was a case of not wanting to look back or get a fix on the point of departure, that was shrinking as I ventured further off-shore. The shock of being out of sight of land is lessened by the belief that a harbor might be just over the horizon. The enchantment of the campfire had become the new beacon. I had been navigating by the penetrating desert stars, this evening they seemed to have dimmed. Seems like Mr. Lonely is ringing the doorbell and I'm trying not to hear him.

In the West Virginia twilight, between Scotts' Hardware and Goodall's Clothing, I stop in Main Street, a canyon of old brick buildings. The window displays of clothes, tools and radios are like museum exhibits, appearing to have been on the shelf since the '50s. The town is a trip into the past, parts of my childhood have been captured and preserved. I can not see a single car that has rolled out of Detroit since the year I finished high school. No foreign cars, VWs or Toyotas. A '59 Pontiac rolls by and heading the other way is a GMC pick-up, the only two vehicles moving, slowly. There is almost no traffic, the stoplight is a boastful statement. Maybe things were booming here, once, years ago.

I scrabble through my pockets and bag in a search for change, a dollar fifty, two bucks, for a phone call. The phonebooth contains remnants of earlier heat. Cigarette butts, predominantly a couple of brands, document long calls of desperation or loneliness. Maybe I've got a touch of the same thing. I find Brandon's number. It will be about six-thirty in California.

Please deposit fifty cents. The phone demands.

The wall-phone rings in the kitchen that I bring into focus.

"Hello."

"Hey man, it's Ian."

"Ian! we were wondering where the old gypsy had gone! How the Hell are you?" Brandon is effusive. "Hey!" says another voice, in the background. "Seems like you've been gone for a couple of months!"

"Yeah, it's been a few weeks now, buddy. I've been all over the place. How are you doing?"

The background voice yells across, "Here, try some of this!" I recognize Mickey Gauvin's voice, resonating in Brandon's kitchen.

"Well, we're just getting round to snortin' a li'l bit o' something ver-r-y special, some zippety-do-dah. Ha!" Mickey choruses, "My oh my what a won-nderful day. Ha, ha." "Hey you should be here. Where are you?"

"I'm somewhere in West Virginia, still. I'm travelling alone now. Barry and Briggs went on ahead. They took-off when we were in Kansas, somewhere."

"Well no wonder they split, who wants to hang 'round out there, in Kansas. You're lucky to have escaped."

"What are you up to?"

"Well, just fine an' dandy. Ha!" Mickey chips-in again, "We're just havin' a good ol' time, out here tonight."

"Well good. What else you been doin?" I ask, again.

"We've been playing. I mean a lot. I just got a re-e-al nice Les Paul. Sounds fan-fuckin'-tastic! And! We're working with a gre-e-at electric piano player, that I met at the Corral."

"Wow, that's cool."

"Hey, we need a bass player!"

"Come on back. Turn around!" Mickey advises.

"We're going to get some gigs, soon as we have a bass. What are you doing?"

"Well, you know, I'm not sure. I'm still just driving… and don't know much else. Have you seen Gram?"

"No, not in awhile now. He's still a Byrd, as far as I know. Last time he was around here, he was, sort of, laying-low. I don't think he wanted to be seen, a bit sneaky, staying in a hotel, maybe dodging Nancy. You know, the usual Gram an' Nancy thing. I don't know what's up with ol' Lulu. Wait a minute.. huh?" I overhear the muffled voices. "Yeah, Mickey says, he heard, GP might have been going to England, or something."

Please deposit fifty cents.

"Aw shit, hold on," several coins chime down the slot. "That's about all of my change. What are you guys playing? What sort of stuff?"

"We-ell, a bit of rock 'n' roll, we worked-up that one, ah, you know," Brandon sings, " Oh-wo-wo Miss Anne.. the other day. A-a-nd a few r 'n' b things, 'There Ain't Nobody Here But Us Chickens'. And, get this, we've been trying 'We're Havin' A Heat Wave', doing it like a blues shuffle."

"That sounds really cool, good idea."

"Oh yeah, fun. We've got some instrumentals that we made up, we just want to use them for, ah, background. Talk or dialogue over the top of them, like.. 'Hi Kids! It's Tiny Tim!' I've been writing a couple of new songs as well. One goes", he signs a bit, "There's nothin' you can't buy for a nickel or a dime.' Something like that. No, things are sounding really good. Mickey's had a break and he's really into playing again."

"Yeah?"

"We tried out an r 'n' b version of 'The Fugitive' that sounded fuckin' dynamite! We've got a good set already! We want to get out and do it! We're thinking about wearing costumes, like Halloween outfits, on stage. Ha! It's great. Wait a second… Gauvin's passing me something here, lets see. Um-m. Oh yes, Ha!"

"Hey, come-on-back-out!" Mickey shouts in the distance. Brandon has grown fainter, I hear.. "Woah yes! Uh-huh, woah-boy, woah-boy, ha!"

Please deposit fifty cents.

"Shit, that's it, my money's almost gone. I shove in a couple of nickels and a dime."

"Woah! Sorry 'bout that. Whoo-hoo!"

"The music thing sounds good, Brandon."

"Hey, think about it, seriously. This band is going to be really a lot of fun!"

Please deposit thirty cents.

"Ok man. Thanks. I'll…"

Please deposit thirty cents.

"..call you again an'…stay in touch.."

Er-r-r-r-r-r-r-r-r-r-r-r-r-r-r. The line went dead but I held the purr against my ear.

"..when I know.… anything."

I step out of the phone booth still hearing remnants of the Topanga-two's boisterousness and the futility of the disconnected-signal. The town has slipped closer to dark and has nothing to say. The stoplight uselessly turns green. Leaning against the van, slightly dazed for a few moments, the fractured sidewalk is enough to hold my attention. The curbstones are actually stone, long slabs of hewn rock, blasted out of a quarry in one of the hills that besiege the town. Horses and wagons might have hauled them here in the town's infancy. Clip-clop-clip-clop.

A guy is coming down the sidewalk toward me, the sound of his footsteps the only buzz in this place. He raises his hand and takes a drag on a cigarette.

"Evenin'." He moves toward the phone, drops the butt on the sidewalk, it bounces, sparks and rolls as he pulls open the door. He must be 'Mr. Lonesome', the smoker. He's going to go in there and start singing that Jim Reeves song; the one that talks about puttin' your sweet lips to the phone. I don't really need to hear this; I've got enough West Virginia melancholy running through me already today. His coins jingle into the slot and, under the phone booth light, he takes center stage.

"Hell-oh, it's me." He turns slightly, his eyes already seeing something else.

No campsite under the stars for me tonight, it's too late now. I head out of town, over rusting railroad tracks, looking for a place to pull over. A bird swoops over the road, lit by the headlights. White, with wide wings and big eyes, an owl. Hey Mr. Night Owl, watch it. Yeah The Night Owl, we had some good times playing there.

We played in Greenwich Village a lot in '66. Sometimes that part of the city was a bit like Bourbon Street but colder. Music swelled out onto the streets from the clubs and coffee houses. Even in the winter there was a buzz as people, back-lit by traffic and puffing warm, breathy clouds, scuttled between doorways and taxis. The Submarine Band's main venue in the Village was The Night Owl and, later in the year, a new band showed up there, The Blues Magoos. Several of the Magoos were young guys. Peppy, who did a lot of the vocals, seemed as if he was just out of high school and Ralph, the piano player, probably was as well. They played rock, a couple of r 'n' b things and dressed in vibrant, bright clothes. I remember thinking that Peppy was too young to sing that James Brown song but he enjoyed himself so much that you couldn't help enjoying it with him. The flowered shirts reflected the band's personality; energetic and effervescent.

We played back-to-back with them several times and the club was usually full. The Magoos brought in passers-by from off the street. People were attracted by the pink, billowing sleeves, swirling locks and fuzz-tone on everything. We became friendly and they came up to the house in the Bronx to hang out. Their manager was trying to get A&R people to come and see them play and knock down another deal. Sometime, later in the year they did get a better deal and began recording. Looking for some more material, they considered recording one of Gram's songs. Gram showed them a few of his ideas, one of them was 'Strong Boy', a new song. The Magoos liked the lyrics and the message, with an underdog story line. Ronnie and Peppy wanted to play it to their producer. That was cool, we'd all been buddies for awhile by then and it would be good if the Magoos covered one of Gram's songs. It didn't work out though, the producer thought that Gram's song had too much of a country sound lurking inside. Too much for the Magoos, who were moving toward 'the psychedelic sound'. Country! No-way, man.

The Blues Magoos' deal with Mercury went ahead later that year. They released a single, 'We Ain't Got Nothing Yet', then an album, Psychedelic Lollipop. The next time we saw them was in the spring of '67 at the end of a tour when they had played The Hollywood Palladium. I noticed that night that they had some new instruments, longer hair and wider bell-bottoms. They filled the hall with plenty of volume but I missed the naïve boisterousness that they used to broadcast at The Night Owl. We met and talked after the gig. The single was beginning to sell and get a lot of airplay. Backstage, they became more lively and animated like in Greenwich Village. Peppy broke out laughing after telling us that they were going on tour with Herman's Hermits and The Who. He giggled, "Man, we're going to be the only Americans there!"

The Magoos had come up with something that a record company wanted. I don't know if it was the shirts or the fuzz-tone. The Submarine Band was wearing the wrong sort of shirt.

A couple of miles past the railroad crossing, I see a rest area loop of road under some trees and turn in. It seems like a long day. I'll sleep in the van tonight.

The television is on, again. They're going round and round until Big Roberta Brown knocks the roller-skaters on their asses. They spin like turtles on their backs, clawing at the sunset and over the waterfall. KRLA's Dick Lane holds the big mic and grimaces in pain. He has a bad toothache from all the microphones he eats, it's going to explode, the shark-nosed X-ray machine moves in for a bite. AH-H-O-O-W-W !!

Awoken by the desperate howl, I lurch up. I'm in the back of the van. Who's driving? It's not moving, I can't remember where I am. Hesitantly I turn and look through the windshield into a dark night. I sigh and begin to decipher the form of a star-lit tree. Again I hear the moan. A distant freight train, wallowing towards dawn, vibrating towns and nudging dreamers en-route. I'm vague about where I am and begin to remember, the slow uphill grades and the phone call to Brandon only a few hours ago. I lay back. Phew.

Some of Brandon's enthusiasm lingers with me, hours after speaking to him on the phone. He often had spontaneous, quirky ideas. He was creative. He enjoyed clowning, getting into a character and finding an animated voice to go with it. We had done hours of un-scripted, improvised recording, playing with the flow of ideas, songs and exchanges as they surfaced. Brandon had often been sitting on the sideline of music. Since the sessions we did with him in the fall of '65, he never quite got back into the game. There had been a couple of times when we had discussed the possibility of him joining The Submarine Band but it never happened. On one occasion, his management had discouraged him from veering-off into music and joining a band. Maybe if that had happened, the ISB would have moved in a slightly different direction.

During this last year, as The Submarine Band began to fragment and his buddies started going off on tangents, he had played less and less music with us. Brandon was a more of a beginner, having only taken up strumming a guitar and writing songs recently, and was intimidated by the guys who had more confidence and experience. Maybe now Brandon was ready to find his voice and do his thing.

Masks, makeup and mayhem: yeah that sounds good. It could be a name.. 'The Makeup and Mayhem Band', 'the Church of Makeup Mayhem.' U-m-m? I liked the idea; I could go that way, more showmanship, childishness and folly. The latter days of The Submarine Band had become too stiff and serious. Before we got The Burritos going, it often seemed that 'Mickey, Ian & Brandon' was an act working on the zany home recordings. Making it up as we went along, what we came up with was usually fresh and was never the same thing twice. We had used a few home-made instruments (rubber bands on cereal boxes, singing through cardboard tubes), that had worked with what we were doing. Spurting banality, stream of consciousness ejaculation, subversive jingles and no-content news programming, were some of the ingredients we pulled together.

Fuck! Maybe I should be working with Brandon and Mickey. We had been paving the way, trying out the ideas and concepts for a new act without even realizing it. Humor had been our platform and the flag we were waving, rather than slick guitar solos or musicianship. We never had any arrangements, it was mostly free-rein. Nonsense had been crowned King.

At three a.m. a fuzzy plan of getting up, starting the engine, turning around and heading back west begins to become believable until the big speaker cabinet, that makes-up part of my berth, nudges, reminding me that I have a delivery to make. The chimera evaporates, Pop! I have to get the cab, an amp top and parts of the motorcycle back to Barry and Briggs. That means Connecticut. I could swing up to Massachusetts, visit my family, refuel and head back to LA with a lighter load. The bus will fly along then. Yeah, maybe that's it. It has taken me all these thousands of miles to get the real picture. What's the future? It's a loop. Future, past, present, past, future, round and round. Here merges with There. I'm holding both of them, one in each hand. I toss them… up… over my head.. they spin, slowly.. hovering … then flutter down… choosing a roost… each lands in the opposite palm.

Just a couple of miles from where I had spent a fretful night in the van, I pull over at a small place that is not much more than a crossroad. A gas station, a smattering of houses, a few trailers and a diner didn't merit a town name. I sit in the van idly looking at the road map half hoping it will be the missing ingredient that will foster an urge to get moving. I still only see what's behind; Charleston, Clay, Sutton; places I drove through yesterday evening. I have racked-up a lot of miles now, getting close to four thousand. I'm tired and don't have the appetite for gobbling-up more highway today. I'm hungry. It's warm, getting close to summer. A parade of cumulus clouds passes, a bloated piglet follows Snoopy and a billowing slipper.

A truck pulls up at the stop sign and a guy gets out. He goes to the back of the pick-up, lifts out an army knapsack and a guitar case, gives the side of the truck a slap and it kicks-off as a horse would. He wears faded jeans, a plaid lumberjack jacket and a baseball cap that pans as he scans the intersection. Crossing the road, he moves toward the diner.

"Howdy", he smiles, "how ya doin'?"

"Hi. Got a good guitar in there?"

"Yep, an old Gibson." The fabric on the weary case is ripped and shredded stickers reveal scuffed wood beneath. The clasps are broken, a couple of knotted cords bind-up the case. "Don't know how I do it, she's been pawned a few times but I always scrape-up the money to bail her out. You passin' through?"

"Well yeah, but I haven't got anywhere much today. Where you headed?"

"That's a good question, yep. I sure know where I've been, nowhere big enough to have a bus come through more than once a day. Ha."

He looks experienced, a few gray hairs in his sideburns, he's ten or fifteen years older than me. "What way you goin'?" I'm hesitant with my reply. Today I still feel unsure about a plan, direction or destination and he picks-up on this. "Hey buddy, don't worry, just askin'. I'm not hustling you or nothing, not a jailbird on the run. I'm not a wanted man, 'cept by a few landlords and maybe the phone company, but they ain't hurtin' that much."

"I was heading towards Boston. Huh," I laugh and relax.

"Boston? Winter's too cold."

"I left LA about a month ago."

"LA. Good life there," he had three-word catalogues for anyplace I mentioned. Lexington; Too many dogs. Flagstaff; Miss them women. Albuquerque; All that whiskey. Taos; Bad ass boyfriend. Knoxville; Never back there.

"Man, you been around."

"Yeah I was in LA 'bout a year ago. All them fumes." I thought he meant the smog. "Worked in a body shop, couldn't last there more than a week. Those guys are gonna die young."

"I was out there then. Playing in a band."

"Well wha'd you know. Small world, an' getting' sma-aller all the time," he smiled and cocked his head. "You know what? It must be shrinking."

"Still seems pretty big to me. I been back an' forth, New York to LA, a couple of times now."

"We-ell that's good. You got a load more times before it sinks in. I'm goin' in for some breakfast, you goin' to join me?"

"Yeah, I think I need some coffee."

We talked about travelling. We talked about music.

"No foolin'," he was surprised, "you been playin' in a country band in New York and LA, I thought they didn't allow none of that up there."

"Well, I guess you're right, they didn't seem to want it. Just don't want to know. We thought they might of. Country is still a bit too weird, sort of scares 'em."

"Did you get down to Nashville?"

"No, we tried to make a stand in the cities. I mean, I know Nashville's a city, we just didn't make any contacts down there. You ever play down there?"

"Hell yeah. Played there a few times. Ha! For tips, lousy tips, mostly. One night I was playin' with this other guy, we were sittin' on the steps of The Ryman. It was about three in the morning, we're playin' away, an' a cop pulls-up, rolled down his window, listened for a bit, then said, 'You boys best go back where you come from, too many guitar players here a'ready.' Ha, that was the closest I got to playin' The Opry, just sittin on the steps."

"At least they didn't throw you in the can, for disturbing the peace."

He rubbed his two-day-growth of whiskers, "Well, I been in the pokey here an' there. Drunk, vagrancy, mistaken identity. Once I just got out of a car, hitched a long ride from Colorado down to Reno, thought I'd see if I could find some work down there, or Tahoe, maybe playing in a bar and, probably, washing dishes. So, I'm sittin' at a lunch counter, State troopers come in, havin' a look at everyone. I'm eating chops and mash potatoes, the cop's walking down, havin' a peek, I see his shadow on the counter, he's stopped, right behind me. Says, 'get up mister', and he checks me over like a damn hawk. I'm asking, 'ah, what's the trouble officer?' He says, 'I think you gotta come with me.' Man, I haven't done anything, I tell him. 'Well,' he says, 'we'll have to check on that down at the station, you gonna give me any trouble?' 'Course, I know better than that, an I get up. The gal at the counter comes skippin' over sayin', 'Hold on, wait a minute, that's a dollar an fifteen cents.' Man, I wanted to finish-off them mash potatoes, before they dragged me away. It was all mistaken identity. I decided, the Hell with Reno. I walked away, got outta there. See, after being on the move for so long, I learned to listen to the little things, and look for the signs, the signals that you gotta read, pointing you in the right direction. Hell, I still get 'em wrong sometimes, but not so much."

"Hm-m. The signs I'm seeing today are pointing in opposite directions. One says, turn right, to Boston, the other one, turn left to LA."

"Boston's closer," he replies.

"Yeah but I don't know if it's the right place."

"Well maybe you'll have to go see."

"It's sort of where I'm from, well near there. Where I grew up."

"You're gonna have to go have a little look-a-see."

"I don't know how much it's changed, there."

"Hell, they don't change all that much. Cities are like people. They've got moods, get a bit pissed-off with you one day, then they're all buddy-buddy again the next day, and, they forget all about ya when you're out of town. You know what? You can go back to a place you knew, hoping things have changed. But usually, you find that some of the best things have died an' some of the worst things are still hangin' around, waiting to get fed."

"We gonna have another coffee?" I suggest.

"What the Hell."

"Where were you coming from, you didn't tell me."

"I'm just coming down from Wheeling, West Virgin-eye-ay. Guitar playin' friend of mine moved back up there. Now he wants to leave, I guess he was in Memphis for a little too long."

"You do anything up there?"

"We played a bit. We were in a band down in Little Rock, two, three years ago. The Rockin' River Boys. Good band, but too much drinkin'. Damn! Had a good gig, pretty regular, played country and party music. Always got the place packed, weekends. I had a room at the club.

Good life. But that went down the drain. Too much drinkin', Man! Led to big trouble."

"Yeah, has a way a doin' that," I agree.

"One of the boys starts dickin' around with the owner's gal. Whiskey and the wrong woman. Uh-uh, I told him, leave it alone. Early one Sunday mornin', before the rooster crows, Wham! My door busts open, I see the dark outline of a guy standing in the doorway, panting. His right hand is raised-up, like someone being sworn-in, an' he's holding a big-ass gun and moaning, 'Where's Marlene, where the Hell is she?' He sees she's not with me and he's gone, running down the hall. I'm just coming to my senses an' hear screaming, 'No, no!' then BAM! That gun's gone off. I ran down the hall, they're in the parking lot. Marlene is on her knees, bare-assed, screamin', 'No, Wayne, No!' A big flash, then BAM! The car window explodes and I see Jamie, the drummer, bail-out of the other door and run off into the dark, all arms and legs. 'I'm gonna kill you!' The guy's screaming. 'You little bastard!' Shit. That was the end a-that gig. He wanted to kill all of us."

"Bands. Never seems long before something explodes."

"Yeah, always a time bomb hiding in there, best not to count your chickens, huh."

"Seems like that's the truth. You ever see the guy he was shootin' at, again?" I ask.

"No. He musta run all the way to the Canadian boarder. Hope the stupid bastard made it."

"Yeah it's funny, how you work with guys for a long time, like every night, an' then it's, just, over. That's it. You never see them again."

"Well you can't be too sure, people got a way of turning up again, a bit further on up the road. Depends if you need them, or if they're holdin' one of the wild cards outta your deck."

After coffee, cornbread and scrambled eggs my stomach is satisfied, maybe it'll spread to my head and I'll get an idea about where I'm going.

"Being settled is fine," he says, "I like it, I've done it dozens of times. Sometimes it comes as a surprise, the whole package drops down right in front of ya. You unwrap it, and there you are, layin' back in bed with a beautiful gal, sippin'a cup of coffee, real cozy. Other times you think you're gonna get settled-in, you pull back the covers and you're lookin' at a bed o' nails. Then you don't want to let the dust hit yer shoes."

"I'd like to settle-down but they won't let me," he sings Merle Haggard, I join him.

"A fugitive must be a rollin' stone.

Down every road there's always one more city,

I'm on the run, the highway is my home."

"Yeah, I'm sort of in love with the road now," I admit.

"Hey that sounds dangerous, you musta got bitten out there somewhere."

"Wanderlust, maybe? It's a high. A trip. You just have to give-in, go with it, keep floating downstream. I keep running into some great things, like prizes, when I'm not expecting them."

"It's a big, big movie."

"Maybe the longer you've been settled into something, the more you need to keep roaming, 'til you find the right trail."

"Like a hound dog, pickin' up that fresh scent. Ah w-o-o-o."

"Yeah, I'm sniffin' around," I take the last slurp of coffee. "Where are you headed now, looking for anymore of the guys from your old band?"

"Oh, they might turn up, somewhere. No, I'm going to swing through Atlanta. I got a couple of songs with a publisher down there and maybe if I bang on his door again, he might get up off his ass and do somethin' with them."

"You write songs?"

"Hell, I got a slew of 'em. Probably lost even more along the way. I left a bunch under the bed when I skipped outta Amarillo, before sun-up." He shook his head, "Amarillo, too much wind. I guess I decided I couldn't take a day more a' that place. Later, I wrote a song about that time, 'That big wind blew me outta town so fast,

I couldn't hear the whisper, sayin' come on back.' Yeah, good ones and bad ones."

"I wrote a few but couldn't seem to finish them. Always seemed like I had a lot of bits and pieces."

"There's a thing about song writing," he squinted, "you have to work 'em through and get something down any way you can. Sometimes, I hitch a couple of them together, to get one that's sort of finished. Give 'em a head and a tail, a little story in the middle, just about all it takes. But then you got to sing 'em."

"Man, they're going to start servin' lunch soon. You headin' out?" he asks.

"Yeah. But I'm still thinking about the guys I spoke to, last night, in LA. I worked with them before. They're trying to put something together. It could be good. On the phone, they were excited about it, you know, really up about it. They were also pretty stoned, out of it."

"Trouble is, with telephones, they have a way of filtering-out the truth. Doesn't matter what people might say, or promise, you can only see what's happening when you walk in through the door. Never is a money-back guarantee on the phone. It's, 'come-on out, the weather's fine!' You hoof-it on out to the promised land, suddenly it's blowin' a damn blizzard. You gotta try a slice, before you buy the whole pie."

"Maybe I've already eaten enough of that Hollywood pie. I heard that, come-on-out-the-weather's-fine thing, the last time."

A newspaper, left on the counter, has a column headline, 'U.S. Pilots Captured: Shot Down Over Hanoi.'

"Woah-boy, what a mess. LBJ doesn't want to see what's goin' on. It's turning into one Hell of a war. Ka-Bam!"

"Were you in the Army?"

"Oh yeah. Worked with radio. Froze my ass off in Korea for six months. This Viet-Nam thing is just sort of an extension of Korea. The reds were sittin' up on the other side of the DMZ; we could only push 'em back so far. The politicians got it in their heads that we can't have that Korea thing happening again. They're crazy, we can't win over there, we're not fighting for anything that's worth a shit. Waste of blood, waste of lives. Leave 'em alone. Get the GIs outta there, bring 'em home and send 'em to college. You weren't over there were you?"

"Uhm-m, nope. I'm not going," I say, quietly, half whispered. My pulse rate goes up.

"Hell no, we won't go?" he winks, "Yeah? I feel sorry for all of the kids, right out of high school, being prodded into that jungle slaughterhouse. You know it's turning this country into a police state."

"Yeah. If I'm not driving, I've been camping in state parks and it's like being out of circulation. When I come out of the sticks and get back on the highway, the cops give me the creeps."

"You lying low, huh?"

I sigh, "Yeah, you know."

"Thought about maybe takin' a little trip to Mexico or Amsterdam? There's a lot of people doin' it."

"I've thought about it. Depends on the heat."

"Well, I got a feelin' you gonna know one way or the other before too long."

"Yeah, unless I stop right here in West Virginia, I guess I'm going to know what's on the cards in a few days. Wow, hard to believe I'm gettin' closer to the East Coast."

"Yep, the sands of time, keep on siftin' through."

"I guess you're not heading south?" he jokes.

"Hey, if I were, you could climb right on in. No, I guess it's north for me." I open-back the side door of the bus.

He stuck his head inside, "You got some cargo squeezed-in here." He turned, sat down on the sill and untied the cords on the battered case. "Well, might as well play one before we say 'so-long."

The old Gibson was scarred, the original black finish had faded to the color of decomposed leaves, deep in a dark forest. A patch above the sound hole was worn to bare spruce by years of pickin'. Thousands of songs had been revived and conjured out of the warm guitar, like a Ouija board, a conduit for the spirits of Hank Williams, Jimmy Rogers, Ira Louvin, Robert Johnson and whoever else drifted in. He began to sing;

Pan-handle cowboys, railroad blues,

Honky-Tonk howlers, hobos' shoes,

Worn-out, patched and singin' the news
About what's inside and how they got through.
Because nothing's new, it's gonna happen to you.
No, nothing's new, it's gonna happen to you.'
"Good meeting ya, buddy."
"Yeah. Great talking to you as well. I hope your man in Atlanta comes through for you."
"Hey what a we been talkin' about? I'll believe it if it happens." He slung the
knapsack over his back and picked up the guitar case.
"Don't sell that guitar!"
"Don't sell yer soul." He ambled towards the road, ready to stick out his thumb.
I wave as I pull out onto the road. I wasn't sure but, over the extended breakfast it
became more clear that I had to complete the trip across before I started flirting with
the schizoid allure of heading back to LA. I'd keep heading east or as near to that as
possible, the roads in West Virginia have to conform to what the steep hills dictate.

Along the road I pass small farms with a few cattle, maybe cows, standing under
trees. Does that mean it's going to rain? There are some clouds, frowning, gray and
grumpy, they are squashing the hills. A small white farmhouse still has last season's
sign, 'Pumpkins'. A guy is looking under the hood of a truck that protrudes from
a barn. The big doors are tied back showing their skeletal Z braces. The humpy
little fields remind me of Brandon's place in Vermont. I remember sitting in a dry,
summer meadow, looking down at the house. Brandon had put stereo speakers on the
windowsill and 'Taxman' was irritating me.

Revolver had just been released and it had been playing almost non-stop since we
arrived from New York a day-and-a-half ago. Brandon had invited us to come up to
Vermont and, along with the instruments we had jammed into the wagon for the half-
day drive up from the City. There had been a heat wave that summer. In the Bronx we
had an air-conditioner in the attic rehearsal room and it was the oasis during the days
of wilting heat. We sat on the floor, against a wall, close to the growling machine, like
being in a bomb shelter, waiting for the heat-raid to end.

One of the features that came with the Vermont farm was a tractor. To adapt the
veteran machine for the new role it might play on a farm that would be producing
frivolity rather than turnips, Brandon had bought several cans of spray paint. Instead of
Farmall red or John Deere green, the colors were fluorescent orange, headache pink
and acid puce.

We had removed the caps and began shaking the cans when Brandon said, "Hold

on. Wait a minute, I want to get my camera. I have to film this." After vibrant tiger
stripes were zigzagged across the hood, the Joker's grin splayed on the radiator and
swirling spirals sprayed on the wheels, Brandon started-up the embarrassed tractor
and backed it, spluttering, out of the barn. "Okay! Come on! Climb aboard. Grab that
movie camera. Great! Let's explore Vermont!" We bumped down the farm track and
turned on to a dirt road. Coincidentally, one of the few cars that ever used the minor
road approached. "Uh-oh. Who's this out here? Oh well. Everyone wave", Brandon
suggested, "might as well let them know we're friendly." As the Ford Falcon passed
I saw only one hand respond to our greeting, a kid in the back seat. The gaunt guy
behind the wheel just stared, open-mouthed.

During a late breakfast around the table, Gram scratched his head. "Hey Brandon.
Your calendar says it's 1965. Wha' do you know, things do move pretty slow up here in
Vermont, just like they say. How are we goin' to git back to 1966? You think it's still '66
in the city? I'm goin' to have to give 'em a call about that. Is that phone working, do I
have to crank a handle or something?" Gram wanted to check-in with our producer,
Jack Lewis, to see what was happening. "Hi, can I speak to Jack please. Who's callin'?
Tell him it's Bullmoose Jackson," Gram smiled and said, "Well that was good enough
for them, but I don't think he's on the label. Yeah, Hi Jack. Yeah, havin' a great time
up here at Boy Scout camp. Campfires, burning marshmallows, got some poison ivy."
Gram needed to hear that Columbia was still ready to make a deal.

After Gram called New York, Brandon asked, "So? Anything new? Are they going to
want you to do an album as well?" He was chuckling about Gram's sense of urgency.
Brandon had plenty of experience and had been talking to agents and producers from
the time he first rode a bicycle. "My agency left a message with the answering service
before we left but I decided to leave it 'til we get back," he sounded blasé and lit a
cigarette. "The last couple of things they called me about were awful, Jesus!" He puffed
the smoke out in disgust. "A guest spot on a Western, a-a-nd the other was, ah, a part
in a comedy about a high school teacher."

"What, like Mr. Peepers?"

"At least Wally Cox was right for that part. I gave up looking at the script after the
third page, maybe the second page. It was crap. I told them, what, are you kidding? I'm
NOT going to do something like that. I'm waiting for something good to come along.
It's a matter of waiting. They are around. Like Dr. Strangelove, that was a good movie.
Even that Russians Are Coming, it was a bit corny but they had a great cast, Alan Arkin,
Jonathan Winters. Must have had fun doing it. You have to have some sort of standards,

I mean look at all of the crappy movies and the people who will do them."

"Well, I guess the price is right."

"Doesn't mean it's any good. There are the right things and the wrong things. Look at The Beatles' album. They've decided to do what they want, and, say the things they want to say. It's great."

"Well yeah, but in a way, they can afford to come up with anything they want to, they've done so many albums that have been big hits. I mean, shit, they're huge."

"Yeah sure, but they're in a position where they could be churning-out anything. They could have already put out a couple of Christmas albums."

"Two, in one year! They could cover all the holidays, Thanksgiving, Fourth of July."

"Hey, seriously, I bet their record company has been pleading with them, begging them, to do that. There are a million people who would do that if they could. That's what most performers end-up doing and they ride it 'til they run out of gas. You have to admire the standards they're sticking to," Brandon insisted. "They keep coming up with something original, on every album."

"Sounds like they spend tons of time recording. All of those sounds, the over-dubs, the strings and arrangements, they're big productions."

"Sure, but look at movies, talk about big productions, they spend more on catering than it would cost to do an album. And, most of them are awful. A good movie stands out a mile. Loads of great ideas never even get into production, people are too scared to gamble on something that's a bit too far-out."

"Well, those Beatles are pretty tricky," Gram agreed. "They write good songs and they found their pace, sorta got into their stride, like a good ol' horse at the Ken-tucky Derby. Yep, Ringo's runnin' at ten-to-one, look at those odds, maybe I ought to put fifty bucks on him in the three o'clock.

"A-a-and they're comin' down the back straight, it's Goiter, stickin'-out, by a neck!"

"Heartbeat's beginning to fail!"

"Ringo's coming-up on the rail!" We were all riding with it now.

"Marijuana is makin' the jockey puff!"

"Junkie's in the back, shootin'-up! Oh no! He's down!"

"They're coming into the corner, It's Chubby Checker, twistin' again!"

"Hooker is spreadin' her legs!"

"Jolly Green Giant is stomping through the field!"

"Scotty's beaming-up!"

"Viet Cong is sneakin' through on the ouside!"

"It's going to be a photo finish!"

"Alcoholic has sobered up!"

"Ringo's still in there. Hey, I want to win."

"There's a cloud of smoke coming through…It's Marlboro Man, smokin' through the pack!"

"Ha!"

"Woah boy!"

We rode the tractor along the edge of a dry field. A crop of stalks and seedpods from summer's weeds had outpaced the parched grass. We unfastened rusty wire to open a wooden gate, stitched to the ground by vines. The track ran into the woods and the tractor crunched over twigs and branches hidden beneath the growth on the rarely used track.

"Hold on," Brandon pushed in the clutch. "See the bend up there?" he shouted above the clunking engine, "Wait a minute, I'll shut it off. Okay. Here, take the camera and go up around the bend and shoot us as we're coming through. Okay? You just press this trigger, here. You shout when you're ready for us." I walked ahead, my sneakers parting the grass on the track. I stepped over a thorny shoot of wild blackberry. There was almost no movement along the trail or in the trees. Large stones rested against tree trunks that had pushed through before I was born. A blue jay shrieked and paddled away between green clouds of maple leaves, his slipstream ruffling some.

"He-ey! Where are you? Don't disappear!" I heard.

"Okay! Roll 'em!" I yelled back. The tractor awakened and yawned with crunching gears, one of the guys laughed. I raised the movie camera and looked through the viewfinder at a thumb-nail green planet. The tractor nosed into the frame, red, with the shocking-pink doodles, the riders shouted and waved frantically as if about to plunge over a cliff. Branches whipped, the engine roared past and a giant hand reached down, scrabbling at the lens. A few weeds sprang back up in the tractor's wake, I let the film run for a few more seconds.

In the barn I found on old kite, dusty and cob-webbed. It had been hung on a bent nail that had ripped its paper skin. The kite was orange once and, to give it some umph, had an image of an F-86 Sabre jet and the motto Hi-Flyer. I followed a thread to the floor and found a ball of string behind a shovel. After performing some first-aid on the lacerated kite with Scotch Tape and I stuffed a bit of newspaper in my pocket, in case it needed a tail.

"Hey Huck, you gonna fly that thing?" Brandon chuckled. I looked through into the living room where he and John were tuning-up acoustic guitars.

"Yeah, well. I'll see if there's any wind."

A small field sloped upward behind the house, I walked toward the top. There was a bit of wind and, after a couple of runs, I encouraged the kite to rise on its short tether. It wobbled aloft, slowly gaining altitude and drifted back toward the house. I fed it more string, beginning to feel connected to the little sail. The kite sagged with a hint of defeat. I jogged backwards a few steps hoping it might revive and crossed the brim of the hill. It caught the scent of a breeze and asked for more string. "Okay Hi-Flyer, go on, that's it." Now it was happy, being up there, yawing against the blue dome. Slumbering clouds slowed the clock as they passed over with some reluctance. I sat down, making friends with the kite.

"Hey you got lift-off," Gram surfaced over the brow of the hill. "I saw it from the house but couldn't see you."

"Yeah, I guess you could use 'em for sending signals or messages."

Gram sat down beside me, "Man that's an old kite. I remember seeing them, with that jet on 'em."

"Yeah, me too. I bought one like this once. Some bigger kids had one and I cycled down to a little old store and bought one. I think they were a dime."

"I used to like kites. My dad used to make them for me. We'd go out to a lake or the fairground with 'em. Somewhere where there wasn't any pine trees. We'd have root beer and a bag o' potato chips, maybe sandwiches that the maid put together. We always had something."

"Well sorry buddy, I didn't bring a picnic. Here you go, you wanna fly it for a bit? The string seems to be holdin'-up."

"Okay, I'll see if I can remember how to run it. Still gotta be inside somewhere. I guess, when we were kids, we'd want to run around a lot, have the kite goin' all over the place, and crashing."

"Yeah, a lot of jumpin' up and down an' yelling. I like this laid-back method. Where was it you used to fly kites, Florida?"

"No. No, in Georgia. Back in Waycross, with my father. Not Bob, I don't think that was his sort of thing. My father was a real outdoors sort of guy. Liked fishin'. Campfires, you know, cookouts, barbecuing chicken, corn-on-the-cob, he used to put them on the coals, they'd get half-burnt, then we'd pour melted butter over them. One of the boys who mowed the lawn had a little melon patch out on the Valdosta Road, we'd get a big watermelon from him. He was called somethin' like Del-ton, when he smiled you'd see a big gap where his teeth got knocked-out. My father used to say somethin' like, 'Delton's a good boy really, he just goes a bit funny when he gets his hands round a bottle'. My father knew a bunch of the black families. Um-m. We used to go out in a canoe on the swamp. Paddle a bit, an' fish. I guess he liked to get away from everythin' once an' awhile. Yeah. It was the South: Watermelon country."

"You were a little kid, then?"

"Yeah. A kid."

We gazed up, along the bow of the string, at the Hi-Flyer and the endless blue. Gram extended his arm and drew it back a couple of times like he was fishin' for a bite, in the sky.

"Flying a kite, every once in awhile, ought to be mandatory. It's re-e-ally good for you. Sort of, um-m, an out-of-body experience," Gram was speaking very slowly.

"Yeah, it's funny but it does, almost, feel like that. Like there's a connection, it's more than just the skimpy string. Weird feeling."

"Yeah. I'm beginning to feel like I can look down on the house roof, huh, an' see the other field, an' the woods. I know it's there, but I, I can see it, or feel it, from some different perspective."

"It's like we're meditating. Just focusing on the kite, an', it's, I don't know, taking us out of ourselves."

"Wow. I haven't flown a kite in years."

"An' this layin'-back is the way to do it." We both stayed fixed on the Hi-Flyer.

"Anybody want a Dubonnet? The end of the day with a Dubonnet." Brandon's favorite aperitif, a summer drink, coral pink.

"Salud!"

"Cheers!"

"Feliz!"

"Bingo!"

"So, did you guys bag any big-game, are we gonna have venison for breakfast?" Mickey, John and Brandon had been cracking-off a .22 rifle out by the woods.

"No. We were looking for Peter Cottontail but he was outta town."

"We made a pretty good spaghetti strainer out of an oilcan. Bam, bam, bam. You ought to see it. I think I'm going to take it back to New York with me."

"I saw a few deer when Susan and I came up in the spring. I came out of the kitchen door and three of them were in the field eating grass. One saw me, his head jerked up and they started running, well, not running, more like leaping, amazing. Like they were springs, boing-boing-boing. They had big white tails that popped up and, it was like, they just flew-w-w over the fence, like six feet high. They hunt them up here. I couldn't do it."

"There were hundreds of them in Connecticut," John said. "One of the men who worked on the farm used to bring one over every year. Venison has a great game taste."

"Well they are good eating but, I know, when the moment came, I wouldn't be able to pull the trigger and, if they all move like the ones I saw, I probably couldn't hit one anyway. Maybe if I drop out and retire to farm I'll have to."

Brandon might have been thinking about what would happen if he kept saying 'no' to lousy TV spots. "So are you guys going to play at all today?" We had brought instruments, intending to rehearse, but, so far, had been enjoying the outdoors. The land, space and silence was shocking, we had hardly seen anyone, even driving by, since we arrived from New York.

"Well, yeah. Anybody feel like it?"

"How 'bout a little poke to get you in the mood?"

"We-e-ell sure."

"I ran through some chords for that song I was writing. We played a bit of it the other day, remember, 'Strong Boy'?"

"Okay, sure. Let's plug in."

Gram played through some chord changes, sang a bit and we jammed on it, feeling our way around.

"Why don't you sing the first part of the verse with me? 'Strong boy you're the wrong boy.' Lets sing it like, Str-r-on-ong boy, you're the wr-r-on-ong boy." It was a country song, with, maybe, a bit of a Buck Owens influence but not as crisp and twangy as a Buckaroos feel. It had the flavour of an older style, a Webb Pierce feeling. Country. More country, less rock. The lyrics were about Mr. Brains and Mr. Brawn competing over a woman. The underlying message was, the pen is mightier than the sword and, sometimes, muscle-flexing, strutting bravado or throbbing Corvettes just don't make it. We ran through it. No one, including Gram, shouted, 'It's a hit! Stop the press! Call the manager!' It was just a good idea expressed in a style of music that no other bands were using. We played and jammed. Brandon picked up his guitar and sang. We ended up bawling-out the song we had played on tour, backing Freddy Cannon. 'Oh baby c'mon, let me take you where the action is, Oh baby come on.'

Revolver was playing again and we had had a pipe of strong hash.

The LP told us to turn off our minds and float. It was loud. I pushed my chair back, got up and went out through the kitchen door into the night. Moths danced a polka around the bulb over the door. I walked toward the barn, leaned against the wall and began to see the crowded night sky. The screen-door's spring croaked like a frog, I looked over to see Gram emerge. He stretched and lit a cigarette, exhaled and noticed me over at the barn.

"Hey."

"I had to get some air and a bit of a break from that record."

"Yeah, that album's gonna be worn-through soon. Sounds like Brandon really likes it."

"I don't like that song. It feels threatening. That horrible vocal sounds like some damn zombie in a dark cellar."

"Yeah, there's a few whirling banshees in there too."

"It sounds like an all-night robot factory, hammering and sawing-up metal. I see blue jolts of electricity and sparks flyin' everywhere."

"Well, it's interesting. Like Brandon says, they keep comin'-up with something new," Gram replied.

"Yeah, I guess. Tonight I find that one more irritating than interesting. Doesn't sound much like relaxing and floating to me. Sounds like pluggin'-in to a mess of turmoil."

"Well, just turn-off your mind. Let them Beatles go where ever they want."

"The record's over anyway. Hey, look, a shooting star!"

"Oh yeah, I just caught the end of it, must have been coming-in low. There sure are a lot of stars over Vermont tonight."

"There's Orion. See those ones in a row, like right above the woods," I pointed.

"Oh yeah. What is Orion?"

"It's a guy holding a sword or something."

"Maybe he's got scales in the other hand." We gazed upward.

"You know, you're new song is okay, I mean, it's a great idea."

"Well, I was thinking about those old ads, in comic books and things, you know the cartoon strip about the guy on the beach getting pushed around by the tough guy; 'I used to be a ninety-seven pound weakling'."

"Yeah, Charles Atlas."

"Yeah, an' it's like; 'An' now that I've been lifting weights all winter, I can go back and sock-it to that other guy, an' grab that girl back. She's just gonna fall in love with me, when I show 'em all my bulging biceps'. You know, they're sellin' that he-man thing. Like Tennessee Williams, Byron or T.S. Eliot ain't worth a dime."

"A bunch of Goddamn sissies and faggots. Yeah, the song is a cool idea. And it's weird sandwiching that idea into country."

"Well, that's what we're doing, I guess."

That was about two years ago. I wonder what's happening at the ol' farm now. I think Brandon put it up for sale after they moved to California. Someone's going to get a surprise when they open up the barn doors and see a psychedelic tractor. It was a great week up there, playing around like kids, getting away from the city heat and being cool in Vermont.

As I go through another one-stoplight town, there's a big moving van ahead of me, Mayflower Moving. They loaded-up the TV, beds and the kids' bikes and are off to a new world. I look in the mirror and see a blue and white car with a gumball machine on the roof. It must be a town cop. Shit! He catches-up with me and just follows. I'm stuck in between the truck and a cop. Okay, okay, stay cool. I don't have any pills, pot or roaches. The van is legal. Insurance, registration, licence, yep, I have all of that stuff. The lights are all working, the tires aren't bald. Shit! The truck is turning-off to a gas station. I didn't see his blinker, I was too busy worrying about the cop.

Outside of the town, the speed limit goes up to 50 and I get the van going up to, on my dial, 80 km/h. I don't want to look like I'm dawdling. The cop could pass me but stays behind. He probably doesn't have much to do today, it's only a one-horse or one-cop car, town. Fuck! I don't need this. Okay, relax, look out the window, like, I'm just a tourist, just passin' through your beautiful state, on my way to somewhere else. The only thing I have to worry about is that draft card I don't have. Shit! He just keeps following me. A sign; Slow Railroad Crossing. There is a ramp and I ease on the brakes and look in the mirror. The cop has disappeared. In the other mirror I see him heading off, down a dirt road. Maybe he was just going home for his dinner of mashed potatoes and meatloaf or to help his cousin jump-start the old pick-up out on the farm. It sure got me wired though, Fuck! Phew. I take a few deep breaths. Nothing happened, relax, it was just uncomfortable for maybe ten minutes. But it seemed like I was in his sights for an hour. I don't want to go through that again in a hurry. It's mid-afternoon. This morning I was just about ready to turn around, now I know I have to keep moving and hit the East Coast.

chapter 10
THE LAST CAMPFIRE
June 1968

RICKETTS GLEN

BENTON

NORTHUMBERLAND

PENNSYLVANIA   RT.512

BURNHAM

RT.220

N
W — E
S

0   25   50   75

CUMBERLAND   MARYLAND

3,225 miles
down the road
The future isn't on the map
12th state

WEST
VIRGINIA

VIRGINIA

I can't seem to get my ass out of West Virginia. I hardly make any progress father east and spend another night in the van having driven less than a couple of hundred miles. Today I had spent more time looking at the roads on the map than driving them.

It has been over four weeks of wandering on highways, backroads, tracks and wilderness trails while scanning the horizon, the constellations and a slide-show of memories for a sign to the next passage, gig or roost. I don't feel the homing instinct or see the harbor lighthouse flashing a welcoming beam. My strongest urge is to keep circling until I have to touch down.

Returning to live and gig in Boston is a vague plan that hasn't crystalized or taken shape. Cambridge and Boston is where this last cycle of my life with the bands began three years ago. The college gigs I used to do with The Refugees, when I was younger, were exciting. We weren't aiming too high and were glad to get out and play on the weekends. It was simple, getting a rush of excitement through playing rock 'n' roll and making people dance. All adrenaline and no music biz, pretty much one hundred percent pure, three or four chords and no bullshit. Maybe the door to that naïve fun is closed because I'm too tainted by the music biz. I've flushed some of that virus out of my system in the desert but there is still some infection that I would like to wash away. Penicillin won't do it and it seems like LSD won't do the trick either. I might need rain from heaven, the fountain of youth, the River Jordan, Holy water or the River Ganges for a baptism.

The last gig I did in Boston with The Submarine Band got pretty whacked-out and it could have used more of that easy going, university fraternity-house atmosphere. Maybe a bit more beer and sweaty dancing would have helped.

We pulled a few of the unpalatable, reactionary country songs out of our pocket when we played that gig in Boston at the end of '66. That's probably how the audience saw it. We didn't plan it that way it just happened. We just rode into town lookin' for a good saloon, hitched the horses and next thing you knew we're standing out front of The Long Horn facin'-down an angry crowd of townsfolks seein' who'd be the first to draw. Them liberals could get mighty ornery if rubbed 'em the wrong way.

An agent had offered us a week playing opposite Phil Ochs, the New York folk musician and songwriter. There wasn't much time to decide, we had to get back to him within a couple of hours with a yes or no and too much scrutiny is a drag so we took the offer. We didn't have a gig that week and in Boston we could have a stab at pushing our Columbia record. It had been almost a year since we left Cambridge.

The Unicorn was probably a folk venue that recently had tried to keep up with the changing times by booking a few bands. Phil Ochs was a purist, he hadn't gone electric and was known for his protest songs. He had attracted the disaffected folk fans who thought that Dylan had become a traitor to the cause. There were loads of them at the gig every night; folkies, with their beards, wire rimmed glasses, ethnic clothes and disapproval. It was Ochs' audience and they glared at us with the recrimination of liberals as we played country music.

On the fist night Gram introduced one of our numbers.

'Hi ya folks, how ya doin', we're gonna start off with a little song about driving trucks through Texas, so look out for the dust. Okay, let's get rollin' boys…' The folk fans did not want to hear about red-neck truck drivin' men, swingin' doors, juke boxes or barstools. Apart from some lonely applause, the seated club audience remained unimpressed. We played a few rock 'n' roll numbers to get through the rest of the set before we gave way to Phil Ochs.

Getting on stage in front of an audience and performing music that might be difficult to accept, or is outside the boundaries of current taste, takes the perseverance of a door-to-door encyclopaedia salesman. Going against the grain was a new experience for us. In our teens, Gram, Mick and I had been in bands that covered the popular rock tunes of the time. You'd play 'Johnny B. Goode' and the kids would dance, everybody had a good time, it was as simple as that. It was almost impossible to do a bad gig at a fraternity house party. If you played 'Twist 'n' Shout' or 'Wha'd I Say', the college crowd would join in, raise their beer bottles in salute, bellow along with the ooows and ahhhs and dance. Mic stands would be knocked over, bottles smashed and after the gig they would stagger over, convivially drape themselves over you and slur, 'Lemme tell ya something, lemme tell ya, you guys are great, you know that, you guys are really good.' Playing country music in the north in the mid '60s was a different ballgame, we had lumbered ourselves with a handicap.

During our break, when Phil Ochs was giving the audience the solo acoustic folk music they had come for, we decided that we had nothing to lose so planned a medley of tear jerkers and gospel songs for the late set. We'd play a few like, 'Sing Me Back Home' (a Merle Haggard song about a death row execution) and a Buck Owens number, 'There's Dust on Mother's Bible'. If they didn't like us so far we'd have some fun and give them a real reason to freak out.

Gram had worked in New York during the summer of '65 and had started writing more songs. He wanted to get into the Village club scene and had played at open mic nights, hootenanny evenings and had opened-up for other acts. He had picked up on the method and style of those folk artists. He had listened to the rap between numbers while they re-tuned the guitar to an open-D or moved the capo up the neck. They usually took their time, keeping a mood, offering some explanation about the next song. 'Well, this is something I wrote in October, a few months ago. Strum, strum. I had read about the volcano in Panama and the church that was locked. Strum, strum. And I thought, why can't we all say what's in our hearts. Strum, strum. How do you survive the night? Strum. This is a song about then, and tomorrow.'

Gram spoke slowly, wistfully, with just a hint of a Southern accent, a little bit lazy and warm, a comforting tone. Even though he wasn't really sure of what was coming next, his delivery was convincing, conveying confidence; hey, why worry, what's the rush? He'd sweep back his hair, raise his sloping eyebrows, blink a couple of times, speak slightly out of the side of his mouth and smile. He could manage to create a boyish, naïve image that was disarming and projected an aura of innocence. He often was nervous and unsure but veiled the uncertainties with a big package of charm. If they didn't like the music they got to like Gram.

A couple of nights into the gig at The Unicorn, we were setting up and tuning instruments when a guy walked up to the stage to say hi. He put down a box that he had carried in holding a tape recorder. He asked if he could record some of the gig. Sure, we thought, why not. 'Yeah, go ahead' and we went back to setting up the gear. Later when we were playing, I noticed the guy sitting close to the side of the stage and wondered if he was running the recorder. At the end of our second set we carried the instruments off stage as Phil Ochs would be coming on to do his last set. If we had the guitars, we could split anytime and wouldn't have to hang around 'til the end of the show. We sometimes went to a bar or Ken's, a late night place in Kenmore Square. There was a knock on the dressing room door and the tape recording guy came in smiling.

"Here you go," he said, holding up two boxes with seven-inch tapes. "I guess I got about twenty minutes on each one. Do you mind if I keep one of them?" That was fine with us. "Okay thanks, just pick one, I guess."

"Eenie-meenie-miney-moe, that one," Gram selected.

"I hope you'll like it. Maybe there's something good on it."

"Oh well, we'll treasure it. We haven't picked up any other souvenirs from Boston, no Bull terriers, beans or salt-water taffy."

"I've got a few tapes now, you know. It's turning into a bit of a collection. I've been taping gigs at clubs around Boston for about a year now."

"That's cool."

"Yeah, mostly everybody's fine about it. I always ask them first and then give the band a tape. It will be interesting to listen to them in a few years, see how things change, maybe." He liked the music scene and this was his way of meeting people and getting into it. I remember playing the tape when we were back in New York. It had some bits that were good but a couple of the slow country songs had some bloopers or bad chords that almost sounded like intentional slapstick sabotage.

As the week at The Unicorn in Boston went by, the character of the club's crowd changed slightly each night. The word had got round that The Submarine Band was a weird outfit; you might not exactly like what they were playing, but it was different. During some nights, Gram played piano, I picked up the sax and our set might include corny lounge music, jazz-tinted jams or cocktail piano with voice-over dialogues. We drifted toward a TV talk-show format including, monologues, joking exchanges with the audience and 'stump the band': "you name it, we'll see if we can play a bit of it." We rambled, improvising on any theme that came to us and used some of the ideas we had found during the home recording sessions at Brandon's.

The dressing room became lively with people and laughter and often the party continued back at the hotel where we got a few requests to keep the noise down. DJ Arnie Ginsberg, on W-MEX in Boston, started playing one of our singles, 'One Day Week' but that wasn't enough to keep us in Boston. That week was our last East Coast gig. We never went back to that club, maybe Phil Ochs would.

On the road, I look at the map. I'm just about into Pennsylvania, a wide state with mountains to cross. It will probably be slow because I don't want to use the turnpike, which is an expensive toll road. I'm aiming to get part of the way across the state and maybe camp in the Pocono Hills. I could get over to Connecticut tomorrow to meet-up with Barry T and unload one of the big amps and some other cargo that I have been hauling. I have to call him later to see if the coast is clear.

As I get into the hills the radio keeps fading out, the signals can't get over the mountains and there are miles of black-out with no reception. There are trucks on the road, heaped with coal and they crawl along at twenty miles-per-hour, I pass them doing about thirty. It is a slow trip, the van is poking along with no radio, no conversation. Having someone to talk to makes a long trip go easier. I remember driving from New York to Florida with Gram in the spring of '66 on our way south to do a tour. We talked a lot.

"How do we get out of here."

"I guess we start by finishing this coffee, puttin' our bags in the car, then making sure our heads are on an' we're wearing sox," Gram suggested.

"Okay, I'll check. Yep, all there. What road are we going to take?"

"I think we should head over to the Hudson and go across the George Washington Bridge. Then, we'll look for a highway south. Maybe they'll make it easy for us, and we'll see a big flashing sign that says, 'Florida; follow the yellow brick road.'"

Gram and I were about to start a long drive. The ISB was doing a tour and we were already running about an hour late. "We'll be fine once we get in the groove. Maybe Washington, DC in a few hours, then Virginia. We'll be writin' truck-drivin' songs by the time we get to the Carolinas, we'll probably be in the right mood by then."

"Let's get out of here."

"Get them wheels a-rollin'."

Wow! It felt like we were flying. The cockpit in the Austin Healey was small, there were a lot of little round dials and instruments. The suspension wasn't like a big car from Detroit, it was stiff and we felt every bump. The seats were low, almost like sitting on the floor, the windshield was tiny. I felt like we were in a World War II fighter 'plane. The engine noise was always there, we're wearing safety belts, the revs increased as if we were getting ready to take off.

"I like this car. I guess the last time I drove it was when we moved to New York, except for starting it up a couple of times," Gram remembers. "It was good having a car in Cambridge, but there really isn't any reason to have it in the city. The parking on the streets downtown is such a pain. If you forget to set your alarm clock, to get out of bed and move it at six in the morning, you get a ticket. I got a ton of them last summer. Sometimes in the Village, I'd go to the car and there'd be about a half-dozen shoved under the wiper. This car is wanted, dead or alive, in New York."

"Wow, glad we escaped onto the New Jersey Turnpike. All the cops are probably getting two-way radio bulletins now, 'Calling all cars, calling all cars, be on the look-out for a green Austin Healey sports car with two, white, male long-hair musicians. Go get 'em boys'. They're screechin' around with lights flashing and sirens blastin'. See ya later, Alice blue gown. Too late now, we're gone!"

"Yeah, a prison break. I can't bring this car back to the city."

"No?"

"No, there must be a couple of thousand dollars worth of tickets. This car's days are numbered in Manhattan. I'm going to leave it in Florida. There aren't any parking problems there, everything's so spread-out. Florida is huge. New York is crowded.

Maybe they'll waive the parking tickets if I tell 'em I've taken one car off the streets. I ought to get paid a bounty. You know, I really wanted to get a motorcycle but Bob and my mother said, 'Forget it, it's a car or nothin'.'"

"What sort of bike did you want?"

"English. Triumph, BSA."

"They're great. I had an old Triumph, at art school. A six-fifty. Great, but it wouldn't be any good in New York, stuck in traffic. They're lousy for long distance. I'm glad we're in this thing, huh."

"Yeah. Maybe I'll get a motorcycle, one day.

As we're driving through North Carolina, the headlights briefly shine on large white letters, sloppily painted on the side of a timber shed.

SINNER REPENT, was the message.

"You got any repentin' to do sinner?" Gram asks.

"Yeah, well, I'm afraid I've been smokin' a bit of weed and playin' rock 'n' roll music, sometimes even on the Sabbath day."

"Uh-oh. My oh my, sounds like you confessed just in the nick of time. See, doesn't that make your soul feel a whole lot cleaner?"

"No, not a lot.

"Well it was worth a try."

"It's funny how, when I was a kid, in church, they'd be up there preachin' that Elvis, and all that mindless rock 'n' roll, was evidence of the Devil's hand at work, trying to steal the hearts of innocent, unsuspecting, young people. Like, when I was ten-years-old and singing along with 'Hound Dog', that was enough to guarantee that I would burn in Hell and be tortured and punished for listening to a guy strumming a guitar and singing a song. What a bunch of nutcases. None of 'em had the brains to define sin. They were using it as a cover to condemn anything they didn't like," I remembered.

"Yeah, they take the name of sin in vain. People get sin confused with law. Laws get changed and they're different, depending on where you are. Sin has, probably, always been the same. I guess there are only a few sins." He listed them. "Like, ah.. don't hurt other people, don't hurt yourself. Maybe there's a couple of other ones, like, don't be a litterbug or don't play Perry Como records at a party, until you're over fifty. Other things aren't so important, people are always gonna cheat at cards, try to get a look at the other guy's hand, that's the law of the jungle, not sin."

"What about desire. Uncontrollable desire. Like, I gotta have this no matter what, I don't care if I have to rob a bank and shoot the teller, I gotta have a million dollars. I need more."

"That's greed, sort of. Those people have a chronic case of it. They've been told so many times that they need a flashy car, a bigger house, or a faster speedboat that they finally reach the breaking point. Maybe advertising is a sin and the devil is the guy behind the ad campaign," Gram figured.

It was late, extra late. We already had been driving for fourteen hours. As we crossed the state line into South Carolina, a loom of light blossomed in the night sky and became a huge yellow sign in the shape of a giant laughing Mexican bandito. From under his wide sombrero, through a walrus moustache, his gap-toothed smile invited us into the vibrant yellow enclave, 'South o' the Border'. After the hours of night driving it was dazzling. Crazy-eyed cabelleros, bandoliers across their chests, waving pistols and playing guitars, were painted on the amarillo walls of the restaurant, gas station and store. The store was a firework warehouse, full of skyrockets, cherry bombs, ashcans and, the one that whistled, jumped along the ground and exploded, 'the nigger chaser'. We creaked out of the Austin Healey, after hours of being folded like jack knives and stretched.

"Woah! God, it's warm! I can't believe it. It's one in the morning and it's almost warm."

Gram smiled, "Hey, welcome to the South." It had been cold when we left New York, late this morning, or yesterday. There were only a few cars in the parking lot, as we walked toward the yellow buildings. "Haven't you been down South before, Ian?"

"Well, I remember driving through Memphis and Little Rock, about four years ago, just going through. I was on the way to California and didn't really stop anywhere much 'til I got to New Mexico. Every where else was a blur."

"Huh, looks like you have a whole new, weird trip ahead of you. I guess I'll have to be your sponsor in Dixie. Let's go and get some of that cornbread."

We walked into the café and in a large mirror behind the counter and under the bright lights I saw the reflection of red-eyed, road-weary travellers.

"I'm goin' to want a coffee, that's for sure. A big one, or two."

The waitress smiled and said, "We got the 'nah-tahm brickfust spayshull' for y-all." I only picked-up part what she had suggested.

"Okay, let's see. I'll have some, eggs, homefries an' toast. Thanks," Gram ordered.

"I'll have the same thing, please."

"Y-all havin' baycun?"

"Okay," I said.

Gram looked at me and whispered, "Maybe not such a good idea, bacon."

"How come?"

"Well, you know."

"M-m, no? I don't."

"Not always such a good idea. You know, trichinous."

"What's that a disease?"

"Well, parasites, worms. You never know. It's all that heat down here."

"Okay, I'll just leave the bacon. I don't need the worms." This was the first bit of local knowledge, from my guide.

The waitress scooted over to fill our cups, "Y-all gonna want coffee."

"Yes mam." I had never heard Gram say yes mam before, it just rolled out. Not the type of phrase you use in New York much.

"Whale, there you go, hun," she replied.

Gram took a big slurp of coffee. "Well, well, my-oh-my. Back in the Southland ag'in."

The waitress returned with our order, "Hair tis hunny."

"Well. Look at that, man. A biscuit," Gram picked it up, admired it, then bit right in. "M-m-m. You forget just how good a biscuit can be. I might have to ask her for another one of those."

"You like 'em?"

"Yeah well, just natural. There seemed to be biscuits at every meal when I was a kid. The table wasn't complete without a basket of biscuits."

"Yeah?"

"Sure, it was the South." He took another bite. "And, some of the best ones were made with grease out of the frying pan. M-m. I remember, one time, we had a new cook and it took awhile for us to get used to the way she made her biscuits." Gram had another swig of coffee. "Ah-h. That's good. My father thought that she didn't bake 'em hot enough. He'd say, 'Could you stick these back in the oven, for another minute'. He wanted them nice an' golden."

"Well, I like them."

"I guess eatin' a biscuit is part of your induction ceremony. Welcome to the South, sir."

"Let's see. I want to have a look at that map, before we get going. I don't know if there are any new highways. They might have finally got around to building one. Okay. We're up the top of South Carolina, here. Hm-m, looks like the ol' boys still can't get it together. Route 95 is still under construction, it says. Looks like we're gonna have to stick to 301, on down into Georgia."

"Then what happens? I can't see, I need to fold the top of this map over." We try spreading the map out, inside the sports car. "Probably, ah, the same road all the way to Jacksonville, I guess."

"If we see that some of that 95 is open, we'll try and get on it, we might make better time, at night."

"Could we be getting close to half-way now?" I wonder.

"Probably gettin' close. Okay, boy. The Or-range Blossom Special is rollin'. Here we go."

"I'm only carrying a tiny piece of hash. I don't think we want the troopers down in South Carolina findin' any on us. Maybe we better smoke some more of it, we won't have to worry so much if the Georgia Patrol starts tailin' us through some little town. We can always eat a little chunk."

"Wha' do you mean, can't you turn-on that Southern Gentleman charm, for the cops, if we need it?"

"Well, sho' 'nuff but this car has Florida plates and Georgia, Florida, well, they sort of got this thing goin'. South Georgia, north Florida, they're just about the same but they think, like, there's an iron curtain runnin' across the state line. It's like the Cold War, as far as they're concerned. If there's a football game between Florida, Georgia colleges, it's like a fight-to-the-death, 'til no one's left standing. Big rivalry goin' on."

"What side would you be on?"

Gram thought, "Hm-m. Well, we used to go to Florida, on the train, to visit my grand-folks and on summer trips. After my dad died, we left. I missed Georgia. You know, friends from school, places where we'd fool around and, the barbecue."

"You used to cook-out a lot?"

"No-o, I mean barbecue. Like barbecue stands. It's, like, smoked ham and a hot sauce. My dad really liked it. Sometimes we'd go over to the black folks' part o' town and get a take-out, like, a quart carton, put it on your bread. It's Southern. No, barbecue is a different thing, not like cooking hot dogs. Maybe we'll get some, there's always a barbecue pit somewhere. There used to be a good one in Winter Park, down in the black neighborhood, Florence Villas."

"Cool, let's go over there."

"Yeah, we could try it, if it's still there. That's a few years ago, now. I haven't been back there in a long time."

"Here. We can roll this hash in a cigarette and keep driving." Gram passed me a little ball of foil. I squeezed the tobacco out of the cigarette and crumbled the hash into it."

"Okay. Here we go. I feel pretty good after that coffee."

"Yeah, we'll be good for another couple of hours, maybe." The interior filled with warm smoke, until we had to roll down a window. The car droned, spurting us further south, at about sixty. The headlights bored through a tunnel of trees. "We're in the pines. There'll be plenty of them, for a long time now."

"Yeah?" We caught up with a trailer truck, loaded with logs.

"Uh-huh, See that truck? They're up all night cuttin' them down but those trees are still growing-up, faster, everywhere. In Georgia, any place where they cut down a patch of pine trees is know as 'civilization'; 'There ain't no pines? Man, this is really living.'"

"Luxury, huh?"

"Yeah. People can get lost in the pines. It's dark, like real dark. Spending too many years in the shadow of the pines, drives people insane. They come running out of the woods, screaming, 'gotta have some light, where's the sun?' They're as blind as a bat, from goin' 'round-and-'round in the dark, with their arms stretched out, feelin' for a way out. If we have to stop and get out for a pee, remember, do it one-handed, right? Keep your other hand 'round the car door handle, and don't, whatever you do, let go. You don't want to go into those pines."

"I'm going to tighten my seatbelt another notch, just in case. Man, those trees aren't gonna get me, even if they reach in through the window with their long, pine-needle fingers to try and pull me into their resiny hearts."

We passed a plywood sign reminding us that, Jesus Saves.

"Yeah, salvation. Jesus, save me from the co-old shadow of the pines."

"They're lonely shadows."

"Going in and out of shadows could be good exercise," Gram suggested. "Maybe, you can't just sit there, in the light or the sun or on Mom's lap, all the time."

"I guess being in the shadows makes you appreciate the sun. But, say, like in Arabia, I bet they can't wait for the sun to go down."

"Yeah. And, Bella Lugosi. Sun and shadows, it's part of a balance. Good and evil, Caroline Kennedy and Lee Harvey Oswald, devils and angels."

"Devils were angels, kicked out of heaven. They were the same thing," so my bible used to say.

"Yeah, they got sick of all that Holy radiance. Like; 'Hey, God!, gimme a break, I can't take it anymore, getting fried all the time. Can't you shut it off once-in-awhile?' Of course God can't, he's sort of a thermo-nuclear generator of flames and creativity, and says, 'Hm-m. Never thought of that one before. It's a full-time job keepin' the universe from fallin' apart. But, if you guys don't like it, you're just gonna have to get out of here. No two-weeks-notice shit, you're fired.'"

"Yeah? The angels say, 'We're already fired, from all your fuckin' heat, see you later, man! They go plummeting down below, all saying, 'ah-h-h, that's more like it. Wow! That feels good, all of this darkness. I never realized it was so oppressive, up there, in heaven."'

The engine purred like a feline bass. I sprung back and opened my eyes. "Shit! I just nodded-off, phew! I'm going to roll down the window, get a blast of air. I was gonna take over and do some drivin' again. Too bad we didn't have a thermos of hot coffee."

"We could have got some bennies," Gram said. "I could use a bit of shock treatment, just about now. I bet there might be a truck stop where they sold 'em in the back room, well, if you knew the right guy to ask. Being tired is a weird thing. It's powerful, like something you can't control. Like rain. When it starts, you get a bit wet, 'til, eventually, you give up and get soaked. In a way, there's something cool about when sleep is trying to swallow you, you get to where you don't care about anything much. The car is droning like a Buddhist monk, you're followin' that white line on the road that just keeps comin' at ya, like unravelling off a big reel, just out-of-sight, in the future. Look in the mirror, nothin' there. It's gone, disappears like smoke. No proof we've ever been here. Leavin' no tracks, except for a bit of exhaust and a few squashed bugs. Whoosh. Hey, are you asleep again?"

"Yeah, I mean, No. I'm just floatin' along too. Hypnotized by headlights lighting up the road and too wasted to care about anything. Just rollin', movin' an' groovin', right on through. Cool. Just breezin' along, not shakin' hands or picking up things to stuff in my pocket. This is the way to live. Like ghosts. Yeah, no tracks."

"Woo-oo-oo, woo-oo-oo-oo, all the way through the woods. That's the good thing about music."

"Singin' woo-oo, woo-oo?" I asked.

"No, I mean, like leaving an invisible trail, an essence, behind you. Like on records. Music is invisible but it can be huge. Mozart, opera, Hank Williams, whatever it is; it's a history and a whole lot different thing than what people think of, as history. Like, Julius Caesar, Napoleon, Abe Lincoln and all the other big shots. Their thing, is really just the size of the mess they kept makin'. Turmoil, disaster."

"And, building big monuments to themselves."

"Duke Ellington's monuments are just sound, not marble. The big characters have their glory story and triumphal arches. They're big heroes, then suddenly, a few years later, it all changes and they're tyrants. They're de-throned or executed, the statues are knocked down, the books get rewritten. Music just stays. People might say Duke Ellington or Pat Boone is crap but you can go out and get the music, listen to it and decide for yourself, without other people's history getting' a foot in the door."

"What's that?" Two dull red dots briefly glowed, like exhausted coals, then shut off. I took my foot off the accelerator. Toffee-colored flanks and a flaring white tail bounded across the road and out of the headlights arc. "A deer?"

"Could be. That was a big one."

"We better be careful around here."

"Yeah. We don't want to crash into the nightlife and end up with a set of antlers welded to the grille."

"I guess it's not hunting season either."

It was still dark a few miles later when I saw another animal and had to stomp on the brakes. The thing was about the size of a racoon, but hugged the ground and had a back like a beetle that shone in the cars lights. It ambled across the road.

"What the hell is that?" I wondered.

"Well, look at that, an armadillo." It moved toward the side of the road with a wobbling scuttle.

"I don't think I've ever seen one before. Weird. It looks like something from the time of the dinosaurs."

"Yeah, they're somethin' else. You see a lot of them down South. In the woods, but mostly, squashed on the road," Gram explained. "They're not much good at getting out o' the way of cars. There's a lot of sleepy animals in the South, possums, 'gators, armadillos. What they like best is stretchin'-out in the sun for a nap, crawl around for a bit, then take another nap. People get a bit that way too. It's sort of like evolution, they learned to take it easy down South, in order to survive. It's all that heat, you know. You don't want to tire yourself out by running around too much. A New Yorker could cram-in a whole sentence, in the time it takes for a Cracker to say 'Howdy'. Kind of makes sense, really. Why get all het-up?"

On Route 301, in Georgia, nearing a town called Jessup, Gram has been silent for awhile. He's awake, he lights a cigarette.

"Hey, what's the matter, you feeling okay?" I ask.

"I didn't think I could remember so much."

"What do you mean, about what?"

"About here. Or, when I was around here. My family, way back then. Ya see, Waycross is only down the road. It's the next town. That's where we lived."

"You want to drive over there?"

"No. Definitely, no," he stated.

"Well, I guess it's a bit out of our way."

"Yeah. Out of the way, alright. No, there's too much shit buried over there. I don't feel like diggin' through that."

"Maybe not so good, now we've been drivin' all night."

"Well, day or night probably doesn't make much difference. It all looks pretty bad, in the sun or under the moon."

"Oh yeah?"

"M-m. That's where my dad shot himself."

"Oh."

"Yeah. On Christmas."

"Oh, Jesus."

"Yeah, a whole lot of tidings of comfort and joy, huh? Fah-la, la, la-la, la-la, la, la. I try to forget it, you know, but, it's hard to, sometimes. I still don't know all of what might have been goin' on." He was silent for awhile. "Probably family stuff, like him having to work for the family business. Maybe he was too independent and the situation was twistin' him out. You know, settling down. Maybe you can begin to feel petrified, fossilized, when it gets to be, like, the same thing, all the time. Some people need it, that's their dream, their goal; they can't wait to be secure, in some sort of mold. Regular job, regular wife, regular kids, regular life. Other people go crazy, like it's a life sentence, with no hope of parole, only chance of an early release is by blowing your brains out."

"What day is it?" I wonder, as we drive in the morning's first sun.

"M-m. It's today. Now. Here we are."

"Is it Tuesday? When did we leave New York, what day was it?"

"Wednesday? Shit, I can't remember. So what. Right now we're not shackled by time, we're just in motion. Like being in some flexible, rubber time zone that has nothing to do with the rest of the country. They're doin' the breakfast news show on TV, back in New York, but, it's already in the past. Okay, see that house up there. Here we go, we're comin' up closer to it, the kids in there are getting ready for school, lookin' around for their homework, grabbin' their coats. No-ow-w, we're past it. It's gone, in the past, history. Will they get to school on time, and pass-in that algebra? Who knows. We're goin' through time zones every minute. We're skatin' over the clock, the weather and the cultures."

"At Stone Age warp-speed, not, z-z-shu-uck, like in Star Trek. Before we left, I remember realizing that it would be my birthday in a couple of days."

"When is your birthday?" He asks.

"The twenty-fourth."

"Hm-m. That could be today. Or tomorrow? Maybe. I don't seem to have the Playboy calendar in the car, opened up to 'the Miss March Bunny' page."

"I guess the birthday can wait."

"We're running outside of time now. What will you be?"

"Twenty-one."

"Hey, now you can go back and drink in Massachusetts."

"Oh yeah, lets turn around. I guess for a lot of people twenty-one is a big deal, like getting your ticket to all the rides in the adult amusement park. Whoopee! Now I can go on the bumper cars, and get a mortgage, do jury service and run for Mayor. Like, I'd just as soon, give 'em their ticket back, turn around and run like hell."

"Well, I've got a feelin' that we're not exactly heading in the solid-citizen direction, anyway," Gram reassured me.

"It's weird, about age, like, havin' a number. It's all over the place, so inconsistent. I mean, the drinking age in Connecticut is twenty-one but you can go a few miles, into New York and it's eighteen. It's like one state is saying, 'No, no, no, they've got it all wrong over there.' You can drive at sixteen in some places but not 'til eighteen somewhere else. I think there are a couple of places, out West, where you can get a licence at fourteen."

"All those laws are good for business. If there is a dry county, you can bet that there are loads of people making a fortune from liquor stores, just over the county line. Like in the roaring twenties and prohibition, they outlawed booze and people actually started drinking more. All that money went right into the black market. If they legalize pot next week, it would put a lot of dealers out on the street. They'd be lining up to collect their unemployment checks," he predicted.

"God! All those idiots, sittin' around makin' laws. Fuck, there already are too many."

"Yeah, why don't they quit and just go out and play golf?"

"When is your birthday? I forgot," I asked

"November. November 5th."

"Yeah, okay, I remember it was in Cambridge. The fifth. Hm-m. You know what? That's the date of some sort of weird English holiday or something, sort of an English Halloween. I remember my mother tellin' me about it, she's English."

"M-m. What is it?" Gram asks.

"Guy Fawkes. They have bonfires, fireworks and make dummies, and burn them. The dummies are 'the Guy' and they stick 'em on top of the big fires. I think he was burned at the stake."

"That was pretty popular back then."

"Yeah. He was an anarchist, or was going to blow-up the government with barrels full of dynamite."

"That's a good idea, once an' awhile."

"Yeah, at least it slows them down, stops them making more laws, for awhile. But, they didn't like that though. I think they caught up with Guy Fawkes and his merry men just when they were lighting the fuse. They dragged 'em off, tortured them, stuffed hot coals up their asses, cut open their stomachs, hung them, cut off their heads, fed their limbs to lions and then burned them at the stake."

"Man, that's what you call over-kill."

"Yeah, really over dramatic. They wanted the public to see what happens if you step out of line too much."

"The establishment doesn't like it, if you disturb 'em when they're having a nap."

"No, those people want to wake up knowing that nothin's gonna change. Well, November 5th, bonfires, treason, I don't know if you want Guy Fawkes for your patron, birthday saint?"

"Well, hm-m. The Revolutionary thing is sort of cool but, no, I could live without the torture and the fire."

"Are we on the right road? It's been awhile since I've seen a sign."

"Yeah, this has been goin' on a bit. We're out in the middle of nowhere again. I'm pretty sure we took the right road out of that last town."

"Well I hope we're not heading for Alabama or somewhere." I wondered. "But, maybe that would be fine, you know, gettin' lost."

"We go around being lost, more times than we think. You never really know what's hiding behind that billboard around the corner or ready to jump out from behind a bush. Could be a Bible salesman, a guy sellin' magic beans, a Playboy bunny, or Santa, wantin' you to give back those electric trains you got last Christmas."

"Yeah, anything could happen. I guess we're always hopin' it's going to be good. Like, Santa's gonna say, 'Hey there you are, I've been lookin' all over the place for you. I forgot to give you this extra caboose for your train set.'"

"Huh. But you know, a couple of weeks ago we didn't know we were going to be driving down here to do a bunch of gigs in Florida, it all just popped up out of nowhere. And here we are."

"Well, we're not really sure exactly where."

"I think we're still goin' in the right direction," Gram said. "We'll see a road sign soon. It'll say, 'Welcome to Florida, enjoy your gigs', then we'll both be saying, 'see, it's okay, we're not lost'. It will convince us that everything is runnin' on schedule, but if you look back, a few months or a year, there is nothing that's running on schedule, the path you've taken looks like spaghetti, it doesn't even fit on the plate."

"M-m. I guess a lot of things happened that I didn't expect. I had a girlfriend, lost a girlfriend, joined a new band, moved to New York. Now we're in Florida."

"I was supposed to be in school at Harvard. We knew where we were going a half-hour ago, now we think we're lost. It's all pretty temporary, knowing where you're going. Really, we're only on, like, a little raft, that's gettin' sucked down this huge, swirling river. We don't know where it takin' us."

"Yeah, he ju-u-st keeps ro-o-llin' a-along."

"There's places where you're paddlin' for all you're worth or you might drift into backwaters, then there are floods and rapids. No goin' back, just downstream."

By mid morning, in North Florida, we've been delivered to summer. We have driven about fourteen-hundred miles south, from the last grip of the northern chill into newly-hatched southern summer. Instead of snow flurries and bleak, skeletal trees, we drive past flowering shrubs, palms and gushing lawn sprinklers. People are wearing short sleeves, straw hats and sunglasses. A red convertible sweeps past, the driver trailing a wake of her hair.

"Hey. We should put the top down."

"Yeah, let's stop and do that. I hope it isn't rusty or jammed shut. Probably the last time it was down was in October, last year. We'll stop for gas and put it down." The clips were stiff but we folded the roof back and headed down the road with a breeze teasing us. The open top resuscitated us from the coma of the all-night drive.

"Yeah!"

"Welcome to the Sunshine State."

"We can start working on our tans. I swear I can't remember the last time I saw the sun," I said, looking up.

"That's the great thing about Florida, there's hardly any winter. You can, just about, go to the beach all year."

"If this is March, the middle of summer must get hot as Hell, though?"

"Sure, sometimes you just can't go outside, you'll fry to death. But, we used to go water skiing a lot. I remember the sun, blazing down so much that I would go water skiing with a hat jammed on my head."

"Maybe we'll get time to do something like that. I feel like I haven't been outside, since we moved to New York."

"Except runnin' for a taxi. We'll be playing over on the coast, the beaches are unbelievable over there, they're huge. You'll want to kick-off your shoes and get your toes in the sand, you know how good that feels."

"Hey, this is sounding promising."

"Well that's mostly what's happenin' in Florida. That's why people are moving here." Gram explained. There's all that sun all the time, beaches, water skiing, golf, lawn mowing, shuffle board, fishing, fruit trees, cheap land an' plenty of space, that's what they're after. But, that's about it, sun and sports, there isn't much of a scene. There sure aren't any record companies in Orlando. That stuff isn't happenin' here."

"Leesburg. Hm-m, maybe less than an hour to go." We had driven through rolling land, some pastures with grazing cattle or horses and had begun to pass by rows of small dark-leafed trees.

"Wow! Look at that, orange trees." I saw the dots of fruit, vibrant, against the leaves.

"Oh-h yeah. There's a lot of them around here alright. We're coming into citrus growing country. That's what my family used to be into. I guess they still are, well, relatives of mine still own some groves."

"Boy I'd love some fresh oranges."

"You won't have to wait too long for that. We'll probably be able to pick 'em off a tree at the house."

"I wonder if Mickey and John have arrived on the train yet?"

"Getting' close, now. At least they might have had some sleep, rockin' in the berth, to the clickity-clack of the track."

"Man, I'm surprised that we got this far without sleeping."

"We're goin' to have crash when we get there."

"This has been a crazy trip, I'm glad we did it," I said.

"Yeah, it's been good. I think we're goin' to have some fun in Florida when we wake up."

In Pennsylvania, I pull into Burnham. I walk down Main Street past a bank with a clock that is a slowly rotating cube. The four faces all agree as if there needs to be a consensus to prove that it is telling the correct time. Cat's Paw Shoe Repairs, Mary's Ladies Fashion, The Courier, the local newspaper, has the front door open emitting the tic-tic-ticking of a typewriter as the high school baseball team's home-game is reported.

A stone railroad bridge straddles Main Street. Under the arch is a guy leaning against the cool supporting wall and holding up a tin cup of pencils. He's wearing big round sunglasses, a white cane leans next to him. A man passing in the other direction says, 'Afternoon Amos.' The blindman hears my steps and turns his head slightly. I pause, fish a couple of coins out of my pocket, he moves the cup closer towards me and I take a new yellow pencil with an eraser that is pink like health gums.

"I guess it never hurts to have another pencil."

"Well, thank you."

"I'd give you more but I'm runnin' a bit low," I say.

"I appreciate it. You from out o' town, huh?" He probably knows everyone by their distinctive footsteps that are accentuated under the arch.

"Yeah, I'm just going through."

"Where have you been?"

"Well, I headed out from the West Coast, LA, almost a month ago."

"You've been stopping-off a lot."

"Yeah, really. I've been to some great places. The deserts, Utah, New Mexico, went across the Mississippi on a little ferryboat. I've seen some amazing stuff," I don't go on, maybe I shouldn't have said seen.

"I went to the Grand Canyon," he says, "what a place. Huge, biggest place I've ever been." I wondered how he could have judged that. "I could hear how deep it was. I went up to this place up top, right to the edge and leaned over a bit. Never heard anything like it."

"Wow."

"If there's no traffic I can hear what's goin' on a few blocks away. I could hear you coming, even though you are wearing sneakers. You stopped to have a look in the window at Stephens' Hardware." He's right, I remember pausing to look in the window at an array of hammers.

"Where are you headed? New England? Boston?"

"Yeah." I was surprised, almost wary. "How do you know?"

He chuckled, "Your accent, hear that a mile away."

"I guess so. Sort of stuck with it now."

"I listen a bit harder when I hear a stranger, I got to know accents that way. You have a girl back there, family?"

"Yeah, family. Haven't seen them in a couple of years now."

"Well that will be something to look forward to."

"Sure. But after that, I'm really not sure what's going to happen."

"Something always does, that's for certain."

"Yeah I hope so. I just couldn't wait to get out of LA, now I don't know what's 'round the corner."

"Just stop and listen a bit more, maybe you'll hear it. I can."

"You know, I have been listening a bit. To the wind, to, well, space but I haven't heard anything tell me where home is."

"Huh," he chuckled, "We all have things around us, like, your chair, a draw full of clothes, a winter hat, a roof over your head at night but really, home is just in here," he pointed to his head.

"That's beginning to make sense to me, lately."

"Oh, it's the truth." He smiled.

"Right now I'm thinkin' about my stomach. Is there a diner in town? I was goin' to get something for lunch."

"There's Emily's Luncheonette, just about a fifty yards down on the right, before the corner," he pointed. "I think they might have meatloaf for the lunch-time special today."

"You think so?"

"Yeah I can smell it from here."

He was right. The meatloaf special was ladled on to one of those sectioned plates that keep the peas from getting too intimate with the mashed potatoes. If you finish your food, the plates look like the circles they use to diagram what percentage of the town budget goes toward education, roads or the Police Department. The cherry pie dessert glows a radioactive red through a lattice of pastry, trying to keep the filling behind bars. I finish my coffee and notice a column in the local paper;

'Vietnam Veteran Attempts Drugstore Hold-up'. That guy has come home with a whole lot of pain.

There is a pay phone in the corner of the diner. I search my pockets looking for change and the scrap of paper with Barry T's phone number. I dial the long distance code for Connecticut and put in fifty cents.

It rang.

"Hello?" A woman's voice.

"Hi, Hello. This is Ian Dunlop. Is Barry around?" She asks me to hold on and I hear footsteps.

"Hey-y. I was wondering where you were," Barry greets, "Thought you might have turned around and gone back to New Mexico."

"Well almost, but I'm in Pennsylvania, about half-way across. Made it that far. I thought I'd let you know that I'm homin'-in on you. I'll probably get into Connecticut tomorrow, maybe in the afternoon."

"Great. You're going to make it. We almost didn't."

"Yeah, really? I got to hear about that but maybe not now, I don't want to start thinking about what could go wrong. I don't have much change, so could I call you when I get closer?"

"Sure, you're going to need that change for all the tolls up here, it's not like out there in Utah."

"Okay buddy. I'll see ya."

" 'Bye."

I head east into the afternoon, fiddling with the radio to see if I can pick up anything. A station playing bluegrass leaks in, it sounds scratchy and stretched, like it had come from a long distance away. The further east I go, the less country music I'll hear. I lost the station and tune into another that is doing the on-the-hour news.

'Hubert Humphrey, who looks like the Democrats front runner, since the assassination of Robert Kennedy, has pledged an end to the bombing, a ceasefire and immediate troop withdrawals in Vietnam,' the announcer says, 'and is promising a fair deal for farm workers. In another story: Residents of New York had better lock-up. Robberies have increased by Sixty percent, according to figures released by the New York Police Department. One of the big winners on Wall Street today was McDonnell Douglas, who have reported profits up by twenty-four per cent.' McDonnell Douglas are probably running the factory twenty-four hours a day, building more F-4 Phantom jets to replace the ones that are getting shot down over Hanoi.

On Route 522, close to Northumberland, I cross a bridge over the Susquehanna River. There is a big factory or steel mill that is pumping out smoke that drapes a muddy cloud over the valley. I bet the people living here hope that the wind will change. It reminds me of the smog in LA, it's just about the some color.

The sky, that afternoon, was the color of the best sky ever, over Hollywood. The blanket of honey-colored smog had been folded up and put away for the day. The wind must have changed, bringing fresh air and a carnival of drifting clouds, from their place of incubation in the distant Sierras, to saunter across the Hollywood hills. The brief change in the LA climate was noticeable. Gram and I went up the few steps to the deck platform on the house roof, to catch some rays. Against the endless blue were feathery streaks, broad, parallel stripes across the sky. A nebulous, dissipating turtle, its skull protruding from the shell, looked down at us before it waned. Vague letters and words, that might have been legible a hundred miles ago, were scrawled above.

"Some God, is layin' on his back, up in the Sierras, with a colossal paint brush and a lake-full of white paint," Gram suggested. "The blue canvas rolls on by and he dips that brush and slaps on the pictures and words. By the time we see them the paint has dripped and smeared."

"Yeah. Like Jackson Pollack, it's all splashes."

"They are really trippy. If you look at one cloud, it keeps changing and turns into something else. Okay, like, I can see a dog, leaping, like a poodle at a circus and, right above him, see, right there," Gram pointed, "is the Sphinx and its wearing a Halloween mask, like a skeleton."

"Yeah, I can see that one."

"Now the poodle has changed, into a hand, like Mickey Mouse, three fingers in a white glove." Gram had phoned earlier saying that he was going to come up to the house, he had some news and wanted to talk me.

"Wow. Look at that one. It's like a huge fossil, a backbone, like one of those dinosaur-type fish."

"Yeah, you can see the vertebrae, all stung along there."

"Hm-m, how come we're seeing all of these bones?"

"I know what you mean, clouds are supposed to be puffy, like piles of whipped cream. Lemon meringue pies."

"Marshmallows and mashed potatoes. Maybe this is the matinee show. The night clouds could get really serious."

"Here come some of those now, two jellyfish, with teeth and a vampire bat."

"Oh yeah, I see them. They're changing, really quickly. Look over there. It looks like a giant mouth. It's spe-e-eaking, ve-e-ery, slo-o-owly. Louder, please! I can't hear you. What's the message?" I ask.

"We have to guess. Maybe we have to be much more receptive," Gram suggested. "Like, we don't spend hours and hours watching the clouds and waiting for messages from the Gods like some ancient societies did. They had people out there all the time, looking at the stars, starring at clouds, cutting up chickens, checking-out the guts to see if there were any urgent bulletins about the future."

"Look at that one. It's like a big question mark. Upside down, but it's definitely a question mark."

"See, there you go. That could be the beginning of a dialogue with the Sky God."

"Yeah, maybe," I looked at the curved cloud. "I think I've been brain washed or sponge brained from watching too much TV. The Gods speak in weird tongues."

"So. I've got some news," Gram said.

"You said you wanted to talk."

"Yeah. I've been talkin' to Suzy Jane Holkum. I had a couple of meetings with her and, after listening to the band and talkin' a bit, she's said that she wants to produce an album for The Submarine Band."

"Yeah? Cool."

"I think so. And, she wants it to be a solid country album."

"Hm-m."

"She said we might be able to get going on it soon. Like in a couple of weeks, a month, maybe. So, I just wanted to talk to you about it," Gram waited for more of a response from me.

"Well, that's good. Finally somebody's come along, after all this time and all o' the doors that slam shut."

"Yeah, it has been rough."

"What about an advance. What are they offering?" I wanted to hear some numbers.

"Well. Nothing."

"What! Nothing?"

"No, they pay for the recording and get the record out."

"No advance?"

"Yep. No advance. I figure, it's a chance to do a country album."

"Shit. These guys in Laurel Canyon, we were jamming with the other day, were talking about getting fifty grand, and they aren't really all that good. How come fuckin' country music isn't worth anything?"

"Hey Ian, you know what's happening. The ISB has been down that road too. Those promises of fifty grand usually never come to anything. And, you know, the big record companies haven't exactly been all over us, recently, have they."

"M-m, no. Not that I've noticed."

"If we sign with Suzy Jane, well, Lee Hazlewood, I mean, we can do it with a producer who's into country music."

"Jesus! No advance?'

Okay, yeah. But, I've found a good pedal steel player, they'll pay him to do the sessions, maybe I'll get a fiddle player too."

"Man, you're talkin' straight, down-the-line country."

"Yeah. That's what I want to do. What about you?"

"Well. I guess so. Sort of. But I'm not sure about, like, solid country. Yeah, we love it. But shit, we've been playing it for over a year and people keep walkin' out on us, when we're playin' country. How is that suddenly going to change? Unless, we go down and play in somewhere like, Arkansas. We'd all have to go right in to the nearest barbershop for a crew-cut. What if they caught us smokin' a joint, between sets down there? We'd get thrown in to the County jail for five years."

"Huh, huh. No, we aren't going to do that."

"Okay. Look what's goin' on. I mean, listen to the records that are comin' out. It's all psychedelic and hu-uge productions. The Submarine Band was actually closer, a year-and-a-half ago, to what was the happenin' thing. Now, we're on another planet."

"Gee. I didn't know that that was buggin' you so much."

"Hey, you know, I'm getting a bit tired of being so broke. The gigs that The Burritos are doing are, at least, bringing in some grocery money for us. The last couple of months have been tough."

"Well, maybe The Submarine Band will get some good gigs after the album is out."

"M-m-m. Maybe. You know, I wanted to see that other woman from that new label. What was it called, ah, Mother's Records. She might want to do somethin'. She's been interested and I think it's more than just talk. She likes us. She's into weird music."

"What about country? Would they respect it like Hazlewood might?"

"Well I don't know about, like, Bakersfield country or Nashville country, but she liked the idea that we're working with a country sound.and wearing country 'n' western clothes. She dug the style thing. I don't know, I want to talk to her about it again. She said that they were going to start signing people. Maybe they'd be offering some money."

"Well, who knows when that will really happen? Lee Hazlewood is talkin' about soon, maybe real soon. Suzy Jane has a record out and she's just produced Warner Mack."

"That's mainstream country."

"Yeah, That's what I want to do. A country record. Not rock, not psychedelic, not r 'n' b. country. Straight country and this is a chance to do it."

"Well, man, that's good. I love country. It's soulful, some of it is, like, so pure. You know, all the tragedy and the hurt. The drinkin'. It's great, I love it. But all of that stuff, it's so, negative."

"M-m-m," Gram thought for a moment then looked up at the sky. "Hey, there goes Dumbo. He's doing a nose dive."

"Yeah, jumpin' off that tower into a barrel of water again."

"Dumbo! You can fly, you can fly," Gram cheered the gaseous elephant. "But, you know, that music, there's so much passion in that negativity. Some good sounds come out from behind them ol' dark curtains."

"Sure, okay. But, look at The Beatles. 'Good Day Sunshine', all those harmonies and key changes. Like you listen to it and you can almost see all of these bands of pink and gold sunbeams, shinin' down on smiling people, all runnin' around, like a chess set, on a big, green pool table. Little flowers start blooming as the song is playing, butterflies, flappin' around in that warm light. You know?"

"Okay, happy, happy, Lucy in the sky, kaleidoscope eyes, yeah?"

"Okay, so country music is mostly about murder, death, drinkin'. The sins of the South.

Really unhappy, morbid lyrics. It's the opposite of 'Good Day Sunshine', yeah? I love all that dark music about prison walls, lonely people drowning in booze, tryin' to hide their pasts and their adultery."

"Yeah. Ha, that's just about it."

"Okay, it's great shit, but it's not chart music, or, something that they're going to be dancing to on Shindig."

Gram wagged his head and looked up again, "Well, I want to do it. I know that John wants to go with Lee Hazlewood. Maybe you don't."

"Well, now that it comes down to it, I really don't know anymore. We've come a long way now. And, worked at it."

"Yeah, hey, we have, and I think this is my chance to do it."

"Maybe. But I'm not sure if I can keep holdin' out. It's been a long time, trying to live on peanut butter sandwiches. The agent we've got for The Burritos, has got us two gigs this week and there might be a week-long gig after that. It's bread. I need it. Man, I still can't believe they don't want to pay an advance."

"Well, it's like an advance for recording sessions and, maybe, bringing in a few studio people. And we've tried it in New York and out here. These are the first people who've said, 'country, sure, let's do it, it's about time there was a country band that could get in the charts'."

I look up at the sky for a sign, but none of the clouds are shaping into a guitar, a submarine, or forming letters that look like 'L P'. I gave it a bit longer, in case the answer took awhile, then said: "No man. The Gods aren't saying yes... for country music."

Gram got out some grass and papers to roll a joint. "A good day for watching those clouds rollin' on by." He lit the joint and passed it over to me. "I guess it's not too early, huh?"

I took a drag and looked up at the big blue, an ocean with clouds sailing downwind. "Man I can't quite believe what I just said."

"About what?"

"About maybe stepping out of The Submarine Band. Jesus! It feels very weird. But, I guess, that's how I feel, right now anyway. Maybe it'll work out for you."

"I don't know either, I just have to grab this chance to get a country record down. In a way, you're right. Nobody has wanted to listen. It has been a rough ride, not having people wanting to sign us, and even trying to get us to drop the country thing, an' all that stuff."

"What a trip."

"Yeah. We've had some laughs."

"I've loved it," I told Gram. "I've probably enjoyed all of the opposition that we've had. The people who shake their heads or stare in disbelief, the jaws that dropped when we sang a country song that mentioned the Bible, all that stuff convinced me that we were doing something right. No matter how many times the music-biz said no, it just seemed to be proof that we were on the right track, even though they kept sayin' we were heading down the wrong road. Weird huh? The opposition was, like, valuable."

"The music-biz really doesn't want to take a lot of chances. They gotta see, at least, three-of-a-kind in their hand before they push those chips over to the middle of the table."

"Right, they don't want to bluff. At least I knew I wasn't one of them. It's amazing how narrow-minded most people are, they can't see below the surface. Makes you want to say fuck 'em and go even further, in the opposite direction. But, you know what? That way of thinking becomes a luxury, like, it costs you. You get more and more isolated. You may be doin' something cool, or different, but you're playin' to an empty room."

"All of the prophets have gone out into that ol' desert, to eat bugs and stare at the sun and have visions, to figure out what the message is. Yeah, we haven't done any gigs for a long time but I've written some good songs. I want to record them. They're country. That's just what happened."

"So what were you doing, eatin' bugs?"

"Yeah. I bet some o' those old bearded prophets ate a few and then found out they were, like, hallucinogenic. That big green-backed-desert-roach was packed full of protein and, if you ate those little antennae, you tripped your ass off, like peyote. Well, they would have had that too, out in the desert, if they got tired of the bug trip. Forty days and forty nights in the wilderness and, by then, you'd of had God come over for supper a few times."

"Yeah, so God comes over, to the cave; 'Hey prophet, had a good day out here? So, what's cookin' tonight, I'm starvin', been really busy up in heaven today. Had to get those pearly gates repaired again. Oh no! Is that all you got? We had bugs the other night.'"

"Yeah. 'Well, God, you send me out here, with no razor blades, I'm tryin' to get the message together for you, but the catering you provide is crap. Is this the way you run the universe?'"

"'Listen prophet, when you've eaten as many bugs as I have, then we'll talk about it. You're still on the children's menu.'"

"Ha, ha. Yeah, maybe more bugs for awhile," he said.

"M-m. Well maybe I've got to step out of the desert. I'm not going to book-in to the penthouse suite but I want to keep a roof over my head and it doesn't look like it's gonna be the Grand Ole Opry."

I drive on small roads toward Ricketts Glen, a state park in the mountains with camping out in the woods. I'll see how it feels, maybe I'll stay for a bit, this might be the last campsite of the trip. Connecticut, where Barry T is staying is about two-hundred miles from Ricketts Glen. Half a day, depending on the roads, until I make contact with people I know. Probably we'll begin putting some of the pieces of the puzzle together by talking about the possibility of getting gigs but maybe they will still be dazed from their cross-country trip and readjusting to the East Coast. They might be rubbing their eyes like someone waking up and saying 'where the Hell am I?' Maybe we'll stare at the puzzle for a bit and decide to put the lid back on it. Creepy, yuck. Don't want to spoil a great drive by thinking about plans and organizing things. During this trip I've never looked at a road map to plan a route coast-to-coast, it has always been one state at a time, no big picture. I've left a zig-zagging trail behind, revealing constantly changing objectives, like the animal tracks I used to follow that meandered in the new-fallen New England snow.

The old bus is pumping along and sounds like it might hold out to do the last four-hundred or more miles to the Atlantic coast. In Benton, Pennsylvania I stop and go into a grocery store to get a couple of things for a cook-out, a small pack of hot-dogs, a couple of potatoes and some juice. The town is mostly wooden houses and small stores. The Stag Horn Bar has antlers mounted above the door and there is an old railroad car-style diner. The gas station is surrounded by rusty pick-ups and a black, smashed-up hearse that was in too much of a hurry to get to the next funeral, or maybe a vampire on tour.

After cutting our first single, the management began to get the Submarine Band some promotional gigs. One of them was a TV spot, in the summer of '66 on the Zacherley Disco-Teen Show. Zacherley was a New York TV personality. In the early '60s he had been the host of a horror movie TV show and became more of a feature than the films they showed. He adopted a vampire persona and broadcast from a crypt where his wife was at rest in her coffin. He had an operating table where he performed brain transplants using cauliflowers and grape juice blood transfusions. Some of his performances had the surrealistic print of Salvador Dali and had made Zach a cult figure.

John Zacherley had also released a couple of singles in the early '60s, I had bought one of them, 'Dinner With Drac', when I was about sixteen. The record had some great honking sax played between the ghoulish, spoken lyrics. More recently, Zach was hosting a music program that went out daily on a weird New York TV channel. The show had developed a following because of Zacherley's spontaneous, unpredictable behavior and it was a showcase for new bands. He had a bit of a habit of getting pulled off the air and being reprimanded for going a little crazy or carried away and saying inappropriate things when a show was going out live. The Disco-Teen Show had suddenly disappeared awhile ago but somehow Zacherley had managed to get back in front of the cameras again. According to Marcia, Tony and some of the other neighborhood kids in the Bronx, it was the hip music show, Zach had re-established his cult status. Sounded cool.

We got out to the W-NJU studios in New Jersey for a late afternoon session. The station was on the ground floor of a brick building in the old industrial section of Newark. We entered the dark studio and found Zacherley in a small office. He was contemplating notes on a clipboard, wearing a long black cape that swished as he grabbed a pen from the desk. He turned with a surprised expression, his mouth open, his hair - parted in the middle - fell down to his cheeks.

"Ah. Hello, hello, hello. Good to have you here." He looked down at the clipboard again. "Ah yes, In-nter-national Submarine Band." He smiled as if it was an intimate secret. "Make yourself at home. Well, that's not really possible is it. Just relax, we'll figure this all out in a minute. Nice to see you. I've got your record, um-m somewhere here." He is working on the running order to give to the floor manager but Zacherley is more like a kid who is trying to get his math homework done on the way to class. He leans towards a mirror on his desk and starts applying makeup, dark circles around his eyes.

A guy wearing headphones comes into the office, "Have you got the order ready yet?" he asks Zach.

"Yes, yes, almost ready. Just a moment please."

"Come on John we need it. Only a half-hour." The guy turns and leaves the office, like this is part of their daily game.

Zach flaps one hand dramatically. "All under control." He looks up, smiles and winks. He likes spontaneity, he knows what he's doing but likes to stay within character of the disorganized vampire, who has been out stalking all night, chasing the wrong victims who are in good shape and leave him behind, panting and drooling, as they outrun him, again. Maybe he has had several nights without a kill and the TV day-job is becoming too much to handle. He could be exhausted and cynical, pissed-off with watching all these teenage nymphs dancing around, exposing so much nubile flesh that remains beyond his reach. He sighs and rolls his eyes, it's all too exasperating.

It's sort of cool though; there is an atmosphere of the Underground. The station's programs are sometimes in Spanish. At night they broadcast old black-and-white movies on The Late Night Movie, showing films from the '30s and '40s, they are probably cheap to rent. They go out on the airwaves to an audience of slumbering night-watchmen, insomniacs, pot-heads and listless vampires. Cool. The studios are in a worn-out, disused brick building. The small staff might have frequent, late night flights, rapidly loading the

cameras, lights and control boards into a truck, evading the bailiff waving the unpaid
bills and setting-up again, in a shut-down bowling alley, just in time to roll the midnight
musical. The whole operation seems barely legal, like they are broadcasting outside the law
from an unknown location in a crumbling city.

The other guest star tonight is Shirley Ellis. She's had several hit records, the best one was
'Nitty Gritty'. Her others are novelty songs, about how to do this or that new dance. She
is very business-like and her manager or agent has paperwork for Zacherley to sign and
wants to know the way to Shirley's dressing room.

"Ah, dressing rooms, yes," Zach scratches his head. "Over there through that door, next
right." He could be sending them to a bathroom, an unoccupied office or a broom closet.

"You got that sheet ready?" the floor manager is back.

"Yes, yes. Send it right out. One more thing, just a sec."

"Okay. We need it." Zach hasn't completed much of the running order. He flips through
a small stack of records scribbling down a few titles, I notice 'Gimmie Some Lovin'' by
Spencer Davis.

Shirley's manager is back. "Where's Makeup?"

"Oh, Makeup. Aren't they here tonight? Hm-m." the manager rolls his eyes and leaves.
Zacherley slips into a Béla Lugosi accent, cloaking the tenuous production facilities behind
vampire sensibilities.

"I do-on't kno-ow what he'll say about the catering, all-l we have tonight is bloo-o-d."
The little room is crowded with teenage girls who giggle and whisper. Zach bends over
the schedule and says, "We'll get you guys up twice. Once near the top then, um-m,
somewhere down here. Let's see, how long is the flip side of your record? Ah, just under
three minutes, good. That'll fit." He scrawls, filling a space across the list, then on the next
line writes, 'another record'. "Could someone take this out to Steve?" A dark teenage-girl
pertly takes the paperwork and scampers out the door. "Thank you Maxine, you're a
darling." She's not a secretary, probably one of the regulars who come to dance around for
the cameras, keeping the party mood going and having fun. They are all having a good
time already, what a fun thing to be doing at 5 pm after school. Zach's show wouldn't be
the same without the energetic teenagers and the production budget probably would not
allow hiring rent-a-crowd dancers.

Zacherley checks his watch, "Ah, tempus fugit. Let's go. On with the show. Forward!"

'Well I'm so glad we made it,
so glad we made it.'

Big loudspeakers are pumping-out Spencer Davis. The crowd is pulsing with the music and raise their arms, flashing the V sign, either V for victory or the Peace sign that has become the greeting used by students and hippies. Zach is shuffling to the rhythm, his long cape sways but he keeps his face set in a slight scowl of aloof disapproval. They shoot a link. Zacherley speaks in a disjointed bored manner, suggesting that getting out of bed and appearing here today is very tedious.

"Ah yes. Spencer Davis. Now, this evening's spectacular show will have more music, to keep my little ones dancing. Now let's have a big hand, or some other welcome for Shirley Ellis." She has been standing on the stage and Zach moves closer, smiles, bares his teeth and gazes at her as if wondering if he could risk an on-stage vampire bite. Shirley is dressed in a sparkling bronze dress and smiles but the angle of her eyebrows, exaggerated by makeup, register a slight hardness, maybe enough to make Zach back-off. She is a pro and has been on the road promoting her records for several years. "Ah-h, lovely to have you on the show my dear."

Shirley flashes a big smile but only answers abruptly: "Thank you, it's good to be here." This isn't going to be an interview.

Zach raises an arm and says, "Shirley Ellis, 'The Name Game.'" There is a slight delay before the record kicks in and Shirley starts moving. She might have already done the same thing in Philadelphia or Albany earlier today, dashing around between TV and radio spots. Her record, 'The Name Game', is one of those novelty songs about short-lived crazes. New dance styles or instant made-up languages were themes that made it into the charts in the late '50s and early '60s. The languages, like Pig Latin, were constructed by adding a couple of letters as a prefix or a suffix to every word. There had been Op, Measurry and others. The lingoes were something that a group of friends could work out and then feel free to speak on the phone, at school or whisper without being understood by little brother, the Math teacher or Mom and Dad. Shirley began singing and revealing the formula for the name game.

'Let's do Shirley.

Shirley, Shirley, bo-hirley,

Banana, fana, fo-hirley.'

This was a renegade record, from an era of music that was long gone and sounded like a chant that little kids used when playing jump-rope.

'Donnie, Donnie, bo-onnie.'

Zacherley's Disco-Teen cut for commercials. I wondered who would be buying ad time on this show. The floor manager raised his hand, pointed at the ceiling then, like a sword thrust, dramatically pointed at Zach, counting him in.

"Welcome back, welcome back. More wonderful things tonight. The International Submarine Band!" The record we are synching to is our Ascot Records single, the 'Russians Are Coming', an instrumental with a few spoken lyrics, a format that is about as dated as Shirley Ellis' song, but it gave us the opportunity to goof around. We strummed the guitars that weren't plugged in and I shaped some vocals. Gram abandoned playing silent guitar chords and began lurching, walking like a zombie and staggered towards Zacherley. Mickey raised his drum sticks, holding them above his head making a vampire-defying cross then left the drum kit and moved towards Zacherley, holding one stick like a wooden stake, the other like a pounding mallet. Zacherley went along with it all. Crouching and half-covering his face with the cape, he cowered flashing his eyes back and forth. The floor manager waved the cameras in, to catch the unrehearsed action.

After the show had wrapped up, the floor manager was clearing people out, herding the chattering kids towards the door. "Okay, everybody, thank you, thank you, that's it." Within a few minutes the studio was empty of bouncing kids. At the exit Zacherley smiled and said,

"Well, thank you for coming along. I enjoyed meeting you guys, that was fun. Good luck with the record," he paused, "but don't believe everything they tell you." Under the outdoor light, I notice the tracks of sweat that had run down the remnants of white makeup on his neck. Zacherley bowed and walked off into the parking lot carrying a sheaf of papers and a box of records. We began walking to our car, Mickey shouted:

"'Bye Zach." Zacherley half turned, waved, and then, vanished.

The campfire is crackling, one of the large branches that I dragged to my campsite had clusters of cones that expand in the heat then pop in the flames. The resin spits. I drove across a bridge over a boulder-strewn stream and up a valley to find the campsite. It's mid-week, there are very few campers and I went around the empty sites collecting half burned logs from the dead fires.

I skewer the hot dogs on the sharpened forks of a couple of whippy saplings that I cut for toasting sticks. No pots or pans tonight, this is cave man cooking, meat on sticks over flames, potatoes singeing in the coals. The flames cast shadows that boil, several kamikaze moths make agitated passes over the fire. A sharp crack and the fire launches a flock of sparks.

I follow their ascension and looking upward see stars that penetrate the dark trees as individuals not constellations. One of the hotdogs begins to curl as it cooks. As the logs burn through, the remnants and coals build-up creating fiery shapes and forms. I see a castle and a misshapen cathedral with spires and an arched doorway, a city on a burning planet. A camel shaped flame rushes past the cathedral, pilgrims bow and kneel on the steps. A pulsating, glowing log appears like a haggard crone and begins to narrate like a tour guide to the burning city. Her eyes close slightly, her mouth opens, 'Ah-h-h' she mouths, like she is bathing in a refreshing pool in the midst of the fire. 'You want to?' she seems to say, 'go on, go on.' I laugh then think, wow I better write this down. What is the rest of the message?

More coals as a burning log collapses and the oracle is gone. That was it, the call has been disconnected. A bird, probably an owl, begins to laugh, 'Hu-hu-who-o-o' Like, 'well stupid, did you get the message?'

The hotdog has curled into a porky smile with severely chapped lips, one of the potatoes bursts. Yes, I tell the owl. After all the campfires, silent mountains, echoing canyons, singing frogs and rolling tires, everything is speaking at once, roaring. The stars are blinking Morse code, the flames speak Neolithic, the Earth is breathing, the trees whisper Uh-huh-h-h-h, the owl whistles, frogs chorus 'yep, yep, yep, yep.' I feel the message, I can hear. I have been deaf, wrapped in a fog of drugs and bullshit. I'm free. Free at last.

The buzz of the natural word is passing through me like an electric charge, lightening streaming through a conductor. For a moment I am live, the current passes through me with a surge that contains no recognizable news, gossip, advertising, clichés or red tape. How did I plug-in, where was the socket, who turned it on for an instant to flush me out? I was sitting on a log, holding a stick that had fleeting kisses with flames. Maybe I completed a circuit of air, fire, water and what else, rock, wood or soil? The spark jumped from the flames into the rocks, in the ground, into the log, up my ass, through my heart and back around to the fire again. A loop of the elements pushing out all the junk that has been harboring inside my head, blasting it out of the way with a shot of unbelievable energy. I'm lucky I'm not frazzled.

Maybe I briefly kissed transcendence, after all the time it has taken to clear the Hollywood demolition derby out of my system.

The remaining heels of unconsumed logs lean into a pool of gray ashes; the remnants of last night's communion. The campfire is lit by the morning sun slanting through the firs. Showing through the trees is a large white camper. A guy with a big belly is turning-on a propane cylinder accompanied by a radio playing polka music. The atmosphere is different this morning, the oracle has packed-up and left. I decide to get going, keep moving and have a look at the map to remind me where I am and what roads will take me through the remainder of Pennsylvania.

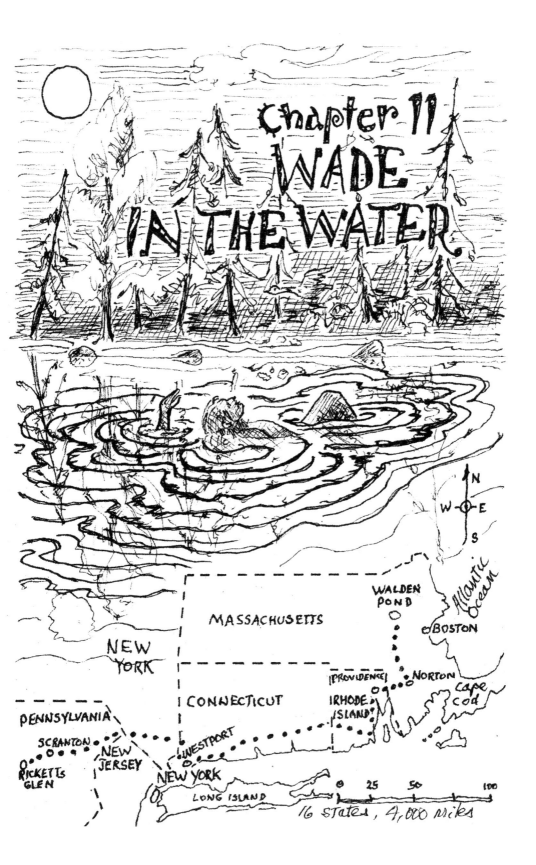

Chapter 11
WADE IN THE WATER

WALDEN POND

MASSACHUSETTS

NEW YORK

Atlantic Ocean

BOSTON

PROVIDENCE

NORTON

CONNECTICUT

RHODE ISLAND

Cape Cod

PENNSYLVANIA

SCRANTON

NEW JERSEY

WESTPORT

RICKETTS GLEN

NEW YORK

LONG ISLAND

N
W   E
S

0   25   50   100

16 STATES, 4,000 miles

Could I use the phone? I really should call my folks place, see if anyone is home and warn them that I'm about to show." From Barry T's family home in Westport, Connecticut, I dial the home number in Massachusetts that had remained the same since we moved there in 1955. It feels like I'm trying to call the past.

"Hello?" I was surprised, my sixteen-year-old brother answered.

"Hey man, its Ian."

"Hi. Where are you?"

"I just made it to Connecticut."

"Wow, you made it."

"Well almost. I thought I'd call an' see what's goin' on. Is it safe to come back?"

"Yeah sure, we're lookin' forward to seeing you."

"I guess that will be tomorrow or the next day. Will you be around?"

"Yeah, school's finished for the summer, I'll be here."

"Cool. I'm sort of out of school myself, not sure what's happening next."

"Oh yeah. Maybe you'll want to go to England with us."

"England?"

"Yeah. We're going to have a family reunion over there."

"Really?"

"You know, everybody has been away for so long that they decided to do it, but there was no way of getting in touch with you."

"Yeah I've been really out of touch. When is this reunion thing going to happen?"

"Like soon, maybe a week and half. You want to go?"

"God, this is a surprise! I don't know. Maybe I should go, huh? Hey look, I'll probably be up there tomorrow. Wow! This is crazy. Hey I'm on somebody's phone, I'll get up there tomorrow, if I don't get a flat tire or anything and I'll see you then. Okay?"

"Okay. But, wait a minute. There's a postcard here for you, from Gram."

"No foolin'?"

"Yeah, it's from London. You want me to read it?"

"Hit me."

"Okay, it says, 'Ian, I'm in London and I'm hanging out with some cool English people. You would really like it over here. You ought to come over. Hope you are doing something cool. Cheers, Gram.'"

"Wow! Isn't that weird. I heard that Gram might have been goin' over there. Is there a date on the card? When did it arrive?"

"Let's see. It says... May. I can't read the rest of the date. It only came in the mail the other day."

"Man! Isn't that something. I wonder what Gram's up to? Thanks for letting me know about everything. England huh? Wow. See you soon, okay?"

"Yeah, great. 'Bye."

I was still blinking from this news when Barry asked me,

"Did you get through? Everything okay?"

"Yeah, good. Some interesting things seem to be brewing."

We unload the big Sun bass amp and the motorcycle frame that was lashed onto the VW's roof.

"I bet this bus is going to fly now. That was a lot of weight I've been hauling."

"We were so relieved to unload all the instruments out of the van, towards the end we didn't think we were goin' to make it," Barry says.

"Really?"

"Well, by the time we got to Ohio the van was burning even more oil, just drinkin' it down. If you looked in the mirror there was this huge cloud of blue smoke blowing out. Man! When we got to the end of the Pennsylvania Turnpike, we handed the guy in the tollbooth the ticket and started counting out change, quarters, dimes, nickels, even pennies. We gave him two handfuls of change and we were still about a dollar short. They were threatening to impound the vehicle. We had to plead with the guy, sayin', that's it, we don't have anything left, maybe even not enough gas in the tank to get back. That was the last of our money. Eventually he let us go through, there were so many cars lined-up behind us. We had to dodge all the tolls after that. We stopped in New Jersey and began searching through everything and found some more change, just about enough to pay the bridge toll. We were lucky to make it."

"I'm not all the way back yet, so I better not say anything about my luck. What does it feel like to be back here?"

"Weird. You know, after about a year in LA and all the gigs... it's strange. Then Joshua Tree, Utah, the road. Man, the last couple of days on the road, phew! Non-stop driving. Crazy," he shook his head, "I still feel like I just got off one of those amusement park rides, that spin around, up-side-down, an' when you get off, you stagger around like a drunk and can't walk in a straight line. I've hooked-up with a couple of people in the last couple of days and they've asked what it was like in LA? Or, what am I doing now? I've told them, 'imagine you've been in a cement mixer since lunch, that's about it'. My head", he shook it again, "I haven't really landed yet. I'm still adjusting."

"Check this out. A couple of days ago I almost turned around and started heading back to California."

"Woah, that sounds like the tell-tale sign of becoming a road junkie. White line fever."

"Yeah. I think I've got a bit of that, I might be strung-out on it. When I get back to Massachusetts, I'll probably have to give the keys to the VW to my brother and tell him, no matter what I say, if I'm climbing the walls or get down on my knees and beg, please don't give me those keys. You know, like goin' cold turkey."

"Maybe you'll just have to sweat it out. Well, except for those last couple of days, the whole trip was great. The other day, I put a sweatshirt in the washing machine and I could smell the smoke from the campfire. M-m-m. Maybe I shouldn't have washed it. It would be like preserving a good memory."

"I guess you haven't been thinking about moving into New York first thing tomorrow morning?"

"Hm-m, not right off. Briggs has phoned a couple of people in Boston to check-out what's happening."

"Thinking about going back up there?" I wondered.

"I don't know. Could go to Cambridge, maybe. Or stay here in Connecticut, it's so close to the city, you know. I don't know yet. We'll talk about the band, later. You have to get up to Massachusetts, unpack and have a shower to wash the road off you. You'll need to rest up a bit."

"Yeah. I really don't know what I'll be doing yet. There's a chance that I might go to England for, like, a vacation."

"Really?"

"Um. Not sure what's goin' on."

"Man! Jump on it, if you can," Barry advised, "I'd love to go back to Europe."

"Could be good huh? I'll have to see what's happening. Maybe I will be able to go to England, I'd like to get out of here for awhile. You know, everything seems to be getting even more screwed-up in the U S of A. It's still hard to believe that Kennedy got bumped-off. And, the whole Vietnam thing looks like it'll be getting' worse before it ever gets better."

"I guess we were on the Pennsylvania Turnpike when we heard about Bobby Kennedy. Man, bad news or what? I think I was dozing in the van, half-heard it on the radio and thought it was a bad dream. I woke up later and it was on every station: 'Bobby Kennedy is dead'. We were driving into the bright, morning sun, it was no dream, welcome to today. We hadn't stopped, except for gas, for about two days, I was pretty much out of my head by then. It made me feel sick, like how bad are things going to get. Like we're on some kind of Heart of Darkness trip, the further you go the more like Hell it becomes. You know, when we finally made it to Connecticut I went to bed and slept for almost two days. I didn't want to know about anything."

"Everyone I talked to after Kennedy was shot, I mean people in Missouri, Kentucky, places like that, were really pissed-off about how fucked-up America is getting and, you know, they're the conservative bunch. I think that things are going to get really bad pretty soon. How long are people going to keep swallowing all this crap? Man!"

"It's getting hard to be optimistic, I think that's dying-out."

"Maybe they're feelin' okay back there in Drop City, being out in the middle of nowhere and spending most their time tryin' to figure out how to run their electricity off a windmill. They've got that attitude of, hey, the United States is goin' the wrong way so fast that we don't want to have anything to do with it. We're not going to pay taxes that go toward bombing peasants in Vietnam, screw that."

"Um-m, it's all getting' crazier."

"Yeah, I'll drink to that." I said. "Well, maybe not. I've hardly been drinkin', I haven't even had a beer for a few days."

"All of that fresh air sort of cleans you up, doesn't it?"

"Funny, but I haven't missed it, or smokin' pot. I've been havin' really crazy trips without any of that stuff."

"Um-m, some of those places that we went to got ya high, just being there. The Grand Canyon, wow! Looking out at all those layers of colors on the cliffs, weaving in and out, wriggling around, it was like hallucinating."

"Yeah, I felt like that a few times. Some of the trails, like in Joshua Tree or Zion Canyon, it was like being in a fantasy land, a dream landscape, like unreal."

"Yeah, and then you'd realize that it was real."

"We're so out of touch with that stuff, drifted so far away from nature that we don't give it a chance anymore. I think that we might have been out there for just long enough to start getting into it, opening up and feeling some of the magic that's oozing around out there."

"It takes a long time to get all the night-club out of your system and be able to open your eyes," Barry T diagnosed.

"Yeah, all of that cheap wine and honky tonk makes you blind. I sort of wonder if my trippin' days are over, I'm beginning to think that acid and all that stuff just screwed me up."

"Maybe. It can be weird."

"Sure. You know, if you are out there in your sleeping bag at Joshua Tree or New Mexico, the stars comin' down at you, some of them are sparkling with color and lighting up the stacks of boulders or makin' the cactus glow, it's like, who needs that chemical crap."

"I guess it's useful if you're locked-up in a small apartment in Cleveland."

"Yeah, or if you're in prison. I'm hoping that I've broken-out now. Maybe that's the main thing that I have learned from this trip, I know where to go to get high now."

After saying 'bye to Barry T and Briggs I'm heading out of Westport, Connecticut to pick up Route 6 and a Mini Cooper pulls out in front of me. They're fun cars. I used to drive one in Hollywood that had been loaned to me by a really cool woman. I remember seeing a few of those mini sports cars in LA.

I was on the way to return a borrowed electric bass to a friend. I really liked the Fender jazz bass. I had become used to the feel of it, after playing it for a couple of weeks at Burritos gigs. It had a great neck but it didn't belong to me, the bass had been loaned to me by Noel Harrison and it was about time to return it. Noel was having a good run, playing a spy on the hit TV series The Girl From UNCLE. He was also doing some song writing and rehearsing for a recording session. I figured he might need to have it.

I drove over to Westwood with the bass to Noel and Sarah Harrison's place. Noel and another guy were standing near the front door when I arrived.

"Hello Ian," Noel still had a strong English accent.

"Hi, how are you? I thought it was about time that I brought your bass back."

"Oh that's good of you. Did you like it?" asked Noel.

"Like it? Man, I love it. It has such a great feel. There is something about it that's really special. It's different from a Fender Precision."

"Really?"

"Yeah I'll tell you, you're lucky to get it back. I really dug it."

"Well thanks. I hope it didn't spoil you." The other guy was still standing there. He had dark curly hair and was wearing a leather jacket, he look a bit like a Greek merchant seaman. Noel introduced us.

"Alan, this is Ian. He's a musician. Ian, this is Alan Arkin, he's, ah, in films." We shook hands.

"Are you playing anywhere or recording?" Arkin asked.

"Yeah, playing in a couple of bands but mostly doing a lot of gigs with one of them, The Flying Burrito Brothers."

"Good name," Arkin laughed.

I thought for a moment. I recognized his name from somewhere, then asked: "Were you in that movie the Russians are Coming?"

"Well, yes. I guess I have to admit it."

"That must have been fun."

"It wasn't bad, nice location on the coast. I got to the beach. Yeah it was a laugh."

"You know, the last band I was in did a promo record for that movie."

"Really? I don't think I ever knew about that."

"Well, I don't think anybody much knew about it. It got a bit of airplay but nothing else happened. That was our first single."

"Have you done any more?" asked Noel.

"Yeah, another one for Columbia but they didn't do anything much with it."

"What are you doing lately?" Arkin asked.

"Playing a lot with The Burritos, we're workin' at clubs all the time. It's a good band, sometimes six-piece with horns. We play a bit of soul, r 'n' b, you know."

"Yeah really. Sounds good. I blow a bit of sax once and awhile."

"No foolin'."

"Well I can just about get by, if it's bluesy," he smiled.

"Cool."

"Whereabouts are you playing? I'll try an' come down."

"We're at a place downtown. It's always a long gig, we sometimes get people to come down and sit-in, makes the night go a bit faster."

"Hm, maybe I'll make it down with the horn one night." Arkin shrugged his shoulders.

"Sure that'll be cool. Do it."

The quiet suburban afternoon was interrupted by the excited drone of a car that was revving through the gears as it approached. It sounded like a sports car, the engine was wound-up tight and shifted as it got nearer. We all turned in the direction of the road as the blare increased and saw the reflections from a metallic bronze Mini Cooper as it flashed by, like it was in a race.

"There goes Steve McQueen," said Noel.

"Man he's scorchin'," said Arkin, "that guy's going to kill himself."

"Yeah. Those crazy young kids and their hot rods. The roads just aren't safe anymore."

At the Rhode Island state border there are several road signs that warn drivers; Rhode Island Enforces Speed Limits. Obey No Passing Regulations. Then there is a big one, a painted billboard depicting a car crash. It is weather beaten and faded; the overturned vehicle is an old '50s-style car. The large red letters spell out the warning; Speeding Can Kill. It looks like an old horror movie poster, a bit Pop-Art. You can get killed speeding, ski-jumping, being hit on the head by a high-fly ball, snake bites, napalm, earthquakes, heart attacks, food poisoning or planes falling out of the sky. It's always waiting, out there somewhere ready to jump out at you around the next corner or in your imagination. Sometimes you can just start making it up, or even go looking for it.

The living room was empty. A confusion of voices seeped in from the kitchen where the others sat around the table. I parted the drapes to look out the window and across a jagged rooftop horizon at midnight in New York. Aerials and water tanks, in silhouette against night light radiance, crowned the buildings with gap-toothed coronets. Lights winked on and off in the cliff of windows that shelved-off to street level. The glass was cold against my forehead. The building opposite contracted and expanded, it was breathing. Some of the illuminated windows showed bars, the inmates were locked-up tonight. A window flashed blue, then disappeared, there were hundreds of them blinking. I heard someone shuffle into the room. Gram sat down on the floor and leaned against the dark green wall, his head bowed, eyes closed. Several of us had taken LSD and it was sloshing around now.

The stereo was soft and emitted a warbling music that bubbled around the room. By candlelight, the wiggly notes of a vibraphone rolled across the carpet like grapes, slowly spilling from the speakers, some of them inflated and floated to the ceiling. The winking windows opposite seemed to light up in synch with the occasional sperm whale bass note that warmed the room. Towering trees swayed. Maybe the building was moving.

I heard a murmuring and turned to see another person standing in the doorway. The other end of the room seemed far away. Brandon leaned forward to say something to Gram, then sat on the floor, his head resting against the wall. Again, he said something to Gram, who shook his head and said 'No'. Gram buried his head in his arms and repeated, 'No, no'.

"Hey, Gram, what's the matter?" Brandon asked. Gram is going through something, not good.

"Somebody hates me," Gram says in a breathy, frightened voice. "Somebody wants to kill me." Gram is having a bad trip, going down the wrong road. "Someone in this room... I know it." Now it's beginning to get creepy, and freaking me a bit. Then I think, wait a minute, I'm not planning to kill him. I don't have a baseball bat or a .38 stuck in my belt.

Brandon is together, Gram isn't rattling him, he replies, "I'm not going to kill you Gram." He asks Mickey, "Are you trying to kill Gram?"

"No, I'm not going to kill you Gram."

"You're not going to kill Gram are you Ian?"

"No. No, of course I'm not."

Brandon's been round the room, the verdict is, no murder is about to happen. "See, Gram, nobody is trying to kill you. We're your friends. Okay? We're your friends." When Brandon leans back, his candlelit shadow is cast on the wall above his shoulder. I watch the shadow as it speaks. Brandon is straddling two worlds, the shadow is telling the truth.

Gram isn't convinced, "Somebody, in this room, wants to kill me!" He insists.

"Gram, listen. We're all in this room, okay? And, nobody is going to kill you. You just heard me ask everybody." Brandon is speaking to Gram as if he were comforting a five-year-old who has awoken from a nightmare. Brandon laughs, "Hey, you're the only one left, Gram."

Gram raises his voice, he's panicking, "It's in this room, it's going to kill me. It's me. It's going to kill me!"

"Gram. Listen to me. Relax. No one is trying to kill you."

"I know who it is!"

"Okay then, who is it? Tell us." Brandon is trying to remain, light and easy-going, to reassure Gram.

"It's me! It's me. I'm going to kill myself."

"Gram. You're having a bad trip. We all took LSD. You don't have to do this. You can stop it, if you want to." Gram was deep into it and beginning to scare everyone else.

"I'm going to kill myself, I've gotta die. It's me."

"Gram, you're not..."

Gram began sobbing, "I'm going to do it. I'm going to kill myself."

Brandon tried again, "Look, Gram. Listen-n-n, to, me-e-e. We're all here with you. We're not going to let you get killed. We're not going to let anything like that happen." Brandon turned to me, "Come on guys, help me out here."

I was just about panting and couldn't take a lot more of this, but managed to say, "Gram, come on, man. You're gonna be alright. It's okay. It's just a trip." Brave fucking words.

"Are you sure?"

"Yes." We chorused, like the Andrews Sisters. "Come on buddy, we're your friends. You gotta try and remember that. We all took acid and you just started going to a bad place."

Gram sighed. He took deep breaths, like someone who just surfaced after trying to swim a lap in the pool, underwater. "I thought I was going to kill myself. I believed it."

At a small road junction in Rhode Island, I see brightly colored clothes and hair. A group of people are in a huddle, talking. Long hair and tie-dye. Chestnut hair trails over the yellow blanket draped across a girl's shoulders. They look like they could be on their way to a festival, waiting for a ride on a big painted bus. They're not thumbing for a ride. Several dark guitar cases lie at their feet. The cases have the figure-eight shape, acoustic guitars. Maybe they are on their way to a beach party, the weather is good enough for that. I wonder what sort of guitars they have; Spanish? Flat-tops? They look like college students and they probably have decent guitars; folk guitars, Gibson or Martin maybe. I don't see that much any more, the folk thing, and acoustic guitars, is pretty much over, everybody has switched to electrics. Kids probably don't even start playing on a cheap acoustic anymore. It used to be part of the normal evolutionary cycle. Gram had a folk style guitar when I first met him.

You have to bash the Hell out of those acoustic guitars to get anything out of them. Filling the room, in a coffee house folk club, demands whacking out the chords, to be heard against the background noise of clinking glasses, whispers and the burble of people who have lost interest in the song by the time the second verse rolls around: even less time if they don't recognize it. Gram had been slamming a Martin for the past few years when we originally got together.

He had worked with a folk group, The Shilos, and had to thrash-out enough volume to compete with a banjo. Usually, when playing next to that wiry, needling thing, being heard is a struggle. After the folk group, Gram played solo and continued with the heavy-handed style, in folk clubs and cafes.

During our first jams and rehearsals, Gram played a small Martin.

It didn't look like most of the other Martins I had seen; the folkie standard was the, big-bodied, D series. Gram's guitar was the smaller New Yorker model that had a different neck and headstock. He used a pick and wailed away on it playing open chords or used a capo to keep the open chord shapes, if a song might be in an awkward key. A folk style, with a lot of songs in D minor.

The first recording sessions in New York, when we cut 'November Night', 'Just Can't Take It Anymore' and some others, had a folk-rock feel and his acoustic worked on those songs. After we moved to New York and were pulling a live act together, Gram had to get an electric.

Manny's was the musical instrument Mecca in the City, it had been for years, maybe decades. Now, the fast breeding range of electric instruments were elbowing-out the clarinets, French horns and violas at the shop. The rock music eruption disgorged novel guitars, basses and keyboards. A vast choice compared with what was on offer at the local music shops, just a few years ago, when Kay, Silvertone and Danelectro dominated the teen rock 'n' roll market. Gram had headed downtown for Manny's, to shop.

With a penchant for style and fashion, Gram passed over the Gibsons, Fenders or Gretschs hanging on the wall, being more attracted by the odd-ball Rickenbacker. His eye was drawn to the red-orange sunburst finish and the thin, semi-acoustic body with a slant-eyed slash of a sound hole. It was a guitar with flair. A couple of over-size pick-ups, a cluster of knobs and switches on a large, teardrop pick guard, white wedge-shaped fret marks and a neck crowned with an off-kilter head, made it a showy guitar. He liked how it felt and looked. Gram returned to the Bronx, excited by his purchase of the guitar and an amp. The amp was another oddity, a Standel Super Custom XV. The 70 watt, single speaker amp featured an illuminated control panel that glowed with a see-in-the-dark neon green. It was the first mass-produced, solid-state amp and it didn't have to warm up, a flick of the switch and it was ready to go. Gram was excited and ready to write a new chapter in his life with the motorcycle of musical instruments, the electric guitar.

John Nuese had reservations about Gram's prize. In his eyes the Rickenbacker was a frivolous guitar. John's personal choice was a stripped-down white Telecaster, lean and basic, but he seemed to think that an electric was a step in the right direction.

"Now we're going to rock 'n' roll, GP," he enthused and grinned.

Within weeks, The Submarine Band was playing several sets a night, pumping it out at The Night Owl in The Village.

'Nadine, honey is that you,

Seems like every time I see you,

You got somethin' else to do'

The stage lights glow orange, the color of excited toaster elements, as we step off the side of the stage into the jumbled, closet-sized dressing room.

"Phew!"

"Man, you are sweating."

"Yeah and if I step outside, it'll turn to ice, I bet."

"No foolin', it's freezing out there tonight."

Gram reaches for a pack of Winstons. "Shit! I'm bleeding." A flap of skin hangs from his knuckle "I thought that pick was getting slippery, I couldn't hardly hold on to it."

"Get some toilet paper."

"You've got to take it easy, you don't have to hit your guitar so hard. Turn up the volume, you don't need to keep banging it, you keep putting it out of tune," John advised. Gram played the electric like it was an unamplified Martin, he couldn't break that acoustic habit.

The next night at The Night Owl, Gram had a Band-Aid on that finger but the dressing had disappeared halfway through the first set.

Looking over at me, he held up the skinned finger, rolled his eyes, shrugged his shoulders, pursed his lips then said, "Oh well, whacha gonna do?"

Offstage, playing at home, learning harmonies and singing country music, Gram used his Martin and in the intimacy of a small room there was no need to slam chords. John played his D series Martin and the acoustic music sounded good, to us.

Soon after moving to Laurel Canyon we melded into a society that seemed to be made of musicians. Unlike New York, LA was awash with guitars and amps. Instruments were being bought, sold or bartered frequently. In amongst the guitar traffic, Gram found a Fender Esquire, a simplified Telecaster. It was idiot-proof, with only two knobs, tone and volume, no switches. Gram had sometimes been befuddled by the bewildering array of controls on the Rickenbacker and would randomly twist the knobs in hope that something would happen. Often he would shut himself off. He had even resorted to turning the volume knobs all the way up, sticking them in position with Scotch Tape and adjusting the volume with the easy-to-see, green-glow amp. The Esquire solved all that.

On gigs in LA, Gram was playing less guitar and would usually sit at the keyboard for several numbers. A few songs could be a considerable part of the set, since we were mostly playing concert style gigs. We weren't doing several sets a night at club gigs any more.

As The Sub's motion changed from full-speed-ahead to a drift, Gram got a big Gibson flat top and was delivered from the claws of electric guitars. He wasn't at ease with solid-body electrics, he was a strummer, really.

After crossing over the state border into Rhode Island I decide I want to see the Atlantic. It can't be far, Rhode Island is so small. Probably several Rhode Islands could be dumped into the Grand Canyon and not come anywhere near to filling it up.

The land weakens closer to the coast, loses its muscle, flattens-out, and I can see the gleam of the sea at the end of the road ahead. I have not seen an ocean for over a month or the Atlantic for several years. I take off my shoes and walk over the sand, crunching over dry seaweed cast up by a spring storm. I walk into the sea and am licked by the Atlantic. I recognize her familiar tongue. The on-shore wind is fresh. Waves rear and spill forward with white rumbles. I close my eyes, the sound of the sea is like a sleeper, unreservedly breathing, deep and guttural, occasionally snoring. The beach is long and most of the houses seem empty, maybe only used on the weekends. I sit, half propped against an overturned skiff. A large flock of gulls had settled beyond the shine of retreating waves. The birds rest in unison, heads to the wind, tails to the land. The group is so large that the distant gulls become a chalky smear. Fresh seaweed, ejected by the swells, is piled above the foam, like a drift of crisp salad, almost appetizing. Each wave applauds as it crosses the finish line, collapses, spent and exhausted from a marathon journey. Foam tongues push through the feeble wall of seaweed. Close to the shore, the disturbed sea is the color of sandstone and glazed with reflections of a sharply contrasting, iridescent sky-blue.

A choir of rumbling, liquid throats begin a chorus as the waves break.

All-l-l-l-l-l. All-l-l-l-l-l. War-r-r-m-m-m-m. Goes-s-s-s-s. In-n-n-n-n.

Yeah well, okay. Let's talk if you want to. You and I go back a long way, don't we. We were friends for a long time. You saw me grow-up. And, you know what? You never hurt me, once. Well, except for that time you got really crazy and smashed up our boat and then knocked our house over. But, you never hurt me, even though I just about invited you to do your worst, a few times. Maybe I swallowed some of you, took communion, drank some of your blood, and that... that's made me part of the family.

Oh-h-h-h-h-h. S-s-s-s-ur-r-re-e-e-e-e-e.

I walk along on the mirror of wet sand. Small shells, bleached the color of a half-moon, against a mid-day sky, litter the sand. The sea swooshes in around me, a bubble blanket of champagne leaving my feet glistening against a porridge of sand. The fine granules of shells have been ground by the constantly chewing sea. Another surge of water covers my feet and possibly washes away some dust from Joshua Tree or that sandy field in New Mexico. That's cool. Take it away. Baptise me, again.

S-s-sure-e-e. W-wash-sh-sh-sh-sh. Kiss-ss-ss-ss-ss-ss. Kiss-ss-ss-ss-ss, the Atlantic says in answer.

I drive through Providence, Rhode Island, up the hill across Benefit Street past RISD, the art school I went to. The semester must have finished but I see several people around who look like art students. There might be a summer term in session. Two students are waiting to cross the street. They are both carrying sketchbooks, an essential part of the art student's attire. You are not properly dressed without a sketchbook.

I kept the sketchbooks going in Cambridge, New York and Los Angeles for doodles, writing and pasting-in bizarre headlines, ads and photos, torn from newspapers. Often the sketchbooks were the 9 x 11 inch, cartridge paper type I had picked up at art school. At RISD, all the students had the plain paper, black covered books. Black as a Bible. We were writing our own Bibles, the sketchbooks were filled with personal revelations, visions and commandments.

I was into the fifth or sixth volume by now, since 1963. Fragments of events were recorded in ink or pencil drawings; an interior, a view from a window or a door step, of whatever neighborhood might be current and sketches of objects and the people I was involved with at the time. Most of the guys in the bands were inked-in on one page or another; Gram watching TV, Brandon playing guitar or various girlfriends. More recently the sketches showed the stacked boulders of Joshua Tree and the soaring spires of Zion Canyon. Other microliths of civilization and little souvenirs collected on the way, ticket stubs, a matchbook cover, bits of packaging labels, were taped-in.

Looking through previous books of mine, the nonsense notes and cartoons could remind me of a bad patch, or when I was running a hundred-and-four fever of love, or times when I was locked in the waiting room, anticipating the arrival of the mystery train. Some of the pages contained a condensed adventure of emotions or a concentrated package of personalities while others showed an exploding, colorful escape from all of them.

During the time I spent with Barry T, he had a sketchbook ticking over that included, lists of songs, doodles, newspaper cut-outs, unusual business cards and bursts of nonsense doggerel. I was always interested in what was going into other books, if they were open to look at.

Gram usually had a few notebooks and frequently had one open. I remember one day, at the house in the Bronx when he was frowning at it and chewing the end of a ballpoint pen. A small hard cover notebook was balanced on his knee, as he sat with his legs crossed on the sofa.

"What's goin' on?" I asked.

"Well. I was trying to figure which way I'm goin' on some lyrics here. And, um-m, I'm not quite sure about it. I had this idea the other day, you know, just tryin' to see if it's going anywhere."

"Yeah? What is it, or is it too soon to tell?"

"Uh-h, I don't have a melody or anything but I'm thinkin' along the lines of a country shuffle. Um-m, maybe. And, the basic idea, it's sort of about meeting-up with old friends, like from high school or, really, anywhere from the past. A-and, ah, remembering some of the things that went down back then. Like, say, one guy stole his best friend's girl or somebody was into, whatever, like always talkin' about getting out of town, you know that sort of stuff. And, one day, you go back there and you see how nothing's changed and how you don't fit-in anymore, at all. Like one line is 'This town is so much smaller than the last time I was here. They're runnin',' I think chasing is better," He scratched running, "They're chasin' smaller circles 'til their shadows disappear. I was even thinkin' about rhyming beer. Still not sure if it's a chorus or what."

"Hey, it's a good idea."

"Um-m. I'm gonna have to let it brew." He closed the book. "There. I'll let 'em simmer. Sometimes it's good to do that, like sticking a chicken in the oven to roast. Pull it out later and it's almost done. Or, throw the clothes in a dryer, they spin round an' round and bingo, they're ready to wear. Might just happen here." He put his thumb and forefinger together and made a twisting motion on the notebook cover. "There, I'll give 'em an extra half hour to cook."

The notebooks were always near, he kept a running list of interesting words, or phrases that he overheard, in conversation, from TV or from the background babble of the street, the subway and the advertising signs and billboards that surrounded us.

"I was looking through another book and found something that I started awhile ago. It could have been from back in Cambridge and I might be able to use part of it in something else. It was a song that was goin' in a completely different direction, but, it's funny, you can take some lines an' stick 'em right next to something else, like where they were never supposed to be and then it all makes sense. Well, maybe docsn't make sense, it just fits. Even though you brought in that line, from some other context, they just want to hook-up. Just happens sometimes. Like makin' an omelette, you take a couple of eggs, bit of pepper, then pour in a shot of brandy." Gram began accompanying the recipe with motions of stirring and pouring. "Then, we'll chop-up a bit of blues, some hangover, a pinch of heartache, ha! there you go. You want coffee with that?"

Gram often carried a notebook with him, as if he might get stuck somewhere hoping for a blizzard to end or waiting to see the dentist and he would have something to do. The notebooks were small, sometimes with a leather or marbled cover, but just too big to slip into a pocket. He carried them like a student on his way to class. One night in New York, in the fall, it was still warm enough not to be wearing winter coats, Gram and I had been running around downtown. It was late and it took awhile to get a taxi, as, sometimes, they wouldn't want to go all that way, up to the Bronx. We zoomed along side of the East River. We crossed through the X's of the Erector Set bridge over the river and up the hill into the Bronx. We decided to get out at the Fordham Road so, maybe, the guy could find a fare and we gave him a tip in case he couldn't.

The door slammed and the cab moved away. Suddenly, Gram sort of gasped, "Oh no!"

and started waving his arm at the retreating taxi.

"My notebook! Shit! Hey, Hey!" We both ran after the taxi but he had a green light, not much other traffic and probably wanted to get the hell out of the Bronx. The two red taillights quickly disappeared. "Fuck! I forgot my notebook."

"Maybe we can call the taxi company. They might have a lost and found." I tried to offer consolation, knowing the book was important to Gram.

"Shit! We don't know anything, what company it was, it's just another yellow cab. There are thousands of them!"

"What was in the book?"

"Oh, man. You know, it was full of things. I can't remember what, except for the last page, maybe. I can't remember." He shook his head. We turned and started walking up the dark street. "Just all of those little things. Words. Lines. Ideas. You know. Gone."

I pick up Route 123, east into Massachusetts, running through a couple of small New England towns near to where I grew-up. The town centers, with one or two stoplights, look unchanged, the same as the last time, apart from a few high school hippies with long hair. Other than a couple of new roadside businesses selling aluminum garage doors or lawnmowers, it seems like I'm driving back into 1963 and my senior year in high school. After passing the village common, the big white Congregationalist Church and a college for women, I drive past Pine Street, turn on to Elm Street and pull into the driveway of my family's old house. I blip the gas pedal and shut off the ignition. The VW engine unwinds and sputters to a stop. I slump back in the seat and sigh. My left hand still grips the steering wheel like it does not want to stop driving. I let go and look at my open my hand. I remember telling Gram my theory about how too much driving could alter the lines on the palm and change fate.

"Hi, Good mornin' how you feeling today?" Gram is slouching back, reading, in his strange bed. The head, foot and one side are a couple of feet high, like a coffin, a crib, away in a manger. "Did you stay up to watch the end of that old movie?" The early morning hours were the time slot for 1930s-40s movies and the stoned-out, night owl fans of Busby Berkley musicals. New York TV Channel 11 began showing the old black and whites at about midnight. The movies became more eccentric, meaningful and bizarre in direct proportion to the lateness of the hour.

"Well, I just surfaced a while ago, m-m." Gram folded the book in his lap. "Gave-up on that Fred MacMurray movie, you know, all those hats and baggy suits. . . m-m."

"What are you reading?"

"It's a book." He held it up for me to see: How to Read the Palm.

"Have you figured out the future?"

"Well no, just looking at the basic lines and shapes. I've got some of these crosses, see. Here, sit down. Let's have a look at your hand." He flipped back a couple of pages. "Um-m-m, here's the life-line, the heart line and on the wrist, these others, like bracelets, see, here. Man, you don't have a lot of lines. Look at mine." Gram opened his hand next to mine revealing a busy network of lines. Scoring, scratches and scrawls threaded from his wrist. His palm, was a seismic frenzy of lines, continuing up the phalanges to eventually blend with his finger print swirls. It looked like the hand of a force-fed mummy. We examined our two specimens spread in supplication, awaiting translation.

"These crosses are supposed to be lucky." Gram touched an X with his long forefinger.

"There's another small one just below your little finger," I pointed out. Gram's palm was long, narrow, compared to my chunky hand.

"Hey, let's see what it says about those lines by your thumb." Numerous fine streaks fanned-out from the fleshy mound at the base of my thumb. He flicked the page over. "Okay, it says, they represent opposition."

"Fuck! There's an awful lot of them. I'm in for a rough ride."

"Well, maybe not. They extend toward the heart line but, see, not many of them go through it."

"I hope so, it kinda looks like ridin' out a long storm to me."

"Ah, you'll be alright," Gram assured.

"Well, with my force-shield heart line and your lucky crosses, maybe we'll make it through the valley of the shadow of death, huh?"

"Yeah, if we keep crouchin' down and run like Hell."

"What else you got on your treasure map?" I asked. We contemplate the web of lines on his hand.

"Well-l-l, I can't figure which one is the life-line, there's about three of 'em where it should be. See, sort of diagonally across and down. They're crossing over, one ends and then another picks up."

"They're woven, or frayed," I suggested.

"Um-m-m. See there's this gap, nothing, then, here it is again."

"Wonder how far along the life line we are already? That would be handy to know."

"Who knows. The line isn't calibrated," he said.

"So, what if you took your hand an' made a fist, then taped it up for a month. That would alter the lines, I bet."

"Aw come on, that's cheatin'."

"What about a guy, drivin' a truck all the time, his hands on the wheel for weeks, he's gonna be creating different lines."

"Yeah, well, he's gonna end up with Route 66 on his palm."

"M-m, guess so."

"Babies are born with lines. Like, they're already there. There's a forecast, you know, a fate, inevitability, where you come from where you're going, what train you hop, what station you stop at and where you get off. I'm tryin' to figure out how to read the station signs as they go flashing past the club car window."

There was a small collection of mail awaiting me at my parents' home. A few envelopes containing unexciting papers; an insurance document, an announcement for a Class of '63 reunion that had happened a couple of months ago and a deposit account statement that showed that I had a couple of hundred dollars that I had forgotten about. There was also a postcard showing Piccadilly Circus, in London. The card was another one from Gram. I recognized his handwriting by the fluid loops of his Ys and Gs.

'Wondering where you are and what you're dreaming?

I'm going to see a gypsy Tarot card reader to look

at my map. I might not be flying with the Byrds

for much longer. You know, bands, how they can get.

London is cool. The road keeps winding. Gram.'

The instruments, boxes of records and odd collections had been unloaded from the exhausted VW. I had reached my temporary destination and was about to leap to another. It seemed to me that England was on the cards. I had travelled across the USA but my journey was not over, there was another place I had to reach, maybe it was the finish line that I still had to cross. Thoreau's retreat, Walden Pond, was the Mecca waiting at the end of my pilgrimage.

Fragments of Henry David Thoreau's writing had taken root in me since I was a teenager when I had heard about this guy who, over one hundred years ago, had decided to walk away from society and went off to live in the woods. His choice makes more sense to me now. The day must have come along when Thoreau said to himself;

'Screw this, man. I'm getting out of here, I can't take all of this bullshit, hype and greed for a second longer, it's doin' my head in. Goodbye, so long, see you later alligator'. And he headed out to shack-up in the boonies. He dropped-out and stayed out there for a couple of years, writing and trying to pick up on the message that nature keeps broadcasting, even when no one wants to listen. Thoreau had written; 'I went to the woods to see if I could learn what it had to teach'.

I had been on the road, in the woods or the desert for over a month. I had been still for just a few days at a time and had only begun to clear some of the whirling confusion and pollution out of my system. I was only beginning to tune-in and feel the signals that were beaming around me.

Instead of the TV blaring out enticements and advising me to buy-buy-buy my way out of inadequacy, I was listening to the great bargains on offer from the wind or crickets or dead leaves that crunched under my feet. The end of the line, my last stop on this trip would be to drink from Walden Pond.

I headed up north toward Concord. Summer had kicked-in, rolling out thick, wall-to-wall sparkling green. I recognize some of the small towns along the road from my years in high school, remembering some of the trips to rural schools on the teams' school bus when I sprinted at track meets. The VW drives well, relieved of the cargo.

The road into the pond led to a small gravel parking lot. There were a couple of cars and a pick-up but no sign of any people or picnics. I had been here once before but today the pond seems much larger than I remember. I walk along the shore in the warm sun and sit straddling the trunk of a large fallen tree, its roots in the edge of the woods, its head drowned in the pond. The pond is surrounded by woods. The trees grow right up to the shore. Opposite, the woods roll back, up to a ridge. A hundred yards away a guy glides along in a canoe. He raises and dips a paddle that connects him to his reflection. The surface of the pond is mirror still. The trees on the opposite shore, the hills behind and the blue sky are replicated. The strong reflections on the pond make perfect opposites. The trees stand pointing at the sky, their reflections point down into another sky. The reflections are as vivid as the originals. A thin horizontal line of sand marks the division between these two worlds. A mallard flies low over the shore and his upside-down double matches each wing beat. He is flying through both worlds. The duck circles and swoops, meeting his reflection as he skates then settles on the pond. The mallard moves across the reflection of the trees, he has splashed down into an inverted world and is paddling through the mirror dimension. He has entered an illusion. The ripples from the duck snake down through the reflections creating mini shock waves of distortion. The worlds of reality and the ethereal are linked, the duck knows the way through.

I pull my sweatshirt over my head and see it glimmer on the water's surface. The water is clear and I can see the bottom as it shelves away. The pond is deep and clean. I bend and swish my hands under the surface, the water is cool and refreshing. I need to follow the duck through to the other world. I take off my T-shirt and shorts and wade into the pond. The bottom is soft, I walk on sand between the rocks. At thigh-depth I ease into the cool water and begin to swim, slowly. If there was someone watching on the other shore they might see me marbling and stirring the reflections of the trees behind me. I might look like an ape climbing through the branches, an illusion that only they could see.

I kick my feet making splashes and eruptions, the ripples radiate across the mirror. I swim on my back looking up into the sky. There are high clouds, delicate strands trail behind a more distinct, rounded form, like a comet of mist. Angel hair flowing behind a head, a face. Angels, the heavenly hosts. One of them might open its mouth and proclaim; Fear not shepherds, or people in canoes, a child is born. Maybe it is Thoreau's spirit up there, keeping an eye on the pond just in case someone pulls in and starts dumping old refrigerators or uncomfortable easy-chairs, burned out by too many asses watching television. I tread water, looking back at the fallen tree and see my clothes draped over the trunk. Clothing from California, another life. I float on my back. The clouds that I saw are thinner, dispersing, I guess Thoreau figures that I'm not a threat.

"Hey it's okay, man, I'm cool. Thanks for showing up. I'm glad I made it."

I take a breath and dive under. The water is more clear than I had expected, I see some of the bottom and a couple of boulders. I'm in the pond. I'm here, a new migrant that has flown in to take refuge with the frogs, turtles and ducks. I'm one of the guys now, a member of the club. I float to the surface and exhale with a roar, taking deep breaths. Now I'm talking in the language of the pond with deep groaning breaths like a bullfrog. I fill my lungs and dive toward the bottom. After a few strokes I roll over on my back and look up through the water.

Above me is a ceiling of slowly undulating glass, it shimmers with a radiant, heavenly glow, some of the most beautiful light I've ever seen.

M. SAUVIN   R. TASSEAU   E. MARQUIS

CLARKSDALE

meet you
at the crossroads

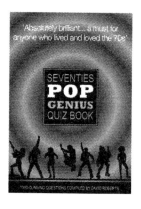

www.clarksdalebooks.co.uk
clarksdale@ovolobooks.co.uk